READINGS IN
ETHICAL
ISSUES

Revised Printing

William Smith
Seton Hall University

KENDALL/HUNT PUBLISHING COMPANY
4050 Westmark Drive   Dubuque, Iowa 52002

Copyright © 1993, 1998 by Kendall/Hunt Publishing Company

Revised Printing

ISBN 0-7872-5077-5

Printed in the United States of America
10   9   8   7   6   5   4   3

Table of Contents

Section III: When Is Killing Murder? 171

Section IV: The Use of Sexuality 229

Preface

I have often wondered about the wisdom of using an anthology, a book of "readings", for a philosophy course. I find it difficult to believe that the writings of all major philosophers were aimed at beginners rather than professionals in the field. We know that many of these writers came from intellectual traditions and formations well beyond those of the average American student. This can present difficulties for the professor, who must now painstakingly explain the philosopher's basic system and thought. Nevertheless, I think the positives outweigh the negatives. The students are made familiar with and can study from the original sources. Time is saved in the classroom because the teacher doesn't have to read the original writings and then give explanations. Students can be given reading assignments ahead of time; this makes them aware of the areas of difficulty in time to question intelligently in the assigned class period. Hopefully, clarification will come in the classroom.

I have tried to make this book of "readings" different from some others by using not only some of the so-called "classic" texts, but also excerpts from more "popular" and modern essayists and journalists. In this way, students will come to realize that active discussion and controversy on these issues are currently taking place around them.

I take this opportunity to thank Kendall/Hunt's editors and staff for all their help and encouragement.

William A. Smith, Ph.D.
South Orange, N.J.
1992

General Introduction

Readings in Ethical Issues is intended to be used as a supplement to textbooks that do not include readings; that is, texts which simply explain and critique theories and analyze issues. I must confess that this book does follow the structure of my own basic text, *Ethical Reflections*, originally published by GINN Press, now in its 4th edition by Simon & Schuster. This book includes many of the readings which were used as background and suggested readings in *Ethical Reflections*. Many professors prefer the combination of text and readings, and this book should complement various textbooks. The book could be used alone, with the professor supplying explanations and analyses. Some professors might prefer this to the explanations and analyses of others. At the end of each section there will be questions and space for answers. These can be done in class or at home and the pages torn out and handed in. Sections I and II deal mainly with the various theories and systems of Ethics which philosophers and theologians have developed down through the centuries. Sections III, IV and V contain readings which relate to issues germane to those sections.

Section III deals with the taking of human life and the question: when is the killing of a human being murder? All essays are contemporary.

Section IV deals with issues relating to the creation of human life and, therefore, the "use of sex," procreation techniques and some analysis of homosexuality. Anthony Perkins' poignant statement on AIDS is included.

Section V deals with various problems in Business Ethics, including the application of the virtue of Justice to wages, job discrimination and problems relating to Affirmative Action. Maximization of Profits as related to plant closings will be examined. Several more articles have been added in the 3rd and latest printing.

The Introduction to each Section is somewhat brief because I believe it is best left to the professor to expand on the topics in his/her own manner. Also, as mentioned, he/she might be using an expository textbook as well.

Of course, many more selections could have been included. The author will welcome critical reports.

Section I

Ethics and Positive Law

Introduction:

Ethicians who have operated in the traditional mode for centuries have always tried to discover the key or route to human happiness in this life if not also in a possible future life. They have studied the human being, the human reality, in order to discern whatever might be the "ingredients" of the "good life." It has often been said that our human nature lies between the angels and the animals, that we are some sort of combination of mind and body, of intellect, will, emotions and sensuality.

Traditional ethicians were always optimistic, believing that if they persevered, ethical truth would eventually be fully revealed. Yet, there were always those who took a more pessimistic view of the human intellect's ability to make the move from a true and full perception of human nature to a superior moral system and thence to a valid and credible resolution of moral problems.

Pessimists left the traditionalists with at least three alternatives:

1. Examine the language of Ethics and the meaning given to ethical statements by those who make them;

2. Turn to your religion and your written divine revelation for your answers;

3. Fall back on the positive civil law.

The first is the view of logical positivists or empiricists like A.J. Ayer (1910-1989) who have a problem with any metaphysical foundation of Ethics (e.g.-human nature) and who might feel that ethical statements express the feelings only of the one stating the view. Members of the Vienna Circle would share this position. Even the meaning of the word "good" would be analyzed.

The second alternative refers the perplexed person to the Old Testament, New Testament or Koran depending on their religious persuasion. Since morality often deals with topics related to the use of sex I have chosen sample texts from the Douay-Rheims version of the Bible that have been used by many in relation to homosexuality and sodomy (Leviticus), birth-control and masturbation ("sin of onan") or all "Onanistic intercourse" in (Genesis) and Paul's condemnation of adultery, fornication and sexual perversion. As always, since this is a book of Readings only, I shall leave it to the professor to evaluate critically these texts. (Students find it interesting to see other biblical translations-especially on sexual perversion). The third alternative includes first and second-level philosophers who believed that the State, through its positive, visible and authoritatively promulgated laws will interpret what is just and right for the people. If something is legal it is right. An unjust law therefore, is a contradiction in terms and in reality.

1

The reading by Niccolo Machiavelli (1469-1527) an Italian statesman and student of politics is taken from *The Prince* (publ. 1532) and that by Thomas Hobbes (1588-1679) an English philosopher is taken from his work *Leviathan.* Since Fascist philosophy taught that the State is supreme I have included a reading by Alfredo Rocco (d. 1935) Minister of Justice under Benito Mussolini, who praised him for his accurate description. National Socialism in Germany was also a Fascist philosophy. Its infamous leader, Adolf Hitler (1889-1945) agreed with Rocco and Mussolini but, unfortunately, had a special version of national and racial superiority which included the "solution" of the problem of the presence of the Jews in Europe. In his book, *Mein Kampf (My Struggle)*, written while in Landsberg prison, Munich, in 1924, he tells of his hatred of the Jews. As dictator and "Leader" he made the civil laws of Germany. Therefore, what happened to the Jews was legal.

In this Section Legal Positivism must also come under some scrutiny as well as Logical Positivism.

The Elimination of Metaphysics

Alfred Jules Ayer

The traditional disputes of philosophers are, for the most part, as unwarranted as they are unfruitful. The surest way to end them is to establish beyond question what should be the purpose and method of a philosophical enquiry. And this is by no means so difficult a task as the history of philosophy would lead one to suppose. For if there are any questions which science leaves it to philosophy to answer, a straightforward process of elimination must lead to their discovery.

We may begin by criticising the metaphysical thesis that philosophy affords us knowledge of a reality transcending the world of science and common sense. Later on, when we come to define metaphysics and account for its existence, we shall find that it is possible to be a metaphysician without believing in a transcendent reality; for we shall see that many metaphysical utterances are due to the commission of logical errors, rather than to a conscious desire on the part of their authors to go beyond the limits of experience. But it is convenient for us to take the case of those who believe that it is possible to have knowledge of a transcendent reality as a starting-point for our discussion. The arguments which we use to refute them will subsequently be found to apply to the whole of metaphysics.

One way of attacking a metaphysician who claimed to have knowledge of a reality which transcended the phenomenal world would be to enquire from what premises his propositions were deduced. Must he not begin, as other men do, with the evidence of his senses? And if so, what valid process of reasoning can possibly lead him to the conception of a transcendent reality? Surely from empirical premises nothing whatsoever concerning the properties, or even the existence, of anything super-empirical can legitimately be inferred. But this objection would be met by a denial on the part of the metaphysician that his assertions were ultimately based on the evidence of his senses. He would say that he was endowed with a faculty of intellectual intuition which enabled him to know facts that could not be known through sense-experience. And even if it could be shown that he was relying on empirical premises, and that his venture into a nonempirical world was therefore logically unjustified, it would not follow that the assertions which he made concerning this nonempirical world could not be true. For the fact that a conclusion does not follow from its putative premise is not sufficient to show that it is false. Consequently one cannot overthrow a system of transcendent metaphysics merely by criticizing the way in which it comes into being. What is required is rather a criticism of the nature of the actual statements which comprise it. And this is the line of argument which we shall, in fact, pursue. For we shall maintain that no statement which refers to a

From *Language, Truth and Logic*, 2nd ed. by Alfred Jules Ayer. Reprinted by permission of Dover Publications, Inc., New York.

"reality" transcending the limits of all possible sense-experience can possibly have any literal significance; from which it must follow that the labours of those who have striven to describe such a reality have all been devoted to the production of nonsense.

It may be suggested that this is a proposition which has already been proved by Kant. But although Kant also condemned transcendent metaphysics, he did so on different grounds. For he said that the human understanding was so constituted that it lost itself in contradictions when it ventured out beyond the limits of possible experience and attempted to deal with things in themselves. And thus he made the impossibility of a transcendent metaphysic not, as we do, a matter of logic, but a matter of fact. He asserted, not that our minds could not conceivably have had the power of penetrating beyond the phenomenal world, but merely that they were in fact devoid of it. And this leads the critic to ask how, if it is possible to know only what lies within the bounds of sense-experience, the author can be justified in asserting that real things do exist beyond, and how he can tell what are the boundaries beyond which the human under standing may not venture, unless he succeeds in passing them himself. As Wittgenstein says, "in order to draw a limit to thinking, we should have to think both sides of this limit,"[1] a truth to which Bradley gives a special twist in maintaining that the man who is ready to prove that metaphysics is impossible is a brother metaphysician with a rival theory of his own.[2]

Whatever force these objections may have against the Kantian doctrine, they have none whatsoever against the thesis that I am about to set forth. It cannot here be said that the author is himself overstepping the barrier he maintains to be impassable. For the fruitlessness of attempting to transcend the limits of possible sense-experience will be deduced, not from a psychological hypothesis concerning the actual constitution of the human mind, but from the rule which determines the literal significance of language. Our charge against the metaphysician is not that he attempts to employ the understanding in a field where it cannot profitably venture, but that he produces sentences which fail to conform to the conditions under which alone a sentence can be literally significant. Nor are we ourselves obliged to talk nonsense in order to show that all sentences of a certain type are necessarily devoid of literal significance. We need only formulate the criterion which enables us to test whether a sentence expresses a genuine proposition about a matter of fact, and then point out that the sentences under consideration fail to satisfy it. And this we shall now proceed to do. We shall first of all formulate the criterion in somewhat vague terms, and then give the explanations which are necessary to render it precise.

The criterion which we use to test the genuineness of apparent statements of fact is the criterion of verifiability. We say that a sentence is factually significant to any given person, if, and only if, he knows how to verify the proposition which it purports to express—that is, if he knows what observations would lead him, under certain conditions, to accept the proposition as being true, or reject it as being false. If, on the other hand, the putative proposition is of such a character that the assumption of its truth, or falsehood, is consistent with any assumption whatsoever concerning the nature of his future experience, then, as far as he is con-

---

1   *Tractatus Logico-Philosophicus*, Preface.
2   Bradley, *Appearance and Reality*, 2nd ed., p. 1.

cerned, it is, if not a tautology, a mere pseudo-proposition. The sentence expressing it may be emotionally significant to him; but it is not literally significant. And with regard to questions the procedure is the same. We enquire in every case what observations would lead us to answer the question, one way or the other; and, if none can be discovered, we must conclude that the sentence under consideration does not, as far as we are concerned, express a genuine question, however strongly its grammatical appearance may suggest that it does.

As the adoption of this procedure is an essential factor in the argument of this book, it needs to be examined in detail.

In the first place, it is necessary to draw a distinction between practical verifiability, and verifiability in principle. Plainly we all understand, in many cases believe, propositions which we have not in fact taken steps to verify. Many of these are propositions which we could verify if we took enough trouble. But there remain a number of significant propositions, concerning matters of fact, which we could not verify even if we chose; simply because we lack the practical means of placing ourselves in the situation where the relevant observations could be made. A simple and familiar example of such a proposition is the proposition that there are mountains on the farther side of the moon.[3] No rocket has yet been invented which would enable me to go and look at the farther side of the moon, so that I am unable to decide the matter by actual observation. But I do know what observations would decide it for me, if, as is theoretically conceivable, I were once in a position to make them. And therefore I say that the proposition is verifiable in principle, if not in practice, and

is accordingly significant. On the other hand, such a metaphysical pseudo-proposition as "the Absolute enters into, but is itself incapable of, evolution and progress,"[4] is not even in principle verifiable. For one cannot conceive of an observation which would enable one to determine whether the Absolute did, or did not, enter into evolution and progress. Of course it is possible that the author of such a remark is using English words in a way in which they are not commonly used by English-speaking people, and that he does, in fact, intend to assert something which could be empirically verified. But until he makes us understand how the proposition that he wishes to express would be verified, he fails to communicate anything to us. And if he admits, as I think the author of the remark in question would have admitted, that his words were not intended to express either a tautology or a proposition which was capable, at least in principle, of being verified, then it follows that he has made an utterance which has no literal significance even for himself.

A further distinction which we must make is the distinction between the "strong" and the "weak" sense of the term "verifiable." A proposition is said to be verifiable, in the strong sense of the term, if, and only if, its truth could be conclusively established in experience. But it is verifiable, in the weak sense, if it is possible for experience to render it probable. In which sense are we using the term when we say that a putative proposition is genuine only if it is verifiable?

It seems to me that if we adopt conclusive verifiability as our criterion of significance, as some positivists have proposed,[5] our argument will prove too much. Consider, for example, the case of general propo-

3   This example has been used by Professor Schlick to illustrate the same point.
4   A remark taken at random from *Appearance and Reality,* by F. H. Bradley.
5   e.g. M. Schlick, "Positivismus and Realismus," *Erkenntnis,* Vol. I, 1930. F. Waismann, "Logische Analyse des Warscheinlichkeitsbegriffs," *Erkenntnis,* Vol. I, 1930.

sitions of law—such propositions, namely, as "arsenic is poisonous"; "all men are mortal"; "a body tends to expand when it is heated." It is of the very nature of these propositions that their truth cannot be established with certainty by any finite series of observations. But if it is recognised that such general propositions of law are designed to cover an infinite number of cases, then it must be admitted that they cannot, even in principle, be verified conclusively. And then, if we adopt conclusive verifiability as our criterion of significance, we are logically obliged to treat these general propositions of law in the same fashion as we treat the statements of the metaphysician.

In face of this difficulty, some positivists[6] have adopted the heroic course of saying that these general propositions are indeed pieces of nonsense, albeit an essentially important type of nonsense. But here the introduction of the term "important" is simply an attempt to hedge. It serves only to mark the authors' recognition that their view is somewhat too paradoxical, without in any way removing the paradox. Besides, the difficulty is not confined to the case of general propositions of law, though it is there revealed most plainly. It is hardly less obvious in the case of propositions about the remote past. For it must surely be admitted that, however strong the evidence in favour of historical statements may be, their truth can never become more than highly probable. And to maintain that they also constituted an important, or unimportant, type of nonsense would be unplausible, to say the very least. Indeed, it will be our contention that no proposition, other than a tautology, can possibly be anything more than a probable hypothesis. And if this is correct, the principle that a sentence can be factually significant only if it expresses what is conclusively verifiable is self-stultifying as a criterion of significance. For it leads to the conclusion that it is impossible to make a significant statement of fact at all.

Nor can we accept the suggestion that a sentence should be allowed to be factually significant if, and only if, it expresses something which is definitely confutable by experience.[7] Those who adopt this course assume that, although no finite series of observations is ever sufficient to establish the truth of a hypothesis beyond all possibility of doubt, there are crucial cases in which a single observation, or series of observations, can definitely confute it. But, as we shall show later on, this assumption is false. A hypothesis cannot be conclusively confuted any more than it can be conclusively verified. For when we take the occurrence of certain observations as proof that a given hypothesis is false, we presuppose the existence of certain conditions. And though, in any given case, it may be extremely improbable that this assumption is false, it is not logically impossible. We shall see that there need be no self-contradiction in holding that some of the relevant circumstances are other than we have taken them to be, and consequently that the hypothesis has not really broken down. And if it is not the case that any hypothesis can be definitely confuted, we cannot hold that the genuineness of a proposition depends on the possibility of its definite confutation.

Accordingly, we fall back on the weaker sense of verification. We say that the question that must be asked about any putative statement of fact is not, Would any observations make its truth or falsehood logically certain? but simply, Would any observations be relevant to the determination of its truth

---

6   e.g. M Schlick, "Die Kausalität in der gegenwärtigen Physik," Naturwissenschaft, Vol. 19, 1931.
7   This has been proposed by Karl Popper in his *Logik der Forschung*.

or falsehood? And it is only if a negative answer is given to this second question that we conclude that the statement under consideration is nonsensical.

To make our position clearer, we may formulate it in another way. Let us call a proposition which records an actual or possible observation an experiential proposition. Then we may say that it is the mark of a genuine factual proposition, not that it should be equivalent to an experiential proposition, or any finite number of experiential propositions, but simply that some experiential propositions can be deduced from it in conjunction with certain other premises without being deducible from those other premises alone.[8]

This criterion seems liberal enough. In contrast to the principle of conclusive verifiability, it clearly does not deny significance to general propositions or to propositions about the past. Let us see what kinds of assertion it rules out.

A good example of the kind of utterance that is condemned by our criterion as being not even false but nonsensical would be the assertion that the world of sense-experience was altogether unreal. It must, of course, be admitted that our senses do sometimes deceive us. We may, as the result of having certain sensations, expect certain other sensations to be obtainable which are, in fact, not obtainable. But, in all such cases, it is further sense-experience that informs us of the mistakes that arise out of sense-experience. We say that the senses sometimes deceive us, just because the expectations to which our sense-experiences give rise do not always accord with what we subsequently experience. That is, we rely on our senses to substantiate or confute the judgements which are based on our sensations. And therefore the fact that our perceptual judgements are sometimes found to be erroneous has not the slightest tendency to show that the world of sense-experience is unreal. And, indeed, it is plain that no conceivable observation, or series of observations, could have any tendency to show that the world revealed to us by sense-experience was unreal. Consequently, anyone who condemns the sensible world as a world of mere appearance, as opposed to reality, is saying something which, according to our criterion of significance, is literally nonsensical.

An example of a controversy which the application of our criterion obliges us to condemn as fictitious is provided by those who dispute concerning the number of substances that there are in the world. For it is admitted both by monists, who maintain that reality is one substance, and by pluralists, who maintain that reality is many, that it is impossible to imagine any empirical situation which would be relevant to the solution of their dispute. But if we are told that no possible observation could give any probability either to the assertion that reality was one substance or to the assertion that it was many, then we must conclude that neither assertion is significant. We shall see later on[9] that there are genuine logical and empirical questions involved in the dispute between monists and pluralists. But the metaphysical question concerning "substance" is ruled out by our criterion as spurious.

A similar treatment must be accorded to the controversy between realists and idealists, in its metaphysical aspect. A simple illustration, which I have made use of in a similar argument elsewhere,[10] will help to

---

8 This is an over-simplified statement, which is not literally correct. I give what I believe to be the correct formulation in the Introduction, p. 13.
9 In Chapter VIII.
10 Vide "Demonstration of the Impossibility of Metaphysics," *Mind*, 1934, p. 339.

demonstrate this. Let us suppose that a picture is discovered and the suggestion made that it was painted by Goya. There is a definite procedure for dealing with such a question. The experts examine the picture to see in what way it resembles the accredited works of Goya, and to see if it bears any marks which are characteristic of a forgery; they look up contemporary records for evidence of the existence of such a picture, and so on. In the end, they may still disagree, but each one knows what empirical evidence would go to confirm or discredit his opinion. Suppose, now, that these men have studied philosophy, and some of them proceed to maintain that this picture is a set of ideas in the perceiver's mind, or in God's mind, others that it is objectively real. What possible experience could any of them have which would be relevant to the solution of this dispute one way or the other? In the ordinary sense of the term "real," in which it is opposed to "illusory," the reality of the picture is not in doubt. The disputants have satisfied themselves that the picture is real, in this sense, by obtaining a correlated series of sensations of sight and sensations of touch. Is there any similar process by which they could discover whether the picture was real, in the sense in which the term "real" is opposed to "ideal"? Clearly there is none. But, if that is so, the problem is fictitious according to our criterion. This does not mean that the realist-idealist controversy may be dismissed without further ado. For it can legitimately be regarded as a dispute concerning the analysis of existential propositions, and so as involving a logical problem which, as we shall see, can be definitively solved.[11] What we have just shown is that the question at issue between idealists and realists becomes fictitious when, as is often the case, it is given a metaphysical interpretation.

There is no need for us to give further examples of the operation of our criterion of significance. For our object is merely to show that philosophy, as a genuine branch of knowledge, must be distinguished from metaphysics. We are not now concerned with the historical question how much of what has traditionally passed for philosophy is actually metaphysical. We shall, however, point out later on that the majority of the "great philosophers" of the past were not essentially metaphysicians, and thus reassure those who would otherwise be prevented from adopting our criterion by considerations of piety.

As to the validity of the verification principle, in the form in which we have stated it, a demonstration win be given in the course of this book. For it will be shown that all propositions which have factual content are empirical hypotheses; and that the function of an empirical hypothesis is to provide a rule for the anticipation of experience.[12] And this means that every empirical hypothesis must be relevant to some actual, or possible, experience, so that a statement which is not relevant to any experience is not an empirical hypothesis, and accordingly has no factual content. But this is precisely what the principle of verifiability asserts.

It should be mentioned here that the fact that the utterances of the metaphysician are nonsensical does not follow simply from the fact that they are devoid of factual content. It follows from that fact, together with the fact that they are not *a priori* propositions. And in assuming that they are not *a priori* propositions, we are once again anticipating the conclusions of a later chapter in this book.[13] For it will be shown there that *a priori* proposi-

---

11   Vide Chapter VIII.
12   Vide Chapter V.
13   Chapter IV.

tions, which have always been attractive to philosophers on account of their certainty, owe this certainty to the fact that they are tautologies. We may accordingly define a metaphysical sentence as a sentence which purports to express a genuine proposition, but does, in fact, express neither a tautology nor an empirical hypothesis. And as tautologies and empirical hypotheses form the entire class of significant propositions, we are justified in concluding that all metaphysical assertions are nonsensical. Our next task is to show how they come to be made.

The use of the term "substance," to which we have already referred, provides us with a good example of the way in which metaphysics mostly comes to be written. It happens to be the case that we cannot, in our language, refer to the sensible properties of a thing without introducing a word or phrase which appears to stand for the thing itself as opposed to anything which may be said about it. And, as a result of this, those who are infected by the primitive superstition that to every name a single real entity must correspond assume that it is necessary to distinguish logically between the thing itself and any, or all, of its sensible properties. And so they employ the term "substance" to refer to the thing itself. But from the fact that we happen to employ a single word to refer to a thing, and make that word the grammatical subject of the sentences in which we refer to the sensible appearances of the thing, it does not by any means follow that the thing itself is a "simple entity," or that it cannot be defined in terms of the totality of its appearances. It is true that in talking of "its" appearances we appear to distinguish the thing from the appearances, but that is simply an accident of linguistic usage. Logical analysis shows that what makes these "appearances" the "appearances of" the same thing is not their relationship to an entity other than themselves, but their relationship to one another. The metaphysician fails to see this because he is misled by a superficial grammatical feature of his language.

A simpler and clearer instance of the way in which a consideration of grammar leads to metaphysics is the case of the metaphysical concept of Being. The origin of our temptation to raise questions about Being, which no conceivable experience would enable us to answer, lies in the fact that, in our language, sentences which express existential propositions and sentences which express attributive propositions may be of the same grammatical form. For instance, the sentences "Martyrs exist" and "Martyrs suffer" both consist of a noun followed by an intransitive verb, and the fact that they have grammatically the same appearance leads one to assume that they are of the same logical type. It is seen that in the proposition "Martyrs suffer," the members of a certain species are credited with a certain attribute, and it is sometimes assumed that the same thing is true of such a proposition as "Martyrs exist." If this were actually the case, it would, indeed, be as legitimate to speculate about the Being of martyrs as it is to speculate about their suffering. But, as Kant pointed out,[14] existence is not an attribute. For, when we ascribe an attribute to a thing, we covertly assert that it exists: so that if existence were itself an attribute, it would follow that all positive existential propositions were tautologies, and all negative existential propositions self-contradictory; and this is not the case.[15] So that those who raise questions about Being which are based on

14   Vide *The Critique of Pure Reason,* "Transcendental Dialectic," Book II, Chapter iii, section 4.
15   This argument is well stated by John Wisdom, *Interpretation and Analysis,* pp. 62, 63.

the assumption that existence is an attribute are guilty of following grammar beyond the boundaries of sense.

A similar mistake has been made in connection with such propositions as "Unicorns are fictitious." Here again the fact that there is a superficial grammatical resemblance between the English sentences "Dogs are faithful" and "Unicorns are fictitious," and between the corresponding sentences in other languages, creates the assumption that they are of the same logical type. Dogs must exist in order to have the property of being faithful, and so it is held that unless unicorns in some way existed they could not have the property of being fictitious. But, as it is plainly self-contradictory to say that fictitious objects exist, the device is adopted of saying that they are real in some non-empirical sense—that they have a mode of real being which is different from the mode of being of existent things. But since there is no way of testing whether an object is real in this sense, as there is for testing whether it is real in the ordinary sense, the assertion that fictitious objects have a special non-empirical mode of real being is devoid of all literal significance. It comes to be made as a result of the assumption that being fictitious is an attribute. And this is a fallacy of the same order as the fallacy of supposing that existence is an attribute, and it can be exposed in the same way.

In general, the postulation of real non-existent entities results from the superstition, just now referred to, that, to every word or phrase that can be the grammatical subject of a sentence, there must somewhere be a real entity corresponding. For as there is no place in the empirical world for many of these "entities," a special non-empirical world is invoked to house them. To this error must be attributed, not only the utterances of a Heidegger, who bases his metaphysics on the assumption that "Nothing" is a name which is used to denote something peculiarly mysterious,[16] but also the prevalence of such problems as those concerning the reality of propositions and universals whose senselessness, though less obvious, is no less complete.

These few examples afford a sufficient indication of the way in which most metaphysical assertions come to be formulated. They show how easy it is to write sentences which are literally nonsensical without seeing that they are nonsensical. And thus we see that the view that a number of the traditional "problems of philosophy" are metaphysical, and consequently fictitious, does not involve any incredible assumptions about the psychology of philosophers.

Among those who recognise that if philosophy is to be accounted a genuine branch of knowledge it must be defined in such a way as to distinguish it from metaphysics, it is fashionable to speak of the metaphysician as a kind of misplaced poet. As his statements have no literal meaning, they are not subject to any criteria of truth or falsehood: but they may still serve to express, or arouse, emotion, and thus be subject to ethical or aesthetic standards. And it is suggested that they may have considerable value, as means of moral inspiration, or even as works of art. In this way, an attempt is made to compensate the metaphysician for his extrusion from philosophy.[17]

I am afraid that this compensation is hardly in accordance with his deserts. The view that the metaphysician is to be reckoned among the poets appears to rest on the

---

16 Vide *Was ist Metaphysik*, by Heidegger: criticised by Rudolf Carnap in his "Überwindung der Metaphysik durch logische Analyse der Sprache," *Erkenntnis*, Vol. II, 1932.
17 For a discussion of this point, see also C. A. Mace, "Representation and Expression," *Analysis*, Vol. I, No. 3; and "Metaphysics and Emotive Language," *Analysis*, Vol. II, Nos. 1 and 2.

assumption that both talk nonsense. But this assumption is false. In the vast majority of cases the sentences which are produced by poets do have literal meaning. The difference between the man who uses language scientifically and the man who uses it emotively is not that the one produces sentences which are incapable of arousing emotion, and the other sentences which have no sense, but that the one is primarily concerned with the expression of true propositions, the other with the creation of a work of art. Thus, if a work of science contains true and important propositions, its value as a work of science will hardly be diminished by the fact that they are inelegantly expressed. And similarly, a work of art is not necessarily the worse for the fact that all the propositions comprising it are literally false. But to say that many literary works are largely composed of falsehoods, is not to say that they are composed of pseudo-propositions. It is, in fact, very rare for a literary artist to produce sentences which have no literal meaning. And where this does occur, the sentences are carefully chosen for their rhythm and balance. If the author writes nonsense, it is because he considers it most suitable for bringing about the effects for which his writing is designed.

The metaphysician, on the other hand, does not intend to write nonsense. He lapses into it through being deceived by grammar, or through committing errors of reasoning, such as that which leads to the view that the sensible world is unreal. But it is not the mark of a poet simply to make mistakes of this sort. There are some, indeed, who would see in the fact that the metaphysician's utterances are senseless a reason against the view that they have esthetic value. And, without going so far as this, we may safely say that it does not constitute a reason for it.

It is true, however, that although the greater part of metaphysics is merely the embodiment of humdrum errors, there remain a number of metaphysical passages which are the work of genuine mystical feeling; and they may more plausibly be held to have moral or esthetic value. But, as far as we are concerned the distinction between the kind of metaphysics that is produced by a philosopher who has been duped by grammar, and the kind that is produced by a mystic who is trying to express the inexpressible, is of no great importance: what is important to us is to realise that even the utterances of the metaphysician who is attempting to expound a vision are literally senseless; so that henceforth we may pursue our philosophical researches with as little regard for them as for the more inglorious kind of metaphysics which comes from a failure to understand the workings of our language.

Critique of Ethics and Theology

Alfred Jules Ayer

There is still one objection to be met before we can claim to have justified our view that all synthetic propositions are empirical hypotheses. This objection is based on the common supposition that our speculative knowledge is of two distinct kinds—that which relates to questions of empirical fact, and that which relates to questions of value. It will be said that "statements of value" are genuine synthetic propositions, but that they cannot with any show of justice be represented as hypotheses, which are used to predict the course of our sensations; and, accordingly, that the existence of ethics and aesthetics as branches of speculative knowledge presents an insuperable objection to our radical empiricist thesis.

In face of this objection, it is our business to give an account of "judgements of value" which is both satisfactory in itself and consistent with our general empiricist principles. We shall set ourselves to show that in so far as statements of value are significant, they are ordinary "scientific" statements; and that in so far as they are not scientific, they are not in the literal sense significant, but are simply expressions of emotion which can be neither true nor false. In maintaining this view, we may confine ourselves for the present to the case of ethical statements. What is said about them will be found to apply, *mutatis mutandis*, to the case of aesthetic statements also.[1]

The ordinary system of ethics, as elaborated in the works of ethical philosophers, is very far from being a homogeneous whole. Not only is it apt to contain pieces of metaphysics, and analyses of non-ethical concepts: its actual ethical contents are themselves of very different kinds. We may divide them, indeed, into four main classes. There are, first of all, propositions which express definitions of ethical terms, or judgements about the legitimacy or possibility of certain definitions. Secondly, there are propositions describing the phenomena of moral experience, and their causes. Thirdly, there are exhortations to moral virtue. And, lastly, there are actual ethical judgements. It is unfortunately the case that the distinction between these four classes, plain as it is, is commonly ignored by ethical philosophers; with the result that it is often very difficult to tell from their works what it is that they are seeking to discover or prove.

In fact, it is easy to see that only the first of our four classes, namely that which comprises the propositions relating to the definitions of ethical terms, can be said to constitute ethical philosophy. The propositions which describe the phenomena of moral experience, and their causes, must be assigned to the science of psychology, or

---

From *Language, Truth and Logic*, 2nd ed. by Alfred Jules Ayer. Reprinted by permission of Dover Publications, Inc., New York.

1   The argument that follows should be read in conjunction with the Introduction, pp. 20-2.

sociology. The exhortations to moral virtue are not propositions at all, but ejaculations or commands which are designed to provoke the reader to action of a certain sort. Accordingly, they do not belong to any branch of philosophy or science. As for the expressions of ethical judgements, we have not yet determined how they should be classified. But inasmuch as they are certainly neither definitions nor comments upon definitions, nor quotations, we may say decisively that they do not belong to ethical philosophy. A strictly philosophical treatise on ethics should therefore make no ethical pronouncements. But it should, by giving an analysis of ethical terms, show what is the category to which all such pronouncements belong. And this is what we are now about to do.

A question which is often discussed by ethical philosophers is whether it is possible to find definitions which would reduce all ethical terms to one or two fundamental terms. But this question, though it undeniably, belongs to ethical philosophy, is not relevant to our present enquiry. We are not now concerned to discover which term, within the sphere of ethical terms, is to be taken as fundamental; whether, for example, "good" can be defined in terms of "right" or "right" in terms of "good," or both in terms of "value." What we are interested in is the possibility of reducing the whole sphere of ethical terms to non-ethical terms. We are enquiring whether statements of ethical value can be translated into statements of empirical fact.

That they can be so translated is the contention of those ethical philosophers who are commonly called subjectivists, and of those who are known as utilitarians. For the utilitarian defines the rightness of actions, and the goodness of ends, in terms of the pleasure, or happiness, or satisfaction, to which they give rise; the subjectivist, in terms of the feelings of approval which a certain person, or group of people, has towards them. Each of these types of definition makes moral judgements into a sub-class of psychological or sociological judgements; and for this reason they are very attractive to us. For, if either was correct, it would follow that ethical assertions were not generically different from the factual assertions which are ordinarily contrasted with them; and the account which we have already given of empirical hypotheses would apply to them also.

Nevertheless we shall not adopt either a subjectivist or a utilitarian analysis of ethical terms. We reject the subjectivist view that to call an action right, or a thing good, is to say that it is generally approved of, because it is not self-contradictory to assert that some actions which are generally approved of are not right, or that some things which are generally approved of are not good. And we reject the alternative subjectivist view that a man who asserts that a certain action is right, or that a certain thing is good, is saying that he himself approves of it, on the ground that a man who confessed that he sometimes approved of what was bad or wrong would not be contradicting himself. And a similar argument is fatal to utilitarianism. We cannot agree that to call an action right is to say that of all the actions possible in the circumstances it would cause, or be likely to cause, the greatest happiness, or the greatest balance of pleasure over pain, or the greatest balance of satisfied over unsatisfied desire, because we find that it is not self-contradictory to say that it is sometimes wrong to perform the action which would actually or probably cause the greatest happiness, or the greatest balance of pleasure over pain, or of satisfied over unsatisfied desire. And since it is not self-contradictory to say that some pleasant things are not good, or that some bad things are desired, it cannot be the case that the sentence "x is good" is equivalent to "*x* is pleasant," or to "*x* is desired." And to every other variant of utilitarianism with which I am acquainted the same objection can be made. And therefore we should, I think, conclude that the validity of ethical judgements is not determined by the felicific tendencies of actions, any more than by the nature of people's feelings; but that it must be regarded as "absolute" or "intrinsic," and not empirically calculable.

If we say this, we are not, of course, denying that it is possible to invent a language in which all ethical symbols are definable in non-ethical terms, or even that it is desirable to invent such a language and adopt it in place of our own; what we are denying is that the suggested reduction of ethical to non-ethical statements is consistent with the conventions of our actual language. That is, we reject utilitarianism and subjectivism, not as proposals to replace our existing ethical notions by new ones, but as analyses of our existing ethical notions. Our contention is simply that, in our language, sentences which contain normative ethical symbols are not equivalent to sentences which express psychological propositions, or indeed empirical propositions of any kind.

It should now be clear that the only information which we can legitimately derive from the study of our aesthetic and moral experiences is information about our own mental and physical make-up. We take note of these experiences as providing data for our psychological and sociological generalisations. And this is the only way in which they serve to increase our knowledge. It follows that any attempt to make our use of ethical and aesthetic concepts the basis of a metaphysical theory concerning the existence of a world of values, as distinct from the world of facts, involves a false analysis of these concepts. Our own analysis has shown that the phenomena of moral experience

cannot fairly be used to support any rationalist or metaphysical doctrine whatsoever. In particular, they cannot, as Kant hoped, be used to establish the existence of a transcendent god.

This mention of God brings us to the question of the possibility of religious knowledge. We shall see that this possibility has already been ruled out by our treatment of metaphysics. But, as this is a point of considerable interest, we may be permitted to discuss it at some length.

It is now generally admitted, at any rate by philosophers, that the existence of a being having the attributes which define the god of any non-animistic religion cannot be demonstratively proved. To see that this is so, we have only to ask ourselves what are the premises from which the existence of such a god could be deduced. If the conclusion that a god exists is to be demonstratively certain, then these premises must be certain; for, as the conclusion of a deductive argument is already contained in the premises, any uncertainty there may be about the truth of the premises is necessarily shared by it. But we know that no empirical proposition can ever be anything more than probable. It is only *a priori* propositions that are logically certain. But we cannot deduce the existence of a god from an *a priori* proposition. For we know that the reason why *a priori* propositions are certain is that they are tautologies. And from a set of tautologies nothing but a further tautology can be validly deduced. It follows that there is no possibility of demonstrating the existence of a god.

What is not so generally recognised is that there can be no way of proving that the existence of a god, such as the God of Christianity, is even probable. Yet this also is easily shown. For if the existence of such a god were probable, then the proposition that he existed would be an empirical hypothesis. And in that case it would be possible to deduce from it, and other empirical hypotheses, certain experiential propositions which were not deducible from those other hypotheses alone. But in fact this is not possible. It is sometimes claimed, indeed, that the existence of a certain sort of regularity in nature constitutes sufficient evidence for the existence of a god. But if the sentence "God exists" entails no more than that certain types of phenomena occur in certain sequences, then to assert the existence of a god will be simply equivalent to asserting that there is the requisite regularity in nature; and no religious man would admit that this was all he intended to assert in asserting the existence of a god. He would say that in talking about God, he was talking about a transcendent being who might be known through certain empirical manifestations, but certainly could not be defined in terms of those manifestations. But in that case the term "god" is a metaphysical term. And if "god" is a metaphysical term, then it cannot be even probable that a god exists. For to say that "God exists" is to make a metaphysical utterance which cannot be either true or false. And by the same criterion, no sentence which purports to describe the nature of a transcendent god can possess any literal significance.

It is important not to confuse this view of religious assertions with the view that is adopted by atheists, or agnostics.[2] For it is characteristic of an agnostic to hold that the existence of a god is a possibility in which there is no good reason either to believe or disbelieve; and it is characteristic of an atheist to hold that it is at least probable that no god exists. And our view that all utterances about the nature of God are nonsensical, so far from being identical with, or even lending any support to, either of these familiar contentions, is actually incompatible with

them. For if the assertion that there is a god is nonsensical, then the atheist's assertion that there is no god is equally nonsensical, since it is only a significant proposition that can be significantly contradicted. As for the agnostic, although he refrains from saying either that there is or that there is not a god, he does not deny that the question whether a transcendent god exists is a genuine question. He does not deny that the two sentences "There is a transcendent god" and "There is no transcendent god" express propositions one of which is actually true and the other false. All he says is that we have no means of telling which of them is true, and therefore ought not to commit ourselves to either. But we have seen that the sentences in question do not express propositions at all. And this means that agnosticism also is ruled out.

Thus we offer the theist the same comfort as we gave to the moralist. His assertions cannot possibly be valid, but they cannot be invalid either. As he says nothing at all about the world, he cannot justly be accused of saying anything false, or anything for which he has insufficient grounds. It is only when the theist claims that in asserting the existence of a transcendent god he is expressing a genuine proposition that we are entitled to disagree with him.

It is to be remarked that in cases where deities are identified with natural objects, assertions concerning them may be allowed to be significant. If, for example, a man tells me that the occurrence of thunder is alone both necessary and sufficient to establish the truth of the proposition that Jehovah is angry, I may conclude that, in his usage of words, the sentence "Jehovah is angry" is equivalent to "It is thundering." But in sophisticated religions, though they may be to some extent based on men's awe of natural process which they cannot sufficiently un-

---

2   This point was suggested to me by Professor H. H. Price.

derstand, the "person" who is supposed to control the empirical world is not himself located in it; he is held to be superior to the empirical world, and so outside it; and he is endowed with super-empirical attributes. But the notion of a person whose essential attributes are nonempirical is not an intelligible notion at all. We may have a word which is used as if it named this "person," but, unless the sentences in which it occurs express propositions which are empirically verifiable, it cannot be said to symbolize anything. And this is the case with regard to the word "god," in the usage in which it is intended to refer to a transcendent object. The mere existence of the noun is enough to foster the illusion that there is a real, or at any rate a possible entity corresponding to it. It is only when we enquire what God's attributes are that we discover that "God," in this usage, is not a genuine name.

It is common to find belief in a transcendent god conjoined with belief in an afterlife. But, in the form which it usually takes, the content of this belief is not a genuine hypothesis. To say that men do not ever die, or that the state of death is merely a state of prolonged insensibility, is indeed to express a significant proposition, though all the available evidence goes to show that it is false. But to say that there is something imperceptible inside a man, which is his soul or his real self, and that it goes on living after he is dead, is to make a metaphysical assertion which has no more factual content than the assertion that there is a transcendent god.

It is worth mentioning that, according to the account which we have given of religious assertions, there is no logical ground for antagonism between religion and natural science. As far as the question of truth or falsehood is concerned, there is no opposition between the natural scientist and the theist who believes in a transcendent god. For since the religious utterances of the theist are not genuine propositions at all, they cannot stand in any logical relation to the propositions of science. Such antagonism as there is between religion and science appears to consist in the fact that science takes away one of the motives which make men religious. For it is acknowledged that one of the ultimate sources of religious feeling lies in the inability of men to determine their own destiny; and science tends to destroy the feeling of awe with which men regard an alien world, by making them believe that they can understand and anticipate the course of natural phenomena, and even to some extent control it. The fact that it has recently become fashionable for physicists themselves to be sympathetic towards religion is a point in favour of this hypothesis. For this sympathy towards religion marks the physicists' own lack of confidence in the validity of their hypotheses, which is a reaction on their part from the anti-religious dogmatism of nineteenth-century scientists, and a natural outcome of the crisis through which physics has just passed.

It is not within the scope of this enquiry to enter more deeply into the causes of religious feeling, or to discuss the probability of the continuance of religious belief. We are concerned only to answer those questions which arise out of our discussion of the possibility of religious knowledge. The point which we wish to establish is that there cannot be any transcendent truths of religion. For the sentences which the theist uses to express such "truths" are not literally significant.

An interesting feature of this conclusion is that it accords with what many theists are accustomed to say themselves. For we are often told that the nature of God is a mystery which transcends the human understanding. But to say that something transcends the human understanding is to say that it is unintelligible. And what is unintelligible cannot significantly be described. Again, we are told that God is not an object of reason but an object of faith. This may be nothing more than an admission that the existence of God must be taken on trust, since it cannot be proved. But it may also be an assertion that God is the object of a purely mystical intuition, and cannot therefore be defined in terms which are intelligible to the reason. And I think there are many theists who would assert this. But if one allows that it is impossible to define God in intelligible terms, then one is allowing that it is impossible for a sentence both to be significant and to be about God. If a mystic admits that the object of his vision is something which cannot be described, then he must also admit that he is bound to talk nonsense when he describes it.

For his part, the mystic may protest that his intuition does reveal truths to him, even though he cannot explain to others what these truths are; and that we who do not possess this faculty of intuition can have no ground for denying that it is a cognitive faculty. For we can hardly maintain *a priori* that there are no ways of discovering true propositions except those which we ourselves employ. The answer is that we set no limit to the number of ways in which one may come to formulate a true proposition. We do not in any way deny that a synthetic truth may be discovered by purely intuitive methods as well as by the rational method of induction. But we do say that every synthetic proposition, however it may have been arrived at, must be subject to the test of actual experience. We do not deny *a priori* that the mystic is able to discover truths by his own special methods. We wait to hear what are the propositions which embody his discoveries, in order to see whether they are verified or confuted by our empirical observations. But the mystic, so far from producing propositions which are empirically verified, is unable to produce any intelligible propositions at all. And therefore we say that his intuition has not revealed to him any facts. It is no use his saying that he has apprehended facts but is unable to express them. For we know that if he really had acquired any information, he would be able to express it. He would be able to indicate in some way or other how the genuineness of his discovery might be empirically determined. The fact that he cannot reveal what he "knows," or even himself devise an empirical test to validate his "knowledge," shows that his state of mystical intuition is not a genuinely cognitive state. So that in describing his vision the mystic does not give us any information about the external world; he merely gives us indirect information about the condition of his own mind.

These considerations dispose of the argument from religious experience, which many philosophers still regard as a valid argument in favour of the existence of a god. They say that it is logically possible for men to be immediately acquainted with God, as they are immediately acquainted with a sense-content, and that there is no reason why one should be prepared to believe a man when he says that he is seeing a yellow patch, and refuse to believe him when he says that he is seeing God. The answer to this is that if the man who asserts that he is seeing God is merely asserting that he is experiencing a peculiar kind of sense-content, then we do not for a moment deny that his assertion may be true. But, ordinarily, the man who says that he is seeing God is saying not merely that he is experiencing a religious emotion, but also that there exists a transcendent being who is the object of this emotion; just as the man who says that he sees a yellow patch is ordinarily saying not merely that his visual sense-field contains a yellow sense-content, but also that there exists a yellow object to which the sense-content belongs.

And it is not irrational to be prepared to believe a man when he asserts the existence of a yellow object, and to refuse to believe him when he asserts the existence of a transcendent god. For whereas the sentence "There exists here a yellow-coloured material thing" expresses a genuine synthetic proposition which could be empirically verified, the sentence "There exists a transcendent god" has, as we have seen, no literal significance.

We conclude, therefore, that the argument from religious experience is altogether fallacious. The fact that people have religious experiences is interesting from the psychological point of view, but it does not in any way imply that there is such a thing as religious knowledge, any more than our having moral experiences implies that there is such a thing as moral knowledge. The theist, like the moralist, may believe that his experiences are cognitive experiences, but, unless he can formulate his "knowledge" in propositions that are empirically verifiable, we may be sure that he is deceiving himself It follows that those philosophers who fill their books with assertions that they intuitively "know" this or that moral or religious "truth" are merely providing material for the psycho-analyst. For no act of intuition can be said to reveal a truth about any matter of fact unless it issues in verifiable propositions. And all such propositions are to be incorporated in the system of empirical propositions which constitutes science.

Genesis

Chapter 38

The sons of Juda: the death of her and Onan: the birth of Phares and Zara

1 At that time Juda went down from his brethren, and turned in to a certain Odollamite, named Hiras.

2 And he saw there the daughter of a man of Chanaan, called Sue: and taking her to wife, he went in unto her.

3 And she conceived, and bore a son, and called his name Her.

4 And conceiving again, she bore a son, and called him Onan.

5 She bore also a third: whom she called Sela. After whose birth, she ceased to bear any more.

6 And Juda took a wife for Her his firstborn, whose name was Thamar.

7 And Her, the firstborn of Juda, was wicked in the sight of the Lord: and was slain by him.

8 Juda therefore said to Onan his son: Go in to thy brother's wife and marry her, that thou mayst raise seed to thy brother.

9 He knowing that the children should not be his, when he went in to his brother's wife, spilled *his* seed upon the ground, lest children should be born in his brother's name.

10 And therefore, the Lord slew him, because he did a detestable thing.

11 Wherefore Juda said to Thamar his daughter in law: Remain a widow in thy father's house, till Sela my son grow up: for he was afraid lest he also might die, as his brethren did. She went her way and dwelt in her father's house.

Leviticus

Chapter 18

Marriage is prohibited in certain degrees of kindred: and all unnatural lusts.

1 And the Lord spoke to Moses, saying:

2 Speak to the children of Israel, and thou shalt say to them: I am the Lord your God.

3 You shall not do according to the custom of the land of Egypt, in which you dwelt: neither shall you act according to the manner of the country of Chanaan, into which I will bring you, nor shall you walk in their ordinances.

4 You shall do my judgments, and shall observe my precepts, and shall walk in them. I am the Lord your God.

5 Keep my laws and my judgments, which if a man do, he shall live in them. I am the Lord.

6 No man shall approach to her that is near of kin to him, to uncover her nakedness. I am the Lord.

7 Thou shalt not uncover the nakedness of thy father, or of the nakedness of thy mother: she is thy mother, thou shalt not uncover her nakedness.

8 Thou shalt not uncover the nakedness of thy father's wife: for it is the nakedness of thy father.

9 Thou shalt not uncover the nakedness of thy sister by father or by mother, whether born at home or abroad.

10 Thou shalt not uncover the nakedness of thy son's daughter, or thy daughter's daughter: because it is thy own nakedness.

11 Thou shalt not uncover the nakedness of thy father's wife daughter, whom she bore to thy father, and who is thy sister.

12 Thou shalt not uncover the nakedness of thy father's sister: because she is the flesh of thy father.

13 Thou shalt not uncover the nakedness of thy mother's sister: because she is thy mother's flesh.

14 Thou shalt now uncover the nakedness of thy father's brother: neither shalt thou approach to his wife, who is joined in thee by affinity.

15 Thou shalt not uncover the nakedness of thy daughter in law: because she is thy son's wife, neither shalt thou discover her shame.

16 Thou shalt not uncover the nakedness of thy brother's wife: because it is the nakedness of thy brother.

17 Thou shalt not uncover the nakedness of thy wife and her daughter. Thou shalt not take her son's daughter or her daughter's daughter, to discover her shame: because they are her flesh, and such copulation is incest.

18 Thou shalt not take thy wife's sister for a harlot, to rival her, neither shalt thou discover her nakedness, while she is yet living.

19 Thou shalt not approach to a women having her flowers, neither shalt that uncover her nakedness.

20 Thou shalt not lie with thy neighbour's wife, nor be defiled with mingling of seed.

21 Thou shalt not give any of thy seed to be consecrated to the idol Moloch, nor defile the name of thy God: I am the Lord.

22 Thou shalt not lie with mankind as with womankind, because it is an abomination.

23 Thou shalt not copulate with any beast, neither shalt thou be defiled with it. A woman shalt not lie down to a beast, nor copulate with it: because it is a *heinous* crime.

24 Defile not yourselves with any of these things with which all the nations have been defiled, which I will cast out before you.

25 And with which the land is defiled: the abominations of which I will visit, that it may vomit out its inhabitants.

26 Keep ye my ordinances and my judgments, and do not any of these abominations: neither any of your own nation, not any stranger that sojourneth among you.

27 For all these detestable things the inhabitants of the land have done, that were before you, and have defiled it.

28 Beware then, lest in like manner, it vomit you also out, if you do the like things, as it vomited out the nation that was before you.

29 Every soul that shall commit any of these abominations, shall perish from the midst of his people.

30 Keep my commandments. Do not the things which they have done, that have been before you, and be not defiled therein. I am the Lord your God.

I Corinthians

Chapter 6

He blames them for going to law before unbelievers. Of sins that exclude from the kingdom of heaven. The evil of fornication.

1 Dare any of you, having a matter against another, go to be judged before the unjust, and not before the saints?

2 Know you not that the saints shall judge this world? And if the world shall be judged by you, are you unworthy to judge the smallest matters?

3 Know you not that we shall judge angels? how much more things of this world?

4 If therefore you have judgments of things pertaining to this world, set them to judge, who are the most despised in the church.

5 I speak to your shame. Is it so that there is not among you any one wise man, that is able to judge between his brethren?

6 But brother goeth to law with brother, and that before unbelievers.

7 Already indeed there is plainly a fault among you, that you have lawsuits one with another. Why do you not rather take wrong? Why do you not rather suffer yourselves to be defrauded?

8 But you do wrong and defraud, and that to *your* brethren.

9 Know you not that the unjust shall not possess the kingdom of God? Do not err: neither fornicators, nor idolators, not adulterers.

10 Nor the effeminate, nor liers with mankind, nor thieves, nor covetous, nor drunkards, nor railers, nor extortioners, shall possess the kingdom of God.

11 And such some of you were; but you are washed, but you are sanctified, but you are justified in the name of our Lord Jesus Christ, and the Spirit of our God.

12 All things are lawful to me, but all things are not expedient. All things are lawful to me, but I will not be brought under the power of any.

13 Meat for the belly, and the belly for the meats; but God shall destroy both it and them: but the body is not for fornication, but for the Lord, and the Lord for the body.

14 Now God hath both raised up the Lord, and will raise us up also by his power.

15 Know you not that your bodies are the members of Christ? Shall I then take the members of Christ, and make them the members of an harlot? God forbid.

16 Or know you not, that he who is joined to a harlot, is made one body? *For they shall be*, saith he, *two in one flesh.*

17 But he who is joined to the Lord, is one spirit.

18 Fly fornication. Every sin that a man doth, is without the body; but he that committeth fornication, sinneth against his own body.

19 Or know you not, that your members are the temple of the Holy Ghost, who is in

you, whom you have from God; and you are not your own?

20 For you are bought with a great price. Glorify and bear God in your body.

Chapter 7

Lessons relating to marriage and celibacy. Virginity is preferable to a married state.

1 Now concerning the things whereof you wrote to me: It is good for a man not to touch a woman.

2 But for fear of fornication, let every man have his own wife, and let every woman have her own husband.

3 Let the husband render the debt to his wife, and the wife also in the like manner to her husband.

from The Prince

Niccolo Machiavelli

Concerning the Things for which Men, and Especially Princes, are Praised or Blamed

It remains now to see what ought to be the rules of conduct for a prince towards subject and friends. . . .

. . . It is necessary for a prince wishing to hold his own to know how do wrong, and to make use of it or not according to necessity . . . It is necessary for him to be sufficiently prudent that he may know how to avoid the reproach of those vices which would lose him his state; and, also to keep himself, if it be possible, from those which would not lose him it; but this not being possible, he may with less hesitation abandon himself to them. And again, he need not make himself uneasy at incurring a reproach for those vices without which the state can only be saved with difficulty, for if everything is considered carefully, it will be found that something which looks like virtue, if followed, would be his ruin; while something else, which looks like vice, yet followed brings him security and prosperity.

Concerning Liberality and Meanness

. . . It would be well to be reputed liberal. Nevertheless, liberality exercised in a way that does not bring you the reputation for it, injures you; for if one exercises it honestly and as it should be exercised, it may not become known, and you will not avoid the reproach of its opposite. Therefore, any one wishing to maintain among men the name of liberal is obliged to avoid no attribute of magnificence; so that a prince thus inclined will consume in such acts all his property, and will be compelled in the end, if he wish to maintain the name of liberal, to unduly weigh down his people, and tax them, and do everything he can to get money. This will soon make him odious to his subjects, and becoming poor he will be little valued by anyone; thus, with his liberality, having offended many and rewarded few, he is affected by the very first trouble and imperiled by whatever may be the first danger; recognizing this himself, and wishing to draw back from it, he runs at once into the reproach of being miserly.

Therefore, a prince, not being able to exercise this virtue of liberality in such a way that it is recognized, except to his cost, if he is wise he ought not to fear the reputation of being mean, for in time he will come to be more considered than if liberal, seeing that with his economy his revenues are enough, that he can defend himself against all attacks, and is able to engage in enterprises without burdening his people; thus it comes to pass that he exercises liberality towards all from whom he does not take, who are numberless, and meanness towards those to whom he does not give, who are few. . . .

A prince, therefore, provided that he has not to rob his subjects, that he can defend himself, that he does not become poor and abject, that he is not forced to become rapacious, ought to hold of little account a reputation for being mean, for it is one of those vices which will enable him to govern.

. . . Either a prince spends that which is his own or his subjects' or else that of others. In the first case he ought to be sparing, in the second he ought not to neglect any opportunity for liberality. And to the prince who goes forth with his army, supporting it by pillage, sack, and extortion, handling that which belongs to others, this liberality is necessary, otherwise he would not be followed by soldiers. And of that which is neither yours nor your subjects' you can be a ready giver, as were Cyrus, Caesar, and Alexander; because it does not take away your reputation if you squander that of others, but adds to it; it is only squandering your own that injures you.

And there is nothing wastes so rapidly as liberality, for even while you exercise it you lose the power to do so, and so become either poor or despised, or else, in avoiding poverty, rapacious and hated. And a prince should guard himself, above all things, against being despised and hated; and liberality leads you to both. Therefore it is wiser to have a reputation for meanness which brings reproach without hatred, than to be compelled through seeking a reputation for liberality to incur a name for rapacity which begets reproach with hatred.

Concerning Cruelty and Clemency, and Whether it is Better to be Loved than Feared

. . . Every prince ought to desire to be considered clement and not cruel. Nevertheless he ought to take care not to misuse this clemency. Cesare Borgia was considered cruel; notwithstanding, his cruelty reconciled the Romagna, unified it, and restored it to peace and loyalty. And if this be rightly considered, he will be seen to have been much more merciful than the Florentine people, who, to avoid a reputation for cruelty permitted Pistoia to be destroyed. Therefore a prince, so long as he keeps his subjects united and loyal, ought not to mind the reproach of cruelty; because with a few examples he will be more merciful than those who, through too much mercy, allow disorders to arise, from which follow murder or robbery; for these are wont to injure the whole people, while those executions which originate with a prince offend the individual only.

And of all princes, it is impossible for the new prince to avoid the imputation of cruelty, owing to new states being full of dangers. . . . Nevertheless he ought to be slow to believe and to act, nor should he himself show fear, but proceed in a temperate manner with prudence and humanity, so that too much confidence may not make him incautious and too much distrust render him intolerable.

Upon this a question arises: whether it be better to be loved than feared or feared than loved? It may be answered that one should wish to be both, but, because it is difficult to unite them in one person, it is much safer to be feared than loved, when, of the two, either must be dispensed with. Because this is to be asserted in general of men, that they are ungrateful, fickle, false, cowards, covetous, and as long as you succeed they are yours entirely; they will offer you their blood, property, life, and children, as is said above, when the need is far distant; but when it approaches they turn against you. And that prince who, relying entirely on their promises, has neglected other precautions, is ruined; because friendships that are obtained by payments, and not by greatness or nobility of mind, may indeed be earned, but they are not secured, and in time of need cannot be relied upon; and men have less scruple in offending one who is beloved than one who is feared, for love is preserved by the link of obligation which, owing to the baseness of men, is broken at every opportunity for their advantage; but fear preserves you by a dread of punishment which never fails.

The Origin and Nature of the State

Thomas Hobbes

Of the Causes, Generation, and Definition of a Commonwealth.

The final cause, end, or design of men, who naturally love liberty, and dominion over others, in the introduction of that restraint upon themselves, in which we see them live in commonwealths, is the foresight of their own preservation, and of a more contented life thereby; that is to say, of getting themselves out from that miserable condition of war, which is necessarily consequent, as hath been shown in chapter xiii, to the natural passions of men, when there is no visible power to keep them in awe, and tie them by fear of punishment to the performance of their covenants, and observation of those laws of nature set down in the fourteenth and fifteenth chapters.

For the laws of nature, as "justice," "equity," "modesty," "mercy," and, in sum, "doing to others as we would be done to," of themselves, without the terror of some power to cause them to be observed, are contrary to our natural passions, that carry us to partiality, pride, revenge, and the like. And covenants, without the sword, are but words, and of no strength to secure a man at all. Therefore notwithstanding the laws of nature, which everyone hath then kept, when he has the will to keep them, when he can do it safely, if there be no power erected, or not great enough for our security, every man will and may lawfully rely on his own strength and art, for caution against all other men. And in all places where men have lived by small families, to rob and spoil one another has been a trade, and so far from being reputed against the law of nature, that the greater spoils they gained, the greater was their honor; and men observed no other laws therein, but the laws of honor; that is, to abstain from cruelty, leaving to men their lives, and instruments of husbandry. And as small families did then, so now do cities and kingdoms, which are but greater families, for their own security, enlarge their dominions, upon all pretenses of danger, and fear of invasion, or assistance that may be given to invaders, and endeavor as much as they can to subdue or weaken their neighbors, by open force and secret arts, for want of other caution, justly; and are remembered for it in after ages with honor.

Not is it the joining together of a small number of men that gives them this security; because in small numbers, small additions on the one side or the other make the advantage of strength so great as is sufficient to carry the victory; and therefore gives encouragement to an invasion. The multitude sufficient to confide in for our security is not determined by any certain number, but by comparison with the enemy we fear; and is then sufficient, when the odds of the enemy is not of so visible and conspicuous moment to determine the event of war, as to move him to attempt.

And be there never so great a multitude; yet if their actions be directed according to their particular judgments and particular appetites, they can expect thereby no defense, nor protection, neither against a common enemy, nor against the injuries of one another. For being distracted in opinions concerning the best use and application of their strength, they do not help but hinder one another; and reduce their strength by mutual opposition to nothing: whereby they are easily, not only subdued by a very few that agree together; but also when there is no common enemy, they make war upon each other, for their particular interests. For if we could suppose a great multitude of men to consent in the observation of justice, and other laws of nature, without a common power to keep them all in awe, we might as well suppose all mankind to do the same; and then there neither would be nor need to be any civil government or commonwealth at all; because there would be peace without subjection.

Nor is it enough for the security, which men desire should last all the time of their life, that they be governed and directed by one judgment, for a limited time: as in one battle, or one war. For though they obtain a victory by their unanimous endeavor against a foreign enemy; yet afterwards, when either they have no common enemy, or he that by one part is held for an enemy is by another part held for a friend, they must needs by the difference of their interests dissolve, and fall again into a war among themselves. . . .

The only way to erect such a common power as may be able to defend them from the invasion of foreigners and the injuries of one another, and thereby to secure them in such sort as that by their own industry, and by the fruits of the earth, they may nourish themselves and live contentedly, is to confer all their power and strength upon one man, or upon one assembly of men, that may reduce all their wills, by plurality of voices, unto one will: which is as much as to say, to appoint one man, or assembly of men, to

bear their person; and everyone to own and acknowledge himself to be author of whatsoever he that so beareth their person shall act, or cause to be acted, in those things which concern the common peace and safety; and therein to submit their wills, every one to his will, and their judgments to his judgment. This is more than consent, or concord; it is a real unity of them all in one and the same person, made by covenant of every man with every man, in such manner as if every man should say to every man, "I authorize and give up my right of governing myself, to this man or to this assembly of men, on this condition, that thou give up thy right to him and authorize all his actions in like manner." This done, the multitude so united in one person is called a "commonwealth," in Latin *civitas*. This is the generation of that great leviathan, or rather, to speak more reverently, of that mortal God, to which we owe under the immortal God, our peace and defense. For by this authority, given him by every particular man in the commonwealth, he hath the use of so much power and strength conferred on him, that by terror thereof, he is enabled to perform the wills of them all, to peace at home, and mutual aid against their enemies abroad. And in him consisteth the essence of the commonwealth; which, to define it, is "one person, of whose acts a great multitude, by mutual covenants one with another, have made themselves every one the author, to the end he may use the strength and means of them all, as he shall think expedient, for their peace and common defense."

And he that carrieth this person is called sovereign, and said to have sovereign power; and everyone besides, his subject.

The attaining to this sovereign power is by two ways. One, by natural force; as when a man maketh his children to submit themselves, and their children, to his government, as being able to destroy them if they refuse;

or by war subdueth his enemies to his will, giving them their lives on that condition. The other is when men agree among themselves to submit to some man, or assembly of men, voluntarily, on confidence to be protected by him against all others. This latter may be called a political commonwealth, or commonwealth by institution; and the former, a commonwealth by acquisition. And first, I shall speak of a commonwealth by institution. . . .

Mein Kampf

Adolf Hitler

The ignorance of the broad masses about the inner nature of the Jew, the lack of instinct and narrow-mindedness of our upper classes, make the people an easy victim for this Jewish campaign of lies.

While from innate cowardice the upper classes turn away from a man whom the Jew attacks with lies and slander, the broad masses from stupidity or simplicity believe everything. The state authorities either cloak themselves in silence or, what usually happens, in order to put an end to the Jewish press campaign, they persecute the unjustly attacked, which, in the eyes of such an official ass, passes as the preservation of state authority and the safeguarding of law and order.

Slowly fear of the Marxist weapon of Jewry descends like a nightmare on the mind and soul of decent people.

They begin to tremble before the terrible enemy and thus have become his final victim.

The Jew's domination in the state seems so assured that now not only can he call himself a Jew again, but he ruthlessly admits his ultimate national and political designs. A section of his race openly owns itself to be a foreign people, yet even here they lie. For while the Zionists try to make the rest of the world believe that the national consciousness of the Jew finds its satisfaction in the creation of a Palestinian state, the Jews again slyly dupe the dumb *Goyim.*[1] It doesn't even enter their heads to build up a Jewish state in Palestine for the purpose of living there; all they want is a central organization for their international world swindle, endowed with its own sovereign rights and removed from the intervention of other states: a haven for convicted scoundrels and a university for budding crooks.

It is a sign of their rising confidence and sense of security that at a time when one section is still playing the German, Frenchman, or Englishman, the other with open effrontery comes out as the Jewish race.

How close they see approaching victory can be seen by the hideous aspect which their relations with the members of other peoples takes on.

With satanic joy in his face, the black-haired Jewish youth lurks in wait for the unsuspecting girl whom he defiles with his blood, thus stealing her from her people. With every means he tries to destroy the racial foundations of the people he has set out to subjugate. Just as he himself systematically ruins women and girls, he does not shrink back from pulling down the blood barriers for others, even on a large scale. It was and it is Jews who bring the Negroes into the Rhineland, always with the same secret thought and clear aim of ruining the

---

1 Yiddish for Gentiles.

hated white race by the necessarily resulting bastardization, throwing it down from its cultural and political height, and himself rising to be its master.

For a racially pure people which is conscious of its blood can never be enslaved by the Jew. In this world he will forever be master over bastards and bastards alone.

And so he tries systematically to lower the racial level by a continuous poisoning of individuals.

And in politics he begins to replace the idea of democracy by the dictatorship of the proletariat.

In the organized mass of Marxism he has found the weapon which lets him dispense with democracy and in its stead allows him to subjugate and govern the peoples with a dictatorial and brutal fist.

He works systematically for revolutionization in a twofold sense: economic and political.

Around peoples who offer too violent a resistance to attack from within he weaves a net of enemies, thanks to his international influence, incites them to war, and finally, if necessary, plants the flag of revolution on the very battlefields.

In economics he undermines the states until the social enterprises which have become unprofitable are taken from the state and subjected to his financial control.

In the political field he refuses the state the means for its self-preservation, destroys the foundations of all national self-maintenance and defense, destroys faith in the leadership, scoffs at its history and past, and drags everything that is truly great into the gutter.

Culturally he contaminates art, literature, the theater, makes a mockery of natural feeling, overthrows all concepts of beauty and sublimity, of the noble and the good, and instead drags men down into the sphere of his own base nature.

Religion is ridiculed, ethics and morality represented as outmoded, until the last props of a nation in its struggle for existence in this world have fallen.

(e)[2] Now begins the great last revolution. In gaining political power the Jew casts off the few cloaks that he still wears. The democratic people's Jew becomes the blood-Jew and tyrant over peoples. In a few years he tries to exterminate the national intelligentsia and by robbing the peoples of their natural intellectual leadership makes them ripe for the slave's lot of permanent subjugation.

The most frightful example of this kind is offered by Russia, where he killed or starved about thirty million people with positively fanatical savagery, in part amid inhuman tortures, in order to give a gang of Jewish journalists and stock exchange bandits domination over a great people.

The end is not only the end of the freedom of the peoples oppressed by the Jew, but also the end of this parasite upon the nations. After the death of his victim, the vampire sooner or later dies too.

* * *

If we pass all the causes of the German collapse in review, the ultimate and most decisive remains the failure to recognize the racial problem and especially the Jewish menace.

The defeats on the battlefield in August, 1918, would have been child's play to bear. They stood in no proportion to the victories of our people. It was not they that caused our downfall; no, it was brought about by that power which prepared these defeats by systematically over many decades robbing our

---

2   The writer has lost track of his letters. Second edition has (i).

people of the political and moral instincts and forces which alone make nations capable and hence worthy of existence.

In heedlessly ignoring the question of the preservation of the racial foundations of our nation, the old Reich disregarded the sole right which gives life in this world. Peoples which bastardize themselves, or let themselves be bastardized, sin against the will of eternal Providence, and when their ruin is encompassed by a stronger enemy it is not an injustice done to them but only the restoration of justice. If a people no longer wants to respect the Nature-given qualities of its being which root in its blood, it has no further right to complain over the loss of its earthly existence.

Everything on this earth is capable of improvement. Every defeat can become the father of a subsequent victory, every lost war the cause of a later resurgence, every hardship the fertilization of human energy, and from every oppression the forces for a new spiritual rebirth can come—as long as the blood is preserved pure.

The lost purity of the blood alone destroys inner happiness forever, plunges man into the abyss for all time, and the consequences can never more be eliminated from body and spirit.

Only by examining and comparing all other problems of life in the light of this one question shall we see how absurdly petty they are by this standard. They are all limited in time—but the question of preserving or not preserving the purity of the blood will endure as long as there are men.

All really significant symptoms of decay of the pre-War period can in the last analysis be reduced to racial causes.

Whether we consider questions of general justice or cankers of economic life, symptoms of cultural decline or processes of political degeneration, questions of faulty schooling or the bad influence exerted on grown-ups by the press, etc., everywhere and always it is fundamentally the disregard of the racial needs of our own people or failure to see a foreign racial menace.

And that is why all attempts at reform, all works for social relief and political exertions, all economic expansion and every apparent increase of intellectual knowledge were futile as far as their results were concerned. The nation, and the organism which enables[3] and preserves its life on this earth, the state, did not grow inwardly healthier, but obviously languished more and more. All the illusory prosperity of the old Reich could not hide its inner weakness, and every attempt really to strengthen the Reich failed again and again, due to disregarding the most important question.

It would be a mistake to believe that the adherents of the various political tendencies which were tinkering around on the German national body—yes, even a certain section of the leaders—were bad or malevolent men in themselves. Their activity was condemned to sterility only because the best of them saw at most the forms of our general disease and tried to combat them, but blindly ignored the virus. Anyone who systematically follows the old Reich's line of political development is bound to arrive, upon calm examination, at the realization that even at the time of the unification, hence the rise of the German nation, the inner decay was already in full swing, and that despite all apparent political successes and despite increasing economic wealth, the general situation was deteriorating from year to year. If nothing else, the elections for the Reichstag announced, with their outward swelling of the Marxist vote, the steadily approaching inward and hence also outward collapse. All the successes of

---

3   *"Die Nation und ihr das Leben auf dieser Erde befähigender und erhaltender Organismus."*

the so-called bourgeois parties were worthless, not only because even with so-called bourgeois electoral victories they were unable to halt the numerical growth of the Marxist flood, but because they themselves above all now bore the ferments of decay in their own bodies. Without suspecting it, the bourgeois world itself was inwardly infected with the deadly poison of Marxist ideas and its resistance often sprang more from the competitor's envy of ambitious leaders than from a fundamental rejection of adversaries determined to fight to the utmost. In these long years there was only one who kept up an imperturbable, unflagging fight, and this was the *Jew*. His Star of David[4] rose higher and higher in proportion as our people's will for self-preservation vanished.

Therefore, in August, 1914, it was not a people resolved to attack which rushed to the battlefield; no, it was only the last flicker of the national instinct of self-preservation in face of the progressing pacifist-Marxist paralysis of our national body. Since even in these days of destiny, our people did not recognize the inner enemy, all outward resistance was in vain and Providence did not bestow her reward on the victorious sword, but followed the law of eternal retribution.

On the basis of this inner realization, there took form in our new movement the leading principles as well as the tendency, which in our conviction were alone capable, not only of halting the decline of the German people, but of creating the granite foundation upon which some day a state will rest which represents, not an alien mechanism of economic concerns and interests, but a national organism.

---

4   Typical Hitlerian metaphor. The Star of David, it will be remembered is not a star, but a shield.

The Political Doctrine of Fascism

Alfredo Rocco

Premier Mussolini's Endorsement of Signor Rocco's Speech

The following message was sent by Benito Mussolini, the Premier of Italy, to Signor Rocco after he had delivered his speech at Perugia.

Dear Rocco,

I have just read your magnificent address which I endorse throughout. You have presented in a masterful way the doctrine of Fascism. For Fascism has a doctrine, or, if you will, a particular philosophy with regard to all the questions which beset the human mind today. All Italian Fascists should read your discourse and derive from it both the clear formulation of the basic principles of our program as well as the reasons why Fascism must be systematically, firmly, and rationally inflexible in its uncompromising attitude towards other parties. Thus and only thus can the word become flesh and the ideas be turned into deeds.

Cordial greetings,
Mussolini

Fascism as Action, as Feeling, and as Thought

Much has been said, and is now being said for or against this complex political and social phenomenon which in the brief period of six years has taken complete hold of Italian life and, spreading beyond the borders of the Kingdom, has made itself felt in varying degrees of intensity throughout the world. But people have been much more eager to extol or to deplore than to understand—which is natural enough in a period of tumultuous fervor and of political passion. The time has not yet arrived for a dispassionate judgment. For even I, who noticed the very first manifestations of this great development, saw its significance from the start and participated directly in its first doings, carefully watching all its early uncertain and changing developments, even I do not feel competent to pass definite judgment. Fascism is so large a part of myself that it would be both arbitrary and absurd for me to try to dissociate my personality from it, to submit it to impartial scrutiny in order to evaluate it coldly and accurately. What can be done, however, and it seldom is attempted, is to make inquiry into the phenomenon which shall not merely consider its fragmentary and adventitious aspects, but strive to get at its inner essence. The undertaking may not be easy, but it is necessary, and no occasion for attempting it is more suitable than the present one afforded me by my friends of Perugia. Suitable it is in time because, at the inauguration of a course of lectures and lessons principally intended to illustrate that old and glorious trend of the life and history of Italy which takes its name from the humble saint of Assisi, it seemed natural to connect it with the greatest achievement of modern Italy, different in so many ways from the Franciscan movement, but united

37

with it by the mighty common current of Italian History. It is suitable as well in place because at Perugia, which witnessed the growth of our religious ideas, of our political doctrines and of our legal science in the course of the most glorious centuries of our cultural history, the mind is properly disposed and almost oriented towards an investigation of this nature.

First of all let us ask ourselves if there is a political doctrine of Fascism; if there is any ideal content in the Fascist state. For in order to link Fascism, both as concept and system, with the history of Italian thought and find therein a place for it, we must first show that it is thought; that it is a doctrine. Many persons are not quite convinced that it is either the one or the other; and I am not referring solely to those men, cultured or uncultured, as the case may be and very numerous everywhere, who can discern in this political innovation nothing except its local and personal aspects, and who know Fascism only as the particular manner of behavior of this or that well-known Fascist, of this or that group of a certain town; who therefore like or dislike the movement on the basis of their likes and dislikes for the individuals who represent it. Nor do I refer to those intelligent and cultivated persons, very intelligent indeed and very cultivated, who because of their direct or indirect allegiance to the parties that have been dispossessed by the advent of Fascism, have a natural cause of resentment against it and are therefore unable to see, in the blindness of hatred, anything good in it. I am referring rather to those—and there are many in our ranks too—who know Fascism as action and feeling but not yet as thought, who therefore have an intuition but no comprehension of it.

It is true that Fascism is, above all, action and sentiment and that such it must continue to be. Were it otherwise, it could not keep up that immense driving force, that renovating power which it now possesses and would merely be the solitary meditation of a chosen few. Only because it is feeling and sentiment, only because it is the unconscious reawakening of our profound racial instinct, has it the force to stir the soul of the people, and to set free an irresistible current of national will. Only because it is action, and as such actualizes itself in a vast organization and in a huge movement, has it the conditions for determining the historical course of contemporary Italy.

But Fascism is thought as well and it has a theory, which is an essential part of this historical phenomenon, and which is responsible in a great measure for the successes that have been achieved. To the existence of this ideal content of Fascism, to the truth of this Fascist logic we ascribe the fact that though we commit many errors of detail, we very seldom go astray on fundamentals, whereas all the parties of the opposition, deprived as they are of an informing, animating principle, of a unique directing concept, do very often wage their war faultlessly in minor tactics, better trained as they are in parliamentary and journalistic maneuvers, but they constantly break down on the important issues. Fascism, moreover, considered as action, is a typically Italian phenomenon and acquire universal validity because of the existence of this coherent and organic doctrine. The originality of Fascism is due in great part to the autonomy of its theoretical principles. For even when, in its external behavior and in its conclusions, it seems identical with other political creeds, in reality it possesses an inner originality due to the new spirit which animates it and to an entirely different theoretical approach.

Common Origins and Common Background of Modern Political Doctrines: From Liberalism to Socialism

Modern political thought remained, until recently, both in Italy and outside Italy under the absolute control of those doctrines which, proceeding from the Protestant Reformation and developed by the adepts of natural law in the seventeenth and eighteenth centuries, were firmly grounded in the institutions and customs of the English, of the American, and of the French Revolutions. Under different and sometimes clashing forms these doctrines have left a determining imprint upon all theories and actions both social and political, of the nineteenth and twentieth centuries down to the rise of Fascism. The common basis of all these doctrines, which stretch from Longuet, from Buchanan, and from Althusen down to Karl Marx, to Wilson and to Lenin is a social and state concept which I shall call mechanical or atomistic.

Society according to this concept is merely a sum total of individuals, a plurality which breaks up into its single components. Therefore the ends of a society, so considered, are nothing more than the ends of the individuals which composed it and for whose sake it exists. An atomistic view of this kind is also necessarily anti-historical, inasmuch as it considers society in its spatial attributes and not in its temporal ones; and because it reduces social life to the existence of a single generation. Society becomes thus a sum of determined individuals, viz., the generation living at a given moment. This doctrine which I call atomistic and which appears to be anti-historical, reveals from under a concealing cloak a strongly materialistic nature. For in its endeavors to isolate the present from the past and the future, it rejects the spiritual inheritance of ideas and sentiments which each generation receives from those preceding and hands down to the following generation thus destroying the unity and the spiritual life itself of human society.

This common basis shows the close logical connection existing between all political doctrines; the substantial solidarity, which unites all the political movements, from Liberalism to Socialism, that until recently have dominated Europe. For these political schools differ from one another in their methods, but all agree as to the ends to be achieved. All of them consider the welfare and happiness of individuals to be the goal of society, itself considered as composed of individuals of the present generation. All of them see in society and in its juridical organization, the state, the mere instrument and means whereby individuals can attain their ends. They differ only in that the methods pursued for the attainment of these ends vary considerably one from the other.

Thus the Liberals insist that the best manner to secure the welfare of the citizens as individuals is to interfere as little as possible with the free development of their activities and that therefore the essential task of the state is merely to coordinate these several liberties in such a way as to guarantee their coexistence. Kant, who was without doubt the most powerful and thorough philosopher of liberalism, said, "man, who is the end, cannot be assumed to have the value of an instrument." And again, "justice, of which the state is the specific organ, is the condition whereby the freedom of each is conditioned upon the freedom of others, according to the general law of liberty."

Having thus defined the task of the state, Liberalism confines itself to the demand of certain guarantees which are to keep the state from overstepping its functions as general coordinator of liberties and from sacrificing the freedom of individuals more than is absolutely necessary for the accomplishment of its purpose. All the efforts are therefore directed to see to it that the ruler, mandatory of all and entrusted with the realization, through and by liberty, of the harmonious happiness of everybody, should never be clothed with undue power. Hence the creation of a system of checks and limitations designed to keep the rulers within bounds; and among these, first and foremost, the principle of the division of powers, contrived as a means for weakening the state in its relation to the individual, by making it impossible for the state ever to appear in its dealings with citizens, in the full plenitude of sovereign powers: also the principle of the participation of citizens in the lawmaking power, as a means for securing, in behalf of the individual, a direct check on this, the strongest branch, and an indirect check on the entire government of the state. This system of checks and limitations, which goes by the name of constitutional government resulted in a moderate and measured liberalism. The checking power was exercised only by those citizens who were deemed worthy and capable, with the result that a small élite was made to represent legally the entire body politic for whose benefit this régime was instituted.

It was evident, however, that this moderate system, being fundamentally illogical and in contradiction with the very principles from which it proceeded, would soon become the object of serious criticism. For if the object of society and of the state is the welfare of individuals, severally considered, how is it possible to admit that this welfare can be secured by the individuals themselves only through the possibilities of such a liberal régime? The inequalities brought about both by nature and by social organizations are so numerous and so serious, that, for the greater part, individuals abandoned to themselves not only would fail to attain happiness, but would also contribute to the perpetuation of their condition of misery and

dejection. The state therefore cannot limit itself to the merely negative function of the defense of liberty. It must become active, in behalf of everybody, for the welfare of the people. It must intervene, when necessary, in order to improve the material, intellectual, and moral conditions of the masses; it must find work for the unemployed, instruct and educate the people, and care for health and hygiene. For if the purpose of society and of the state is the welfare of individuals, and if it is just that these individuals themselves control the attainment of their ends, it becomes difficult to understand why Liberalism should not go the whole distance, why it should see fit to distinguish certain individuals from the rest of the mass, and why the functions of the people should be, restricted to the exercise of a mere check. Therefore the state, if it exists for all, must be governed by all, and not by a small minority: if the state is for the people, sovereignty must reside in the people: if all individuals have the right to govern the state, liberty is no longer sufficient; equality must be added: and if sovereignty is vested in the people, the people must wield all sovereignty and not merely a part of it. The power to check and curb the government is not sufficient. The people must be the government. Thus, logically developed, Liberalism leads to Democracy, for Democracy contains the promises of Liberalism but oversteps its limitations in that it makes the action of the state positive, proclaims the equality of all citizens through the dogma of popular sovereignty. Democracy therefore necessarily implies a republican form of government even though at times, for reasons of expediency, it temporarily adjusts itself to a monarchical régime.

Once started on this downward grade of logical deductions it was inevitable that this atomistic theory of state and society should pass on to a more advanced position. Great industrial developments and the existence of a huge mass of working men, as yet badly treated and in a condition of semi-servitude, possibly endurable in a régime of domestic industry, became intolerable after the industrial revolution. Hence a state of affairs which towards the middle of the last century appeared to be both cruel and threatening. It was therefore natural that the following question be raised: "If the state is created for the welfare of its citizens, severally considered, how can it tolerate an economic system which divides the population into a small minority of exploiters, the capitalists, on one side, and an immense multitude of exploited, the working people, on the other?" No! The state must again intervene and give rise to a different and less iniquitous economic organization, by abolishing private property, by assuming direct control of all production, and by organizing it in such a way that the products of labor be distributed solely among those who create them, viz., the working classes. Hence we find Socialism, with its new economic organization of society, abolishing private ownership of capital and of the instruments and means of production, socializing the product, suppressing the extra profit of capital, and turning over to the working class the entire output of the productive processes. It is evident that Socialism contains and surpasses Democracy in the same way that Democracy comprises and surpasses Liberalism, being a more advanced development of the same fundamental concept. Socialism in its turn generates the still more extreme doctrine of Bolshevism which demands the violent suppression of the holders of capital, the dictatorship of the proletariat, as means for a fairer economic organization of society and for the rescue of the laboring classes from capitalistic exploitation.

Thus Liberalism, Democracy, and Socialism, appear to be, as they are in reality, not only the offspring of one and the same

theory of government, but also logical derivations one of the other. Logically developed Liberalism leads to Democracy; the logical development of Democracy issues into Socialism. It is true that for many years, and with some justification, Socialism was looked upon as antithetical to Liberalism. But the antithesis is purely relative and breaks down as we approach the common origin and foundation of the two doctrines, for we find that the opposition is one of method, not of purpose. The end is the same for both, viz., the welfare of the individual members of society. The difference lies in the fact that Liberalism would be guided to its goal by liberty, whereas Socialism strives to attain it by the collective organization of production. There is therefore no antithesis nor even a divergence as to the nature and scope of the state and the relation of individuals to society. There is only a difference of evaluation of the means for bringing about these ends and establishing these relations, which difference depends entirely on the different economic conditions which prevailed at the time when the various doctrines were formulated. Liberalism arose and began to thrive in the period of small industry; Socialism grew with the rise of industrialism and of world-wide capitalism. The dissension therefore between these two points of view, or the antithesis, if we wish so to call it, is limited to the economic field. Socialism is at odds with Liberalism only on the question of the organization of production and of the division of wealth. In religious, intellectual, and moral matters it is liberal, as it is liberal and democratic in its politics. Even the anti-liberalism and anti-democracy of Bolshevism are in themselves purely contingent. For Bolshevism is opposed to Liberalism only in so far as the former is revolutionary, not in its socialistic aspect. For if the opposition of the Bolsheviki to liberal and democratic doctrines were to continue, as now seems more and more probable, the result might be a complete break between Bolshevism and Socialism notwithstanding the fact that the ultimate aims of both are identical.

Fascism as an Integral Doctrine of Sociality Antithetical to the Atomism of Liberal, Democratic, and Socialistic Theories

The true antithesis, not to this or that manifestation of the liberal-democratic-socialistic conception of the state but to the concept itself, is to be found in the doctrine of Fascism. For while the disagreement between Liberalism and Democracy, and between Liberalism and Socialism lies in a difference of method, as we have said, the rift between Socialism, Democracy, and Liberalism on one side and Fascism on the other is caused by a difference in concept. As a matter of fact, Fascism never raises the question of methods, using in its political praxis now liberal ways, now democratic means and at times even socialistic devices. This indifference to method often exposes Fascism to the charge of incoherence on the part of superficial observers, who do not see that what counts with us is the end and that therefore even when we employ the same means we act with a radically different spiritual and strive for entirely different results. The Fascist concept then of the nation, of the scope of the state, and of the relations obtaining between society and its individual components, rejects entirely the doctrine which I said proceeded from the theories of natural law developed in the course of the sixteen, seventeenth, and eighteenth centuries and which form the basis of the liberal, democratic, and socialistic ideology.

I shall not try here to expound this doctrine but shall limit myself to a brief résumé of its fundamental concepts.

Man—the political animal—according to the definition of Aristotle, lives and must live in society. A human being outside the pale of society is an inconceivable thing—a non-man. Humankind in its entirety lives in social groups that are still, today, very numerous and diverse, varying in importance and organization from the tribes of Central Africa to the great Western Empires. These various societies are fractions of the human species each one of them endowed with a unified organization. And as there is no unique organization of the human species, there is not "one" but there are "several" human societies. Humanity therefore exists solely as a biological concept not as a social one.

Each society on the other hand exists in the unity of both its biological and its social contents. Socially considered it is a fraction of the human species endowed with unity of organization for the attainment of the peculiar ends of the species.

This definition brings out all the elements of the social phenomenon and not merely those relating to the preservation and perpetuation of the species. For man is not solely matter; and the ends of the human species, far from being the materialistic ones we have in common with other animals, are, rather, and predominantly, the spiritual finalities which are peculiar to man and which every form of society strives to attain as well as its stage of social development allows. Thus the organization of every social group is more or less pervaded by the spiritual influxes of: unity of language, of culture, of religion, of tradition, of customs, and in general of feeling and of volition, which are as essential as the material elements: unity of economic interests, of living conditions, and of territory. The definition given above demonstrates another truth, which has been ignored by the political doctrines that for the last four centuries have been the foundations of political systems, viz., that the social concept has a biological aspect, because social groups are fractions of the human species, each one possessing a peculiar organization, a particular rank in the development of civilization with certain needs and appropriate ends, in short, a life which is really its own. If social groups are then fractions of the human species, they must possess the same fundamental traits of the human species, which means that they must be considered as a succession of generations and not as a collection of individuals.

It is evident therefore that as the human species is not the total of the living human beings of the world, so the various social groups which compose it are not the sum of the several individuals which at a given moment belong to it, but rather the infinite series of the past, present, and future generations constituting it. And as the ends of the human species are not those of the several individuals living at a certain moment, being occasionally in direct opposition to them, so the ends of the various social groups are not necessarily those of the individuals that belong to the groups but may even possibly be in conflict with such ends, as one sees clearly whenever the preservation and the development of the species demand the sacrifice of the individual, to wit, in times of war.

Fascism replaces therefore the old atomistic and mechanical state theory which was at the basis of the liberal and democratic doctrines with an organic and historic concept. When I say organic I do not wish to convey the impression that I consider society as an organism after the manner of the so-called "organic theories of the state"; but rather to indicate that the social groups as fractions of the species receive thereby a life and scope which transcend the scope and life of the individuals identifying themselves with the history and finalities of the uninter-rupted series of generations. It is irrelevant in this connection to determine whether social groups, considered as fractions of the species, constitute organisms. The important thing is to ascertain that this organic concept of the state gives to society a continuous life over and beyond the existence of the several individuals.

The relations therefore between state and citizens are completely reversed by the Fascist doctrine. Instead of the liberal-democratic formula, "society for the individual," we have, "individuals for society" with this difference however: that while the liberal doctrines eliminated society, Fascism does not submerge the individual in the social group. It subordinates him, but does not eliminate him; the individual as a part of his generation even remaining an element of society however transient and insignificant he may be. Moreover the development of individuals in each generation, when coordinated and harmonized, conditions the development and prosperity of the entire social unit.

At this juncture the antithesis between the two theories must appear complete and absolute. Liberalism, Democracy, and Socialism look upon social groups as aggregates of living individuals; for Fascism they are the recapitulating unity of the indefinite series of generations. For Liberalism, society has no purposes other than those of the members living at a given moment. For Fascism, society has historical and immanent ends of preservation, expansion, improvement, quite distinct from those of the individuals which at a given moment compose it; so distinct in fact that they may even be in opposition. Hence the necessity, for which the older doctrines make little allowance, of sacrifice, even up to the total immolation of individuals, in behalf of society; hence the true explanation of war, eternal law of mankind, interpreted by the liberal-democratic doctrines as a degenerate absurdity or as a maddened monstrosity.

For Liberalism, society has no life distinct from the life of the individuals, or as the phrase goes: *solvitur in singularitates*. For Fascism, the life of society overlaps the existence of individuals and projects itself into the succeeding generations through centuries and millennia. Individuals come into being, grow, and die, followed by others, unceasingly; social unity remains always identical to itself. For Liberalism, the individual is the end and society the means; nor is it conceivable that the individual, considered in the dignity of an ultimate finality, be lowered to mere instrumentality. For Fascism, society is the end, individuals the means, and its whole life consists in using individuals as instruments for its social ends. The state therefore guards and protects the welfare and development of individuals not for their exclusive interest, but because of the identity of the needs of individuals with those of society as a whole. We can thus accept and explain institutions and practices, which like the death penalty, are condemned by Liberalism in the name of the preeminence of individualism.

The fundamental problem of society in the old doctrines is the question of the rights of individuals. It may be the right to freedom as the Liberals would have it; or the right to the government of the commonwealth as the Democrats claim it, or the right to economic justice as the Socialists contend; but in every case it is the right of individuals, or groups of individuals (classes). Fascism on the other band faces squarely the problem of the right of the state and of the duty of individuals. Individual rights are only recognized in so far as they are implied in the rights of the state. In this preeminence of duty we find the highest ethical value of Fascism.

The Problems of Liberty, of Government, and of Social Justice in the Political Doctrine of Fascism

This, however, does not mean that the problems raised by the other schools are ignored by Fascism. It means simply that it faces them and solves them differently, as, for example, the problem of liberty.

There is a Liberal theory of freedom, and there is a Fascist concept of liberty. For we, too, maintain the necessity of safeguarding the conditions that make for the free development of the individual; we, too, believe that the oppression of individual personality can find no place in the modern state. We do not, however, accept a bill of rights which tends to make the individual superior to the state and to empower him to act in opposition to society. Our concept of liberty is that the individual must be allowed to develop his personality in behalf of the state, for these ephemeral and infinitesimal elements of the complex and permanent life of society determine by their normal growth the development of the state. But this individual growth must be normal. A huge and disproportionate development of the individual of classes, would prove as fatal to society as abnormal growths are to living organisms. Freedom therefore is due to the citizen and to classes on condition that they exercise it in the interest of society as a whole and within the limits set by social exigencies, liberty being, like any other individual right, a concession of the state. What I say concerning civil liberties applies to economic freedom as well. Fascism does not look upon the doctrine of economic liberty as an absolute dogma. It does not refer economic problems to individual needs, to individual interest, to individual solutions. On the contrary it considers the economic development, and especially the production of wealth, as an eminently social concern, wealth being for society an essential element of power and prosperity. But Fascism maintains that in the ordinary run of events economic liberty serves the social purposes best; that it is profitable to entrust to individual initiative the task of economic development both as to production and as to distribution; that in the economic world individual ambition is the most effective means for obtaining the best social results with the least effort. Therefore, on the question also of economic liberty the Fascists differ fundamentally from the Liberals; the latter see in liberty a principle, the Fascists accept it as a method. By the Liberals, freedom is recognized in the interest of the citizens; the Fascist grant it in the interest of society. In other terms, Fascists make of the individual an economic instrument for the advancement of society, an instrument which they use so long as it functions and which they subordinate when no longer serviceable. In this guise Fascism solves the eternal problem of economic freedom and of state interference, considering both as mere methods which may or may not be employed in accordance with the social needs of the moment.

What I have said concerning political and economic Liberalism applies also to Democracy. The latter envisages fundamentally the problem of sovereignty; Fascism does also, but in an entirely different manner. Democracy vests sovereignty in the people, that is to say, in the mass of human beings. Fascism discovers sovereignty to be inherent in society when it is juridically organized as a state. Democracy therefore turns over the government of the state to the multitude of living men that they may use it to further their own interests; Fascism insists that the government be entrusted to men capable of rising above their own private interests and of realizing the aspirations of the social collectivity, considered in its unity and in its relation to the past and future. Fascism therefore not only rejects the dogma

of popular sovereignty and substitutes for it that of state sovereignty, but it also proclaims that the great mass of citizens is not a suitable advocate of social interests for the reason that the capacity to ignore individual private interests in favor of the higher demands of society and of history is a very rare gift and the privilege of the chosen few. Natural intelligence and cultural preparation are of great service in such tasks. Still more valuable perhaps is the intuitiveness of rare great minds, their traditionalism and their inherited qualities. This must not however be construed to mean that the masses are not to be allowed to exercise any influence on the life of the state. On the contrary, among peoples with a great history and with noble traditions, even the lowest elements of society possess an instinctive discernment of what is necessary for the welfare of the race, which in moments of great historical crises reveals itself to be almost infallible. It is therefore as wise to afford to this instinct the means of declaring itself as it is judicious to entrust the normal control of the commonwealth to a selected élite. . . .

Historical Value of the Doctrine of Fascism

. . . At this point it will not be very difficult to assign a fitting place in history to this great trend of thought which is called Fascism and which, in spite of the initial difficulties, already gives clear indication of the magnitude of its developments.

The liberal-democratic speculation both in its origin and in the manner of its development appears to be essentially a non-Italian formation. Its connection with the Middle Ages already shows it to be foreign to the Latin mind, the medieval disintegration being the result of the triumph of Germanic individualism over the political mentality of the Romans. The barbarians, boring from within and hacking from without, pulled down the great political structure raised by Latin genius and put nothing in its place. Anarchy lasted eight centuries during which time only one institution survived and that a Roman one—the Catholic Church. But, as soon as the laborious process of reconstruction was started with the constitution of the great national states backed by the Roman Church the Protestant Reformation set in followed by the individualistic currents of the seventeenth and eighteenth centuries, and the process of disintegration was started anew. This anti-state tendency was the expression of the Germanic spirit and it therefore became predominant among the Germanic peoples and wherever Germanism had left a deep imprint even if afterward superficially covered by a veneer of Latin culture. . . .

While therefore in other countries such as France, England, Germany, and Holland, the general tradition in the social and political sciences worked in behalf of anti-state individualism, and therefore of liberal and democratic doctrines, Italy, on the other hand, clung to the powerful legacy of its past in virtue of which she proclaims the rights of the state, the preeminence of its authority, and the superiority of its ends. The very fact that the Italian political doctrine in the Middle Ages linked itself with the great political writers of antiquity, Plato and Arisotle, who in a different manner but with an equal firmness advocated a strong state and the subordination of individuals to it, is a sufficient index of the orientation of political philosophy in Italy. We all know how thorough and crushing the authority of Aristotle was in the Middle Ages. But for Aristotle the spiritual cement of the state is "virtue" not absolute virtue but political virtue, which is social

devotion. His state is made up solely of its citizens, the citizens being either those who defend it with their arms or who govern it as magistrates. All others who provide it with the materials and services it needs are not citizens. They become such only in the corrupt forms of certain democracies. Society is therefore divided into two classes, the free men or citizens who give their time to noble and virtuous occupations and who profess their subjection to the state, and the laborers and slaves who work for the maintenance of the former. No man in this scheme is his own master. The slaves belong to the freemen, and the freemen belong to the state.

It was therefore natural that St. Thomas Aquinas, the greatest political writer of the Middle Ages, should emphasize the necessity of unity in the political field, the harm of plurality of rulers, the dangers and damaging effects of demagogy. The good of the state, says St. Thomas Aquinas, is unity. And who can procure unity more fittingly than he who is himself one? Moreover the government must follow, as far as possible, the course of nature and in nature power is always one. In the physical body only one organ is dominant—the heart; in the spirit only one faculty has sway—reason. Bees have one sole ruler; and the entire universe one sole sovereign—God. Experience shows that the countries, which are ruled by many, perish because of discord while those that are ruled over by one enjoy peace, justice, and plenty. The States which are not ruled by one are troubled by dissensions, and toil unceasingly. On the contrary the states which are ruled over by one king enjoy peace, thrive in justice and are gladdened by affluence.[1] The rule of the multitudes cannot be sanctioned, for where the crowd rules it oppresses the rich as would a tyrant. . . .[2]

---

1   De reg. princ. I. c. 2.
2   Comm. In Polit. L. III. lectio VIII.

The Roman tradition, which was one of practice but not of theories—for Rome constructed the most solid state known to history with extraordinary statesmanship but with hardly any political writings—influenced considerably the founder of modern political science, Niccolo Machiavelli, who was himself in truth not a creator of doctrines but a keen observer of human nature who derived from the study of history practical maxims of political import. He freed the science of politics from the formalism of the scholastic and brought it close to concrete reality. His writings, an inexhaustible mine of practical remarks and precious observations, reveal dominant in him the state idea, no longer abstract but in the full historical concreteness of the national unity of Italy.

Machiavelli therefore is not only the greatest of modern political writers, he is also the greatest of our countrymen in full possession of a national Italian consciousness. To liberate Italy, which was in his day "enslaved, torn and pillaged," and to make her more powerful, he would use any means, for to his mind the holiness of the end justified them completely. In this he was sharply rebuked by foreigners who were not as hostile to his means as they were fearful of the end which he propounded. He advocated therefore the constitution of a strong Italian state, supported by the sacrifices and by the blood of the citizens, not defended by mercenary troops; well-ordered internally, aggressive and bent on expansion. . . .

Questions

Section I

1. What was the "Vienna Circle"? What were the basic philosophical views of Logical Positivism?

2. What was Ayer's opinion on the possibility of "doing" Metaphysics?

3. Describe the relationship between Metaphysics and Ethics as Ayer saw it.

4. If Ethics cannot be studied in a "scientific" manner, how should we deal with ethical issues and precepts?

5. After considering the event depicted in the town of Sodom according to *Genesis*, what do you think *was* the "sin of Sodom": attempted homosexual rape or, as some in the gay community view it, "inhospitality"?

6. After reading *Leviticus* 18:
   a. What would be the meaning of incest in the "direct line" and in the "collateral line"?

   b. Why might it be that incest is almost universally condemned?

   c. Regarding male homosexuality, which passage is the most significant?

   d. Why do you think female homosexuality (lesbianism) is not mentioned?

7. The text from St. Paul seems to condemn fornication and homosexual behavior. Leaving aside translation controversies from the orginial Greek:
   a. What is the exact meaning of fornication and how does it differ from adultery?

   b. Regarding what most consider a reference to homosexual behaviour, our version of the New Testament differs from other versions (although *not* the King James version). Check your bibles at home or in a local library: do they have a different wording (e.g., sodomite, homosexual)?

   c. Why are these passages cited in this book?

   d. Can you find out when the term "homosexual" began to be used in English?

Turning now to the use of civil positive law rather than divine law:

8. What is meant by "the State"?

9. What is the purpose of the State for Machiavelli and Hobbes?

10. Does the individual citizen have any rights over against the State?

11. According to Machiavelli and Hobbes, what would be the possibility of a justification for civil disobedience?

12. Give three reasons for Hitler's hatred of Jews.
    a.

    b.

    c.

13. Are you aware of any personal or psychological reasons for this negative view of Jews?

14. Between 1940 and 1945, were the appropriation of Jewish properties and the death camps for Jews *legal* throughout territories controlled by the Third Reich?

15. What are the main elements of the philosophy of Fascism?

16. What were Rocco's main objections against a democratic form of government?

Section II

Selected Ethical Theories/Systems

Introduction

When addressing moral issues we must come to them armed with principles and ethical theories which we can bring to bear upon the problem. We might use one or even a mixture of theories in more complicated cases. However, as someone once stated: "We stand on the shoulders of giants." We are not starting "from scratch". We have a long ethical tradition in the Western world going back 2400 years to Socrates, Plato and Aristotle.

The dialogue, the *Crito* continues the theme of the first section: respect for the state, its laws and authority. And yet we do see Plato and Socrates raising the question of justice and civil disobedience. Aristotle (384-322 B.C.) then addresses the topic of virtue in general and the relationship of various virtues to the elements which would go to make up what we might call "the good life": wealth, health, pleasure, etc.

With Cicero (106-43 B.C.), St. Thomas Aquinas (1225-1274) and John Locke (1632-1704) we return to the problem of Law and its relation to human happiness. Our authors examine Law in general but also the relationship or complementariness of positive law and natural law with Locke even establishing the basis for a "right to revolution." Thomas Jefferson applies this view to the Declaration of Independence. John Rawls (b.1921) of Harvard, adds the concept of "So-cial" justice to the other "parts" of Justice mentioned by Aristotle in Book V of the *Nicomachean Ethics* which, while not included in this book, might profitably be read by students.

St. Thomas Aquinas although considered for centuries to be the foremost Catholic theologian is nevertheless highly respected for his philosophical work which is found in various sections of his *Summa of Theology*. John Locke is famous in the area of Epistemology as well as political philosophy. In our reading he gives the reasons for the very existence of the State (which could be related to the Capital Punishment and War issue) as well as the duties of magistrates and civil disobedience.

Jeremy Bentham (1738-1832) [in his *Principles of Morals and Legislation*] relates law and the state to happiness through pleasure. A calculus of pleasure is presented as well as the notion of "consequences" as justifying actions. The democratic principle of rule by majority is also present in this work. John Stuart Mill (1806-1873) in *Utilitarianism* clarifies the relationships of pleasure, happiness and intellectual pursuits.

Inmanuel Kant (1724-1804) the Great German philosopher who won his fame (for some) in the combined areas of epistemology and what might be termed "anti-metaphysics" in his *Metaphysics of Morals* states the "Categorical Imperative." This does not allow for relativistic or situational ethics, nor for utilitarian, consequentialist or teleological considerations. The article by John Rawls of Harvard University is considered one of the more significant writings on the virtue of Justice in the latter part of the 20th century.

The final reading is by Dr. Joseph Fletcher, who died in 1991. Dr. Fletcher, a native of Newark, N.J., was an ordained Episcopal Minister and taught at the Episcopal Theological School in Cambridge, Massachusetts, and at the University of Virginia. His *New York Times* obituary sees him as "a founder of the field of biomedical ethics whose 1966 book, *Situation Ethics*, sparked both scholarly and popular debate." Briefly put, Fletcher taught that rather than adhere to inflexible laws or abstract principles (or believe that there are no laws), we should choose the theory or principle in the ethical situation with the overriding principle of "love of neighbor" present in each conscience decision.

Crito

Plato

SOCRATES: Why have you come so early, Crito? Or is it not still early?

CRITO: It certainly is.

S: How early?

C: Early dawn.

S: I am surprised that the warder was willing to listen to you.

C: He is quite friendly to me by now, Socrates. I have been here often and I have given him something.

S: Have you just come, or have you been here for some time?

C: A fair time.

S: Then why did you not wake me right away but sit there in silence?

C: By Zeus no, Socrates. I would not myself want to be in distress and awake so long. I have been surprised to see you so peacefully asleep. It was on purpose that I did not wake you, so that you should spend your time most agreeably. Often in the past throughout my life, I have considered the way you live happy, and especially so now that you bear your present misfortune so easily and lightly.

S: It would not be fitting at my age to resent the fact that I must die now.

C: Other men of your age are caught in such misfortunes, but their age does not prevent them resenting their fate.

S: That is so. Why have you come so early?

C: I bring bad news, Socrates, not for you, apparently, but for me and all your friends the news is bad and hard to bear. Indeed, I would count it among the hardest.

S: What is it? Or has the ship arrived from Delos, at the arrival of which I must die?

C: It has not arrived yet, but it will, I believe, arrive today, according to a message brought by some men from Sunium, where they left it. This makes it obvious that it will come today, and that your life must end tomorrow.

S: May it be for the best. If it so please the gods, so be it. However, I do not think it will arrive today.

C: What indication have you of this?

S: I will tell you. I must die the day after the ship arrives.

C: That is what those in authority say.

S: Then I do not think it will arrive on this coming day, but on the next. I take to witness of this a dream I had a little earlier during this night. It looks as if it was the right time for you not to wake me.

C: What was your dream?

· S: I thought that a beautiful and comely woman dressed in white approached me. She called me and said: "Socrates, may you arrive at fertile Phthia[1] on the third day."

From Plato, *Five Dialogues*, translated by G.M.A. Grube, 1981. By permission of Hackett Publishing Company, Inc., Indianapolis, IN and Cambridge, MA. All rights reserved.

1 [A quotation from the ninth book of the *Iliad* (363). Achilles has rejected all the presents of Agamemnon for him to return to the battle, and threatens to go home. He says his ships will sail in the morning, and with good weather he might arrive on the third day "in fertile Phthia" (which is his home). The dream means, obviously, that on the third day Socrates' soul, after death, will find its home. As always, counting the first member of a

C: A strange dream, Socrates.

S: But it seems clear enough to me, Crito

C: Too clear it seems, my dear Socrates, but listen to me even now and be saved. If you die, it will not be a single misfortune only for me. Not only will I be deprived of a friend, the like of whom I shall never find again, but many people who do not know you or me very well will think that I could have saved you if I were willing to spend money, but that I did not care to do so. Surely there can be no worse reputation than to be thought to value money more highly than one's friends, for the majority will not believe that you yourself were not willing to leave prison while we were eager for you to do so.

S: My good Crito, why should we care so much for what the majority think? The most reasonable people, to whom one should pay more attention, will believe that things were done as they were done.

C: You see, Socrates, that one must also pay attention to the opinion of the majority. Your present situation makes clear that the majority can inflict not the least but pretty well the greatest evils if one is slandered among them.

S: Would that the majority could inflict the greatest evils, for they would then be capable of the greatest good, and that would be fine, but now they cannot do either. They cannot make a man either wise or foolish, but they inflict things haphazardly.

C: That may be so. But tell me this, Socrates, are you anticipating that I and your other friends would have trouble with the informers if you escape from here, as having stolen you away, and that we should be compelled to lose all our property or pay heavy fines and suffer other punishment besides? If you have any such fear, forget it. We would be justified in running this risk to save you, and

worse, if necessary. Do follow my advice, and do not act differently.

S: I do have these things in mind, Crito, and also many others.

C: Have no such fear. It is not much money that some people require to save you and get you out of here. Further, do you not see that those informers are cheap, and that not much money would be needed to deal with them? My money is available and is, I think, sufficient. If, because of your affection for me, you feel you should not spend any of mine, there are those strangers here ready to spend money. One of them, Simmias the Theban, has brought enough for this very purpose. Cebes, too, and a good many others. So, as I say, do not let this fear make you hesitate to save yourself, nor let what you said in court trouble you, that you would not know what to do with yourself if you left Athens, for you would be welcomed in many places to which you might go. If you want to go to Thessaly, I have friends there who will greatly appreciate you and keep you safe, so that no one in Thessaly will harm you.

Besides, Socrates, I do not think that what you are doing is right, to give up your life when you can save it, and to hasten your fate as your enemies would hasten it, and indeed have hastened it in their wish to destroy you. Moreover, I think you are betraying your sons by going away and leaving them, when you could bring them up and educate them. You thus show no concern for what their fate may be. They will probably have the usual fate of orphans. Either one should not have children, or one should share with them to the end the toil of upbringing and education. You seem to me to choose the easiest path, whereas one should choose the path a good and courageous man would choose, particularly when one claims throughout one's life to care for virtue.

series, the third day is the day after tomorrow—G.M.A.G.]

I feel ashamed on your behalf and on behalf of us, your friends, lest all that has happened to you be thought due to cowardice on our part: the fact that your trial came to court when it need not have done so, the handling of the trial itself, and now this absurd ending which will be thought to have got beyond our control through some cowardice and unmanliness on our part, since we did not save you, or you save yourself, when it was possible and could be done if we had been of the slightest use. Consider, Socrates, whether this is not only evil, but shameful, both for you and for us. Take counsel with yourself, or rather the time for counsel is past and the decision should have been taken, and there is no further opportunity, for this whole business must be ended tonight. If we delay now, then it will no longer be possible, it will be too late. Let me persuade you on every count, Socrates, and do not act otherwise.

S: My dear Crito, your eagerness is worth much if it should have some right aim; if not, then the greater your keenness the more difficult it is to deal with. We must therefore examine whether we should act in this way or not, as not only now but at all times I am the kind of man who listens only to the argument that on reflection seems best to me. I cannot, now that this fate has come upon me, discard the arguments I used; they seem to me much the same. I value and respect the same principles as before, and if we have no better arguments to bring up at this moment, be sure that I shall not agree with you, not even if the power of the majority were to frighten us with more bogeys, as if we were children, with threats of incarcerations and executions and confiscation of property. How should we examine this matter most reasonably? Would it be by taking up first your argument about the opinions of men, whether it is sound in every case that one should pay attention to some opinions, but not to others? Or was that well-spoken be-

fore the necessity to die came upon me, but now it is clear that this was said in vain for the sake of argument, that it was in truth play and nonsense? I am eager to examine together with you, Crito, whether this argument will appear in any way different to me in my present circumstances, or whether it remains the same, whether we are to abandon it or believe it. It was said on every occasion by those who thought they were speaking sensibly, as I have just now been speaking, that one should greatly value some people's opinions, but not others. Does that seem to you a sound statement?

You, as far as a human being can tell, are exempt from the likelihood of dying tomorrow, so the present misfortune is not likely to lead you astray. Consider then, do you not think it a sound statement that one must not value all the opinions of men, but some and no others, nor the opinions of all men, but those of some and not of others? What do you say? Is this not well said?

C: It is.

S: One should value the good opinions, and not the bad ones?

C: Yes.

S: The good opinions are those of wise men, the bad ones those of foolish men?

C: Of course.

S: Come then, what of statements such as this: Should a man professionally engaged in physical training pay attention to the praise and blame and opinion of any man, or to those of one man only, namely a doctor or trainer?

C: To those of one only.

S: He should therefore fear the blame and welcome the praise of that one man, and not those of the many?

C: Obviously.

S: He must then act and exercise, eat and drink in the way the one, the trainer and the one who knows, thinks right, not all the others?

C: That is so.

S: Very well. And if he disobeys the one, disregards his opinion and his praises while valuing those of the many who have no knowledge, will he not suffer harm?

C: Of course.

S: What is that harm, where does it tend, and what part of the man who disobeys does it affect?

C: Obviously the harm is to his body, which it ruins.

S: Well said. So with other matters, not to enumerate them all, and certainly with actions just and unjust, shameful and beautiful, good and bad, about which we are now deliberating, should we follow the opinion of the many and fear it, or that of the one, if there is one who has knowledge of these things and before whom we feel fear and shame more than before all the others. If we do not follow his directions, we shall harm and corrupt that part of ourselves that is improved by just actions and destroyed by unjust actions. Or is there nothing in this?

C: I think there certainly is, Socrates.

S: Come now, if we ruin that which is improved by health and corrupted by disease by not following the opinions of those who know, is life worth living for us when that is ruined? And that is the body, is it not?

C: Yes.

S: And is life worth living with a body that is corrupted and in bad condition?

C: In no way.

S: And is life worth living for us with that part of us corrupted that unjust action harms and just action benefits? Or do we think that part of us, whatever it is, that is concerned with justice and injustice, is inferior to the body?

C: Not at all.

S: It is more valuable?

C: Much more.

S: We should not then think so much of what the majority will say about us, but what he will say who understands justice and injustice, the one, that is, and the truth itself. So that, in the first place, you were wrong to believe that we should care for the opinion of the many about what is just, beautiful, good, and their opposites. "But," someone might say, "the many are able to put us to death."

C: That too is obvious, Socrates, and someone might well say so.

S: And, my admirable friend, that argument that we have gone through remains, I think, as before. Examine the following statement in turn as to whether it stays the same or not, that the most important thing is not life, but the good life.

C: It stays the same.

S: And that the good life, the beautiful life, and the just life are the same; does that still hold, or not?

C: It does hold.

S: As we have agreed so far, we must examine next whether it is right for me to try to get out of here when the Athenians have not acquitted me. If it is seen to be right, we will try to do so; if it is not, we will abandon the idea. As for those questions you raise about money, reputation, the upbringing of children, Crito, those considerations in truth belong to those people who easily put men to death and would bring them to life again if they could, without thinking; I mean the majority of men. For us, however, since our argument leads to this, the only valid consideration, as we were saying just now, is whether we should be acting rightly in giving money and gratitude to those who will lead me out of here, and ourselves helping with the escape, or whether in truth we shall do wrong in doing all this. If it appears that we shall be acting unjustly, then we have no need at all to take into account whether we shall have to die if we stay here and keep quiet, or suffer in another way, rather than do wrong.

C: I think you put that beautifully, Socrates, but see what we should do.

S: Let us examine the question together, my dear friend, and if you can make any objection while I am speaking, make it and I will listen to you, but if you have no objection to make, my dear Crito, then stop now from saying the same thing so often, that I must leave here against the will of the Athenians. I think it important to persuade you before I act, and not to act against your wishes. See whether the start of our enquiry is adequately stated, and try to answer what I ask you in the way you think best.

C: I shall try.

S: Do we say that one must never in any way do wrong willingly, or must one do wrong in one way and not in another? Is to do wrong never good or admirable, as we have agreed in the past, or have all these former agreements been washed out during the last few days? Have we at our age failed to notice for some time that in our serious discussions we were no different from children? Above all, is the truth such as we used to say it was, whether the majority agree or not, and whether we must still suffer worse things than we do now, or will be treated more gently, that nonetheless, wrongdoing is in every way harmful and shameful to the wrongdoer? Do we say so or not?

C: We do.

S: So one must never do wrong.

C: Certainly not.

S: Nor must one, when wronged, inflict wrong in return, as the majority believe, since one must never do wrong.

C: That seems to be the case.

S: Come now, should one injure anyone or not, Crito?

C: One must never do so.

S: Well then, if one is oneself injured, is it right, as the majority say, to inflict an injury in return, or is it not?

C: It is never right.

S: Injuring people is no different from wrongdoing.

C: That is true.

S: One should never do wrong in return, nor injure any man, whatever injury one has suffered at his hands. And Crito, see that you do not agree to this, contrary to your belief. For I know that only a few people hold this view or will hold it, and there is no common ground between those who hold this view and those who do not, but they inevitably despise each other's views. So then consider very carefully whether we have this view in common, and whether you agree, and let this be the basis of our deliberation, that neither to do wrong or to return a wrong is ever right, not even to injure in return for an injury received. Or do you disagree and do not share this view as a basis for discussion? I have held it for a long time and still hold it now, but if you think otherwise, tell me now. If, however, you stick to our former opinion, then listen to the next point.

C: I stick to it and agree with you. So say on.

S: Then I state the next point, or rather I ask you: when one has come to an agreement that is just with someone, should one fulfill it or cheat on it?

C: One should fulfill it.

S: See what follows from this: if we leave here without the city's permission, are we injuring people whom we should least injure? And are we sticking to a just agreement, or not?

C: I cannot answer your question, Socrates. I do not know.

S: Look at it this way. If, as we were planning to run away from here, or whatever one should call it, the laws and the state came and confronted us and asked: "Tell me, Socrates, what are you intending to do? Do you not by this action you are attempting intend to destroy us, the laws, and indeed the whole city, as far as you are concerned? Or do you think it possible for a city not to be destroyed if the verdicts of its courts have no force but are nullified and set at naught by private individuals?" What shall we answer to this and other such arguments? For many things could be said, especially by an orator on behalf of this law we are destroying, which orders that the judgments of the courts shall be carried out. Shall we say in answer, "The city wronged me, and its decision was not right." Shall we say that, or what?

C: Yes, by Zeus, Socrates, that is our answer.

S: Then what if the laws said: "Was that the agreement between us, Socrates, or was it to respect the judgments that the city came to?" And if we wondered at their words, they would perhaps add: "Socrates, do not wonder at what we say but answer, since you are accustomed to proceed by question and answer. Come now, what accusation do you bring against us and the city, that you should try to destroy us? Did we not, first, bring you to birth, and was it not through us that your father married your mother and begat you? Tell us, do you find anything to criticize in those of us who are concerned with marriage?" And I would say that I do not criticize them. "Or in those of us concerned with the nurture of babies and the education that you too received? Were those assigned to that subject not right to instruct your father to educate you in the arts and in physical culture?" And I would say that they were right. "Very well," they would continue, "and after you were born and nurtured and educated, could you, in the first place, deny that you are our offspring and servant, both you and your forefathers? If that is so, do you think that we are on an equal footing as regards the right, and that whatever we do to you it is right for you to do to us? You were not on an equal footing with your father as regards the right, nor with your master if you had one, so as to retaliate for anything they did to you,

to revile them if they reviled you, to beat them if they beat you, and so with many other things. Do you think you have this right to retaliation against your country and its laws? That if we undertake to destroy you and think it right to do so, you can undertake to destroy us, as far as you can, in return? And will you say that you are right to do so, you who truly care for virtue? Is your wisdom such as not to realize that your country is to be honoured more than your mother, your father and all your ancestors, that it is more to be revered and more sacred, and that it counts for more among the gods and sensible men, that you must worship it, yield to it and placate its anger more than your father's? You must either persuade it or obey its orders, and endure in silence whatever it instructs you to endure, whether blows or bonds, and if it leads you into war to be wounded or killed, you must obey. To do so is right, and one must not give way or retreat or leave one's post, but both in war and in courts and everywhere else, one must obey the commands of one's city and country, or persuade it as to the nature of justice. It is impious to bring violence to bear against your mother or father, it is much more so to use it against your country." What shall we say in reply, Crito, that the laws speak the truth, or not?

C: I think they do.

S: "Reflect now, Socrates," the laws might say, "that if what we say is true, you are not treating us rightly by planning to do what you are planning. We have given you birth, nurtured you, educated you, we have given you and all other citizens a share of all the good things we could. Even so, by giving every Athenian the opportunity, after he has reached manhood and observed the affairs of the city and us the laws, we proclaim that if we do not please him, he can take his possessions and go wherever he pleases. Not one of our laws raises any obstacle or forbids him, if he is not satisfied with us or the city, if one of you wants to go and live in a colony or wants to go anywhere else, and keep his property. We say, however, that whoever of you remains, when he sees how we conduct our trials and manage the city in other ways, has in fact come to an agreement with us to obey our instructions. We say that the one who disobeys does wrong in three ways, first because in us he disobeys his parents, also those who brought him up, and because, in spite of his agreement, he neither obeys us nor, if we do something wrong, does he try to persuade us to do better. Yet we only propose things, we do not issue savage commands to do whatever we order; we give two alternatives, either to persuade us or to do what we say. He does neither. We do say that you too, Socrates, are open to those charges if you do what you have in mind; you would be among not the least but the most guilty of the Athenians." And if I should say "Why so?" they might well be right to upbraid me and say that I am among the Athenians who most definitely came to that agreement with them. They might well say: "Socrates, we have convincing proofs that we and the city were congenial to you. You would not have dwelt here most consistently of all the Athenians if the city had not been exceedingly pleasing to you. You have never left the city, even to see a festival, nor for any other reason except military service; you have never gone to stay in any other city, as people do; you have had no desire to know another city or other laws; we and our city satisfied you.

"So decisively did you choose us and agree to be a citizen under us. Also, you have had children in this city, thus showing that it was congenial to you. Then at your trial you could have assessed your penalty at exile if you wished, and you are now attempting to do against the city's wishes what you could then have done with her consent. Then you prided yourself that you did not resent death, but you chose, as you said, death in preference to exile. Now, however, those words do not make you ashamed, and you pay no heed to us, the laws, as you plan to destroy us, and you act like the meanest type of slave by trying to run away, contrary to your undertakings and your agreement to live as a citizen under us. First then, answer us on this very point, whether we speak the truth when we say that you agreed, not only in words but by your deeds, to live in accordance with us." What are we to say to that, Crito? Must we not agree?

C: We must, Socrates.

S: "Surely," they might say, "you are breaking the undertakings and agreements that you made with us without compulsion or deceit, and under no pressure of time for deliberation. You have had seventy years during which you could have gone away if you did not like us, and if you thought our agreements unjust. You did not choose to go to Sparta or to Crete, which you are always saying are well governed, nor to any other city, Greek or foreign. You have been away from Athens less than the lame or the blind or other handicapped people. It is clear that the city has been outstandingly more congenial to you than to other Athenians, and so have we, the laws, for what city can please without laws? Will you then not now stick to our agreements? You will, Socrates, if we can persuade you, and not make yourself a laughingstock by leaving the city.

"For consider what good you will do yourself or your friends by breaking our agreements and committing such a wrong. It is pretty obvious that your friends will themselves be in danger of exile, disfranchisement and loss of property. As for yourself, if you go to one of the nearby cities—Thebes or Megara, both are well governed—you will arrive as an enemy to their government; all who care for their city will look on you with suspicion, as a destroyer of the laws. You will also strengthen the conviction of the jury that they passed the right sentence on you, for anyone who destroys the laws could easily be thought to corrupt the young and the ignorant. Or will you avoid cities that are well governed and men who are civilized? If you do this, will your life be worth living? Will you have social intercourse with them and not be ashamed to talk to them? And what will you say? The same as you did here, that virtue and justice are man's most precious possession, along with lawful behaviour and the laws? Do you not think that Socrates would appear to be an unseemly kind of person? One must think so. Or will you leave those places and go to Crito's friends in Thessaly? There you will find the greatest license and disorder, and they may enjoy hearing from you how absurdly you escaped from prison in some disguise, in a leather jerkin or some other things in which escapees wrap themselves, thus altering your appearance. Will there be no one to say that you, likely to live but a short time more, were so greedy for life that you transgressed the most important laws? Possibly, Socrates, if you do not annoy anyone, but if you do, many disgraceful things will be said about you.

"You will spend your time ingratiating yourself with all men, and be at their beck and call. What will you do in Thessaly but feast, as if you had gone to a banquet in Thessaly? As for those conversations of yours about justice and the rest of virtue, where will they be? You say you want to live for the sake of your children, that you may bring them up and educate them. How so? Will you bring them up and educate them by taking them to Thessaly and making strangers of them, that they may enjoy that too? Or not so, but they will be better brought up and educated here, while you are alive, though absent? Yes, your friends will look after them. Will they look after them if you go and live in Thessaly, but not if you go away to the underworld? If those who profess themselves your friends are any good at all, one must assume that they will.

"Be persuaded by us who have brought you up, Socrates. Do not value either your children or your life or anything else more than goodness, in order that when you arrive in Hades you may have all this as your defence before the rulers there. If you do this deed, you will not think it better or more just or more pious here, nor will any one of your friends, nor will it be better for you when you arrive yonder. As it is, you depart, if you depart, after being wronged not by us, the laws, but by men; but if you depart after shamefully returning wrong for wrong and injury for injury, after breaking your agreement and contract with us, after injuring those you should injure least—yourself, your friends, your country and us—we shall be angry with you while you are still alive, and our brothers, the laws of the underworld, will not receive you kindly, knowing that you tried to destroy us as far as you could. Do not let Crito persuade you, rather than us, to do what he says."

Crito, my dear friend, be assured that these are the words I seem to hear, as the Corybants hear the music of their flutes, and the echo of these words resounds in me, and makes it impossible for me to hear anything else. As far as my present beliefs go, if you speak in opposition to them, you will speak in vain. However, if you think you can accomplish anything, speak.

C: I have nothing to say, Socrates.

S: Let it be then, Crito, and let us act in this way, since this is the way the god is leading us.

Ethica Nicomachea
Nicomachean Ethics

Aristotle
Translated by W. D. Ross

Book I

Every art and every inquiry, and similarly every action and pursuit, is thought to aim at some good; and for this reason the good has rightly been declared[1] to be that at which all things aim. But a certain difference is found among ends; some are activities, others are products apart from the activities that produce them. Where there are ends apart from the actions, it is the nature of the products to be better than the activities. Now, as there are many actions, arts, and sciences, their ends also are many; the end of the medical art is health, that of shipbuilding a vessel, that of strategy victory, that of economics wealth. But where such arts fall under a single capacity—as bridlemaking and the other arts concerned with the equipment of horses fall under the art of riding, and this and every military action under strategy, in the same way other arts fall under yet others—in all of these the ends of the master arts are to be preferred to all the subordinate ends; for it is for the sake of the former that the latter are pursued. It makes no difference whether the activities themselves are the ends of the actions, or something else apart from the activities, as in the case of the sciences just mentioned.

If, then, there is some end of the things we do, which we desire for its own sake (everything else being desired for the sake of this), and if we do not choose everything for the sake of something else (for at that rate the process would go on to infinity, so that our desire would be empty and vain), clearly this must be the good and the chief good. Will not the knowledge of it, then, have a great influence on life? Shall we not, like archers who have a mark to aim at, be more likely to bit upon what is right? If so, we must try, in outline at least to determine what it is, and of which of the sciences or capacities it is the object. It would seem to belong to the most authoritative art and that which is most truly the master art. And politics appears to be of this nature; for it is this that ordains which of the sciences should be studied in a state, and which each class of citizens should learn and up to what point they should learn them; and we see even the most highly esteemed of capacities to fall under this, e. g. strategy, economics, rhetoric; now, since politics uses the rest of the sciences, and since, again, it legislates as to what we are to do and what we are to abstain from, the end of this science must include those of the others, so that this end must be the good for man. For even if the

From *Introduction to Aristotle* by R. McKeon, copyright 1965, 309-341. Reprinted by permission of McGraw-Hill, Inc.

1   Perhaps by Eudoxus; Cf. 1172^b 9.

end is the same for a single man and for a state, that of the state seems at all events something greater and more complete whether to attain or to preserve; though it is worth while to attain the end merely for one man, it is finer and more godlike to attain it for a nation or for city-states. These, then, are the ends at which our inquiry aims, since it is political science, in one sense of that term.

Our discussion will be adequate if it has as much clearness as the subject-matter admits of, for precision is not to be sought for alike in all discussions, any more than in all the products of the crafts. Now fine and just actions, which political science investigates, admit of much variety and fluctuation of opinion, so that they may be thought to exist only by convention, and not by nature. And goods also give rise to a similar fluctuation because they bring harm to many people; for before now men have been undone by reason of their wealth, and others by reason of their courage. We must be content, then, in speaking of such subjects and with such premisses to indicate the truth roughly and in outline, and in speaking about things which are only for the most part true and with premisses of the same kind to reach conclusions that are no better. In the same spirit, therefore, should each type of statement be *received*; for it is the mark of an educated man to look for precision in each class of things just so far as the nature of the subject admits; it is evidently equally foolish to accept probable reasoning from a mathematician and to demand from a rhetorician scientific proofs.

Now each man judges well the things he knows, and of these he is a good judge. And so the man who has been educated in a subject is a good judge of that subject, and the man who has received an all-round education is a good judge in general. Hence a young man is not a proper hearer of lectures on political science; for he is inexperienced in the actions that occur in life, but its discussions start from these and are about these; and, further, since he tends to follow his passions, his study will be vain and unprofitable, because the end aimed at is not knowledge but action. And it makes no difference whether he is young in years or youthful in character; the defect does not depend on time, but on his living, and pursuing each successive object, as passion directs. For to such persons, as to the incontinent, knowledge brings no profit; but to those who desire and act in accordance with a rational principle knowledge about such matters will be of great benefit.

These remarks about the student, the sort of treatment to be expected, and the purpose of the inquiry, may be taken as our preface.

Let us resume our inquiry and state, in view of the fact that all knowledge and every pursuit aims at some good, what it is that we say political science aims at and what is the highest of all goods achievable by action. Verbally there is very general agreement; for both the general run of men and people of superior refinement say at it is happiness, and identify living well and doing well with being happy; but with regard to what happiness is they differ, and the many do not give the same account as the wise. For the former think it is some plain and obvious thing, like pleasure, wealth, or honour; they differ, however, from one another—and often even the same man identifies it with different things, with health when he is ill, with wealth when he is poor; but conscious of their ignorance, they admire those who proclaim some great ideal that is above their comprehension. Now some[2] thought that apart from these many goods there is another which is self-subsistent and causes the

---

2   The Platonic School; Cf. ch. 6.

goodness of all these as well. To examine all the opinions that have been held were perhaps somewhat fruitless; enough to examine those that are most prevalent or that seem to be arguable.

Let us not fail to notice, however, that there is a difference between arguments from and those to the first principles. For Plato, too, was right in raising this question and asking, as he used to do, "are we on the way from or to the first principles?"[3] There is a difference, as there is in a race-course between the course from the judges to the turning-point and the way back. For, while we must begin with what is known, things are objects of knowledge in two senses— some to us, some without qualification. Presumably, then, we must begin with things known to *us*. Hence any one who is to listen intelligently to lectures about what is noble and just and, generally, about the subjects of political science must have been brought up in good habits. For the fact is the starting-point, and if this is sufficiently plain to him, he will not at the start need the reason as well; and the man who has been well brought up has or can easily get starting-points. And as for him who neither has nor can get them, let him hear the words of Hesiod:

> Far best is he who knows all things himself;
> Good, he that hearkens when men counsel right;
> But he who neither knows, nor lays to heart
> Another's wisdom, is a useless wight.

Let us, however, resume our discussion from the point at which we digressed. To judge from the lives that men lead, most men, and men of the most vulgar type, seem (not without some ground) to identify the good, or happiness, with pleasure; which is the reason why they love the life of enjoyment. For there are, we may say, three prominent types of life—that just mentioned, the political, and thirdly the contemplative life. Now the mass of mankind are evidently quite slavish in their tastes, preferring a life suitable to beasts, but they get some ground for their view from the fact that many of those in high places share the tastes of Sardanapallus. A consideration of the prominent types of life shows that people of superior refinement and of active disposition identify happiness with honour; for this is, roughly speaking, the end of the political life. But it seems too superficial to be what we are looking for, since it is thought to depend on those who bestow honour rather than on him who receives it, but the good we divine to be something proper to a man and not easily taken from him. Further, men seem to pursue honour in order that they may be assured of their goodness; at least it is by men of practical wisdom that they seek to be honoured, and among those who know them, and on the ground of their virtue; clearly, then, according to them, at any rate, virtue is better. And perhaps one might even suppose this to be rather than honour, the end of the political life. But even this appears somewhat incomplete; for possession of virtue seems actually compatible with being asleep, or with lifelong inactivity, and, further, with the greatest sufferings and misfortunes; but a man who was living so no one would call happy, unless he were maintaining a thesis at all costs. But enough of this; for the subject has been sufficiently treated even in the current discussions. Third comes the contemplative life, which we shall consider later.[4]

---

3   Cf. *Rep.* 511 B
4   1177^a 12–1178^a 8, 1178^a 22–1179^a 32.

The life of money-making is one undertaken under compulsion, and wealth is evidently not the good we are seeking; for it is merely useful and for the sake of something else. And so one might rather take the aforenamed objects to be ends; for they are loved for themselves. But it is evident that not even these are ends; yet many arguments have been thrown away in support of them. Let us leave this subject, then.

We had perhaps better consider the universal good and discuss thoroughly what is meant by it, although such an inquiry is made an uphill one by the fact that the Forms have been introduced by friends of our own. Yet it would perhaps be thought to be better, indeed to be our duty, for the sake of maintaining the truth even to destroy what touches us closely, especially as we are philosophers or lovers of wisdom; for, while both are dear, piety requires us to honour truth above our friends.

The men who introduced this doctrine did not posit Ideas of classes within which they recognized priority and posteriority (which is the reason why they did not maintain the existence of an Idea embracing all numbers); but the term "good" is used both in the category of substance and in that of quality and in that of relation, and that which is *per se*, i.e. substance, is prior in nature to the relative (for the latter is like an offshoot and accident of being); so that there could not be a common Idea set over all these goods. Further, since "good" has as many senses as "being" (for it is predicated both in the category of substance, as of God and of reason, and in quality, i.e. of the virtues, and in quantity, i.e. of that which is moderate, and in relation, i.e. of the useful, and in time, i.e. of the right opportunity, and in place, i.e. of the right locality and the like), clearly it cannot be something universally present in

all cases and single; for then it could not have been predicated in all the categories but in one only. Further, since of the things answering to one Idea there is one science, there would have been one science of all the goods; but as it is there are many sciences even of the things that fall under one category, e. g. of opportunity, for opportunity in war is studied by strategics and in disease by medicine, and the moderate in food is studied by medicine and in exercise by the science of gymnastics. And one might ask the question, what in the world they *mean* by "a thing itself," if (as is the case) in "man himself" and in a particular man the account of man is one and the same. For in so far as they are man, they will in no respect differ,; and if this is so, neither will "good itself" and particular goods, in so far as they are good. But again it will not be good any the more for being eternal, since that which lasts long is no whiter than that which perishes in a day. The Pythagoreans seem to give a more plausible account of the good, when they place the one in the column of goods; and it is they that Speusippus seems to have followed.

But let us discuss these matters elsewhere;[5] an objection to what we have said, however, may be discerned in the fact that the Platonists have not been speaking about *all* goods, and that the goods that are pursued and loved for themselves are called good by reference to a single Form, while those which tend to produce or to preserve these somehow or to prevent their contraries are called so by reference to these, and in a secondary sense. Clearly, then, goods must be spoken of in two ways, and some must be good in themselves, the others by reason of these. Let us separate, then, things good in themselves from things useful, and consider whether the former are called good by refer-

---

5   Cf. *Met.* 986^a, 22–6, 1028^b 21–4, 1072^b 30–1073^a 3, 1091^a 29–^{b} 3, ^{b} 13–1092^a 17.

ence to a single Idea. What sort of goods would one call good in themselves? Is it those that are pursued even when isolated from others, such as intelligence, sight, and certain pleasures and honours? Certainly, if we pursue these also for the sake of something else, yet one would place them among things good in themselves. Or is nothing other than the Idea of good good in itself? In that case the Form will be empty. But if the things we have named are also things good in themselves, the account of the good will have to appear as something identical in them all, as that of whiteness is identical in snow and in white lead. But of honour, wisdom, and pleasure, just in respect of their goodness, the accounts are distinct and diverse. The good, therefore, is not some common clement answering to one Idea.

But what then do we mean by the good? It is surely not like the things that only chance to have the same name. Are goods one, then, by being derived from one good or by all contributing to one good, or are they rather one by analogy? Certainly as sight is in the body, so is reason in the soul, and so on in other cases. But perhaps these subjects had better be dismissed for the present; for perfect precision about them would be more appropriate to another branch of philosophy.[6] And similarly with regard to the Idea; even if there is some one good which is universally predicable of goods or is capable of separate and independent existence, clearly it could not be achieved or attained by man; but we are now seeking something attainable. Perhaps, however, some one might think it worth while to recognize this with a view to the goods that are attainable and achievable; for having this as a sort of pattern we shall know better the goods that are good for us, and if we know them shall attain them. This argument has some plausibility,

but seems to clash with the procedure of the sciences; for all of these, though they aim at some good and seek to supply the deficiency of it, leave on one side the knowledge of *the* good. Yet that all the exponents of the arts should be ignorant of, and should not even seek, so great an aid is not probable. It is hard, too, to see how a weaver or a carpenter will be benefitted in regard to his own craft by knowing this "good itself," or how the man who has viewed the Idea itself will be a better doctor or general thereby. For a doctor seems not even to study health in this way, but the health of man, or perhaps rather the health of a particular man; it is individuals that he is healing. But enough of these topics.

Let us again return to the good we are seeking, and ask what it can be. It seems different in different actions and arts; it is different in medicine, in strategy, and in the other arts likewise. What then is the good of each? Surely that for whose sake everything else is done. In medicine this is this is health, in strategy victory, in architecture a house, in any other sphere something else, and in every action and pursuit the end; for it is for the sake of this that all men do whatever else they do. Therefore, if there is an end for all that we do, this will be the good achievable by action, and if there are more than one, these will be the goods achievable by action.

So the argument has by a different course reached the same point; but we must try to state this even more clearly. Since there are evidently more than one end, and we choose some of these (e. g. wealth, flutes, and in general instruments) for the sake of something else, clearly not all ends are final ends; but the chief good is evidently something final. Therefore, if there is only one final end, this will be what we are seeking, and if there are more than one, the most final of these will

---

6 Cf. *Met.* iv. 2.

be what we are seeking. Now we call that which is in itself worthy of pursuit more final than that which is worthy of pursuit for the sake of something else, and that which is never desirable for the sake of something else more final than the things that are desirable both in themselves and for the sake of that other thing, and therefore we call final without qualification that which is always desirable in itself and never for the sake of something else.

Now such a thing happiness, above all else, is held to be; for this we choose always for itself and never for the sake of something else, but honour, pleasure, reason, and every virtue we choose indeed for themselves (for if nothing resulted from them we should still choose each of them), but we choose them also for the sake of happiness, judging that by means of them we shall be happy. Happiness, on the other hand, no one chooses for the sake of these, nor, in general, for anything other than itself.

From the point of view of self-sufficiency the same result seems to follow; for the final good is thought to be self-sufficient. Now by self-sufficient we do not mean that which is sufficient for a man by himself, for one who lives a solitary life, but also for parents, children, wife, and in general for his friends and fellow citizens, since man is born for citizenship. But some limit must be set to this; for if we extend our requirement to ancestors and descendants and friends' friends we are in for an infinite series. Let us examine this question, however, on another occasion;[7] the self-sufficient we now define as that which when isolated makes life desirable and lacking in nothing; and such we think happiness to be; and further we think it most desirable of all things, without being counted as one good thing among others—if it were so counted it would clearly be made

more desirable by the addition of even the least of goods; for that which is added becomes an excess of goods, and of goods the greater is always more desirable. Happiness, then, is something final and self-sufficient, and is the end of action.

Presumably, however, to say that happiness is good seems a platitude, and a clearer account of what it is is still desired. This might perhaps be given, if we could first ascertain the function of man. For just as for a fluteplayer, a sculptor, or any artist, and, in general, for all things that have a function or activity, the good and the "well" is thought to reside in the function, so would it seem to be for man, if he has a function. Have the carpenter, then, and the tanner certain functions or activities, and has man none? Is he born without a function? Or as eye, hand, foot, and in general each of the parts evidently has a function, may one lay it down that man similarly has a function apart from all these? What then can this be? life seems to be common even to plants, but we are seeking what is peculiar to man. Let us exclude, therefore, the life of nutrition and growth. Next there would be a life of perception, but it also seems to be common even to the horse, the ox, and every animal. There remains, then, an active life of the element that has a rational principle; of this, one part has such a principle in the sense of being obedient to one, the other in the sense of possessing one and exercising thought. And, as "life of the rational element" also has two meanings, we must state that life in the sense of activity is what we mean; for this seems to be the more proper sense of the term. Now if the function of man is an activity of soul which follows or implies a rational principle, and if we say "a so-and-so" and "a good so-and-so" have a function which is the same in kind, e.g. a lyre-player and a good lyre-

7   i. 10, 11, ix. 10.

player, and so without qualification in all cases, eminence in respect of goodness being added to the name of the function (for the function of a lyre-player is to play the lyre, and that of a good lyre-player is to do so well): if this is the case, [and we state the function of man to be a certain kind of life, and this to be an activity or actions of the soul implying a rational principle, and the function of a good man to be the good and noble performance of these, and if any action is well performed when it is performed in accordance with the appropriate excellence: if this is the case,] human good turns out to be activity of soul in accordance with virtue, and if there are more than one virtue, in accordance with the best and most complete.

But we must add "in a complete life." For one swallow does not make a summer, not does one day; and so too one day, or a short time, does not make a man blessed and happy.

Let this serve as an outline of the good; for we must presumably first sketch it roughly, and then later fill in the details. But it would seem that any one is capable of carrying on and articulating what has once been well outlined, and that time is a good discoverer or partner in such a work; to which facts the advances of the arts are due; for any one can add what is lacking. And we must also remember what has been said before,[8] and not look for precision in all things alike, but in each class of things such precision as accords with the subject-matter, and so much as is appropriate to the inquiry. For a carpenter and a geometer investigate the right angle in different ways; the former does so in so far as the right angle is useful for his work, while the latter inquires what it is or what sort of thing it is; for he is a spectator of the truth. We must act in the same way, then,

in all other matters as well, that our main task may not be subordinated to minor questions. Nor must we demand the cause in all matters alike; it is enough in some cases that the *fact* be well established, as in the case of the first principles; the fact is the primary thing or first principle. Now of first principles we see some by induction, some by perception, some by a certain habituation, and others too in other ways. But each set of principles we must try to investigate in the natural way, and we must take pains to state them definitely, since they have a great influence on what follows. For the beginning is thought to be more than half of the whole, and many of the questions we ask are cleared up by it.

We must consider it, however, in the light not only of our conclusion and our premises, but also of what is commonly said about it; for with a true view all the data harmonize, but with a false one the facts soon clash. Now goods have been divided into three classes,[9] and some are described as external, others as relating to soul or to body; we call those that relate to soul most properly and truly goods, and psychical actions and activities we class as relating to soul. Therefore our account must be sound, at least according to this view, which is an old one and agreed on by philosophers. It is correct also in that we identify the end with certain actions and activities; for thus it falls among goods of the soul and not among external goods. Another belief which harmonizes with our account is that the happy man lives well and does well; for we have practically defined happiness as a sort of good life and good action. The characteristics that are looked for in happiness seem also, all of them, to belong to what we have defined happiness as being. For some identify hap-

---

8   1094^b 11–27.
9   Pl *Eutlyd.* 279 AB, *Phil.* 48 E, *Laws*, 743 E.

piness with virtue, some with practical wisdom, others with a kind of philosophic wisdom, others with these, or one of these, accompanied by pleasure or not without pleasure; while others include also external prosperity. Now some of these views have been held by many men and men of old, other by a few eminent persons; and it is not probable that either of these should be entirely mistaken, but rather that they should be right in at least some one respect or even in most respects.

With those who identify happiness with virtue or some one virtue our account is in harmony; for to virtue belongs virtuous activity. But it makes, perhaps, no small difference whether we place the chief good in possession or in use, in state of mind or in activity. For the state of mind may exist without producing any good result, as in a man who is asleep or in some other way quite inactive, but the activity cannot; for one who has the activity will of necessity be acting and acting well. And as in the Olympic Games it is not the most beautiful and the strongest that are crowned, but those who compete (for it is some of these that are victorious), so those who act win, and rightly win, the noble and good things in life.

Their life is also in itself pleasant. For pleasure is a state of *soul*, and to each man that which he is said to be a lover of is pleasant; e.g. not only is a horse pleasant to be the lover of horses, and a spectacle to the lover of sights, but also in the same way just acts are pleasant to the lover of justice and in general virtuous acts to the lover of virtue. Now for most men their pleasures are in conflict with one another because these are not be nature pleasant, but the lovers of what is noble find pleasant the things that are by

nature pleasant; and virtuous actions are such, so that these are pleasant for such men as well as in their own nature. Their life, therefore, has no further need of pleasure as a sort of adventitious charm, but has its pleasure in itself. For, besides what we have said, the man who does not rejoice in noble actions is not even good; since no one would call a man just who did not enjoy acting justly, nor any man liberal who did not enjoy liberal actions; and similarly in all other cases. If this is so, virtuous actions must be in themselves pleasant. But they are also *good* and *noble*, and have each of these attributes in the highest degree, since the good man judges well about these attributes; his judgement is such as we have described.[10] Happiness then is the best, noblest, and most pleasant thing in the world, and these attributes are not severed as in the inscription at Delos—

> Most noble is that which is justest, and best is health;
> But pleasantest is it to win what we love.

For all these properties belong to the best activities; and these, or one—the best—of these, we identify with happiness.

Yet evidently, as we said, [11] it needs the external goods as well; for it is impossible, or not easy, to do noble acts without the proper equipment. In many actions we use friends and riches and political power as instruments; and there are some things the lack of which takes the lustre from happiness, as good birth, goodly children, beauty; for the man who is very ugly in appearance or ill-born or solitary and childless is not very likely to be happy, and perhaps a man would be still less likely if he had thoroughly bad children or friends or had lost good children

---

10   i.e., he judges that virtuous actions are good and noble in the highest degree.
11   1098^b 26–9.

or friends by death. As we said, [12] then, happiness seems to need this sort of prosperity in addition; for which reason some identify happiness with good fortune, though others identify it with virtue.

For this reason also the question is asked, whether happiness is to be acquired by learning or by habituation or some other sort of training, or comes in virtue of some divine providence or again by chance. Now if there is *any* gift of the gods to men, it is reasonable that happiness should be god-given, and most surely god-given of all human things inasmuch as it is the best. But this question would perhaps be more appropriate to another inquiry; happiness seems, however, even if it is not god-sent but comes as a result of virtue and some process of learning or training, to be among the most god-like things; for that which is the prize and end of virtue seems to be the best thing in the world, and something godlike and blessed.

It will also on this view be very generally shared; for all who are not maimed as regards their potentiality for virtue may win it by a certain kind of study and care. But if it is better to be happy thus than by chance, it is reasonable that the facts should be so, since everything that depends on the action of nature is by nature as good as it can be, and similarly everything that depends on art or any rational cause, and especially if it depends on the best of all causes. To entrust to chance what is greatest and most noble would be a very defective arrangement.

The answer to the question we are asking is plain also from the definition of happiness; for it has been said[13] to be a virtuous activity of soul, of a certain kind. Of the remaining goods, some must necessarily pre-exist as conditions of happiness, and others are naturally co-operative and useful as instruments. And this will be found to agree with what we said at the outset; [14] for we stated the end of political science to be the best end, and political science spends most of its pains on making the citizens to be of a certain character, viz. good and capable of noble acts.

It is natural, then, that we call neither ox nor horse nor any other of the animals happy; for none of them is capable of sharing in such activity. For this reason also a boy is not happy, for he is not yet capable of such acts, owing to his age; and boys who are called happy are being congratulated by reason of the hopes we have for them. For there is required, as we said,[15] not only complete virtue but also a complete life, since many changes occur in life, and all manner of chances, and the most prosperous may fall into great misfortunes in old age, as it is told of Priam in the Trojan Cycle; and one who has experienced such chances and has ended wretchedly no one calls happy.

Must no one at all, then, be called happy while he lives; must we, as Solon says, see the end? Even if we are to lay down this doctrine, is it also the case that a man is happy when he is *dead*? Or is not this quite absurd, especially for us who say that happiness is an activity? But if we do not call the dead man happy, and if Solon does not mean this, but that one can then safely *call* a man blessed as being at last beyond evils and misfortunes, this also affords matter for discussion; for both evil and good are thought to exist for a dead man, as much as for one who is alive but not aware of them; e.g. honours and dishonours and the good or bad fortunes of children and in general of descendants. And this also presents a prob-

---

12   1098^b 26–9.
13   1098^a 16.
14   1094^a 27.
15   1098^a 16–18.

lem; for though a man has lived happily up to old age and has had a death worthy of his life, many reverses may befall his descendants—some of them may be good and attain the life they deserve, while with others the opposite may be the case; and clearly too the degrees of relationship between them and their ancestors may vary indefinitely. It would be odd, then, if the dead man were to share in these changes and become at one time happy, at another wretched; while it would also be odd if the fortunes of the descendants did not for *some* time have *some* effect on the happiness of their ancestors.

But we must return to our first difficulty; for perhaps by a consideration of it our present problem might be solved. Now if we must see the end and only then call a man happy, not as being happy but as having been so before, surely this is a paradox, that when he is happy the attribute that belongs to him is not to be truly predicated of him because we do not wish to call living men happy, on account of the changes that may befall them, and because we have assumed happiness to be something permanent and by no means easily changed, while a single man may suffer many turns of fortune's wheel. For clearly if we were to keep pace with his fortunes, we should often call the same man happy and again wretched, making the happy man out to be a "chameleon and insecurely based." Or is this keeping pace with his fortunes quite wrong? Success or failure in life does not depend on these, but human life, as we said,[16] needs these as mere additions, while virtuous activities or their opposites are what constitute happiness or the reverse.

The question we have now discussed confirms our definition. For no function of man has so much permanence as virtuous activities (these are thought to be more durable even than knowledge of the sciences), and of these themselves the most valuable are more durable because those who are happy spend their life most readily and most continuously in these; for this seems to be the reason why we do not forget them. The attribute in question,[17] then, will belong to the happy man, and he will be happy throughout his life; for always, or by preference to everything else, he will be engaged in virtuous action and contemplation, and he will bear the chances of life most nobly and altogether decorously, if he is "truly good" and "foursquare beyond reproach."[18]

Now many events happen by chance, and events differing in importance; small pieces of good fortune or of its opposite clearly do not weigh down the scales of life one way or the other, but a multitude of great events if they turn out well will make life happier (for not only are they themselves such as to add beauty to life, but the way a man deals with them may be noble and good), while if they turn out ill they crush and maim happiness; for they both bring pain with them and hinder many activities. Yet even in these nobility shines through, when a man bears with resignation many great misfortunes, not through insensibility to pain but through nobility and greatness of soul.

If activities are, as we said,[19] what gives life its character, no happy man can become miserable; for he will never do the acts that are hateful and mean. For the man who is truly good and wise, we think, bears all the chances of life becomingly and always makes the best of circumstances, as a good general makes the best military use of the

---

16 1099^a 31–^{b} 7.
17 Durability.
18 Simonides.
19 I. 9.

army at his command and a good shoemaker makes the best shoes out of the hides that are given him; and so with all other craftsmen. And if this is the case, the happy man never become miserable—though he will not reach *blessedness*, if he meet with fortunes like those of Priam.

Nor, again, is he many-coloured and changeable; for neither will he be moved from his happy state easily or by any ordinary misadventures, but only by many great ones, nor, if he has had many great misadventures, will be recovering his happiness in a short time, but if at all, only in a long and complete one in which he has attained many splendid successes.

Why then should we not say that he is happy who is active in accordance with complete virtue and is sufficiently equipped with external goods, not for some chance period but throughout a complete life? Or must we add "and who is destined to live thus and die as befits his life"? Certainly the future is obscure to us, while happiness, we claim, is an end and something in every way final. If so, we shall call happy those among living men in whom these conditions are, and are to be, fulfilled—but happy *men*. So much for these questions.

[20]That the fortunes of descendants and of all a man's friends should not affect his happiness at all seems a very unfriendly doctrine, and one opposed to the opinions men hold; but since the events that happen are numerous and admit of all sorts of difference, and some come more near to us and others less so, it seems a long—nay, an infinite—task to discuss each in detail; a general outline will perhaps suffice. If, then, as some of a man's own misadventures have a certain weight and influence on life while others are, as it were, lighter, so too there are differences among the misadventures of our friends taken as a whole, and it makes a difference whether the various sufferings befall the living or the dead (much more even than whether lawless and terrible deeds are presupposed in a tragedy done on the stage), this difference also must be taken into account; or rather, perhaps, the fact that doubt is felt whether the dead share in any good or evil. For it seems, from these considerations, that even if anything whether good or evil penetrates to them, it must be something weak and negligible, either in itself or for them, or if not, at least it must be such in degree and kind as not to make happy those who are not happy nor to take away their blessedness from those who are. The good or bad fortunes of friends, then, seem to have some effects on the dead, but effects of such a kind and degree as neither to make the happy unhappy nor to produce any other change of the kind.

These questions having been definitely answered, let us consider whether happiness is among the things that are praised or rather among the things that are prized; for clearly it is not to be placed among *potentialities*.[21] Everything that is praised because it is of a certain kind and is related somehow to something else; for we praise the just or brave man and in general both the good man and virtue itself because of the actions and functions involved, and we praise the strong man, the good runner, and so on, because he is of a certain kind and is related in a certain way to something good and important. This is clear also from the praises of the gods; for it seems absurd that the gods should be referred to our standard, but this *is* done because praise involves a reference, as we said, to something else. But if praise is for things such as we have described, clearly what ap-

---

20   Aristotle now returns to the question stated in 1100^a 18–30.
21   Cf. *Top.* 126^b 4; M. M. 1183^b 20.

plies to the best things is not praise, but something greater and better, as is indeed obvious; for what we do to the gods and the most godlike of men is to call them blessed and happy. And so too with good *things*; no one praises happiness as he does justice, but rather calls it blessed, as being something more divine and better.

Eudoxus also seems to have been right in his method of advocating the supremacy of pleasure; he thought that the fact that, though a good, it is not praised indicated it to be better than the things that are praised, and that this is what God and the good are; for by reference to these all other things are judged. *Praise* is appropriate to virtue, for as a result of virtue men tend to do noble deeds; but *encomia* are bestowed on acts, whether of the body or of the soul. But perhaps nicety in these matters is more proper to those who have made a study of encomia; to us it is clear from what has been said that happiness is among the things that are prized and perfect. It seems to be so also from the fact that it is a first principle; for it is for the sake of this that we all do all that we do, and the first principle and cause of goods is, we claim, something prized and divine.

Since happiness is an activity of soul in accordance with perfect virtue, we must consider the nature of virtue; for perhaps we shall thus see better the nature of happiness. The true student of politics, too, is thought to have studied virtue above all things; for he wishes to make his fellow citizens good and obedient to the laws. As an example of this we have the lawgivers of the Cretans and the Spartans, and any others of the kind that there may have been. And if this inquiry belongs to political science, clearly the pursuit of it will be in accordance with our original plan. But clearly the virtue we must study is human virtue; for the good we were seeking was human good and the happiness human happiness. By human virtue we mean not that of the body but that of the soul; and happiness also we call an activity of soul. But if this is so, clearly the student of politics must know somehow the facts about soul, as the man who is to heal the eyes or the body as a whole must know about the eyes or the body; and all the more since politics is more prized and better than medicine; but even among doctors the best educated spend much labour on acquiring knowledge of the body. The student of politics, then, must study the soul, and must study it with these objects in view, and do so just to the extent which is sufficient for the questions we are discussing; for further precision is perhaps something more laborious than our purposes require.

Some things are said about it, adequately enough, even in the discussions outside our school, and we must use these; e.g. that one element in the soul is irrational and one has a rational principle. Whether these are separated as the parts of the body or of anything divisible are, or are distinct by definition but by nature inseparable, like convex and concave in the circumference of a circle, does not affect the present question.

Of the irrational element one division seems to be widely distributed, and vegetative in its nature, I mean that which causes nutrition and growth; for it is this kind of power of the soul that one must assign to all nurslings and to embryos, and this same power to full-grown creatures; this is more reasonable than to assign some different power to them. Now the excellence of this seems to be common to all species and not specifically human; for this part or faculty seems to function most in sleep, while goodness and badness are least manifest in sleep (whence comes the saying that the happy are no better off than the wretched for half their lives; and this happens naturally enough, since sleep is an inactivity of the soul in that respect in which it is called good or bad), unless perhaps to a small extent some of the movements actually penetrate to the soul, and in this respect the dreams of good men are better than those of ordinary people. Enough of this subject, however; let us leave the nutritive faculty alone, since it has by its nature no share in human excellence.

There seems to be also another irrational element in the soul—one which in a sense, however, shares in a rational principle. For we praise the rational principle of the continent man and of the incontinent, and the part of their soul that has such a principle, since it urges them aright and towards the best objects; but there is found in them also another element naturally opposed to the rational principle, which fights against and resists that principle. For exact as paralysed limbs when we intend to move them to the right turn on the contrary to the left, so is it with the soul; the impulses of incontinent people move in contrary directions. But while in the body we see that which moves astray, in the soul we do not. No doubt, however, we must none the less suppose that in the soul too there is something contrary to the rational principle, resisting and opposing it. In what sense it is distinct from the other elements does not concern us. Now even this seems to have a share in a rational principle, as we said;[22] at any rate in the continent man it obeys the rational principle—and presumably in the temperate and brave man it is still more obedient; for in him it speaks, on all matters, with the same voice as the rational principle.

Therefore the irrational element also appears to be twofold. For the vegetative element in no way shares in a rational principle, but the appetitive, and in general the desiring element in a sense shares in it, in so far as it listens to and obeys it; this is the sense in which we speak of "taking account" of one's father or one's friends, not that in which we speak of "accounting" for a mathematical property. That the irrational element is in some sense persuaded by a rational principle is indicated also by the giving of advice and by all reproof and exhortation. And if this element also must be said to have a rational principle, that which has a rational principle (as well as that which has not) will be twofold, one subdivision having it in the strict sense and in itself, and the other having a tendency to obey as one does one's father.

Virtue too is distinguished into kinds in accordance with this difference; for we say that some of the virtues are intellectual and others moral, philosophic wisdom and understanding and practical wisdom being intellectual, liberality and temperance moral. For in speaking about a man's character we do not say that he is wise or has understanding but that he is good-tempered or temperate; yet we praise the wise man also with respect to his state of mind; and of states of mind we call those which merit praise virtues.

Book II

Virtue, then, being of two kinds, intellectual and moral, intellectual virtue in the main owes both its birth and its growth to teaching (for which reason it requires experience and time), while moral virtue comes about as a result of habit, whence also its name *ethike* is one that is formed by a slight variation from the word *ethos* (habit). From this it is also plain that none of the moral virtues arises in us by nature; for nothing that exists by nature can form a habit contrary to its nature. For instance the stone which by nature moves downwards cannot be habituated to move upwards, not even if

---

22   1. 13.

one tries to train it by throwing it up ten thousand times; nor can fire be habituated to move downwards, nor can anything else that by nature behaves in one way be trained to behave in another. Neither by nature, then, nor contrary to nature do the virtues arise in us; rather we are adapted by nature to receive them, and are made perfect by habit.

Again, of all the things that come to us by nature we first acquire the potentiality and later exhibit the activity (this is plain in the case of the senses; for it was not by often seeing or often hearing that we got these senses, but on the contrary we had them before we used them, and did not come to have them by using them); but the virtues we get by first exercising them, as also happens in the case of the arts as well. For the things we have to learn before we can do them, we learn by doing them, e.g. men become builders by building and lyre-players by playing the lyre; so too we become just by doing just acts, temperate by doing temperate acts, brave by doing brave acts.

This is confirmed by what happens in states; for legislators make the citizens good by forming habits in them, and this is the wish of every legislator, and those who do not effect it miss their mark, and it is in this that a good constitution differs from a bad one.

Again, it is from the same causes and by the same means that every virtue is both produced and destroyed, and similarly every art; for it is from playing the lyre that both good and bad lyre-players are produced. And the corresponding statement is true of builders and of all the rest; men will be good or bad builders as a result of building well or badly. For if this were not so, there would have been no need of a teacher, but all men would have been born good or bad at their craft. This, then, is the case with the virtues also; by doing the acts that we do in our transactions with other men we become just or unjust, and by doing the acts that we do in the presence of danger, and being habituated to feel fear or confidence, we become brave or cowardly. The same is true of appetites and feelings of anger; some men become temperate and good-tempered, others self-indulgent and irascible, by behaving in one way or the other in the appropriate circumstances. Thus, in one word, states of character arise out of like activities. This is why the activities we exhibit must be of a certain kind; it is because the states of character correspond to the differences between these. It makes no small difference, then, whether we form habits of one kind or of another from our very youth; it make a very great difference, or rather *all* the difference.

Since, then, the present inquiry does not aim at theoretical knowledge like the others (for we are inquiring not in order to know what virtue is, but in order to become good, since otherwise our inquiry would have been of no use), we must examine the nature of actions, namely how we ought to do them; for these determine also the nature of the states of character that are produced, as we have said.[23] Now, that we must act according to the right rule is a common principle and must be assumed—it will be discussed later,[24] i.e. both what the right rule is, and how it is related to the other virtues. But this must be agreed upon beforehand, that the whole account of matters of conduct must be given in outline and not precisely, as we said at the beginning[25] that the accounts we demand must be in accordance with the subject-matter; matters concerned with conduct

23   ᵃ 31–ᵇ 25.
24   vi. 13.
25   1094ᵇ 11–27.

and questions of what is good for us have no fixity, any more than matters of health. The general account being of this nature, the account of particular cases is yet more lacking in exactness; for they do not fall under any art or precept but the agents themselves must in each case consider what is appropriate to the occasion, as happens also in the art of medicine or of navigation.

But though our present account is of this nature we must give what help we can. First, then, let us consider this, that it is the nature of such things to be destroyed by defect and excess, as we see in the case of strength and of health (for to gain light on things imperceptible we must use the evidence of sensible things); both excessive and defective exercise destroys the strength, and similarly drink or food which is above or below a certain amount destroys the health, while that which is proportionate both produces and increases and preserves it. So too is it, then, in the case of temperance and courage and the other virtues. For the man who flies from and fears everything and does not stand his ground against anything becomes a coward, and the man who fears nothing at all but goes to meet every danger becomes rash; and similarly the man who indulges in every pleasure and abstains from none becomes self-indulgent, while the man who shuns every pleasure, as boors do, becomes in a way insensible; temperance and courage, then, are destroyed by excess and defect, and preserved by the mean.

But not only are the sources and causes of their origination and growth the same as those of their destruction, but also the sphere of their actualization will be the same; for this is also true of the things which are more evident to sense, e.g. of strength; it is produced by taking much food and undergoing much exertion, and it is the strong man that will be most able to do these things. So too is it with the virtues; by abstaining from pleasures we become temperate, and it is when we have become so that we are most able to abstain from them; and similarly too in the case of courage; for by being habituated to despise things that are terrible and to stand our ground against them we become brave, and it is when we have become so that we shall be most able to stand our ground against them.

We must take as a sign of states of character the pleasure or pain that ensues on acts; for the man who abstains from bodily pleasures and delights in this very fact is temperate, while the man who is annoyed at it is self-indulgent, and he who stands his ground against things that are terrible and delights in this or at least is not pained is brave, while the man who is pained is a coward. For moral excellence is concerned with pleasures and pains; it is on account of the pleasure that we do bad things, and on account of the pain that we abstain from noble ones. Hence we ought to have been brought up in a particular way from our very youth, as Plato says,[26] so as both to delight in and to be pained by the things that we ought; for this is the right education.

Again, if the virtues are concerned with actions and passions, and every passion and every action is accompanied by pleasure and pain, for this reason also virtue will be concerned with pleasures and pains. This is indicated also by the fact that punishment is inflicted by these means; for it is a kind of cure, and it is the nature of cures to be effected by contraries.

Again, as we said but lately,[27] every state of soul has a nature relative to and concerned with the kind of things by which it tends to

26   *Laws,* 653 A ff., *Rep.* 401 E–402 A.
27   [a] 27–[b] 3.

be made worse or better; but it is by reason of pleasures and pains that men become bad, by pursuing and avoiding these—either the pleasures and pains they ought not or when they ought not or as they ought not, or by going wrong in one of the other similar ways that may be distinguished. Hence men[28] even define the virtues as certain states of impassivity and rest; not well, however, because they speak absolutely, and do not say "as one ought" and "as one ought not" and "when one ought or ought not," and the other things that may be added. We assume, then, that this kind of excellence tends to do what is best with regard to pleasures and pains, and vice does the contrary.

The following facts also may show us that virtue and vice are concerned with these same things. There being three objects of choice and three of avoidance, the noble, the advantageous, the pleasant, and their contraries, the base, the injurious, the painful, about all of these the good man tends to go right and the bad man to go wrong, and especially about pleasure; for this is common to the animals, and also it accompanies all objects of choice; for even the noble and the advantageous appear pleasant.

Again, it has grown up with us all from our infancy; this is why it is difficult to rub off this passion, engrained as it is in our life. And we measure even our actions, some of us more and others less, by the rule of pleasure and pain. For this reason, then, our whole inquiry must be about these; for to feel delight and pain rightly or wrongly has no small effect on our actions.

Again, it is harder to fight with pleasure than with anger, to use Heraclitus' phrase, but both art and virtue are always concerned with what is harder; for even the good is

better when it is harder. Therefore for this reason also the whole concern both of virtue and of political science is with pleasures and pains; for the man who uses these well will be good, he who uses them badly bad.

That virtue, then, is concerned with pleasures and pains, and that by the acts from which it arises it is both increased and, if they are done differently, destroyed, and that the acts from which it arose are those in which it actualizes itself—let this be taken as said.

The question might be asked, what we mean by saying[29] that we must become just by doing just acts, and temperate by doing temperate acts; for if men do just and temperate acts, they are already just and temperate, exactly as, if they do what is in accordance with the laws of grammar and of music, they are grammarians and musicians.

Or is this not true even of the arts? It is possible to do something that is in accordance with the laws of grammar, either by change or at the suggestion of another. A man will be a grammarian, then, only when he has both done something grammatical and done it grammatically; and this means doing it in accordance with the grammatical knowledge in himself.

Again, the case of the arts and that of the virtues are not similar; for the products of the arts have their goodness in themselves, so that it is enough that they should have a certain character, but if the acts that are in accordance with the virtues have themselves a certain character it does not follow that they are done justly or temperately. The agent also must be in a certain condition when he does them; in the first place he must have knowledge, secondly he must choose the acts, and choose them for their own

---

28   Probably Speusippus is referred to.
29   1103[a] 31-[b] 25. 1104[a] 27–[b] 3.

sakes, and thirdly his action must proceed from a firm and unchangeable character. These are not reckoned in as conditions of the possession of the arts, except the bare knowledge; but as a condition of the possession of the virtues knowledge has little or no weight, while the other conditions count not for a little but for everything, i.e. the very conditions which result from often doing just and temperate acts.

Actions, then, are called just and temperate when they are such as the just or the temperate man would do; but it is not the man who does these that is just and temperate, but the man who also does them *as* just and temperate men do them. It is well said, then, that it is by doing just acts that the just man is produced, and by doing temperate acts the temperate man; without doing these no one would have even a prospect of becoming good.

But most people do not do these, but take refuge in theory and think they are being philosophers and will become good in this way, behaving somewhat like patients who listen attentively to their doctors, but do none of the things they are ordered to do. As the latter will not be made well in body by such a course of treatment, the former will not be made well in soul by such a course of philosophy.

Next we must consider what virtue is. Since things that are found in the soul are of three kinds—passions, faculties, states of character, virtue must be one of these. By passions I mean appetite, anger, fear, confidence, envy, joy, friendly feeling, hatred, longing, emulation, pity, and in general the feelings that are accompanied by pleasure or pain; by faculties the things in virtue of which we are said to be capable of feeling these, e.g. of becoming angry or being pained or feeling pity; by states of character

the things in virtue of which we stand well or badly with reference to the passions, e.g. with reference to anger we stand badly if we feel it violently or too weakly, and well if we feel it moderately; and similarly with reference to the other passions.

Now neither the virtues nor the vices are *passions*, because we are not called good or bad on the ground of our passions, but are so called on the ground of our virtues and our vices, and because we are neither praised nor blamed for our passions (for the man who feels fear or anger is not praised, nor is the man who simply feels anger blamed, but the man who feels it in a certain way), but for our virtues and our vices we *are* praise or blamed.

Again, we feel anger and fear without choice, but the virtues are modes of choice or involve choice. Further, in respect of the passions we are said to be moved, but in respect of the virtues and the vices we are said not to be moved but to be disposed in a particular way.

For these reasons also they are not *faculties*; for we are neither called good nor bad, nor praised nor blamed, for the simple capacity of feeling the passions; again, we have the faculties by nature; but we are not made good or bad by nature, we have spoken of this before.[30]

If, then, the virtues are neither passions nor faculties, all that remains is that they should be *states of character*.

Thus we have stated what virtue is in respect of its genus.

We must, however, not only describe virtue as a state of character, but also so what sort of state it is. We may remark, then, that every virtue or excellence both brings into good condition the thing of which it is the excellence and makes the work of that thing be done well; e.g. the excellence of the eye

---

30   1103ᵃ 18–ᵇ 2.

makes both the eye and its work good; for it is by the excellence of the eye that we see well. Similarly the excellence of the horse makes a horse both good in itself and good at running and at carrying its rider and at awaiting the attack of the enemy. Therefore, if this is true in every case, the virtue of man also will be the state of character which makes a man good and which makes him do his own work well.

How this is to happen we have stated already,[31] but it will be made plain also by the following consideration of the specific nature of virtue. In everything that is continuous and divisible it is possible to take more, less, or an equal amount, and that either in terms of the thing itself or relatively to us; and the equal is an intermediate between excess and defect. By the intermediate in the object I mean that which is equidistant from each of the extremes, which is one and the same for all men; by the intermediate relatively to us that which is neither too much nor too little—and this is not one, nor the same for all. For instance, if ten is many and two is few, six is the intermediate, taken in terms of the object; for it exceeds and is exceeded by an equal amount; this is intermediate according to arithmetical proportion. But the intermediate relatively to us is not to be taken so; if ten pounds are too much for a particular person to eat and two too little, it does not follow that the trainer will order six pounds; for this also is perhaps too much for the person who is to take it, or too little—too little for Milo,[32] too much for the beginner in athletic exercises. The same is true of running and wrestling. Thus a master of any art avoids excess and defect, but seeks the intermediate and chooses this—the intermediate not in the object but relatively to us.

If it is thus, then, that every art does its work well—by looking to the intermediate and judging its works by this standard (so that we often say of good works of art that it is not possible either to take away or to add anything, implying that excess and defect destroy the goodness of works of art, while the mean preserves it; and good artists, as we say, look to this in their work), and if, further, virtue is more exact and better than any art, as nature also is, then virtue must have the quality of aiming at the intermediate. I mean moral virtue; for it is this that is concerned with passions and actions, and in these there is excess, defect, and the intermediate. For instance, both fear and confidence and appetite and anger and pity and in general pleasure and pain may be felt both too much and too little, and in both cases not well; but to feel them at the right times, with reference to the right objects, towards the right people, with the right motive, and in the right way, is what is both intermediate and best, and this is characteristic of virtue. Similarly with regard to actions also there is excess, defect, and the intermediate. Now virtue is concerned with passions and actions, in which excess is a form of failure, and so is defect, while the intermediate is praised and is a form of success; and being praised and being successful are both characteristics of virtue. Therefore virtue is a kind of mean, since, as we have seen, it aims at what is intermediate.

Again, it is possible to fail in many ways (for evil belongs to the class of the unlimited, as the Pythagoreans so conjectured, and good to that of the limited), while to succeed is possible only in one way (for which reason also one is easy and the other difficult—to miss the mark easy, to his it difficult); for these reasons also, then, excess and defect

---

31   1104^a 11–27.
32   A famous wrestler.

are characteristic of vice, and the mean of virtue.

For men are good in but one way, but bad in many.

Virtue, then, is a state of character concerned with choice, lying in a mean, i.e. the mean relative to us, this being determined by a rational principle, and by that principle by which the man of practical wisdom would determine it. Now it is a mean between two vices, that which depends on excess and that which depends on defect; and again it is a mean because the vices respectively fall short of or exceed what is right in both passions and actions, while virtue both finds and chooses that which is intermediate. Hence in respect of its substance and the definition which states its essence virtue is a mean, with regard to what is best and right an extreme.

But not every action nor every passion admits of a mean; for some have names that already imply badness, e.g. spite, shamelessness, envy, and in the case of actions adultery, theft, murder; for all of these and suchlike things imply by their names that they are themselves bad, and not the excesses or deficiencies of them. It is not possible, then ever to be right with regard to them; one must always be wrong. Nor does goodness or badness with regard to such things depend on committing adultery with the right woman, at the right time, and in the right way, but simply to do any of them is to go wrong. It would be equally absurd, then, to expect that in unjust, cowardly, and voluptuous action there should be a mean, an excess, and a deficiency; for at that rate there would be a mean of excess and of deficiency, an excess of excess, and a deficiency of deficiency. But as there is no excess and deficiency of temperance and courage because what is intermediate is in a sense an extreme, so too of the actions we have mentioned there is no mean nor any excess and deficiency, but however they are done they are wrong; for in general there is neither a mean of excess and deficiency, nor excess and deficiency of a mean.

We must, however, not only make this general statement, but also apply it to the individual facts. For among statements about conduct those which are general apply more widely, but those which are particular are more genuine, since conduct has to do with individual cases, and our statements must harmonize with the facts in these cases. We may take these cases from our table. With regard to feelings of fear and confidence courage is the mean; of the people who exceed, he who exceeds in fearlessness has no name (many of the states have no name), while the man who exceeds in confidence is rash, and he who exceeds in fear and falls short in confidence is a coward. With regard to pleasures and pains—not all of them, and not so much with regard to the pains—the mean is temperance, the excess self-indulgence. Persons deficient with regard to the pleasures are not often found; hence such persons also have received no name. But let us call them "insensible."

On the Commonwealth

Marcus Tullius Cicero

True law is right reason conformable to nature, universal, unchangeable, eternal, whose commands urge us to duty, and whose prohibitions restrain us from evil. Whether it enjoins or forbids, the good respect its injunctions, and the wicked treat them with indifference. This law cannot be contradicted by any other law, and is not liable either to derogation or abrogation. Neither the senate nor the people can give us any dispensation for not obeying this universal law of justice. It needs no other expositor and interpreter than our own conscience. It is not one thing at Rome, and another at Athens; one thing to-day, and another to-morrow; but in all times and nations this universal law must for ever reign, eternal and imperishable. It is the sovereign master and emperor of all beings. God himself is its author, its promulgator, its enforcer. And he who does not obey it flies from himself, and does violence to the very nature of man. And by so doing he will endure the severest penalties even if he avoid the other evils which are usually accounted punishments.

On the Laws

It is therefore an absurd extravagance in some philosophers to assert, that all things are necessarily just which are established by the evil laws and the institutions of nations. Are then the laws of tyrants just, simply because they are laws? Suppose the thirty tyrants of Athens had imposed certain laws on the Athenians? Or, suppose again that these Athenians were delighted with these tyrannical laws, would these laws on that account have been considered just? For my own part, I do not think such laws deserve any greater estimation than that passed during our own interregnum, which ordained that the dictator should be empowered to put to death with impunity whatever citizens he pleased, without hearing them in their own defence.

For there is but one essential justice which cements society, and one law which establishes this justice. This law is right reason, which is the true rule of all commandments and prohibitions. Whoever neglects this law, whether written or unwritten, is necessarily unjust and wicked.

Summa of Theology

Saint Thomas Aquinas

Question XCI

On the Various Kinds of Law
(In Six Articles)

We must now consider the various kinds of law, under which head there are six points of inquiry: (1) Whether there is an eternal law? (2) Whether there is a natural law? (3) Whether there is a human law? (4) Whether there is a divine law? (5) Whether there is one divine law, or several? (6) Whether there is a law of sin?

First Article

Whether There is an Eternal Law?

We proceed thus to the First Article:—

Objection 1. It would seem that there is no eternal law. For every law is imposed on someone. But there was not someone from eternity on whom a law could be imposed, since God alone was from eternity. Therefore no law is eternal.

Obj. 2. Further, promulgation is essential to law. But promulgation could not be from eternity, because there was no one to whom it could be promulgated from eternity. Therefore no law can be eternal.

Obj. 3. Further, law implies order to an end. But nothing ordained to an end is eter-

nal, for the last end alone is eternal. Therefore no law is eternal.

On the contrary, Augustine says: *That Law which is the Supreme Reason cannot be understood to be otherwise than unchangeable and eternal.*[1]

I answer that, As we have stated above, law is nothing else but a dictate of practical reason emanating from the ruler who governs a perfect community.[2] Now it is evident, granted that the world is ruled by divine providence, as was stated in the First Part,[3] that the whole community of the universe is governed by the divine reason. Therefore the very notion of the government of things in God, the ruler of the universe, has the nature of a law. And since the divine reason's conception of things is not subject to time, but is eternal, according to *Prov.* viii. 23, therefore it is that this kind of law must be called eternal.

Reply Obj. 1. Those things that do not exist in themselves exist in God, inasmuch as they are known and preordained by Him, according to *Rom.* iv. 17: *Who calls those things that are not, as those that are.* Accordingly, the eternal concept of the divine law bears the character of an eternal law in so far as it is ordained by God to the government of things foreknown by Him.

Reply Obj. 2. Promulgation is made by word of mouth or in writing, and in both

From *Introduction to Saint Thomas Aquinas* by A. Pegis, copyright 1965, 616-619, 628-638. Reprinted by permission of McGraw-Hill, Inc.

1   *De Lib. Arb.,* I, 6 (PL 32, 1229).
2   Q. 90, a. 1, ad 2; a. 3 and 4.
3   *S. T.,* I, q. 22, a. 1, ad 2.

ways the eternal law is promulgated, because both the divine Word and the writing of the Book of Life are eternal. But the promulgation cannot be from eternity on the part of the creature that hears or reads.

Reply Obj. 3. Law implies order to the end actively, namely, in so far as it directs certain things to the end; but not passively, —that is to say, the law itself is not ordained to the end, except accidentally, in a governor whose end is extrinsic to him, and to which end his law must needs be ordained. But the end of the divine government is God Himself, and His law is not something other than Himself. Therefore the eternal law is not ordained to another end.

Second Article

Whether There is in Us a Natural Law?

We proceed thus to the Second Article:—

Objection 1. It would seem that there is no natural law in us. For man is governed sufficiently by the eternal law, since Augustine says that *the eternal law is that by which it is right that all things should be most orderly.*[4] But nature does not abound in superfluities as neither does she fail in necessaries. Therefore man has no natural law.

Obj. 2. Further, by the law man is directed, in his acts, to the end, as was stated above.[5] But the directing of human acts to their end is not a function of nature, as is the case in irrational creatures, which act for an end solely by their natural appetite; whereas man acts for an end by his reason and will. Therefore man has no natural law.

Obj. 3. Further, the more a man is free, the less is he under the law. But man is freer than all the animals because of his free choice, with which he is endowed in distinction from all other animals. Since, therefore, other animals are not subject to a natural law, neither is man subject to a natural law.

On the contrary, The *Gloss* on *Rom. ii.* 14 (*When the Gentiles, who have not the law, do by nature those things that are of the law*) comments as follows: *Although they have no written law, yet they have the natural law, whereby each one knows, and is conscious of, what is good and what is evil.*[6]

I answer that, As we have stated above,[7] law, being a rule and measure, can be in a person in two ways: in one way, as in him that rules and measures; in another way, as in that which is ruled and measured, since a thing is ruled and measured in so far as it partakes of the rule or measure. Therefore, since all things subject to divine providence are ruled and measured by the eternal law, as was stated above, it is evident that all things partake in some way in the eternal law, in so far as, namely, from its being imprinted on them, they derive their respective inclinations to their proper acts and ends. Now among all others, the rational creature is subject to divine providence in a more excellent way, in so far as it itself partakes of a share of providence, by being provident both for itself and for others. Therefore it has a share of the eternal reason, whereby it has a natural inclination to its proper act and end; and this participation of the eternal law in the rational creature is called the natural law. Hence the Psalmist, after saying (*Ps. iv.* 6): *Offer up the sacrifice of justice,* as though someone asked what the works of justice are, adds: *Many say, Who showeth us good things?* in answer to which question he says: *The light of Thy countenance, O Lord, is signed upon us.* He thus implies that the light of natural rea-

---

4   *De Lib. Arb.,* I, 6 (PL 32, 1229)
5   Q. 90, a. 2.
6   *Gloss ordin.* (VI, 7E); Peter Lómbard, *In Rom.,* super II, 14 (PL 191, 1345).
7   Q. 90, a. 1, ad 1.

son, whereby we discern what is good and what is evil, which is the function of the natural law, is nothing else than an imprint on us of the divine light. It is therefore evident that the natural law is nothing else than the rational creature's participation of the eternal law.

Reply Obj. 1. This argument would hold if the natural law were something different from the eternal law; whereas it is nothing but a participation thereof, as we have stated above.

Reply Obj. 2. Every act of reason and will in us is based on that which is according to nature, as was stated above.[8] For every act of reasoning is based on principles that are known naturally, and every act of appetite in respect of the means is derived from the natural appetite in respect of the last end. Accordingly, the first direction of our acts to their end must needs be through the natural law.

Reply Obj. 3. Even irrational animals partake in their own way of the eternal reason, just as the rational creature does. But because the rational creature partakes thereof in an intellectual and rational manner, therefore the participation of the eternal law in the rational creature is properly called a law, since a law is something pertaining to reason, as was stated above.[9] Irrational creatures, however, do not partake thereof in a rational manner, and therefore there is no participation of the eternal law in them, except by way of likeness.

Third Article

Whether There is a Human Law?

We proceed thus to the Third Article:—

Objection 1. It would seem that there is not a human law. For the natural law is a participation of the eternal law, as was stated above. Now through the eternal law *all things are most orderly*, as Augustine states.[10] Therefore the natural law suffices for the ordering of all human affairs. Consequently there is not need for a human law.

Obj. 2. Further, law has the character of a measure, as was stated above.[11] But human reason is not a measure of things, but *vice versa*, as is stated in *Metaph.* X.[12] Therefore no law can emanate from the human reason.

Obj. 3. Further, a measure should be most certain, as is stated in *Metaph.* X.[13] But the dictates of the human reason in matters of conduct are uncertain, according to *Wis.* ix. 14: *The thoughts of mortal men are fearful, and our counsels uncertain.* Therefore no law can emanate from the human reason.

Question XCIII

The Eternal Law (In Six Articles)

We must now consider each law by itself: (1) the eternal law; (2) the natural law;[14] (3) the human law;[15] (4) the Old Law;[16] (5) the New Law, which is the law of the Gospel.[17] Of the sixth law, which is the law of the "fomes," what we have said when treating of original sin must suffice.[18]

---

8   Q. 10, a. 1.
9   Q. 90, a. 1.
10   *De Lib. Arb.*, I, 6 (PL 32, 1229).
11   Q. 90, a. 1.
12   Aristotle, *Metaph.*, IX, 1 (1053a 31).
13   *Ibid.*
14   Q. 94.
15   Q. 95.
16   Q. 98.
17   Q. 106.

Concerning the first there are six points of inquiry: (1) What is the eternal law? (2) Whether it is known to all? (3) Whether every law is derived from it? (4) Whether necessary things are still subject to the eternal law? (5) Whether natural contingents are subject to the eternal law? (6) Whether all human things are subject to it?

First Article

Whether the Eternal Law is a Supreme Exemplar Existing in God?

We proceed thus to the First Article:—

Objection 1. It would seem that the eternal law is not a supreme exemplar existing in God. For there is only one eternal law. But there are many exemplars of things in the divine mind, for Augustine says that God *made each thing according to its exemplar.*[19] Therefore the eternal law does not seem to be the same as an exemplar existing in the divine mind.

Obj. 2. Further, it is of the nature of a law that it be promulgated by word, as was stated above.[20] But *Word* is a Personal name in God, as was stated in the First Part,[21] whereas *exemplar* refers to the essence. Therefore the eternal law is not the same as a divine exemplar.

Obj. 3. Further, Augustine says: *We see law above our minds, which is called truth.*[22] But the law which is above our minds is the eternal law. Therefore truth is the eternal law. But the notion of truth is not the same as the notion of an exemplar. Therefore the eternal law is not the same as the supreme exemplar.

On the contrary, Augustine says that *the eternal law is the supreme exemplar to which we must always conform.*[23]

I answer that, just as in every artificer there preexists an exemplar of the things that are made by his art, so too in every governor there must preexist the exemplar of the order of those things that are to be done by those who are subject to his government. And just as the exemplar of the things yet to be made by an art is called the art or model of the products of that art, so, too, the exemplar in him who governs the acts of his subjects bears the character of a law, provided the other conditions be present which we have mentioned above as belonging to the nature of law.[24] Now God, by His wisdom, is the Creator of all things, in relation to which He stands as the artificer to the products of his art, as was stated in the First Part.[25] Moreover, He governs all the acts and movements that are to be found in each single creature, as was also stated in the First Part.[26] Therefore, just as the exemplar of the divine wisdom, inasmuch as all things are created by it, has the character of an art, a model or an idea, so the exemplar of divine wisdom, as moving all things to their due end, bears the character of law. Accordingly, the eternal law is nothing else than the exemplar of divine wisdom, as directing all actions and movements.

Reply Obj. 1. Augustine is speaking in that passage of the ideal exemplars which refer to the proper nature of each single thing; and consequently in them there is a certain distinction and plurality, according to their different relations to things, as was stated in the First

---

18   Q. 81, 82, 83.
19   *Lib. 83 Quaest.*, q. 46 (PL 40, 30).
20   Q. 90, a. 4; q. 91, a. 1, ad 2.
21   *S. T., I*, q. 34, a. 1.
22   *De Vera Relig.*, XXX (PL 34, 147).
23   *De Lib. Arb.*, I, 6 (PL 32, 1229).
24   Q. 90.
25   *S. T.*, I, q. 14 a. 8.
26   *S. T.*, I, q. 103, a. 5.

Part.[27] But law is said to direct human acts by ordaining them to the common good, as was stated above.[28] Now things which are in themselves diverse may be considered as one, according as they are ordained to something common. Therefore the eternal law is one since it is the exemplar of this order.

Reply Obj. 2. With regard to any sort of word, two points may be considered: viz., the word itself, and that which is expressed by the word. For the spoken word is something uttered by the mouth of man, and expresses that which is signified by the human word. The same applies to the human mental word, which is nothing else than something conceived by the mind, by which man expresses mentally the things of which he is thinking. So, too, in God, therefore, the Word conceived by the intellect of the Father is the name of a Person; but all things that are in the Father's knowledge, whether they refer to the essence or to the Persons, or to the works of God, are expressed by this Word, as Augustine declares.[29] But among other things expressed by this Word, the eternal law itself is expressed thereby. Nor does it follow that the eternal law is a Personal name in God. Nevertheless, it is appropriated to the Son, because of the suitability of *exemplar* to *word*.

Reply Obj. 3. The exemplars of the divine intellect do not stand in the same relation to things as do the exemplars of the human intellect. For the human intellect is measured by things, so that a human concept is not true by reason of itself, but by reason of its being consonant with things, since *an opinion is true or false according as things are or are not.* But the divine intellect is the measure of things, since each thing has truth in it in so far as it is like the divine intellect, as was stated in the First Part.[30] Consequently the divine intellect is true in itself, and its exemplar is truth itself.

Second Article

Whether the Eternal Law is Known to All?

We proceed thus to the Second Article:—

Objection 1. It would seem that the eternal law is not known to all. For, as the Apostle says (*I. Cor.* ii. 11), *the things that are of God no man knoweth, but the Spirit of God.* But the eternal law is an exemplar existing in the divine mind. Therefore it is unknown to all save God alone.

Obj. 2. Further, as Augustine says, *the eternal law is that by which it is right that all things should be most orderly.*[31] But all do not know how all things are most orderly. Therefore all do not know the eternal law.

Obj. 3. Further, Augustine says that *the eternal law is not subject to the judgment of man.*[32] But according to *Ethics* i., *any man can judge well of what he knows.*[33] Therefore the eternal law is not known to us.

On the contrary, Augustine says that *knowledge of the eternal law is imprinted on us.*[34]

I answer that, A thing may be known in two ways: first, in itself; secondly, in its effect, in which some likeness of that thing is found: *e.g.,* someone, not seeing the sun in its substance, may know it by its rays. Hence we must say that no one can know the eternal

---

27   *S. T.,* I, q. 15, a. 2.
28   Q. 90, a. 2.
29   *De Trin.,* XV, 14 (PL 42, 1076).
30   *S. T.,* I, q. 16, a. 1.
31   *De Lib. Arb.,* I, 6 (PL 32, 1229).
32   *De Vera Relig.,* XXXI (PL 34, 148).
33   Aristotle, *Eth.,* I, 3 (1094b 27).
34   *De Lib. Arb.,* I, 6 (PL 32, 1229).

law as it is in itself, except God and the blessed who see God in His essence. But every rational creature knows it according to some reflection, greater or less. For every knowledge of truth is a kind of reflection and participation of the eternal law, which is the unchangeable truth, as Augustine says.[35] Now all men know the truth to a certain extent, at least as to the common principles of the natural law. As to the other truths, they partake of the knowledge of truth, some more, some less; and in this respect they know the eternal law in a greater or lesser degree.

Reply Obj. 1. We cannot know the things that are of God as they are in themselves; but they are made known to us in their effects, according to *Rom.* i. 20: *The invisible things of God . . . are clearly seen, being understood by the things that are made.*

Reply Obj. 2. Although each one knows the eternal law according to his own capacity, in the way explained above, yet none can comprehend it, for it cannot be made perfectly known by its effects. Therefore it does not follow that anyone who knows the eternal law, in the aforesaid way, knows also the whole order of things whereby they are most orderly.

Reply Obj. 3. To judge of a thing may be understood in two ways. First, as when a cognitive power judges of its proper object, according to *Job* xii. 11: *Doth not the ear discern words, and the palate of him that eateth, the taste?* It is to this kind of judgment that the Philosopher alludes when he says that *anyone judges well of what he knows,*[36] by judging, namely, whether what is put forward is true. In another way, we speak of a superior judging of a subordinate by a kind of practical judgment, as to whether he should be such and

such or not. And thus none can judge of the eternal law.

Third Article

Whether Every Law is Derived from the Eternal Law?

We proceed thus to the Third Article:—

Objection 1. It would seem that not every law is derived from the eternal law. For there is a law of the "fomes," as was stated above,[37] which is not derived from the divine law which is the eternal law, since to it pertains the *prudence of the flesh,* of which the Apostle says (*Rom.* viii. 7) that *it cannot be subject to the law of God.* Therefore, not every law is derived from the eternal law.

Obj. 2. Further, nothing unjust can be derived from the eternal law, because, as was stated above, *the eternal law is that according to which it is right that all things should be most orderly.* But some laws are unjust, according to *Isa.* X. 1: *Woe to them that make wicked laws.* Therefore, not every law is derived from the eternal law.

Obj. 3. Further, Augustine says that *the law which is framed for ruling the people rightly permits many things which are punished by the divine providence.*[38] But the exemplar of the divine providence is the eternal law, as was stated above. Therefore not even every good law is derived from the eternal law.

On the contrary, Divine Wisdom says (*Prov.* viii. 15): *By Me kings reign, and lawgivers decree just things.* But the exemplar of divine Wisdom is the eternal law, as was stated above. Therefore all laws proceed from the eternal law.

I answer that, As was stated above, law denotes a kind of plan directing acts towards

35   *De Vera Relig.,* XXXI (PL 34, 147).
36   *Eth.,* I, 3 (1094b 27).
37   Q. 91, a. 6.
38   *De Lib. Arb.,* I, 5 (PL 32 1228).

an end.[39] Now wherever there are movers ordained to one another, the power of the second mover must needs be derived from the power of the first mover, since the second mover does not move except in so far as it is moved by the first. Therefore we observe the same in all those who govern, namely, that the plan of government is derived by secondary governors from the governor in chief. Thus the plan of what is to be done in a state flows from the king's command to his inferior administrators; and again in things of art the plan of whatever is to be done by art flows from the chief craftsman to the under-craftsmen who work with their hands. Since, then, the eternal law is the plan of government in the Chief Governor, all the plans of government in the inferior governors must be derived from the eternal law. But these plans of inferior governors are all the other laws which are in addition to the eternal law. Therefore all laws, in so far as they partake of right reason, are derived from the eternal law. Hence Augustine says that *in temporal law there is nothing just and lawful but what man has drawn from the eternal law.*[40]

Reply Obj. 1. The "fomes" has the nature of law in man in so far is it is a punishment resulting from the divine justice; and in this respect it is evident that it is derived from the eternal law. But in so far as it denotes a proneness to sin, it is contrary to the divine law, and has not the nature of law, as was stated above.[41]

Reply Obj. 2. Human law has the nature of law in so far as it partakes of right reason; and it is clear that, in this respect, it is derived from the eternal law. But in so far as it deviates from reason, it is called an unjust law, and has the nature, not of law, but of violence. Nevertheless, even an unjust law, in so far as it retains some appearance of law, through being framed by one who is in power, is derived from the eternal law; for all power is from the Lord God, according to *Rom.* xiii. 1.

Reply Obj. 3. Human law is said to permit certain things, not as approving of them, but as being unable to direct them. And many things are directed by the divine law, which human law is unable to direct, because more things are subject to a higher than to a lower cause. Hence the very fact that human law does not concern itself with matters it cannot direct comes under the ordination of the eternal law. It would be different, were human law to sanction what the eternal law condemns. Consequently, it does not follow that human law is not derived from the eternal law; what follows is rather that it is not on a perfect equality with it.

Question XCIV

The Natural Law
(In Six Articles)

We must now consider the natural law, concerning which there are six points of inquiry: (I) What is the natural law? (2) What are the precepts of the natural law? (3) Whether all the acts of the virtues are prescribed by the natural law? (4) Whether the natural law is the same in all? (5) Whether it is changeable? (6) Whether it can be abolished from the mind of man?

First Article

Whether the Natural Law is a Habit?

We proceed thus to the First Article:—
Objection 1. It would seem that the natural law is a habit. For, as the Philosopher says, *there are three things in the soul, power, habit and passion.*[42] But the natural law is not

---

39   Q. 90, a. 1 and 2.
40   *De Lib. Arb.*, I, 6 (PL 32, 1229).
41   Q. 91, a. 6.

one of the soul's powers, nor is it one of the passions, as we may see by going through them one by one. Therefore the natural law is a habit.

Obj. 2. Further, Basil says that the *conscience or synderesis is the law of our mind;*[43] which can apply only to the natural law. But *synderesis* is a habit, as was shown in the First Part.[44] Therefore the natural law is a habit.

Obj. 3. Further, the natural law abides in man always, as will be shown further on. But man's reason, which the law regards, does not always think about the natural law. Therefore the natural law is not an act, but a habit.

On the contrary, Augustine says that *a habit is that whereby something is done when necessary.*[45] But such is not the natural law, since it is in infants and in the damned who cannot act by it. Therefore the natural law is not a habit.

I answer that, A thing may be called a habit in two ways. First, properly and essentially, and thus the natural law is not a habit. For it has been stated above that the natural law is something appointed by reason, just as a proposition is a work of reason.[46] Now that which a man does is not the same as that whereby he does it, for he makes a becoming speech by the habit of grammar. Since, then, a habit is that by which we act, a law cannot be a habit properly and essentially.

Secondly, the term habit may be applied to that which we hold by a habit. Thus *faith* may mean *that which we hold by faith.* Accordingly, since the precepts of the natural law are sometimes considered by reason actually, while sometimes they are in the reason only habitually, in this way the natural law may be called a habit. So, too, in speculative matters, the indemonstrable principles are not the habit itself whereby we hold these principles; they are rather the principles of which we possess the habit.

Reply Obj. 1. The Philosopher proposes there to discover the genus of virtue;[47] and since it is evident that virtue is a principle of action, he mentions only those things which are principles of human acts, viz., powers, habits and passions. But there are other things in the soul besides these three: *e.g.,* acts, as *to will* is in the one that wills; again, there are things known in the knower; moreover its own natural properties are in the soul, such as immortality and the like.

Reply Obj. 2. Synderesis is said to be the law of our intellect because it is a habit containing the precepts of the natural law, which are the first principles of human actions.

Reply Obj. 3. This argument proves that the natural law is held habitually; and this is granted.

To the argument advanced in the contrary sense we reply that sometimes a man is unable to make use of that which is in him habitually, because of some impediment. Thus, because of sleep, a man is unable to use the habit of science. In like manner, through the deficiency of his age, a child cannot use the habit of the understanding of principles, or the natural law, which is in him habitually.

---

42   *Eth.,* II, 5 (1105b 20).
43   Cf. *In Hexaëm.,* hom. VII (PG 29, 158); St. John Damascene, *De Fide Orth.,* IV, 22 (PG 94, 1200).
44   *S. T.,* I, q. 79, a. 12.
45   *De Bono Coniug.,* XXI (PL 40, 390).
46   Q. 90 , a. 1, ad 2.
47   *Eth.,* II, 5 (1105b 20).

Second Article

Whether the Natural Law Contains Several Precepts, or Only One?

We proceed thus to the Second Article:—
Objection 1. It would seem that the natural law contains not several precepts, but only one. For law is a kind of precept, as was stated above.[48] If therefore there were many precepts of the natural law, it would follow that there are also many natural laws.

Obj. 2. Further, the natural law is consequent upon human nature. But human nature, as a whole, is one, though, as to its parts, it is manifold. Therefore, either there is but one precept of the law of nature because of the unity of nature as a whole, or there are many by reason of the number of parts of human nature. The result would be that even things relating to the inclination of the concupiscible power would belong to the natural law.

Obj. 3. Further, law is something pertaining to reason, as was stated above.[49] Now reason is but one in man. Therefore there is only one precept of the natural law.

On the contrary, The precepts of the natural law in man stand in relation to operable matters as first principles do to matters of demonstration. But there are several first indemonstrable principles. Therefore there are also several precepts of the natural law.

I answer that, As was stated above, the precepts of the natural law are to the practical reason what the first principles of demonstrations are to the speculative reason, because both are self-evident principles.[50] Now a thing is said to be self-evident in two ways: first, in itself; secondly, in relation to us. Any proposition is said to be self-evident in itself, if its predicate is contained in the notion of the subject; even though it may happen that to one who does not know the definition of the subject, such a proposition is not self-evident. For instance, this proposition, *Man is a rational being,* is, in its very nature, self-evident, since he who says *man,* says *a rational being;* and yet to one who does not know what a man is, this proposition is not self-evident. Hence it is that, as Boethius says,[51] certain axioms or propositions are universally self-evident to all; and such are the propositions whose terms are known to all, as, *Every whole is greater than its part,* and, *Things equal to one and the same are equal to one another.* But some propositions are self-evident only to the wise, who understand the meaning of the terms of such propositions. Thus to one who understands that an angel is not a body, it is self-evident that an angel is not circumscriptively in a place. But this is not evident to the unlearned, for they cannot grasp it.

Now a certain order is to be found in those things that are apprehended by men. For that which first falls under apprehension is *being,* the understanding of which is included in all things whatsoever a man apprehends. Therefore the first indemonstrable principle is that *the same thing cannot be affirmed and denied at the same time,* which is based on the notion of *being* and *not-being*: and on this principle all others are based, as is stated in *Metaph.* iv.[52] Now as *being* is the first thing that falls under the apprehension absolutely, so *good* is the first thing that falls under the apprehension of the practical reason, which is directed to action (since every agent acts for an end, which has the nature of good). Consequently, the first principle in the practical reason is one founded on the nature of good, viz., that *good is that*

---

48   Q. 92, a. 2.
49   Q. 90, a. 1.
50   Q. 91, a. 3.
51   *De Hebdom.* (PL 64, 1311).
52   Aristotle, *Metaph.,* III, 3 (1005b 29).

which all things seek after. Hence this is the first precept of law, that *good is to be done and promoted, and evil is to be avoided.* All other precepts of the natural law are based upon this; so that all the things which the practical reason naturally apprehends as man's good belong to the precepts of the natural law under the form of things to be done or avoided.

Since, however, good has the nature of an end, and evil, the nature of the contrary, hence it is that all those things to which man has a natural inclination are naturally apprehended by reason as being good, and consequently as objects of pursuit, and their contraries as evil, and objects of avoidance. Therefore, the order of the precepts of the natural law is according to the order of natural inclinations. For there is in man, first of all, an inclination to good in accordance with the nature which he has in common with all substances, inasmuch, namely, as every substance seeks the preservation of its own being, according to its nature; and by reason of this inclination, whatever is a means of preserving human life and warding off its obstacles, belongs to the natural law. Secondly, there is in man an inclination to things that pertain to him more specially, according to that nature which he has in common with other animals; and in virtue of this inclination, those things are said to belong to the natural law *which nature has taught to all animals,* [53] such as sexual intercourse, the education of offspring and so forth. Thirdly, there is in man an inclination to good according to the nature of his reason, which nature is proper to him. Thus man has a natural inclination to know the truth about God, and to live in society; and in this respect, whatever pertains to this inclination belongs to the natural law: *e.g.,* to shun ignorance, to avoid offending those among whom one has to live, and other such things regarding the above inclination.

Reply Obj. 1. All these precepts of the law of nature have the character of one natural law, inasmuch as they flow from one first precept.

Reply Obj. 2. All the inclinations of any parts whatsoever of human nature, *e.g.,* of the concupiscible and irascible parts, in so far as they are ruled by reason, belong to the natural law, and are reduced to one first precept, as was stated above. And thus the precepts of the natural law are many in themselves, but they are based on one common foundation.

Reply Obj. 3. Although reason is one in itself, yet it directs all things regarding man; so that whatever can be ruled by reason is contained under the law of reason.

---

53   *Dig.,* I, i, 1 (I, 29a).—Cf. O. Lottin, *Le droit naturel,* pp. 34, 78.

Second Treatise on Civil Government

John Locke

Chapter II The State of Nature

4. To understand political power aright, and derive it from its original, we must consider what estate all men are naturally in, and that is, a state of perfect freedom to order their actions, and dispose of their possessions and persons as they think fit, within the bounds of the law of Nature, without asking leave or depending upon the will of any other man.

A state also of equality, wherein all the power and jurisdiction is reciprocal, no one having more than another, there being nothing more evident than that creatures of the same species and rank, promiscuously born to all the same advantages of Nature, and the use of the same faculties, should also be equal one amongst another, without subordination or subjection, unless the lord and master of them all should, by any manifest declaration of his will, set one above another, and confer on him, by an evident and clear appointment, an undoubted right to dominion and sovereignty.

6. But though this be a state of liberty, yet it is not a state of license; though man in that state have an uncontrollable liberty to dispose of his person or possessions, yet he has not liberty to destroy himself, or so much as any creature in his possession, but where some nobler use than its bare preservation calls for it. The state of Nature has a law of Nature to govern it, which obliges everyone, and reason, which is that law, teaches all mankind who will but consult it, that being all equal and independent, no one ought to harm another in his life, health, liberty or possessions; for men being all the workmanship of one omnipotent and infinitely wise Maker; all the servants of one sovereign Master, sent into the world by His order and about His business; they are His property, whose workmanship they are made to last during His, not one another's pleasure. And, being furnished with like faculties, sharing all in one community of Nature, there cannot be supposed any such subordination among us that may authorize us to destroy one another, as if we were made for one another's uses, as the inferior ranks of creatures are for ours. Everyone as he is bound to preserve himself, and not to quit his station willfully, so by the like reason, when his own preservation comes not in competition, ought he as much as he can to preserve the rest of mankind, and not unless it be to do justice on an offender, take away or impair the life, or what tends to the preservation of the life, the liberty, health, limb, or goods of another.

7. And that all men may be restrained from invading others' rights, and from doing hurt to one another, and the law of Nature be observed, which willeth the peace and preservation of all mankind, the execution of the law of Nature is in that state put into every man's hands, whereby everyone has a right to punish the transgressors of that law to such a degree as may hinder its violation. For the law of Nature would, as all other laws that concern men in this world, be in

vain if there were nobody that in the state of Nature had a power to execute that law, and thereby preserve the innocent and restrain offenders; and if anyone in the state of Nature may punish another for any evil he has done, everyone may do so. For in that state of perfect equality, where naturally there is no superiority or jurisdiction of one over another, what any may do in prosecution of that law, everyone must needs have a right to do.

8. And thus, in the state of Nature, one man comes by a power over another, but yet no absolute or arbitrary power to use a criminal, when he has got him in his hands, according to the passionate heats or boundless extravagancy of his own will, but only to retribute to him so far as calm reason and conscience dictate, what is proportionate to his transgression, which is so much as may serve for reparation and restraint. For these two are the only reasons why one man may lawfully do harm to another, which is that we call punishment. In transgressing the law of Nature, the offender declares himself to live by another rule than that of reason and common equity, which is that measure God has set to the actions of men for their mutual security, and so he becomes dangerous to mankind; the tie which is to secure them from injury and violence being slighted and broken by him, which being a trespass against the whole species, and the peace and safety of it, provided for by the law of Nature, every man upon this score, by the right he hath to preserve mankind in general, may restrain, or where it is necessary, destroy things noxious to them, and so may bring such evil on anyone who hath transgressed that law, as may make him repent the doing of it, and thereby deter him, and, by his example, others from doing the like mischief. And in this case, and upon this ground, every man hath a right to punish the offender, and be executioner of the law of Nature.

13. To this strange doctrine—viz., That in the state of Nature everyone has the executive power of the law of Nature—I doubt not but it will be objected that it is unreasonable for men to be judges in their own cases, that self-love will make men partial to themselves and their friends; and, on the other side, ill-nature, passion, and revenge will carry them too far in punishing others, and hence nothing but confusion and disorder will follow, and that therefore God hath certainly appointed government to restrain the partiality and violence of men. I easily grant that civil government is the proper remedy for the inconveniences of the state of Nature, which must certainly be great where men may be judges in their own case, since it is easy to be imagined that he who was so unjust as to do his brother an injury will scarce be so just as to condemn himself for it. But I shall desire those who make this objection to remember that absolute monarchs are but men; and if government is to be the remedy of those evils which necessarily follow from men being judges in their own cases, and the state of Nature is therefore not to be endured, I desire to know what kind of government that is, and how much better it is than the state of Nature, where one man commanding a multitude has the liberty to be judge in his own case, and may do to all his subjects whatever he pleases without the least question or control of those who execute his pleasure? and in whatsoever he doth, whether led by reason, mistake, or passion, must be submitted to? which men in the state of Nature are not bound to do one to another. And if he that judges, judges amiss in his own or any other case, he is answerable for it to the rest of mankind.

14. It is often asked as a mighty objection, where are, or ever were, there any men in

such a state of Nature? To which it may suffice as an answer at present, that since all princes and rulers of "independent" governments all through the world are in a state of Nature, it is plain the world never was, nor never will be, without numbers of men in that state. I have named all governors of "independent" communities, whether they are, or are not, in league with others; for it is not every, compact that puts an end to the state of Nature between men, but only this one of agreeing together mutually to enter into one community, and make one body politic; other promises and compacts men may make one with another, and yet still be in the state of Nature. The promises and bargains for truck, etc., between the two men in Soldania, in or between a Swiss and an Indian, in the woods of America, are binding to them, though they are perfectly in a state of Nature in reference to one another for truth, and keeping of faith belongs to men as men, and not as members of society.

15. To those that say there were never any men in the state of Nature, I will not only oppose the authority of the judicious Hooker (*Eccl. Pol.* i. 10), where he says, "the laws which have been hitherto mentioned"—i.e., the laws of Nature—"do bind men absolutely, even as they are men, although they have never any settled fellowship, never any solemn agreement amongst themselves what to do or not to do; but for as much as we are not by ourselves sufficient to furnish ourselves with competent store of things needful for such a life as our Nature doth desire, a life fit for the dignity of man, therefore to supply those defects and imperfections which are in us, as living single and solely by ourselves, we are naturally induced to seek communion and fellowship with others; this was the cause of men uniting themselves at first in politic societies." But I, moreover, affirm that all men are naturally in that state, and remain so till, by their own consents, they make themselves members of some politic society, and I doubt not, in the sequel of this discourse, to make it very clear.

16. The state of war is a state of enmity and destruction; and therefore declaring by word or action, not a passionate and hasty, but sedate, settled design upon another man's life puts him in a state of war with him against whom he has declared such an intention, and so has exposed his life to the other's power to be taken away by him, or anyone that joins with him in his defense, and espouses his quarrel; it being reasonable and just I should have a right to destroy that which threatens me with destruction; for by the fundamental law of Nature, man being to be preserved as much as possible, when all cannot be preserved, the safety of the innocent is to be preferred, and one may destroy a man who makes war upon him, or has discovered an enmity to his being, for the same reason that he may kill a wolf or a lion, because they are not under the ties of the common law of reason, have no other rule but that of force and violence, and so may be treated as a beast of prey, those dangerous and noxious creatures that will be sure to destroy him whenever he falls into their power.

17. And hence it is that he who attempts to get another man into his absolute power does thereby put himself into a state of war with him; it being to be understood as a declaration of a design upon his life. For I have reason to conclude that he who would get me into his power without my consent would use me as he pleased when he had got me there, and destroy me too when he had a fancy to it; for nobody can desire to have me in his absolute power unless it be to compel me by force to that which is against the right of my freedom—i.e., make me a slave. To be free from such force is the only security of my preservation, and reason bids me look on

him as an enemy to my preservation who would take away that freedom which is the fence to it; so that he who makes an attempt to enslave me thereby puts himself into a state of war with me. He that in the state of Nature would take away the freedom that belongs to anyone in that state must necessarily be supposed to have a design to take away everything else, that freedom being the foundation of all the rest; as he that in the state of society would take away the freedom belonging to those of that society or commonwealth must be supposed to design to take away from them everything else, and so be looked on as in a state of war.

18. This makes it lawful for a man to kill a thief who has not in the least hurt him, or declared any design upon his life, any farther than by the use of force, so to get him in his power as to take away his money, or what he pleases, from him; because using force, where he has no right to get me into his power, let his pretense be what it will, I have no reason to suppose that he who would take away my liberty would not, when he had me in his power, take away everything else. And, therefore, it is lawful for me to treat him as one who has put himself into a state of war with me—i.e., kill him if I can; for to that hazard does he justly expose himself whoever introduces a state of war, and is aggressor in it.

19. And here we have the plain difference between the state of Nature and the state of war, which however some men have confounded, are as far distant as a state of peace, goodwill, mutual assistance, and preservation; and a state of enmity, malice, violence and mutual destruction are one from another. Men living together according to reason with a common superior on earth, with authority to judge between them, is properly the state of Nature. But force, or a declared design of force upon the person of another, where there is no common superior

on earth to appeal to for relief, is the state of war; and it is the want of such an appeal gives a man the right of war even against an aggressor, though he be in society and a fellow-subject. Thus, a thief whom I cannot harm, but by appeal to the law, for having stolen all that I am worth, I may kill when he sets on me to rob me but of my horse or coat, because the law, which was made for my preservation, where it cannot interpose to secure my life from present force, which if lost is capable of no reparation, permits me my own defense and the right of war, a liberty to kill the aggressor, because the aggressor allows not time to appeal to our common judge, nor the decision of the law, for remedy in a case where the mischief may be irreparable. Want of a common judge with authority puts all men in a state of Nature; force without right upon a man's person makes a state of war both where there is, and is not, a common judge.

20. But when the actual force is over, the state of war ceases between those that are in society and are equally on both sides subject to the judge; and, therefore, in such controversies, where the question is put, "Who shall be judge?" it cannot be meant who shall decide the controversy; everyone knows what Jephtha here tells us, that "the Lord the Judge" shall judge. Where there is no judge on earth the appeal lies to God in Heaven. That question then cannot mean who shall judge, whether another hath put himself in a state of war with me, and whether I may, as Jephtha did, appeal to Heaven in it? Of that I myself can only judge in my own conscience, as I will answer it at the great day to the Supreme Judge of all men.

Chapter IV Of Slavery

21. The natural liberty of man is to be free from any superior power on earth, and not to be under the will or legislative authority

of man, but to have only the law of Nature for his rule. The liberty of man in society is to be under no other legislative power but that established by consent in the commonwealth, nor under the dominion of any will, or restraint of any law, but what the legislative shall enact according to the trust put in it. Freedom, then, is not what Sir Robert Filmer tells us: "A liberty for everyone to do what he lists, to live as he pleases, and not to be tied by any laws"; but freedom of men under government is to have a standing rule to live by, common to everyone of that society, and made by the legislative power erected in it. A liberty to follow my own will in all things where that rule prescribes not, not to be subject to the inconstant, uncertain, unknown, arbitrary will of another man, as freedom of nature is to be under no other restraint but the law of Nature.

22. This freedom from absolute, arbitrary power is so necessary to, and closely joined with, a man's preservation, that he cannot part with it but by what forfeits his preservation and life together. For a man, not having the power of his own life, cannot by compact or his own consent enslave himself to anyone, nor put himself under the absolute, arbitrary power of another to take away his life when he pleases. Nobody can give more power than he has himself, and he that cannot take away his own life cannot give another power over it. Indeed, having by his fault forfeited his own life by some act that deserves death, he to whom he has forfeited it may, when he has him in his power, delay to take it, and make use of him to his own service; and he does him no injury by it. For, whenever he finds the hardship of his slavery outweigh the value of his life, it is in his power, by resisting the will of his master, to draw on himself the death he desires.

23. This is the perfect condition of slavery, which is nothing else but the state of war continued between a lawful conqueror and a captive, for if once compact enter between them, and make an agreement for a limited power on the one side, and obedience on the other, the state of war and slavery ceases as long as the compact endures; for, as has been said, no man can by agreement pass over to another that which he hath not in himself—a power over his own life. . . .

Chapter V Of Property

25. God, who hath given the world to men in common, hath also given them reason to make use of it to the best advantage of life and convenience. The earth and all that is therein is given to men for the support and comfort of their being. And though all the fruits it naturally produces, and beasts it feeds, belong to mankind in common, as they are produced by the spontaneous hand of Nature, and nobody has originally a private dominion exclusive of the rest of mankind in any of them, as they are thus in their natural state, yet being given for the use of men, there must of necessity be a means to appropriate them some way or other before they can be of any use, or at all beneficial, to any particular men. The fruit or venison which nourishes the wild Indian, who knows no enclosure, and is still a tenant in common, must be his, and so his—i.e., a part of him, that another can no longer have any right to it before it can do him any good for the support of his life.

26. Though the earth and all inferior creatures be common to all men, yet every man has a "property" in his own "person." This nobody has any right to but himself. The "labor" of his body and the "work" of his hands, we may say, are properly his. Whatsoever, then, he removes out of the state that Nature hath provided and left it in, he hath mixed his labor with it, and joined to it something that is his own, and thereby makes it his property. It being by him re-

moved from the common state Nature placed it in, it hath by this labor something annexed to it that excludes the common right of other men. For this "labor" being the unquestionable property of the laborer, no man but he can have a right to what that is once joined to, at least where there is enough, and as good left in common for others.

27. He that is nourished by the acorns he picked up under an oak, or the apples he gathered from the trees in the wood, has certainly appropriated them to himself. Nobody can deny but the nourishment is his. I ask, then, when did they begin to be his? when he digested? or when he ate? or when he boiled? or when he brought them home? or when he picked them up? And it is plain, if the first gathering made them not his, nothing else could. That labor put a distinction between them and common. That added something to them more than Nature, the common mother of all, had done, and so they became his private right. And will anyone say he had no right to those acorns or apples he thus appropriated because he had not the consent of all mankind to make them his? Was it a robbery thus to assume to himself what belonged to all in common? If such a consent as that was necessary, man had starved, notwithstanding the plenty God had given him. We see in commons, which remain so by compact, that it is the taking any part of what is common, and removing it out of the state Nature leaves it in, which begins the property, without which the common is of no use. And the taking of this or that part does not depend on the express consent of all the commoners. Thus, the grass my horse has bit, the turfs my servant has cut, and the ore I have digged in any place, where I have a right to them in common with others, become my property without the assignation or consent of anybody. The labor that was mine, removing them out

of that common state they were in, hath fixed my property in them.

28. By making an explicit consent of every commoner necessary to anyone's appropriating to himself any part of what is given in common, children or servants could not cut the meat which their father or master had provided for them in common without assigning to everyone his peculiar part. Though the water running in the fountain be everyone's, yet who can doubt but that in the pitcher is his only who drew it out? His labor hath taken it out of the hands of Nature where it was common, and belonged equally to all her children, and hath thereby appropriated it to himself.

30. It will, perhaps, be objected to this, that if gathering the acorns or other fruits of the earth, etc., makes a right to them, then anyone may engross as much as he will. To which I answer, Not so. The same law of Nature that does by this means give us property, does also bound that property too. "God has given us all things richly." Is the voice of reason confirmed by inspiration? But how far has He given it us "to enjoy"? As much as anyone can make use of to any advantage of life before it spoils, so much he may by his labor fix a property in. Whatever is beyond this is more than his share, and belongs to others. Nothing was made by God for man to spoil or destroy. And thus considering the plenty of natural provisions there was a long time in the world, and the few spenders, and to how small a part of that provision the industry of one man could extend itself and engross it to the prejudice of others, especially keeping within the bounds set by reason of what might serve for his use, there could be then little room for quarrels or contentions about property so established.

31. But the chief matter of property being now not the fruits of the earth and the beasts that subsist on it, but the earth itself, as that

which takes in and carries with it all the rest, I think it is plain that property in that too is acquired as the former. As much land as a man tills, plants, improves, cultivates, and can use the product of, so much is his property. He by his labor does, as it were, enclose it from the common. Nor will it invalidate his right to say everybody else has an equal title to it, and therefore he cannot appropriate, he cannot enclose, without the consent of all his fellow-commoners, all mankind. God, when He gave the world in common to all mankind, commanded man also to labor, and the penury of his condition required it of him. God and his reason commanded him to subdue the earth—i.e., improve it for the benefit of life and therein lay out something upon it that was his own, his labor. He that, in obedience to this command of God, subdued, tilled, and sowed any part of it, thereby annexed to it something that was his property, which another had no title to, nor could without injury take from him.

32. Nor was this appropriation of any parcel of land, by improving it, any prejudice to any other man, since there was still enough and as good left, and more than the yet unprovided could use. So that, in effect, there was never the less left for others because of his enclosure for himself. For he that leaves as much as another can make use of does as good as take nothing at all. Nobody could think himself injured by the drinking of another man, though he took a good draught, who had a whole river of the same water left him to quench his thirst. And the case of land and water, where there is enough of both, is perfectly the same.

33. God gave the world to men in common, but since He gave it them for their benefit and the greatest conveniences of life they were capable to draw from it, it cannot be supposed He meant it should always remain common and uncultivated. He gave it to the use of the industrious and rational (and labor was to be his title to it); not to the fancy or covetousness of the quarrelsome and contentious. He that had as good left for his improvement as was already taken up needed not complain, ought not to meddle with what was already improved by another's labor; if he did it is plain he desired the benefit of another's pains, which he had no right to, and not the ground which God had given him, in common with others, to labor on, and whereof there was as good left as that already possessed, and more than he knew what to do with, or his industry could reach to.

35. The measure of property Nature well set, by the extent of men's labor and the conveniency of life. No man's labor could subdue or appropriate all, nor could his enjoyment consume more than a small part; so that it was impossible for any man, this way, to entrench upon the right of another or acquire to himself a property to the prejudice of his neighbor, who would still have room for as good and as large a possession (after the other had taken out his) as before it was appropriated. Which measure did confine every man's possession to a very moderate proportion, and such as he might appropriate to himself without injury to anybody in the first ages of the world, when men were more in danger to be lost, by wandering from their company, in the then vast wilderness of the earth than to be straitened for want of room to plant in.

36. The same measure may be allowed still, without prejudice to anybody, full as the world seems. . . . Nay, the extent of ground is of so little value without labor that I have heard it affirmed that in Spain itself a man may be permitted to plow, sow, and reap, without being disturbed, upon land he has no other title to, but only his making use of it. But, on the contrary, the inhabitants think themselves beholden to him who, by his industry on neglected, and consequently

waste land, has increased the stock of corn, which they wanted. But be this as it will, which I lay no stress on, this I dare boldly affirm, that the same rule of propriety—viz., that every man should have as much as he could make use of, would hold still in the world, without straitening anybody, since there is land enough in the world to suffice double the inhabitants, had not the invention of money, and the tacit agreement of men to put a value on it, introduced (by consent) larger possessions and a right to them. . . .

37. This is certain, that in the beginning, before the desire of having more than men needed had altered the intrinsic value of things, which depends only on their usefulness to the life of man, or had agreed that a little piece of yellow metal, which would keep without wasting or decay, should be worth a great piece of flesh or a whole heap of corn, though men had a right to appropriate by their labor, each one to himself, as much of the things of Nature as he could use, yet this could not be much, nor to the prejudice of others, where the same plenty was still left, to those who would use the same industry.

Before the appropriation of land, he who gathered as much of the wild fruit, killed, caught, or tamed as many of the beasts as he could—he that so employed his pains about any of the spontaneous products of Nature as any way to alter them from the state Nature put them in, by placing any of his labor on them, did thereby acquire a propriety in them; but if they perished in his possession without their due use—if the fruits rotted or the venison putrefied before he could spend it, he offended against the common law of Nature, and was liable to be punished: he invaded his neighbor's share, for he had no right farther than his use called for any of them, and they might serve to afford him conveniences of life.

38. The same measures governed the possession of land, too. Whatsoever he tilled and reaped, laid up and made use of before it spoiled, that was his peculiar right; whatsoever he enclosed, and could feed and make use of, the cattle and product was also his. But if either the grass of his enclosure rotted on the ground, or the fruit of his planting perished without gathering and laying up, this part of the earth, notwithstanding his enclosure, was still to be looked on as waste, and might be the possession of any other. Thus, at the beginning, Cain might take as much ground as he could till and make it his own land, and yet leave enough to Abel's sheep to feed on: a few acres would serve for both their possessions. But as families increased and industry enlarged their stocks, their possessions enlarged with the need of them; but yet it was commonly without any fixed property in the ground they made use of till they incorporated, settled themselves together, and built cities, and then, by consent, they came in time to set out the bounds of their distinct territories and agree on limits between them and their neighbors, and by laws within themselves settled the properties of those of the same society. For we see that in that part of the world which was first inhabited, and therefore like to be best peopled, even as low down as Abraham's time, they wandered with their flocks and their herds, which was their substance, freely up and down—and this Abraham did in a country where he was a stranger; whence it is plain that, at least, a great part of the land lay in common, that the inhabitants valued it not, nor claimed property in any more than they made use of; but when there was not room enough in the same place for their herds to feed together, they, by consent, as Abraham and Lot did (Gen. xiii. 5), separated and enlarged their pasture where it best liked them. And for the same reason,

Esau went from his father and his brother, and planted in Mount Seir (Gen. xxxvi. 6).

39. And thus, without supposing any private dominion and property in Adam over all the world, exclusive of all other men, which can no way be proved, nor anyone's property be made out from it, but supposing the world, given as it was to the children of men in common, we see how labor could make men distinct titles to several parcels of it for their private uses, wherein there could be no doubt of right, no room for quarrel.

40. Nor is it so strange as, perhaps, before consideration, it may appear, that the property of labor should be able to overbalance the community of land, for it is labor indeed that puts the difference of value on everything; and let anyone consider what the difference is between an acre of land planted with tobacco or sugar, sown with wheat or barley, and an acre of the same land lying in common without any husbandry upon it, and he will find that the improvement of labor makes the far greater part of the value. I think it will be but a very modest computation to say, that of the products of the earth useful to the life of man, nine-tenths are the effects of labor. Nay, if we will rightly estimate things as they come to our use, and cast up the several expenses about them—what in them is purely owing to Nature and what to labor—we shall find that in most of them ninety-nine hundredths are wholly to be put on the account of labor.

44. From all which it is evident, that though the things of Nature are given in common, man (by being master of himself, and proprietor of his own person, and the actions or labor of it) had still in himself the great foundation of property; and that which made up the great part of what he applied to the support or comfort of his being, when invention and arts had improved the con-

veniences of life, was perfectly his own, and did not belong in common to others.

46. The greatest part of things really useful to the life of man, and such as the necessity of subsisting made the first commoners of the world look after—as it doth the Americans now—are generally things of short duration, such as—if they are not consumed by use—will decay and perish of themselves. Gold, silver, and diamonds are things that fancy or agreement hath put the value on, more than real use and the necessary support of life. Now of those good things which Nature hath provided in common, everyone has a right (as has been said) to as much as he could use, and had a property in all he could effect with his labor; all that his industry could extend to, to alter from the state Nature had put it in, was his. He that gathered a hundred bushels of acorns or apples had thereby a property in them; they were his goods as soon as gathered. He was only to look that he used them before they spoiled, else he took more than his share, and robbed others. And, indeed, it was a foolish thing, as well as dishonest, to hoard up more than he could make use of. If he gave away a part to anybody else, so that it perished not uselessly in his possession, these he also made use of. And if he also bartered away plums that would have rotten in a week, for nuts that would last good for his eating a whole year, he did no injury; he wasted not the common stock; destroyed no part of the portion of goods that belonged to others, so long as nothing perished uselessly in his hands. Again, if he would give his nuts for a piece of metal, pleased with its color, or exchange his sheep for shells, or wool for a sparkling pebble or a diamond, and keep those by him all his life, he invaded not the right of others; he might heap up as much of these durable things as he pleased; the exceeding of the bounds of his just property not

lying in the largeness of his possession, but the perishing of anything uselessly in it.

47. And thus came in the use of money; some lasting thing, that men might keep without spoiling, and that, by mutual consent, men would take in exchange for the truly useful but perishable supports of life.

48. And as different degrees of industry were apt to give men possessions in different proportions, so this invention of money gave them the opportunity to continue and enlarge them. For supposing an island, separate from all possible commerce with the rest of the world, wherein there were but a hundred families, but there were sheep, horses, and cows, with other useful animals, wholesome fruits, and land enough for corn for a hundred thousand times as many, but nothing in the island, either because of its commonness or perishableness, fit to supply the place of money. What reason could anyone have there to enlarge his possessions beyond the use of his family, and a plentiful supply to its consumption, either in what their own industry produced, or they could barter for like perishable, useful commodities with others? Where there is not something both lasting and scarce, and so valuable to be hoarded up, there men will not be apt to enlarge their possessions of land, were it never so rich, never so free for them to take. For I ask, what would a man value ten thousand or a hundred thousand acres of excellent land, ready cultivated and well stocked, too, with cattle, in the middle of the inland parts of America, where he had no hopes of commerce with other parts of the world, to draw money to him by the sale of the product? It would not be worth the enclosing, and we should see him give up again to the wild common of Nature whatever was more than would supply the conveniences of life, to be had there for him and his family.

50. But since gold and silver, being little useful to the life of man, in proportion to food, raiment, and carriage, has its value only from the consent of men—whereof labor yet makes in great part the measure—it is plain that the consent of men have agreed to a disproportionate and unequal possession of the earth—I mean out of the bounds of society and compact; for in governments the laws regulate it; they having, by consent, found out and agreed in a way how a man may, rightfully and without injury, possess more than he himself can make use of by receiving gold and silver, which may continue long in a man's possession without decaying for the overplus, and agreeing those metals should have a value.

51. And thus, I think, it is very easy to conceive without any difficulty, how labor could at first begin a title of property in the common things of Nature, and how the spending it upon our uses bounded it; so that there could then be no reason of quarreling about title, nor any doubt about the largeness of possession it gave. Right and conveniency went together. For as a man had a right to all he could employ his labor upon, so he had no temptation to labor for more than he could make use of. This left no room for controversy about the title, nor for encroachment on the right of others. What portion a man carved to himself was easily seen; and it was useless, as well as dishonest, to carve himself too much, or take more than he needed.

Chapter VI Law and Authority

57. The law that was to govern Adam was the same that was to govern all his posterity, the law of reason. But his offspring having another way of entrance into the world, different from him, by a natural birth, that produced them ignorant, and without the use of reason, they were not presently

under that law. For nobody can be under a law that is not promulgated to him; and this law being promulgated or made known by reason only, he that is not come to the use of his reason cannot be said to be under this law; and Adam's children being not presently as soon as born under this law of reason, were not presently free. For law, in its true notion, is not so much the limitation as the direction of a free and intelligent agent to his proper interest, and prescribes no farther than is for the general good of those under that law. Could they be happier without it, the law, as a useless thing would of itself vanish; and that ill deserves the name of confinement which hedges us in only from bogs and precipices. So that however it may be mistaken, the end of law is not to abolish or restrain. but to preserve and enlarge freedom. For in all the states of created beings, capable of laws, where there is no law there is no freedom. For liberty is to be free from restraint and violence from others, which cannot be where there is no law; and is not, as we are told, "a liberty for every man to do what he lists." For who could be free, when every other man's humor might domineer over him? But a liberty to dispose and order freely as he lists his person, actions, possessions, and his whole property within the allowance of those laws under which he is, and therein not to be subject to the arbitrary will of another, but freely follow his own.

58. The power, then, that parents have over their children arises from that duty which is incumbent on them, to take care of their offspring during the imperfect state of childhood. To inform the mind, and govern the actions of their yet ignorant nonage, till reason shall take its place and ease them of that trouble, is what the children want, and the parents are bound to. For God having given man an understanding to direct his actions, has allowed him a freedom of will and liberty of acting, as properly belonging thereunto within the bounds of that law he is under. But whilst he is in an estate wherein he has no understanding of his own to direct his will, he is not to have any will of his own to follow. He that understands for him must will for him too; he must prescribe to his will, and regulate his actions, but when he comes to the estate that made his father a free man, the son is a free man too.

59. This holds in all the laws a man is under, whether natural or civil. Is a man under the law of Nature? What made him free of that law? What gave him a free disposing of his property, according to his own will, within the compass of that law? I answer, an estate wherein he might be supposed capable to know that law, that so he might keep his actions within the bounds of it. When he has acquired that state, he is presumed to know how far that law is to be his guide, and how far he may make use of his freedom, and so comes to have it; till then, somebody else must guide him, who is presumed to know how far the law allows a liberty. If such a state of reason, such an age of discretion made him free, the same shall make his son free too. Is a man under the law of England? What made him free of that law—that is, to have the liberty to dispose of his actions and possessions, according to his own will, within the permission of that law? A capacity of knowing that law. Which is supposed, by that law, at the age of twenty-one, and in some cases sooner. If this made the father free, it shall make the son free too. Till then, we see the law allows the son to have no will, but he is to be guided by the will of his father or guardian, who is to understand for him. And if the father die and fail to substitute a deputy in this trust, if he hath not provided a tutor to govern his son during his minority, during his want of understanding, the law takes care to do it: some other must govern him and be a will to him

till he has attained to a state of freedom, and his understanding be fit to take the government of his will. But after that the father and son are equally free, as much as tutor and pupil, after nonage, equally subjects of the same law together, without any dominion left in the father over the life, liberty, or estate of his son, whether they be only in the state and under the law of Nature, or under the positive laws of an established government.

60. But if through defects that may happen out of the ordinary course of Nature, anyone comes not to such a degree of reason wherein he might be supposed capable of knowing the law, and so living within the rules of it, he is never capable of being a free man, he is never let loose to the disposure of his own will; because he knows no bounds to it, has not understanding, its proper guide, but is continued under the tuition and government of others all the time his own understanding is incapable of that charge. And so lunatics and idiots are never set free from the government of their parents. . . .

61. Thus we are born free as we are born rational; not that we have actually the exercise of either: age that brings one, brings with it the other too. And thus we see how natural freedom and subjection to parents may consist together, and are both founded on the same principle. A child is free by his father's title, by his father's understanding, which is to govern him till he hath it of his own. . . .

63. The freedom then of man, and liberty of acting according to his own will, is grounded on his having reason, which is able to instruct him in that law he is to govern himself by, and make him know how far he is left to the freedom of his own will. To turn him loose to an unrestrained liberty, before he has reason to guide him, is not the allowing him the privilege of his nature to be free, but to thrust him out amongst brutes, and abandon him to a state as wretched and as

much beneath that of a man as theirs. This is that which puts the authority into the parents' hands to govern the minority of their children. God has made it their business to employ this care on their offspring, and has placed in them suitable inclinations of tenderness and concern to temper this power, to apply it as His wisdom designed it, to the children's good as long as they should need to be under it.

Chapter VII Of Political or Civil Society

77. God, having made man such a creature that, in His own judgment, it was not good for him to be alone, put him under strong obligations of necessity, convenience, and inclination, to drive him into society, as well as fitted him with understanding and language to continue and enjoy it. The first society was between man and wife, which gave beginning to that between parents and children, to which, in time, that between master and servant came to be added. . . .

85. Master and servant are names as old as history, but given to those of far different condition; for a free man makes himself a servant to another by selling him for a certain time the service he undertakes to do in exchange for wages he is to receive; and though this commonly puts him into the family of his master, and under the ordinary discipline thereof, yet it gives the master but a temporary power over him, and no greater than what is contained in the contract between them. But there is another sort of servant which by a peculiar name we call slaves, who being captives taken in a just war are, by the right of Nature, subjected to the absolute dominion and arbitrary power of their masters. These men having, as I say, forfeited their lives and, with it, their liberties, and lost their estates, and being in the state of slavery, not capable of any property, can-

not in that state be considered as any part of civil society, the chief end hereof is the preservation of property.

87. Man being born, as has been proved, with a title to perfect freedom and an uncontrolled enjoyment of all the rights and privileges of the law of Nature, equally with any other man, or number of men in the world, has by nature a power not only to preserve his property—that is, his life, liberty, and estate, against the injuries and attempts of other men, but to judge of and punish the breaches of that law in others, as he is persuaded the offense deserves, even with death itself, in crimes where the heinousness of the fact, in his opinion, requires it. But because no political society can be, nor subsist, without having in itself the power to preserve the property, and in order thereunto punish the offenses of all those of that society, there, and there only, is political society where every one of the members has quitted this natural power, resigned it up into the hands of the community in all cases that exclude him not from appealing for protection to the law established by it. And thus all private judgment of every particular member being excluded, the community comes to be umpire, and by understanding indifferent rules and men authorized by the community for execution, decides all the differences that may happen between any members of that society concerning any matter of right, and punishes those offenses which any member hath committed against the society with such penalties as the law has established; whereby it is easy to discern who are, and are not, in political society together. Those who are united into one body, and have a common established law and judicature to appeal to, with authority to decide controversies between them and punish offenders, are in civil society one with another; but those who have no such common appeal, I mean on earth, are still in the state of Nature, each being where there is no other, judge for himself and executioner; which is, as I have before showed it, the perfect state of Nature.

88. And thus the commonwealth comes by a power to set down what punishment shall belong to the several transgressions they think worthy of it, committed amongst the members of that society (which is the power of making laws), as well as it has the power to punish any injury done unto any of its members by anyone that is not of it (which is the power of war and peace); and all this for the preservation of the property of all the members of that society, as far as is possible. But though every man entered into society has quitted his power to punish offenses against the law of Nature in prosecution of his own private judgment, yet with the judgment of offenses which he has given up to the legislative, in all cases where he can appeal to the magistrate, he has given up a right to the commonwealth to employ his force for the execution of the judgments of the commonwealth whenever he shall be called to it, which, indeed, are his own judgments, they being made by himself or his representative. And herein we have the original of the legislative and executive power of civil society, which is to judge by standing laws how far offenses are to be punished when committed within the commonwealth; and also by occasional judgments founded on the present circumstances of the fact, how far injuries from without are to be vindicated, and in both these be employ all the force of all the members when there shall be need.

89. Wherever, therefore, any number of men so unite into one society as to quit every one his executive power of the law of Nature, and to resign it to the public, there and there only is a political or civil society. And this is done wherever any number of men, in the state of Nature, enter into society to make

one people one body politic under one supreme government: or else when anyone joins himself to, and incorporates with any government already made. For hereby he authorizes the society, or which is all one, the legislative thereof, to make laws for him as the public good of the society shall require, to the execution whereof his own assistance (as to his own decrees) is due. And this puts men out of a state of Nature into that of a commonwealth, by setting up a judge on earth with authority to determine all the controversies and redress the injuries that may happen to any member of the commonwealth, which judge is the legislative or magistrates appointed by it. And wherever there are any number of men, however associated, that have no such decisive power to appeal to, there they are still in the state of Nature go.

90. And hence it is evident that absolute monarchy, which by some men is counted for the only government in the world, is indeed inconsistent with civil society, and so can be no form of civil government at all. For the end of civil society being to avoid and remedy those inconveniences of the state of Nature necessarily follow from every man's being judge in his own case, by setting up a known authority to which every one of that society may appeal upon any injury received, or controversy that may arise, and which every one of the society ought to obey. Wherever any persons are who have not such an authority to appeal to, and decide any difference between them there, those persons are still in the state of Nature. And so is every absolute prince in respect of those who are under his dominion.

91. For he being supposed to have all, both legislative and executive, power in himself alone, there is no judge to be found, no appeal lies open to anyone, who may fairly and indifferently, and with authority decide, and from whence relief and redress may be expected of any injury or inconveniency that may be suffered from him, or by his order. ... For wherever any two men are, who have no standing rule and common judge to appeal to on earth, for the determination of controversies of right betwixt them, there they are still in the state of Nature, and under all the inconveniencies of it, with only this woeful difference to the subject, or rather slave of an absolute prince.

Chapter VIII Of the Beginning of Political Societies

96. When any number of men have, by the consent of every individual, made a community, they have thereby made that community one body, with a power to act as one body, which is only by the will and determination of the majority. For that which acts any community, being only the consent of the individuals of it, and it being one body, must move one way, it is necessary the body should move that way whither the greater force carries it, which is the consent of the majority, or else it is impossible it should act or continue one body, one community, which the consent of every individual that united into it agreed that it should; and so everyone is bound by that consent to be concluded by the majority. And therefore we see that in assemblies empowered to act by positive laws where no number is set by that positive law which empowers them, the act of the majority passes for the act of the whole, and of course determines as having, by the law of Nature and reason, the power of the whole.

97. And thus every man, by consenting with others to make one body politic under one government, puts himself under an obligation to everyone of that society to submit to the determination of the majority, and to be concluded by it; or else this original compact, whereby he with others incorporates

into one society, would signify nothing, and be no compact if he be left free and under no other ties than he was in before in the state of Nature. For what appearance would there be of any compact? What new engagement if he were no farther tied by any decrees of the society than he himself thought fit and did actual consent to? This would be still as great a liberty as he himself had before compact, or anyone else in the state of Nature, who may submit himself and consent to any acts of it if he thinks fit.[1]

119. Every man being, as has been showed, naturally free, and nothing being able to put him into subjection to any earthly power, but only his own consent, it is to be considered what shall be understood to be a sufficient declaration of a man's consent to make him subject to the laws of any government. There is a common distinction of an express and a tacit consent, which will concern our present case. Nobody doubts but an express consent of any man, entering into any society, makes him a perfect member of that society, a subject of that government. The difficulty is, what ought to be looked upon as a tacit consent, and how far it binds—i.e., how far anyone shall be looked on to have consented, and thereby submitted to any government, where he has made no expressions of it at all. And to this I say, that every man that hath any possession or enjoyment of any part of the dominions of any government doth hereby give his tacit consent, and is as far forth obliged to obedience to the laws of that government, during such enjoyment, as anyone under it, whether this his possession be of land to him and his heirs forever, or a lodging only for a week; or whether it be barely traveling freely on the highway; and, in effect, it reaches as far as

the very being of anyone within the territories of that government.

Chapter IX Of the Ends of Political Society and Government

123. If man in the state of Nature be so free as has been said, if he be absolute lord of his own person and possessions, equal to the greatest and subject to nobody, why will he part with his freedom, this empire, and subject himself to the dominion and control of any other power? To which it is obvious to answer, that though in the state of Nature he has such a right, yet the enjoyment of it is very uncertain and constantly exposed to the invasion of others; for all being kings as much as he, every man his equal, and the greater part no strict observers of equity and justice, the enjoyment of the property he has in this state is very unsafe, very insecure. This makes him willing to quit this condition which, however free, is full of fears and continual dangers; and it is not without reason that he seeks out and is willing to join in society with others who are already united, or have a mind to unite for the mutual preservation of their lives, liberties and estates, which I call by the general name—property.

124. The great and chief end, therefore, of men uniting into commonwealths, and putting themselves under government, is the preservation of their property; to which in the state of Nature there are many things wanting.

Firstly, there wants an established, settled, known law, received and allowed by common consent to be the standard of right and wrong, and the common measure to decide all controversies between them. For though the law of Nature be plain and intel-

---

1   "The public power of all society is above every soul contained in the same society, and the principal use of that power is to give laws unto all that are under it, which laws in such cases we must obey, unless there be reason showed which may necessarily enforce that the law of reason or of God doth enjoin the contrary."—Hooker, *Eccl. Pol.*, lib. i., s. 16.

ligible to all rational creatures, yet men, being biased by their interest, as well as ignorant for want of study of it, are not apt to allow of it as a law binding to them in the application of it to their particular cases.

125. Secondly, in the state of Nature there wants a known and indifferent judge, with authority to determine all differences according to the established law. For everyone in that state being both judge and executioner of the law of nature, men being partial to themselves, passion and revenge is very apt to carry them too far, and with too much heat in their own cases, as well as negligence and unconcernedness, make them too remiss in other men's.

126. Thirdly, in the state of Nature there often wants power to back and support the sentence when right, and to give it due execution. They who by any injustice offended will seldom fail where they are able by force to make good their injustice. Such resistance many times makes the punishment dangerous, and frequently destructive to those who attempt it.

127. Thus mankind, notwithstanding all the privileges of the state of Nature, being but in an ill condition while they remain in it are quickly driven into society. Hence it comes to pass, that we seldom find any number of men live any time together in this state. The inconveniences that they are therein exposed to by the irregular and uncertain exercise of the power every man has of punishing the transgressions of others, make them take sanctuary under the established laws of government, and therein seek the preservation of their property. It is this makes them so willingly give up everyone his single power of punishing to be exercised by such alone as shall be appointed to it amongst them, and by such rules as the community, or those authorized by them to that purpose, shall agree on. And in this we have the original right and rise of both the legislative and executive power as well as of the governments and societies themselves.

131. But though men when they enter into society give up the equality, liberty, and executive power they had in the state of Nature into the hands of the society, to be so far disposed of by the legislative as the good of the society shall require, yet it being only with an intention in everyone the better to preserve himself, his liberty and property (for no rational creature can be supposed to change his condition with an intention to be worse), the power of the society or legislative constituted by them can never be supposed to extend farther than the common good, but is obliged to secure everyone's property by providing against those three defects above mentioned that made the state of Nature so unsafe and uneasy. And so, whoever has the legislative or supreme power of any commonwealth, is bound to govern by established standing laws, promulgated and known to the people, and not by extemporary decrees, by indifferent and upright judges, who are to decide controversies by those laws; and to employ the force of the community at home only in the execution of such laws, or abroad to prevent or redress foreign injuries and secure the community from inroads and invasion. And all this to be directed to no other end but the peace, safety, and public good of the people.

Chapter XI Of the Extent of the Legislative Power

134. The great end of men's entering into society being the enjoyment of their properties in peace and safety, and the great instrument and means of that being the laws established in that society, the first and fundamental positive law of all commonwealths is the establishing of the legislative power, as the first and fundamental natural law which is to govern even the legislative.

Itself is the preservation of the society and (as far as will consist with the public good) of every person in it. This legislative is not only the supreme power of the commonwealth, but sacred and unalterable in the hands where the community have once placed it. Nor can any edict of anybody else, in what form soever conceived, or by what power soever backed, have the force and obligation of a law which has not its sanction from that legislative which the public has chosen and appointed; for without this the law could not have that which is absolutely necessary to its being a law, the consent of the society, over whom nobody can have a power to make laws[2] but by their own consent and by authority received from them; and therefore all the obedience, which by the most solemn ties anyone can be obliged to pay, ultimately terminates in this supreme power, and is directed by those laws which it enacts. . . .

135. Though the legislative, whether placed in one or more, whether it be always in being or only by intervals, though it be the supreme power in every commonwealth, yet, first, it is not, nor can possibly be, absolutely arbitrary over the lives and fortunes of the people. For it being but the joint power of every member of the society given up to that person or assembly which is legislator, it can be no more than those persons had in a state of Nature before they entered into society, and gave it up to the community. For nobody can transfer to another more power than he has in himself, and nobody has an absolute arbitrary power over himself, or over any other, to destroy his own life, or take away the life or property of another.

136. Secondly, the legislative or supreme authority cannot assume to itself a power to rule by extemporary arbitrary decrees, but is bound to dispense justice and decide the rights of the subject by promulgated standing laws,[3] and known authorized judges. For the law of Nature being unwritten, and so nowhere to be found but in the minds of men, they who, through passion or interest, shall miscite or misapply it, cannot so easily be convinced of their mistake where there is no established judge; and so it serves not as it ought, to determine the rights and fence the properties of those that live under it, especially where everyone is judge, interpreter, and executioner of it too, and that in his own case; and he that has right on his side, having ordinarily but his own single strength, hath not force enough to defend himself from injuries or punish delinquents. . . .

138. Thirdly, the supreme power cannot take from any man any part of his property without his own consent. For the preservation of property being the end of govern-

---

2   The lawful power of making laws to command whole politic societies of men, belonging so properly unto the same entire societies, that for any prince or potentate, of what kind soever upon earth, to exercise the same of himself, and not by express commission immediately and personally received from God, or elm by authority derived at the first from their consent, upon whose persons they impose laws, it is no better than mere tyranny. Laws they are not, therefore, which public approbation hath not made so.—Hooker (*Eccl. Pol.*, lib. i., s. 10). "Of this point, therefore, we are to note that such men naturally have no full and perfect power to command whole politic multitudes of men, therefore utterly without our consent we could in such sort be at no man's commandment living. And to be commanded, we do consent when that society, whereof we be a part, hath at any time before consented, without revoking the same after by the like universal agreement. "Laws therefore human, of what kind soever, are available by consent."—Hooker, *Eccl. Pol.*

3   "Human laws are measures in respect of men whose actions they must direct, howbeit such measures they are as have also their higher rules to be measured by. which rules are two—the law of God and the law of Nature; so that laws human must be made according to the general laws of Nature, and without contradiction to any positive law of Scripture, otherwise they are ill made."—Hooker, *Eccl. Pol.*, lib. iii., s. 9.
"To constrain men to anything inconvenient doth seem unreasonable."—*Ibid.*, i., 10.

ment, and that for which men enter into society, it necessarily supposes and requires that the people should have property, without which they must be supposed to lose that by entering into society which was the end for which then entered into it; too gross an absurdity for any man to own. . . .

140. It is true governments cannot be supported without great charge, and it is fit every one who enjoys his share of the protection should pay out of his estate his proportion for the maintenance of it. But still it must be with his own consent—i.e., the consent of the majority, giving it either by themselves or their representatives chosen by them; for if anyone shall claim a power to lay and levy taxes on the people by his own authority, and without such consent of the people, he thereby invades the fundamental law of property, and subverts the end of government. For what property have I in that which another may by right take when he pleases to himself?

141. Fourthly, the legislative cannot transfer the power of making laws to any other hands, for it being but a delegated power from the people, they who have it cannot pass it over to others. The people alone can appoint the form of the commonwealth, which by constituting the legislative, and appointing in whose hands that shall be. And when the people have said, "We will submit, and be governed by laws made by such men, and in such forms," nobody else can say other men shall make laws for them; nor can they be bound by any.

Chapter XIX Of the Dissolution of Government

212. Besides this overturning from without, governments are dissolved from within:

First, when the legislative is altered, civil society being a state of peace amongst those who are of it, from whom the state of war is excluded by the umpirage which they have provided in their legislative for the ending all differences that may arise amongst any of them; it is in their legislative that the members of a commonwealth are united and combined together into one coherent living body. This is the soul that gives form, life, and unity to the commonwealth; from hence the several members have their mutual influence, sympathy, and connection; and therefore when the legislative is broken, or dissolved, dissolution and death follows. For the essence and union of the society consisting in having one will, the legislative, when once established by the majority, has the declaring and, as it were, keeping of that will. The constitution of the legislative is the first and fundamental act of society, whereby provision is made for the continuation of their union under the direction of persons and bonds of laws, made by persons authorized thereunto, by the consent and appointment of the people, without which no one man, or number of men, amongst them can have authority of making laws that shall be binding to the rest. When any one, or more, shall take upon them to make laws whom the people have not appointed so to do, they make laws without authority, which the people are not therefore bound to obey; by which means they come again to be out of subjection, and may constitute to themselves a new legislative, as they think best, being in full liberty to resist the force of those who, without authority, would impose anything upon them. Everyone is at the disposure of his own will, when those who had, by the delegation of the society, the declaring of the public will, are excluded from it, and others usurp the place who have no such authority or delegation.

221. There is, secondly, another way whereby governments are dissolved, and that is, when the legislative, or the prince, either of them act contrary to their trust.

For the legislative acts against the trust reposed in them when they endeavor to invade the property of the subject, and to make themselves, or any part of the community, masters or arbitrary disposers of the lives, liberties, or fortunes of the people.

222. The reason why men enter into society is the preservation of their property and the end while they choose and authorize a legislative is that there may be laws made, and rules set, as guards and fences to the properties of all the society, to limit the power and moderate the dominion of every part and member of the society. For since it can never be supposed to be the will of the society that the legislative should have a power to destroy that which everyone designs to secure by entering into society, and for which the people submitted themselves to legislators of their own making: whenever the legislators endeavor to take away and destroy the property of the people, or to reduce them to slavery under arbitrary power, they put themselves into a state of war with the people, who are thereupon absolved from any farther obedience, and are left to the common refuge which God hath provided for all men against force and violence. Whensoever, therefore, the legislative shall transgress this fundamental rule of society, and either by ambition, fear, folly, or corruption, endeavor to grasp themselves, or put into the hands of any other, an absolute power over the lives, liberties, and estates of the people, by this breach of trust they forfeit the power the people had put into their hands for quite contrary ends, and it devolves to the people, who have a right to resume their original liberty, and by the establishment of a new legislative (such as they shall think fit), provide for their own safety and security, which is the end for which they are in society. . . .

223. To this, perhaps, it will be said that the people being ignorant and always dis-

contented, to lay the foundation of government in the unsteady opinion and uncertain humor of the people, is to expose it to certain ruin; and no government will be able long to subsist if the people may set up a new legislative whenever they take offense at the old one. To this I answer, quite the contrary. People are not so easily got out of their old forms as some are apt to suggest. They are hardly to be prevailed with to amend the acknowledged faults in the frame they have been accustomed to. And if there be any original defects, or adventitious ones introduced by time or corruption, it is not an easy thing to get them changed, even when all the world sees there is an opportunity for it. This slowness and aversion in the people to quit their old constitutions has in the many revolutions we have seen in this kingdom, in this and former ages, still kept us to, or after some interval of fruitless attempts, still brought us back again to our old legislative of king, lords and commons; and whatever provocations have made the crown be taken from some of our princes' heads, they never carried the people so far as to place it in another line.

224. But it will be said this hypothesis lays a ferment for frequent rebellion. To which I answer:

First, no more than any other hypothesis. For when the people are made miserable, and find themselves exposed to the ill usage of arbitrary power, cry up their governors as much as you will for sons of Jupiter, let them be scared and divine, descended or authorized from Heaven; give them out for whom or what you please, the same will happen. The people generally ill treated, and contrary to right, will be ready upon any occasion to ease themselves of a burden that sits heavy upon them. They will wish and seek for the opportunity, which in the change, weakness, and accidents of human affairs, seldom delays long to offer itself. He must have lived but a little while in the world, who has not seen examples of this in his time; and he must have read very little who cannot produce examples of it in all sorts of governments in the world.

225. Secondly, I answer, such revolutions happen not upon every little mismanagement in public affairs. Great mistakes in the ruling part, many wrong and inconvenient laws, and all the slips of human frailty will be borne by the people without mutiny or murmur. But if a long train of abuses, prevarications and artifices, all tending the same way, make the design visible to the people, and they cannot but feel what they lie under, and see whither they are going, it is not to be wondered that they should then rouse themselves, and endeavor to put the rule into such hands which may secure to them the ends for which government was at first erected, and without which, ancient names and specious forms are so far from being better, that they are much worse than the state of Nature or pure anarchy; the inconveniences being all as great and as near, but the remedy farther off and more difficult.

226. Thirdly, I answer, that this power in the people of providing for their safety anew by a new legislative when their legislators have acted contrary to their trust by invading their property, is the best fence against rebellion, and the probablest means to hinder it. For rebellion being an opposition, not to persons, but authority, which is founded only in the constitutions and laws of the government: those, whoever they be, who, by force, break through, and, by force, justify their violation of them, are truly and properly rebels. For when men, by entering into society and civil government, have excluded force, and introduced laws for the preservation of property, peace, and unity amongst themselves, those who set up force again in opposition to the laws, do *rebellare*—that is, bring back again the state of war, and are properly rebels, which they who are in power, by the pretense they have to authority, the temptation of force they have in their hands, and the flattery of those about them being likeliest to do, the properest way to prevent the evil is to show them the danger and injustice of it who are under the greatest temptation to run into it.

The Declaration of Independence

Thomas Jefferson

When in the Course of human events it becomes necessary for one people to dissolve the political bands which have connected them with another, and to assume among the powers of the earth, the separate and equal station to which the Laws of Nature and of Nature's God entitle them, a decent respect to the opinions of mankind requires that they should declare the causes which impel them to the separation.

We hold these truths to be self-evident, that all men are created equal, that they are endowed by their Creator with certain unalienable Rights, that among these are Life, Liberty and the pursuit of Happiness.—That to secure these rights, Governments are instituted among Men, deriving their just powers from the consent of the governed.—That whenever any Form of Government becomes destructive of these ends, it is the Right of the People to alter or to abolish it, and to institute new Government, laying its foundation on such principles, and organizing its powers in such form, as to them shall seem most likely to effect their Safety and Happiness. Prudence, indeed, will dictate that Governments long established should not be changed for light and transient causes; and accordingly all experience hath shewn, that mankind are more disposed to suffer while evils are sufferable, than to right themselves by abolishing the forms to which they are accustomed. But when a long train of abuses and usurpations, pursuing invariably the same Object, evinces a design to reduce them under absolute Despotism, it is their right, it is their duty to throw off such Government, and to provide new Guards for their future security.—Such has been the patient sufferance of these Colonies, and such is now the necessity which constrains them to alter their former Systems of Government. The history of the present King of Great Britain is a history of repeated injuries and usurpations, all having in direct object the establishment of an absolute Tyranny over these States. To prove this, let Facts be submitted to a candid world. . . .

In every stage of these Oppressions We have Petitioned for Redress in the most humble terms: Our repeated Petitions have been answered only by repeated injury. A Prince, whose character is thus marked by every act which may define a Tyrant, is unfit to be the ruler of a free people.

Nor have We been wanting in attentions to our British brethren. We have warned them from time to time of attempts by their legislature to extend an unwarrantable jurisdiction over us. We have reminded them of the circumstances of our emigration and settlement here. We have appealed to their native justice and magnanimity, and we have conjured them by the ties of our common kindred to disavow these usurpations, which would inevitably interrupt our connections and correspondence. They too have been deaf to the voice of justice and of consanguinity. We must, therefore, acquiesce in the necessity, which denounces our Separation, and hold them, as we hold the rest of mankind, Enemies in War, in Peace Friends.

We, therefore, the Representatives of the united States of America, in General Congress, Assembled, appealing to the Supreme Judge of the world for the rectitude of our intentions, do, in the Name, and by Authority of the good People of these Colonies solemnly publish and declare, That these United Colonies are, and of Right ought to be Free and Independent States; that they are Absolved from all Allegiance to the British Crown, and that all political connection between them and the State of Great Britain, is and ought to be totally dissolved; and that as Free and Independent States, they have full Power to levy War, conclude Peace, contract Alliances, establish Commerce, and to do all other Acts and Things which Independent States may of right do.

And for the support of this Declaration, with a firm reliance on protection of divine Providence, we mutually pledge to each other Lives, our Fortunes and our sacred Honor.

Transition from Popular Moral Philosophy to the Metaphysics of Morals

Immanuel Kant
Translated by Carl J. Friedrich

If hitherto we have drawn our concept of duty from the common use of our practical reason, it is by no means to be inferred that we have treated it as an empirical concept. On the contrary, if we attend to the experience of men's conduct, we meet frequent and, as we admit ourselves, just complaints that there is not to be found a single certain example of the disposition to act from pure duty. Although many things are done *in conformity* to what duty prescribes, it is nevertheless always doubtful whether they are done strictly *out of duty* [which would have to be the case if they are] to have a moral value. Hence, in all ages there have been philosophers who have denied altogether that this disposition actually exists in human actions at all, and who have ascribed everything to a more or less refined self-love. Not that they have on that account questioned the soundness of the conception of morality; on the contrary they have spoken with sincere regret of the frailty and corruption of human nature, which though noble enough to take as its law an idea so worthy of respect, is yet too weak to follow it, and employs reason, which ought to give it the law, only for the purpose of accommodating the inclinations, whether single or, at best, in the greatest possible harmony with one another. In fact it is absolutely impossible to ascertain by experience with complete certainty a single case in which the maxim of an action, however right in itself, rested simply on moral grounds and on the conception of duty. Sometimes it happens that with the sharpest self-examination we can find nothing, besides the moral principle of duty, powerful enough to move us to this or that action and to such a great sacrifice; yet we cannot infer from this with certainty that it was not some really secret impulse of self-love, under the false appearance of that idea [of the moral principle of duty] that was the actual determining cause of the will. We then like to flatter ourselves by falsely taking credit for a more noble motive. In fact we can never, even by the strictest self-examination, penetrate completely [to the causes] behind the secret springs of action, since when we ask about moral worth, we are not concerned with actions but with their inward principles which we do not see.

Moreover, we cannot better serve the wishes of those people, who ridicule all morality as a mere chimera of human imagination overstepping itself through vanity, than by conceding to them that concepts of duty must be drawn only from experience, just as people are ready to think out of indolence that this is also the case with all other notions; doing this would prepare a certain triumph for them. Out of love for humanity, I am willing to admit that most of our actions accord with duty, but on examining them more closely we encounter everywhere the cherished self which is always dominant. It is this self that men have consideration for and not the strict command of duty which would often require self-denial. Without being an enemy to virtue, a cool observer who does not mistake an ardent wish for good for goodness itself, may sometimes doubt whether true virtue is actually found anywhere in the world, and do this especially as his years increase and his judgment is in part made wiser by experience and in part more acute by observation. This being so, nothing can save us from altogether abandoning our ideas of duty, nothing can maintain in our soul a well-grounded respect for the law; nothing but the clear conviction that, although there have never been actions really springing from such pure sources, yet . . . . reason, by itself and independent of all experience, ordains what ought to be done. Accordingly actions, of which hitherto the world has perhaps never had an example and of which the feasibility might even be very much doubted by anyone basing everything on experience, are nevertheless inflexibly commanded by reason; e.g., even though a sincere friend might never have existed up till now, [just the same] pure sincerity in friendship is required of every man not a whit less, because above and beyond all experience this duty is obligatory in the idea of a reason that determines the will by *a priori* principles.

Unless we deny that the notion of morality has any truth or reference to any possible object, we must admit that its law must be valid not only for men, but for all *rational creatures generally*, not only under certain contingent conditions or with exceptions, but with *absolute necessity*. [When we admit this] then it is clear that no experience could

enable us even to infer the possibility of such apodictic laws. What right have we to demand unbounded respect, as for a universal precept of every rational creature, for something that only holds true under the contingent conditions of humanity? Or, how could laws determining *our* will be regarded as laws determining the will of rational beings generally, if these laws were only empirical and did not originate wholly *a priori* from pure and practical reason?

Nor could an thing be more ill-advised for morality than out wishing to derive it from examples. Every example set before me must first be tested by principles of morality [to determine] whether it is worthy of serving as an original example; that is, as a model or pattern. An example can by no means furnish authoritatively the concept of morality. Even the Holy One of the Gospels must first be compared with our ideal of moral perfection before we can recognize Him as such; and so He says of himself, "Why call ye Me (whom ye see) good? None is good (the model of good) but God only (whom ye do not see)!" But whence do we acquire the concept of God as the supreme good? Simply from the *idea* of moral perfection which reason sketches *a priori* and connects inseparably with the concept of a free will. Imitation has no place at all in morality, and examples serve only for encouragement; that is, they make feasible beyond any doubt what the law commands and they make visible what the practical rule expresses more generally, but they can never authorize us to set aside the true original existing in reason and to guide ourselves by examples. Therefore, if there is no genuine supreme principle of morality, but only that which rests on pure reason independent of all experience, I think it is unnecessary even to put the question as to whether it is good to exhibit these concepts in their generality (*in abstracto*) as they are established *a priori* along with the principles belonging to them, if our knowledge is to be distinguished from the *vulgar* and called philosophical. Indeed, in our time this question might perhaps be necessary; for if we collected votes on whether pure rational knowledge, apart from everything empirical, that is to say, a metaphysic of morals, is to be preferred to a popular practical philosophy; it is easy to guess which side would carry more weight.

This descent to popular notions is certainly very commendable if the ascent to the principles of pure reason has taken place first and has been accomplished satisfactorily. This implies that first we should establish ethics on metaphysics and, when it is firmly founded, procure a hearing for ethics by giving it a popular character. But it is quite absurd to try to be popular in the first inquiry on which the soundness of the principles depends. Not only can this procedure never lay claim to having the very rare merit of a true *philosophical popularity* for there is no sense in being intelligible if one renounces all thoroughness of insight, but this procedure also produces a disgusting medley of compiled observations and half-reasoned principles. Shallow pates enjoy this because it can be used for everyday chat, but those with deeper understanding find only confusion in this method and, being unsatisfied and unable to assist themselves, turn away their eyes, while philosophers, seeing quite clearly through this confusion, are little heeded when they call men away for a time from this pretended popularity, so they may be rightfully popular after attaining a definite insight.

We only need to look at the attempts of moralists in [using] that favorite fashion and

we shall find [a variety of things:] at one point the special destination of human nature including the idea of a rational nature generally, at another point perfection, at another happiness, here moral sense, there fear of God, a little of this and a little of that, all in a marvelous mixture. It does not occur to them to ask whether the principles of morality are to be sought at all in the knowledge of human nature which we can have only from experience. If this is not so, if these principles are completely *a priori* and are to be encountered free from everything empirical only in pure rational concepts and nowhere else, not even in the smallest degree, shall we then adopt the method of making this a separate inquiry as a pure practical philosophy? Or [shall we construct], if one may use a name so decried, a metaphysic of morals[1] and complete it by itself and ask the public wishing for popular treatment to await the outcome of this undertaking?

Such a metaphysic of morals, completely isolated and unmixed with any anthropology, theology, physics, or hyperphysics, and still less with occult qualities which we might call superphysical, is not only an indispensable condition for all sound theoretical knowledge of duties, but at the same time it is a *desideratum* highly important to the actual fulfillment of the precepts of duties. For the pure concept of duty unmixed with any foreign element of experienced attractions, in a word, the pure concept of moral law in general, exercises an influence on the human heart through reason alone. . . . This influence is so much more powerful than all other impulses[2] which may be derived from the field of experience, that in the consciousness of its dignity it

---

1   Just as pure mathematics is differentiated from applied and pure logic from applied, so, if we choose, we may also differentiate pure philosophy of morals (metaphysics) from applied (viz., applied to human nature). Also, by this designation we are at once reminded that moral principles are not based on properties of human nature, but must exist *a priori* of themselves; practical rules for every rational nature must be capable of being deduced from such principles and accordingly deduced for the rational nature of man.

despises such impulses and by degrees can become their master. An eclectic ethics compounded partly of motives drawn from feelings and inclinations and partly from concepts of reason, will necessarily make the mind waver between motives which cannot be brought under any one principle, and will therefore lead to good only by mere accident, and may often lead to evil.

It is clear from what has been said that all moral concepts have their seat and origin completely *a priori* in the reason, and have it in the commonest reason just as truly as in what is speculative in the highest degree. Moral concepts cannot be obtained by abstraction from any empirical and hence merely contingent knowledge. It is exactly this purity in origin that makes them worthy of serving our supreme practical principle [for right action] and, as we add anything empirical, we detract in proportion from their genuine influence and from the absolute value of actions. It is not only very necessary from a purely speculative point of view, but it is also of the greatest practical importance to derive these notions and laws from pure reason, to present them pure and unmixed, and even to determine the compass of this practical or pure rational knowledge; that is, to determine the entire faculty of pure practical reason. In doing so we must not make the principles of pure practical reason dependent on the particular nature of human reason, though in speculative philosophy this may be permitted and even necessary at times. Since moral laws ought to hold true for every rational creature we must

derive them from the general concept of a rational being. Although morality has need of anthropology for its application to man, yet in this way, as in the first step, we must treat morality independently as pure philosophy; that is, as metaphysics, complete in itself. . . . We must fully realize that unless we are in possession of this pure philosophy not only would it be vain to determine the moral element of duty in right actions for purposes of speculative criticism, but it would be impossible to base morals on their genuine principles. This is true even for common practical purposes, but more especially for moral instruction which is to produce pure moral dispositions and to engraft them on men's minds for promoting the greatest possible good in the world.

Our purpose in this study must be not only to advance by natural steps from common moral judgment, which is very worthy of respect, to the philosophical, as has been done already, but also to progress from a popular philosophy which only gets as far as it can by groping with the help of examples, to metaphysics, which does not allow itself to be held back by anything empirical and which goes as far as ideal concepts in measuring the whole extent of this kind of rational knowledge wherever examples fail us. [In order to accomplish this purpose] we must clearly describe and trace the practical faculty of reason, advancing from general rules to the point where the notion of duty springs from it.

Everything in nature works according to laws. Rational beings alone have the faculty

---

2   I have a letter from the late excellent Sulzer, in which he asks me what might be the reason for moral instruction accomplishing so little although it contains much that is convincing to reason. My answer was postponed in order that I might make it complete. But it is simply this: teachers themselves do not have their own notions clear, and often they endeavor to make up for this by suggesting all kinds of motives for moral goodness and in trying to make their medicine strong they spoil it. For, the most ordinary observations show that this is an act of honesty done with steadfast mind and without regard for any advantage in this world or another, and when [persisted in] even under the greatest temptations of need or allurement it will . . . elevate the soul and inspire one with the wish to be able to act in a like manner. Even fairly young children feel this impression and one should never represent duties to them in any other light.

for acting according *to the concept* of laws; that is, according to principles. [In other words, rational beings alone] have a will. Since deriving actions from principles requires *reason,* the will is nothing more than practical reason. If reason infallibly determines the will, then the actions of such a being that are recognized as objectively necessary are also subjectively necessary. The will is a faculty for choosing *only that* which reason, independently of inclination, recognizes as practically necessary; that is, as good. But if reason does not sufficiently determine the will by itself, if the latter is also subject to the subjective conditioning of particular impulses which do not always coincide with the objective conditions; in a word, if the will *in itself* does not completely accord with reason, as is actually the case with men, then the actions which are objectively recognized as necessary are subjectively contingent. Determining such a will according to objective laws is compulsory (*Nötigung*). This means that the relation of objective laws to a will not thoroughly good is conceived as the determination of the will of a rational being by principles of reason which the will, because of its nature, does not necessarily follow.

The concept of an objective principle, in so far as it is compulsory for a will, is called a command of reason and the formulation of such a command is called an IMPERATIVE.

All imperatives are expressed by the word *ought* (or *shall*) and are indicating thereby the relation of an objective law of reason to a will, which, because of its subjective constitution, is not necessarily determined by this [compulsion]. Such imperatives may state that something would be good to do or to forbear from doing, but they are addressing themselves to a will which does not always do a thing merely because that thing is represented as good to do. The practically *good* determines the will by means of the concepts of reason, and consequently from objective, not subjective causes; that is, [it determines them] on principles which are valid for every rational being as such. The practically good is distinguishable from the *pleasant* which influences the will only by means of sensations from subjective causes and which is valid only for the particular sense of this or that man and is not a principle of reason holding true for every one.[3]

Therefore a perfectly good will would be equally subject to objective laws of good [action], but could not be conceived thereby as *compelled* to act lawfully by itself. Because of its subjective constitution it can only be determined by the concept of the good. Consequently no imperatives hold true for the Divine will, or in general for a *holy* will. *Ought* is out of place here because the act of willing is already necessarily in unison with the law. Therefore imperatives are only formulations for expressing the relation of the objective laws of all volition to the subjective

---

3 The dependence of the desires on sensations is called inclination, and accordingly always indicates a *want.* The dependence of a contingently determinable will on principles of reason is called an *interest.* Therefore, this dependence is only found in the case of a dependent will, which of itself does not always conform to reason. We cannot conceive of the Divine will having any interest. But the human will can *take an interest* without necessarily acting *from interest.* The former signifies practical interest in the action, the latter *psychological* interest in the object of the action. The first merely indicates dependence of the will on principles of reason in themselves and the second merely indicates dependence on principles of reason for the sake of inclination, reason supplying only the practical rules of how the demands of inclination may be satisfied. In the first case the action interests me in the object of the action, inasmuch as it is pleasant for me. We have seen, in the first section, that in an action done from duty we must not look to the interest in the object but only to the interest in the action itself, and in its rational principle: the law.

imperfections of the will of this or that rational being; that is, the human will.

All *imperatives* command either *hypothetically* or *categorically*. . . . Since every practical law represents a possible action as good, and on this account as necessary for a subject who can determine practically by reason, all imperatives are formulations determining an action which is necessary according to the principle of a will in some respects good. If the action is good only as a means *to something else,* then the imperative is *hypothetical.* If the action is conceived as good *in itself* and consequently as necessarily being the principle of a will which of itself conforms to reason then it is *categorical.*

Thus the imperative declares what, of my possible actions, would be good. It presents the practical rule in relation to a will which does not perform an action forthwith simply because it is good. For, either the subject does not always know that such action is good or, even should the subject know this, its maxims might be opposed to the objective principles of practical reason.

Consequently the hypothetical imperative only states that an action is good for some purpose, *potential* or *actual.* In the first case the principle is *problematical,* in the second it is *assertorial* [positively asserting a claim and may be called a] practical principle. The categorical imperative which declares an action to be objectively necessary in itself without reference to any purpose, i.e., without any other end, is valid as an *apodictic* (practical) principle.

Whatever is possible through the ability of some rational being may also be considered as a possible purpose of some will. Therefore the principles of action concerning the means needed to attain some possible purpose are really infinitely numerous. All

sciences have a practical aspect consisting of problems expressing that some end is possible for us, and of imperatives directing how it may be attained. Therefore, these may, in general, be called imperatives of *skill.* There is no question as to whether the end is rational and good, but only as to what one must do in order to attain it. The precepts for the physician to make his patient thoroughly healthy, and for a poisoner to ensure certain death, are equivalent in that each serves to effect its purpose perfectly. Since in early youth it cannot be known what purposes are likely to occur to us in the course of life, parents seek to have their children taught a *great many things* and provide for their *skill* in using means for all sorts of purposes. They cannot be sure whether any particular purpose may perhaps hereafter be an objective for their pupil; it is possible that he might aim at any of them. This anxiety is so great that parents commonly neglect to form and correct their judgment on the value of the things which may be chosen as ends.

However there is *one* end which may actually be assumed to be an end for all rational beings, there is one purpose which they not only *may* have, but which we may assume with certainty that they all actually *do have* by natural necessity; that is *happiness.* The hypothetical imperative expressing the practical necessity of an action as a means for the advancement of happiness is assertorial. We are not presenting it as necessary for an uncertain and merely possible purpose, but for a purpose which we may presuppose with certainty and *a priori* for every man, because it belongs to his being. Now a man's skill in choosing the means to his own greatest well-being may be called *prudence* in the most specific sense.[4] Thus the imperative

---

4   The word prudence is taken in two senses: In one it may mean knowledge of the world, in the other, private prudence. The first is a man's ability to influence others so as to use them for his own purposes. The second is the insight to combine all these purposes for his own lasting benefit. This latter is properly that to which the

which refers to the choice of means to one's own happiness, that is, the precept of prudence, is still hypothetical. The action is not commanded absolutely but only as a means to another purpose. Whereas, the categorical imperative directly commands a certain conduct without being conditioned by any other attainable purpose. . . . This imperative may be called the imperative of morality (*Sittlichkeit*).

There is also a marked distinction among the acts of willing according to these three kinds of principles resulting from the *dissimilarity* in the obligation of the will. In order to differentiate them more clearly, I think they would be most suitably classified as either *rules of* skill, *counsels* of prudence, or *commands* or laws of morality. For it is only *law* that involves the concept of an *unconditional necessity* which is objective and hence universally valid. Commands are laws that must be obeyed; that is, must be adhered to even when inclination is opposed. Indeed, counsels involve [a certain kind of] necessity, but only one which can hold true under a contingent subjective condition. They depend on whether this or that man counts this or that [object] as essential to his happiness. By contrast, the categorical imperative is not limited by any condition. . . . We might also call the first kind of imperatives *technical* as belonging to art, the second *pragmatic*[5] as belonging to welfare, and the third *moral* as belonging to free conduct generally, that is, to morals.

The question now arises: How are all these imperatives possible? This question is to ascertain, not how the action commanded by the imperative can be carried out, but merely how the compulsion of will expressed by the imperative can be conceived. I should think that no special explanation is needed to show how an imperative related to skill is possible. Whoever wills the end, also wills, so far as reason decisively influences his conduct, the means in his power which are indispensable for achieving this end. This proposition is analytical in regard to the volition. For, in willing an object as an effect, there is already implied therein that I myself am acting as a cause, that is, I make use of the means. From the concept of the willed end, the imperative derives the concept of the actions necessary for achieving this end. No doubt synthetic propositions will have to be employed in defining the means to a proposed end, but they do not concern the principle, the act of the will but only the object and its realization. To give an example: in order to bisect a line I must draw two intersecting arcs from its end points. Admittedly, this is taught by mathematics in synthetic propositions. But if I know that the intended operation can only be performed by this process, then it is an analytical proposition to say that in fully willing the operation, I also will the action required for it. For [assuming that I want a certain thing] it is just the same to conceive that thing as an effect which I can only produce in a certain way as to conceive of myself as acting in this way.

If it were equally easy to give a definite concept of happiness [as of simpler ends], the imperatives of prudence would correspond exactly with those of skill, and would

---

value of even the former is reduced, and when a man is prudent in the former sense, but not in the latter, we might better say of him that he is clever and cunning, but on the whole, imprudent.

5   It seems to me that the proper meaning of the word *pragmatic* may be most accurately defined in this way: *Sanctions* are called pragmatic when they flow properly not from the law of the states as necessary enactments, but from *precaution* for the general welfare. A history is composed pragmatically when it teaches *prudence*; i.e., instructs the world how it can better provide for its interests, or at least as well as did the men of former times.

likewise be analytical. It could then be said that whoever wills the end also wills the indispensable means thereto which are in his power. But unfortunately the notion of happiness is so indefinite that although every man wishes to attain it, he never can say definitely and consistently what it is that he really wishes and wills. The reason is that the elements belonging to the notion of happiness are altogether empirical; that is, they must be borrowed from experience. Nevertheless, the idea of happiness implies something absolute and whole; a maximum of well-being in my present and all future circumstances. Now, it is impossible for even the most clear-sighted and most powerful being, as long as it is supposedly finite, to frame for itself a definite concept of what it really wills [when it wants to be happy]. If he wills riches, how much anxiety, envy, and snares might not be drawn upon his shoulders thereby? If he wills knowledge and discernment, perhaps such knowledge might only prove to be so much sharper sight showing him much more fearfully the unavoidable evils now concealed from him, or suggesting more wants for his desires which already give him concern enough. If he should will a long life, who can guarantee him that it will not be a long misery? If he should at least have health, how often has infirmity of the body restrained a man from excesses into which perfect health would have allowed him to fall? And so on. In short, a human being is unable with certainty to determine by any principle what would make him truly happy, because to do so he would have to be omniscient. Therefore, we cannot act on any definite principles to secure happiness, but only on counsels derived from experience; e.g., the frugality, courtesy, reserve, etc., which experience teaches·us will promote well-being, for the most part. Hence it follows that the imperatives of prudence do not command at all,

strictly speaking; that is, they cannot present actions objectively as practically *necessary* so that they are to be regarded as *counsels (consilia)* of reason rather than precepts *(praecepta)*. The problem of determining certainly and generally which action would most promote the happiness of a rational being is completely insoluble. Consequently, no imperative respecting happiness is possible, for such a command should, in a strict sense, command men to do what makes them happy. Happiness is an ideal, not of reason, but of imagination resting solely on empirical grounds. It is vain to expect that these grounds should define an action for attaining the totality of a series of consequences that are really endless. However, this imperative of prudence could be an analytical proposition if we assume that the means to happiness could, with certainty, be assigned. For, this imperative is distinguished from the imperative of skill only by this; in the latter the end is merely possible [and available to be chosen]; in the former the end is given. However, both only prescribe the means to an end which we assume to have been willed. It follows that the imperative which calls for the willing of the means by him who wins the end is analytical in both cases. Thus there is no difficulty in regard to the possibility of this kind of imperative either.

On the other hand, the question of how the imperative of *morality* is possible is undoubtedly the only question demanding a solution as this imperative is not at all hypothetical, and the objective necessity it presents cannot rest on any hypothesis, as is the case with hypothetical imperatives. Only we must never leave out of consideration the fact that we *cannot* determine *by any example*, i.e., empirically, whether there is any such imperative at all. Rather is it to be feared that all those apparently categorical imperatives may actually be hypothetical. For instance, when you have a precept such as: thou shalt not promise deceitfully, and it is assumed that the [normative] necessity of this is not a mere counsel to avoid some other evil, [in which case] it might mean: you shall not make a lying promise lest it become known and your credit would be destroyed. On the contrary, an action of this kind should be regarded as evil in itself so that the imperative of the prohibition is categorical. Yet we cannot show with certainty in any instance that the will is determined merely by the law without an other source of action though this may appear to be so. It is always possible that fear of disgrace, also perhaps obscure dread of other dangers, may have a secret influence on the will. Who can prove by experience the non-existence of a cause when all that experience tells us is that we do not perceive it? In such a case the so-called imperative, which appears to be categorical and unconditional, would really only be a pragmatic precept, drawing our attention to our own interests, and merely teaching us to take these interests into consideration.

Therefore we shall have to investigate *a priori* the possibility of a *categorical* imperative, since, in this case, we do not have the advantage that the imperative's reality is given in experience, so that the elucidation of its possibility would be needed only for explaining it, not for establishing it. It can be discerned that the categorical imperative has the purport of a practical law. All the rest may certainly be called *principles* of the will but not laws, since whatever is merely necessary for attaining some cas-

ual purpose may be considered contingent in itself, and at any time we can be free from the precept if we give up the purpose. However, the unconditional command leaves the will no liberty to choose the opposite, and consequently only the will carries with it that necessity we require in a law.

Secondly, in the case of this categorical imperative or law of morality the difficulty [of discerning its possibility] is very profound. It is *a prior*, a synthetic, practical proposition[6] and as there is so much difficulty in discerning the possibility of speculative propositions of this kind, it may readily be supposed that the difficulty will be no less with the practical.

In [approaching] this problem we will first inquire whether the mere concept of a categorical imperative may not perhaps supply us with its formula also, which contains the proposition that alone can be a categorical imperative. Even if we know the tenor of such an absolute command, yet how it is possible will require further special and laborious study which we win postpone to the last section.

When I conceive of a hypothetical imperative at all, I do not know previously what it will contain until I am given the condition. But when I conceive of a categorical imperative I know at once what it contains. In addition to the law, the imperative contains only the necessity that the maxim[7] conform to this law. As the maxim The former contains the practical rule set by reason according to the conditions of the subject (often its ignorance or its inclinations); hence it is the principle on which the subject *acts;*

---

6   I connect the act with the will without presupposing a condition resulting from any inclination but *a priori*, and therefore necessarily (though only objectively; that is, assuming the idea of a reason possessing full power over all subjective motives). Therefore this is a practical proposition which does not analytically deduce the willing for an action from another already presupposed proposition (for we have not such a perfect will), but connects it immediately with the concept of the will of a rational being, as something not contained in it.

7   A maxim is a subjective principle of action and must be distinguished from an *objective principle;* namely, practical law.

but the law is the objective principle valid for every rational being and is the principle on which the being *ought to act;* that is, an imperative. contains no condition restricting the maxim, nothing remains but the general statement of the law to which the maxim of the action should conform, and it is only this conformity that the imperative properly represents as necessary.

Therefore there is only one categorical imperative, namely this: *Act only on a maxim by which you can will that it, at the same time, should become a general law.*

Now, if all imperatives of duty can be deduced from this one imperative as easily as from their principle, then we shall be able at least to show what we understand by it and what this concept means, although it would remain undecided whether what is called duty is not just a vain notion.

Since the universality of the law constitutes what is properly called *nature* in the most general sense [as to form]; that is, the existence of things as far as determined by general laws, the general imperative duty may be expressed thus: *Act as if the maxim of your action were to become by your will a general law of nature.*

We will now enumerate a few duties, adopting the usual division of duties to ourselves and to others, and of perfect and imperfect duties.[8]

1. A man, while reduced to despair by a series of misfortunes and feeling wearied of life, is still so far in possession of his reason that he can ask himself whether it would not be contrary to his duty to himself to take his own life. Now he inquires whether the maxim of his action could become a general law of nature. His maxim is: Out of self-love I

consider it a principle to shorten my life when continuing it is likely to bring more misfortune than satisfaction. The question then simply is whether this principle of self-love could become a general law of nature. Now we see at once that a system of nature, whose law would be to destroy life by the very feeling designed to compel the maintenance of life, would contradict itself, and therefore could not exist as a system of nature; hence that maxim cannot possibly be a general law of nature and consequently it would be wholly inconsistent with the supreme principle of all duty.

2. Another man finds himself forced by dire need to borrow money. He knows that he will not be able to repay it, but he also sees that nothing will be lent him unless he promises firmly to repay it within a definite time. He would like to make this promise but he still has enough conscience to ask himself: Is it not unlawful and contrary to my duty to get out of a difficulty in this way? However, suppose that he does decide to do so, the maxim of his action would then be expressed thus: When I consider myself in want of money, I shall borrow money and promise to repay it although I know that I never can. Now this principle of self-love or of one's own advantage may perhaps be agreeable to my whole future well-being; but the question is now: Is it right? Here I change the suggestion of self-love into a general law and state the question thus: How would it be if my maxim were a general law? I then realize at once that it could never hold as a general law of nature but would necessarily contradict

---

8   It must be noted here that I reserve the classification of duties for a future metaphysic of morals; so here I only give a few arbitrary duties as examples.

itself. For if it were a general law that anyone considering himself to be in difficulties would be able to promise whatever he pleases intending not to keep his promise, the promise itself and its object would become impossible since no one would believe that anything was promised him, but would ridicule all such statements as vain pretenses.

3. A third man finds in himself a talent which with the help of some education might make him a useful man in many respects. But he finds himself in comfortable circumstances, and prefers to indulge in pleasure rather than to take pains in developing and improving his fortunate natural capacities. He asks, however, whether his maxim of neglecting his natural gifts, besides agreeing with his inclination toward indulgence, agrees also with what is called duty. He sees then that nature could indeed subsist according to such a general law, though men (like the South Sea Islanders) let their talents rust and devote their lives merely to idleness, amusement, and the propagation of their species, in a word, to enjoyment. But he cannot possibly *will* that this should be a general law of nature or be implanted in us as such by an instinct of nature. For, as a rational being he necessarily wills that his faculties be developed, since they have been given to serve him for all sorts of possible purposes.

4. A fourth, prosperous man, while seeing others whom he could help having to struggle with great hardship thinks: What concern is it of mine? Let everyone be as happy as heaven pleases or as he can make himself. I will take nothing from him nor even envy him, but I do not wish either to contribute anything to his welfare or assist him in his distress. There is no doubt that if such a way of thinking were a general law, society might get along very well and doubtless even better than if everyone were to talk of sympathy and good will or even endeavor occasionally to put it into practice, but then [were to] cheat when one could and so betray the rights of man or otherwise violate them. But although it is possible that a general law of nature might exist in terms of that maxim, it is impossible to *will* that such a principle should have the general validity of a law of nature. For a will which resolved this would contradict itself, inasmuch as many a time one would need the love and sympathy of others and by such a law of nature, sprung from one's own will, one would deprive himself of all hope of the aid he desires.

These are a few of the many actual duties, or at least what we regard as such, which derive clearly from the one principle that we have established. We must be *able to will* that a maxim of our action should be a general law. This is the canon of any moral assessment at all of such action. Some actions are such that their maxims cannot even be *conceived* as a general law of nature without contradiction, let alone that one could *will* that these maxims *should* become such laws. Other actions reveal no such intrinsic impossibility, but still it is impossible to *will* that their maxim should be elevated to the universality of a law of nature, since such a will would contradict itself. It can be easily seen that the former would conflict with strict or more specific, inexorable duty, the latter merely with a broader (meritorious) duty. Therefore, all duties, in regard to their compulsory nature (not the object of their action), depend on the same principle as the above illustrations conclusively show.

If we now watch ourselves for any transgression of duty, we shall find that we actually do not will that our maxim should be a general law in such cases. On the contrary, we will that the opposite should remain a general law. We merely take the liberty of making an *exception* in our own favor or (just for this time) in favor of our inclination. Consequently, if we considered all cases from the point of view of reason, we should find a contradiction in our own will; namely, that a certain principle is objectively necessary as a general law and yet is subjectively not general but has exceptions. In regarding our action on the one hand from the point of view of a will wholly conformed to reason, and on the other hand looking at the same action from the point of view of a will affected by inclination, there is really no contradiction but an antagonism on the part of inclination to the precept of reason which turns the universality of the principle into a mere generality, so that the principle of practical reason can meet the maxim half way.

Now although our own impartial judgment cannot justify this, it can prove that we do really acknowledge the validity of the categorical imperative and (with due respect) take just a few liberties with it, which we consider unimportant and the same time forced upon us.

Thus we have at least established this much; that if duty is a concept which is to have any import and real controlling authority over our actions, it can only be expressed in a categorical and never in hypothetical imperatives. It is also of great importance that the content of the categorical imperative be presented clearly and definitely for every purpose; the categorical imperative must contain the principle of all duty if there is

such a thing at all. However, we cannot yet prove *a priori* that such an imperative actually exists; that there is a practical law which commands absolutely by itself and without any other impulse and that compliance with this law is duty.

To be able to do that, it is extremely important to heed the warning that we cannot possibly think of deducing the reality of this principle from *particular attributes of human nature.* Duty is to be the practical, unconditional necessity for action; it must hold therefore for all rational beings (to whom an imperative can refer at all), and *for this reason only* it must also be a law for all human wills. On the other hand, whatever is deduced from the particular natural make-up of human beings, from certain feelings and propensities[9] and, if possible, even from any particular tendency of human reason proper which does not need to show in the will of every rational being. [Whatever is so deduced] may indeed furnish a maxim, but not a law. It may offer us a subjective principle on which we may act and may have propensities and inclinations, but [it does not give us] an objective principle by which we should be *constrained* to act, even though all our propensities, inclinations, and natural dispositions were opposed to it. In fact, the maxim evinces the sublime quality and intrinsic dignity of the command that the more clearly duty holds true, the less its subjective impulses favor it and the more they oppose such duty without being able in the slightest to weaken the binding character of the law, or to diminish its validity. . . .

Therefore, every empirical element is not only quite incapable of aiding the principle of morality, but is even highly prejudicial to the purity of morals. For the proper and

9 [Kant distinguishes *Hang* (propensity) from *Neigung* (inclination) as follows: *Hang* is a predisposition to the desire of some enjoyment; in other words, it is the subjective possibility of excitement of a certain desire preceding the concept of its object. When the enjoyment has been experienced it produces a *Neigung* (inclination) for it, which accordingly is defined "habitual, sensible desire." See below Pp 368 ff.-Ed.]

inestimable value of a genuine good will consists just in the principle of action being free from all contingent causes which experience alone can furnish. We cannot repeat our warning too often against this lax and even low habit of thought which searches empirical motives and laws for principles. Human reason when weary likes to rest on this cushion and in a dream of sweet illusions it substitutes for morality a bastard made up of limbs of quite different origin which appears as anything one chooses to see in it, save as virtue to one who has once beheld her in her true form.[10]

The question then is this: Is it a necessary law *for all rational beings* that they should always judge their actions by maxims which they can will themselves to serve as general laws? If this is so, then this must be related (altogether *a priori*) to the very concept of the will of a rational being. But in order to discover this relationship we must, however

reluctantly, take a step into metaphysics, although into a domain of it distinct from speculative philosophy; namely, into the metaphysic of morals. In practical philosophy, where one is not concerned with the reasons of what *happens* but with the law of what *ought to happen* though it never may, that is, with objective practical laws, we need not inquire into the reasons why anything pleases or displeases, how the pleasure of mere sensation differs from taste, and whether the latter differs from a general rational enjoyment. [There we need not ask] for the grounds of pleasure or pain, how desires and inclinations arise from it, and how through the influence of reason from these in turn arise maxims. All this belongs to an empirical psychology which would constitute the second part of the natural sciences viewed as the *philosophy of nature* so far as it is based on *empirical laws*.

---

10 To behold virtue in her proper form is but to contemplate morality divested of all admixture of sensible things and of every spurious ornament of reward or self-love. To what extent she then eclipses everything else that charms the inclinations one may readily perceive with the feast exertion of his reason, if it be not wholly spoiled for abstraction.

Dignity and Self-Respect

Immanuel Kant
Translated by Louis Enfield

I

By way of introduction it is to be noted that there is no question in moral philosophy which has received more defective treatment than that of the individual's duty towards himself. No one has framed a proper concept of self-regarding duty. It has been regarded as a detail and considered by way of an afterthought, as an appendix to moral philosophy, on the view that man should give a thought to himself only after he has completely fulfilled his duty towards others. . . . It was taken for granted that a man's duty towards himself consisted . . . in promoting his own happiness. In that case everything would depend on how an individual determined his own happiness; for our self-regarding duties would consist in the universal rule to satisfy all our inclinations in order to further our happiness. This would, however, militate seriously against doing our duty towards others. In fact, the principle of self-regarding duties is a very different one, which has no connexion with our well-being or earthly happiness. Far from ranking lowest in the scale of precedence, our duties towards ourselves are of primary importance and should have pride of place; for (deferring for the moment the definition of what constitutes this duty) it is obvious that nothing can be expected from a man who dishonours his own person. He who transgresses against himself loses his manliness and becomes incapable of doing his duty towards his fellows. A man who performed his duty to others badly, who lacked generosity, kindness and sympathy, but who nevertheless did his duty to himself by leading a proper life, might yet possess a certain inner worth; but he who has transgressed his duty towards himself, can have no inner worth whatever. Thus a man who fails in his duty to himself loses worth absolutely; while a man who fails in his duty to others loses worth only relatively. It follows that the prior condition of our duty to others is our duty to ourselves; we can fulfil the former only in so far as we first fulfil the latter. Let us illustrate our meaning by a few examples of failure in one's duty to oneself A drunkard does no harm to another, and if he has a strong constitution he does no harm to himself, yet he is an object of contempt. We are not indifferent to cringing servility; man should not cringe and fawn; by so doing he degrades his person and loses his manhood. If a man for gain or profit submits to all indignities and makes himself the plaything of another, he casts away the worth of his manhood. Again, a lie is more a violation of one's duty to oneself than of one's duty to others. A liar, even though by his lies he does no harm to any one, yet becomes an object of

From *Lectures on Ethics* by Immanuel Kant. Translated by Louis Enfield. Reprinted by permission of Methuen & Company, London.

contempt, he throws away his personality; his behaviour is vile, he has transgressed his duty towards himself. We can carry the argument further and say that to accept favours and benefits is also a breach of one's duty to oneself. If I accept favours, I contract debts which I can never repay, for I can never get on equal terms with him who has conferred the favours upon me; he has stolen a march upon me, and if I do him a favour I am only returning a *quid pro quo*; I shall always owe him a debt of gratitude, and who will accept such a debt? For to be indebted is to be subject to an unending constraint. I must for ever be courteous and flattering towards my benefactor, and if I fail to be so he will very soon make me conscious of my failure; I may even be forced to using subterfuge so as to avoid meeting him. But he who pays promptly for everything is under no constraint; he is free to act as he please; none will hinder him. Again, the faint-hearted who complain about their luck and sigh and weep about their misfortunes are despicable in our eyes; instead of sympathizing with them we do our best to keep away from them. But if a man shows a steadfast courage in his misfortune, and though greatly suffering, does not cringe and complain but puts a bold face upon things, to such a one our sympathy goes out. Moreover, if a man gives up his freedom and barters it away for money, he violates his manhood. Life itself ought not to be rated so highly as to warrant our being prepared, in order only not to lose it, to live otherwise than as a man should, i.e. not a life of ease, but so that we do not degrade our manhood. We must also be worthy of our manhood; whatsoever makes us unworthy of it makes us unfit for anything, and we cease to be men. Moreover, if a man offers his body for profit for the sport of others—if, for instance, he agrees in return for a few pints of beer to be knocked about—he throws himself away, and the perpetrators who pay him for it are acting as vilely as he. Neither can we without destroying our person abandon ourselves to others in order to satisfy their desires, even though it be done to save parents and friends from death; still less can this be done for money. If done in order to satisfy one's own desires, it is very immodest and immoral, but yet not so unnatural; but if it be done for money, or for some other reason, a person allows himself to be treated as a thing, and so throws away the worth of his manhood. It is the same with the vices of the flesh *(crimina carnis)*, which for that reason are not spoken of. They do no damage to anyone, but dishonour and degrade a man's own person; they are an offence against the dignity of manhood in one's own person. The most serious offence against the duty one owes to oneself is suicide. But why should suicide be so abominable? It is no answer to say "because God forbids it." Suicide is not an abomination because God has forbidden it; it is forbidden by God because it is abominable. If it were the other way about, suicide would not be abominable if it were not forbidden; and I should not know why God had forbidden it, if it were not abominable in itself. The ground, therefore, for regarding suicide and other transgressions as abominable and punishable must not be found in the divine will, but in their inherent heinousness. Suicide is an abomination because it implies the abuse of man's freedom of action: he uses his freedom to destroy himself. His freedom should be employed to enable him to live as a man. He is free to dispose as he pleases of things appertaining to his person, but not of his person; he may not use his freedom against himself. For a man to recognize what his duty is towards himself in this respect is far from easy: because although man has indeed a natural horror of suicide, yet we can argue and quibble ourselves into believing that, in order to rid himself of trouble and misery, a man may destroy himself. The argument makes a strong appeal; and in terms of the rule of prudence suicide may often be the surest and best course; none the less suicide is in itself revolting. The rule of morality, which takes precedence of all rules of reflective prudence, commands apodeictically and categorically that we must observe our duties to ourselves; and in committing suicide and reducing himself to a carcass, man uses his powers and his liberty against himself. Man is free to dispose of his condition but not of his person; he himself is an end and not a means; all else in the world is of value only as a means, but man is a person and not a thing and therefore not a means. It is absurd that a reasonable being, an end for the sake of which all else is means, should use himself as a means. It is true that a person can serve as a means for others (e.g. by his work), but only in a way whereby he does not cease to be a person and an end. Whoever acts in such a way that he cannot be an end, uses himself as a means and treats his person as a thing. . . .

The duties we owe to ourselves do not depend on the relation of the action to the ends of happiness. If they did, they would depend on our inclinations and so be governed by rules of prudence. Such rules are not moral, since they indicate only the necessity of the means for the satisfaction of inclinations, and cannot therefore bind us. The basis of such obligation is not to be found in the advantages we reap from doing our duty towards ourselves, but in the worth of manhood. This principle does not allow us an unlimited freedom in respect of our own persons. It insists that we must reverence humanity in our own person, because apart from this man becomes an object of contempt, worthless in the eyes of his fellows and worthless in himself. Such faultiness is absolute. Our duties towards ourselves constitute the supreme condition and the principle of all morality; for moral worth is the worth of the person as such; our capacities have a value only in regard to the circumstances in which we find ourselves. Socrates lived in a state of wretchedness; his circumstances were worthless; but though his circumstances were so ill-conditioned, yet he himself was of the highest value. Even though we sacrifice all life's amenities we can make up for their loss and sustain approval by maintaining the worth of our humanity. We may have lost everything else, and yet still retain our inherent worth. Only if our worth as human beings is intact can we perform our other duties; for it is the foundation stone of all other duties. A man who has destroyed and cast away his personality, has no intrinsic worth, and can no longer perform any manner of duty.

Let us next consider the basis of the principle of all self-regarding duties.

Freedom is, on the one hand, that faculty which gives unlimited usefulness to all other faculties. It is the highest order of life, which serves as the foundation of all perfections and is their necessary condition. All animals have the faculty of using their powers according to will. But this will is not free. It is necessitated through the incitement of *stimuli,* and the actions of animals involve a *bruta necessitas.* If the will of all beings were so bound to sensuous impulse, the world would possess no value. The inherent value of the world, the *summum bonum,* is freedom in accordance with a will which is not necessitated to action. Freedom is thus the inner value of the world. But on the other hand, freedom unrestrained by rules of its conditional employment is the most terrible of all things. The actions of animals are regular; they are performed in accordance with rules which necessitate them subjectively. Mankind apart, nature is not free; through it all there runs a subjectively necessitating principle in accordance with which everything happens regularly. Man alone is free; his actions are not regulated by any such subjectively necessitating principle; if they were, he would not be free. And what then? If the freedom of man were not kept within bounds by objective rules, the result would be the completest savage disorder. There could then be no certainty that man might not use his powers to destroy himself, his fellows, and the whole of nature. I can conceive freedom as the complete absence of orderliness, if it is not subject to an objective determination. The grounds of this objective determination must lie in the understanding, and constitute the restrictions to freedom. Therefore the proper use of freedom is the supreme rule. What then is the condition under which freedom is restricted? It is the law. The universal law is therefore as follows: Let thy procedure be such that in all thine actions regularity prevails. What does this restraint imply when applied to the individual? That he should not follow his inclinations. The fundamental rule, in terms of which I ought to restrain my freedom, is the conformity of free behaviour to the essential ends of humanity. I shall not then follow my inclinations, but bring them under a rule. He who subjects his person to his inclinations, acts contrary to the essential end of humanity; for as a free being he must not be subjected to inclinations, but ought to determine them in the exercise of his freedom; and being a free agent he must have a rule, which is the essential end of humanity. In the case of animals inclinations are already determined by subjectively compelling factors; in their case, therefore, disorderliness is impossible. But if man gives free rein to his inclinations, he sinks lower than an animal because he then lives in a state of disorder which does not exist among animals. A man is then in contradiction with the essential ends of humanity in his own

person, and so with himself. All evil in the world springs from freedom. Animals, not being free, live according to rules. But free beings can only act regularly, if they restrict their freedom by rules. Let us reflect upon the actions of man which refer to himself and consider freedom in them. These spring from impulse and inclinations or from maxims and principles. It is essential, therefore, that man should take his stand upon maxims and restrain by rules the free actions which relate to himself. These are the rules of his self-regarding duties. For if we consider man in respect of his inclinations and instincts, he is loosed from them and determined by neither. In all nature there is nothing to injure man in the satisfaction of his desires; all injurious things are his own invention, the outcome of his freedom. We need only instance strong drink and the many dishes concocted to tickle his palate. In the unregulated pursuit of an inclination of his own devising, man becomes an object of utter contempt, because his freedom makes it possible for him to turn nature inside out in order to satisfy himself. Let him devise what he pleases for satisfying his desires, so long as he regulates the use of his devices; if he does not, his freedom is his greatest misfortune. It must therefore be restricted, though not by other properties or faculties, but by itself. The supreme rule is that in all the actions which affect himself a man should so conduct himself that every exercise of his power is compatible with the fullest employment of them. Let us illustrate our meaning by examples. If I have drunk too much I am incapable of using my freedom and my powers. Again, if I kill myself, I use my powers to deprive myself of the faculty of using them. That freedom, the principle of the highest order of life, should annul itself and abrogate the use of itself conflicts with the fullest use of freedom. But freedom can only be in harmony with itself under certain conditions; otherwise it comes into collision with itself. If there were no established order in Nature, everything would come to an end, and so it is with unbridled freedom. Evils are to be found, no doubt, in Nature, but the true moral evil, vice, only in freedom. We pity the fortunate, but we hate the vicious and rejoice at their punishment. The conditions under which alone the fullest use of freedom is possible, and can be in harmony with itself, are the essential ends of humanity. It must conform with these. The principle of all duties is that the use of freedom must be in keeping with the essential ends of humanity. Thus, for instance, a human being is not entitled to sell his limbs for money, even if he were offered ten thousand thalers for a single finger. If he were so entitled, he could sell all his limbs. We can dispose of things which have no freedom but not of a being which has free will. A man who sells himself makes himself a thing and, as he has jettisoned his person, it is open to anyone to deal with him as he pleases. Another instance of this kind is where a human being makes himself a thing by making himself an object of enjoyment for some one's sexual desire. It degrades humanity, and that is why those guilty of it feel ashamed. We see, therefore, that just as freedom is the source of virtue which ennobles mankind, so is it also the root of the most dreadful vices—such as, for instance, a *crimen carnis contra naturam*, since it can devise all manner of means to satisfy its inclinations. Some crimes and vices, the result of freedom (e.g. suicide), make us shudder, others are nauseating; the mere mention of them is loathsome; we are ashamed of them because they degrade us below the level of beasts; they are grosser even than suicide, for the mention of suicide makes us shudder, but those other crimes and vices cannot be mentioned without producing nausea. Suicide is the most abominable of the vices which inspire dread and hate,

but nausea and contempt indicate a lower level still.

Not self-favour but self-esteem should be the principle of our duties towards ourselves. This means that our actions must be in keeping with the worth of man. There are in us two grounds of action; inclinations, which belong to our animal nature, and humanity, to which the inclinations must be subjected. Our duties to ourselves are negative; they restrict our freedom in respect of our inclinations, which aim at our own welfare. Just as law restricts our freedom in our relations with other men, so do our duties to ourselves restrict our freedom in dealing with ourselves. All such duties are grounded in a certain love of honour consisting in self-esteem; man must not appear unworthy in his own eyes; his actions must be in keeping with humanity itself if he is to appear in his own eyes worthy of inner respect. . . .

II Proper Self-respect

Humility, on the one hand, and true, noble pride on the other, are elements of proper self-respect; shamelessness is its opposite. We have reason to have but a low opinion of ourselves as individuals, but as representatives of mankind we ought to hold ourselves in high esteem. In the light of the law of morality, which is holy and perfect, our defects stand out with glaring distinctness and on comparing ourselves with this standard of perfection we have sufficient cause to feel humble. But if we compare ourselves with others, there is no reason to have a low opinion of ourselves; we have a right to consider ourselves as valuable as another. This self-respect in comparison with others constitutes noble pride. A low opinion of oneself in relation to others is no humility; it is a sign of a little spirit and of a servile character. To flatter oneself that this is virtue is to mistake an imitation for the genuine article; it is monk's virtue and not at all natural; this form of humility is in fact a form of pride. There is nothing unjust or unreasonable in self-esteem; we do no harm to another if we consider ourselves equal to him in our estimation. But if we are to pass judgment upon ourselves we must draw a comparison between ourselves and the purity of the moral law, and we then have cause to feel humble. We should not compare ourselves with other righteous men who, like ourselves, model themselves on the moral law. The Gospel does not teach humility, but it makes us humble.

Our self-esteem may arise from self-love and then it is favour and partiality towards ourselves. This pragmatic self-respect in accordance with rules of prudence is reasonable and possible inasmuch as it keeps us in confidence. No one can demand of me that I should humiliate myself and value myself less than others; but we all have the right to demand of a man that he should not think himself superior. Moral self-esteem, however, which is grounded in the worth of humanity, should not be derived from comparison with others, but from comparison with the moral law. Men are greatly inclined to take others as the measure of their own moral worth, and if they find that there are some whom they surpass it gives them a feeling of moral pride; but it is much more than pride if a man believes himself perfect as measured by the standard of the moral law. I can consider myself better than some others; but it is not very much only to be better than the worst, and there is really not much moral pride in that. Moral humility, regarded as the curbing of our self-conceit in face of the moral law, can thus never rest upon a comparison of ourselves with others, but with the moral law. Humility is therefore the limitation of the high opinion we have of our moral worth by comparison of our actions with the moral law. The comparison of our actions with the moral law makes us humble. Man has reason to have but a low opinion of himself because his actions not only contravene the moral law but are also lacking in purity. His frailty causes him to transgress the law, and his weakness makes his actions fall short of its purity. If an individual takes a lenient view of the moral law, he may well have a high opinion of himself and be conceited, because he judges himself by a false standard. The conceptions which the ancients had of humility and all moral virtues were impure and not in keeping with the moral law. The Gospel first presented morality in its purity, and there is nothing in history to compare with it. But if this humility is wrongly construed, harm may result; for it does not bring courage, but the reverse. Conscious of his shortcomings, a man may feel that his actions can never attain to the level of the moral law and he may give up trying, and simply do nothing. Self-conceit and dejection are the two rocks on which man is wrecked if he deviates, in the one direction or the other, from the moral law. On the one hand, man should not despair, but should believe himself strong enough to follow the moral law, even though he himself is not conformable to it. On the other hand, he ought to avoid self-conceit and an exaggerated notion of his powers; the purity of the moral law should prevent him from falling into this pitfall, for no one who has the law explained to him in its absolute purity can be so foolish as to imagine that it is within his powers fully to comply with it. The existence of this safeguard makes the danger of self-conceit less than that of inertia grounded in faith. It is only the lazy, those who have no wish to do anything themselves but to leave it all to God, who interpret their religion thus. The remedy against such dejection and inertia is to be found in our being able to hope that our weakness and infirmity will be supplemented by the help of God if we but do the utmost that the consciousness of our capacity tells us we are able to do. This is the one and indispensable condition on which we can be worthy of God's help, and have a right to hope for it. In order to convince man of his weakness, make him humble and induce him to pray to God for help, some writers have tried to deny to man any good disposition. This can do no good. It is certainly right and proper that man should recognize how weak he is, but not by the sacrifice of his good dispositions, for if he is to receive God's help he must at least be worthy of it. If we depreciate the value of human virtues we do harm, because if we deny good intentions to the man who lives aright, where is the difference between him and the evil-doer? Each of us feels that at some time or other we have done a good action from a good disposition and that we are capable of doing so again. Though our actions are all very imperfect, and though we can never hope that they will attain to the standard of the moral law, yet they may approach ever nearer and nearer to it.

An Introduction to the Principles of Morals and Legislation

Jeremy Bentham

Chapter I Of the Principle of Utility

I. Nature has placed mankind under the governance of two sovereign masters, *pain* and *pleasure*. It is for them alone to point out what we ought to do, as well as to determine what we shall do. On the one hand the standard of right and wrong, on the other the chain of causes and effects, are fastened to their throne. They govern us in all we do, in all we say, in all we think: every effort we can make to throw off our subjection, will serve but to demonstrate and confirm it. In words a man may pretend to abjure their empire: but in reality he will remain subject to it all the while. The *principle of utility*[1] recognises this subjection, and assumes it for the foundation of that system, the object of which is to rear the fabric of felicity by the hands of reason and of law. Systems which attempt to question it, deal in sounds instead of sense, in caprice instead of reason, in darkness instead of light.

But enough of metaphor and declamation: it is not by such means that moral science is to be improved.

II. The principle of utility is the foundation of the present work: it will be proper therefore at the outset to give an explicit and determinate account of what is meant by it. By the principle[2] of utility is meant that principle which approves or disapproves of

---

1   Note by the Author, July 1822.

To this denomination has of late been added, or substituted, by the *greatest happiness* or *greatest felicity* principle: this for shortness, instead of saying at length *that principle* which states the greatest happiness of all those whose interest is in question, as being the right and proper, and only right and proper and universally desirable, end of human action: of human action in every situation, and in particular in that of a functionary or set of functionaries exercising the powers of Government. The word *utility* does not so clearly point to the ideas of *pleasure* and *pain* as the words *happiness* and *felicity* do: nor does it lead us to the consideration of the *number*, of the interests affected; to the *number*, as being circumstance, which contributes, in the largest proportion, to the formation of the standard here in question; the *standard of right and wrong*, by which alone the propriety of human conduct, in every situation, can with propriety be tried. This want of a sufficiently manifest connexion between the ideas of *happiness* and *pleasure* on the one hand, and the idea of *utility* on the other, I have every now and then found operating, and with but too much efficiency, as a bar to the acceptance, that might otherwise have been given, to this principle.

2   The word principle is derived from the Latin *principium*: which seems to be compounded of the two words *primus*, first, or chief, and *cipium*, a termination which seems to be derived from *capio*, to take, as in *mancipium, municipium;* to which are analogous, *auceps, forceps,* and others. It is a term of very vague and very extensive signification: it is applied to any thing which is conceived to serve as a foundation or beginning to any series of operations: in some cases, of physical operations; but of mental operations in the present case.

The principle here in question may be taken for an act of the mind; a sentiment; a sentiment of approbation; a sentiment which, when applied to an action, approves of its utility, as that quality of it by which the measure of approbation or disapprobation bestowed upon it ought to be governed.

every action whatsoever, according to the tendency which it appears to have to augment or diminish the happiness of the party whose interest is in question: or, what is the same thing in other words, to promote or to oppose that happiness. I say of every action whatsoever; and therefore not only of every action of a private individual, but of every measure of government.

III. By utility is meant that property in any object, whereby it tends to produce benefit, advantage, pleasure, good, or happiness, (all this in the present case comes to the same thing) or (what comes again to the same thing) to prevent the happening of mischief, pain, evil, or unhappiness to the party whose interest is considered: if that party be the community in general, then the happiness of the community: if a particular individual, then the happiness of that individual.

IV. The interest of the community is one of the most general expressions that can occur in the phraseology of morals: no wonder that the meaning of it is often lost. When it has a meaning, it is this. The community is a fictitious *body*, composed of the individual persons who are considered as constituting as it were its *members*. The interest of the community then is, what?—the sum of the interests of the several members who compose it.

V. It is in vain to talk of the interest of the community, without understanding what is the interest of the individual.[3] A thing is said to promote the interest, or to be *for* the interest, of an individual, when it tends to add to the sum total of his pleasures: or, what comes to the same thing, to diminish the sum total of his pain.

VI. An action then may be said to be conformable to the principle of utility, or, for shortness sake, to utility, (meaning with respect to the community at large) when the tendency it has to augment the happiness of the community is greater than any it has to diminish it.

VII. A measure of government (which is but a particular kind of action, performed by a particular person or persons) may be said to be conformable to or dictated by the principle of utility, when in like manner the tendency which it has to augment the happiness of the community is greater than any which it has to diminish it.

VIII. When an action, or in particular a measure of government, is supposed by a man to be conformable to the principle of utility, it may be convenient, for the purposes of discourse, to imagine a kind of law or dictate, called a law or dictate of utility: and to speak of the action in question, as being conformable to such law or dictate.

IX. A man may be said to be a partizan of the principle of utility, when the approbation or disapprobation he annexes to any action, or to any measure, is determined by and proportioned to the tendency which he conceives it to have to augment or to diminish the happiness of the community: or in other words, to its conformity or unconformity to the laws or dictates of utility.

X. Of an action that is conformable to the principle of utility one may always say either that it is one that ought to be done, or at least that it is not one that ought not to be done. One may say also, that it is right it should be done; at least that it is not wrong it should be done; that it is a right action; at least that it is not a wrong action. When thus interpreted, the words *ought*, and *right* and *wrong*, and others of that stamp, have a meaning: when otherwise, they have none.

XI. Has the rectitude of this principle been ever formally contested? It should seem that it had, by those who have not known

---

3   Interest is one of those words, which not having any superior *genus*, cannot in the ordinary way be defined.

what they have been meaning. Is it susceptible of any direct proof? it should seem not: for that which is used to prove every thing else, cannot itself be proved: a chain of proofs must have their commencement somewhere. To give such proof is as impossible as · it is needless.

XII. Not that there is or ever has been that human creature breathing, however stupid or perverse, who has not on many, perhaps on most occasions of his life, deferred to it. By the natural constitution of the human frame, on most occasions of their lives men in general embrace this principle, without thinking of it: if not for the ordering of their own actions, yet for the trying of their own actions, as well as of those of other men. There have been, at the same time, not many, perhaps, even of

the most intelligent, who have been disposed to embrace it purely and without reserve. There are even few who have not taken some occasion or other to quarrel with it, either on account of their not understanding always how to apply it, or on account of some prejudice or other which they were afraid to examine into, or could not bear to part with. For such is the stuff that man is made of: in principle and in practice, in a right track and in a wrong one, the rarest of all human qualities is consistency.

XIII. When a man attempts to combat the principle of utility, it is with reasons drawn, without his being aware of it, from that very principle itself.[4] His arguments, if they prove any thing, prove not that the principle is *wrong*, but that, according to the applications he supposes to be made of it, it is *misapplied*.

---

4 'The principle of utility, (I have heard it said) is a dangerous principle: it is dangerous on certain occasions to consult it.' This is as much as to say, what? that it is not consonant to utility, to consult utility: in short, that it is *not* consulting it, to consult it.
Addition by the Author, July 1822.
Not long after the publication of the Fragment on Government, anno 1776, in which, in the character of an all-comprehensive and all-commanding principle, the principle of *utility* was brought to view, one person by whom observation to the above effect was made was *Alexander Wedderburn*, at that time Attorney or Solicitor General, afterwards successively Chief Justice of the Common Pleas, and Chancellor of England, under the successive titles of Lord Loughborough and Earl of Rosslyn. It was made—not indeed in my hearing, but in the hearing of a person by whom it was almost immediately communicated to me. So far from being self-contradictory, it was a shrewd and perfectly true one. By that distinguished functionary, the state of the Government was thoroughly understood: by the obscure individual, at that time not so much as supposed to be so: his disquisitions had not been as yet applied, with any thing like a comprehensive view, to the field of Constitutional Law, now therefore to those features of the English Government, by which the greatest happiness of the ruling *one* with or without that of a favoured few, are now so plainly seen to be the only ends to which the course of it has at any time been directed. The *principle of utility* was an appellative, at that time employed—employed by me, as it had been by others, to design that which, in a more perspicuous and instructive manner, may as above be designated by the name of the *greatest happiness principle*. "This principle (said Wedderburn) is a dangerous one." Saying so, he said that which, to a certain extent, is strictly true: a principle, which lays down, as the only *right* and justifiable end of Government, the greatest happiness of the greatest number—how can it be denied to be a dangerous one? dangerous it unquestionably is, to every government which has for its *actual* end or object, the greatest happiness of a certain *one*, with or without the addition of some comparatively small number of others, whom it is matter of pleasure or accommodation to him to admit, each of them, to a share in the concern, on the footing of so many junior partners. *Dangerous* it therefore really was, to the interest—the sinister interest—of all of those functionaries himself included, whose interest it was, to maximize delay, vexation, and expense, in judicial and other modes of procedure, for the sake of the profit, extractible out of the expense. In a Government which had for its end in view the greatest happiness of the greatest number. Alexander Weddberburn might have been Attorney General and then Chancellor: but he would not have been Attorney General with £15,000 a year, nor Chancellor, with a peerage with a veto upon all justice, with £25,000 a year, and with 500 sinecures at his disposal, under the name of Ecclesiastical Benefices, besides *et coeteras*.

Is it possible for a man to move the earth? Yes; but he must first find out another earth to stand upon.

XIV. To disprove the propriety of it by arguments is impossible; but, from the causes that have been mentioned, or from some confused or partial view of it, a man may happen to be disposed not to relish it. Where this is the case, if he thinks the settling of his opinions on such a subject worth the trouble, let him take the following steps, and, at length, perhaps, he may come to reconcile himself to it.

1. Let him settle with himself, whether he would wish to discard this principle altogether; if so, let him consider what it is that all his reasonings (in matters of politics especially) can amount to?
2. If he would, let him settle with himself, whether he would judge and act without any principle, or whether there is any other he would judge and act by?
3. If there be, let him examine and satisfy himself whether the principle he thinks he has found is really any separate intelligible principle; or whether it be not a mere principle in words, a kind of phrase, which at bottom expresses neither more nor less than the mere averment of his own unfounded sentiments; that is, what in another person he might be apt to call caprice?
4. If he is inclined to think that his own approbation or disapprobation, annexed to the idea of an act, without any regard to its consequences, is a sufficient foundation for him to judge and act upon, let him ask himself whether his sentiment is to be a standard of right and wrong, with respect to every other man, or whether every man's sentiment has the same privilege of being a standard to itself?
5. In the first case, let him ask himself whether his principle is not despotical, and hostile to all the rest of human race?
6. In the second case, whether it is not anarchial, and whether at this rate there are not as many different standards of right and wrong as there are men? and whether even to the same man, the same thing, which is right today, may not (without the least change in its nature) be wrong tomorrow? and whether the same thing is not right and wrong in the same place at the same time? and in either case, whether all argument is not at an end? and whether, when two men have said, 'I like this,' and 'I don't like it,' they can (upon such a principle) have any thing more to say?
7. If he should have said to himself, No: for that the sentiment which he proposes as a standard must be grounded on reflection, let him say on what particulars the reflection is to turn? if on particulars having relation to the utility of the act, then let him say whether this is not deserting his own principle, and borrowing assistance from that very one in opposition to which he sets it up: or if not on those particulars, on what other particulars?
8. If he should be for compounding the matter, and adopting his own principle in part, and the principle of utility in part, let him say how far he will adapt it?
9. When he has settled with himself where he will stop, then let him ask himself how he justifies to himself the adopting it so far? and why he will not adopt it any farther?
10. Admitting any other principle than the principle of utility to be a right principle, a principle that it is right for a man to pursue; admitting (what is not true) that the word *right* can have a meaning without reference to utility, let him say

whether there is any such thing as a *motive* that man can have to pursue the dictates of it: if there is, let him say what that motive is, and how it is to be distinguished from those which enforce the dictates of utility: if not, then lastly let him say what it is this other principle can be good for?

Chapter IV Value of a Lot of Pleasure or Pain, How to be Measured

I. Pleasures then, and the avoidance of pains, are the *ends* which the legislator has in view: it behoves him therefore to understand their *value*. Pleasures and pains are the *instruments* he has to work with: it behoves him therefore to understand their force, which is again, in other words, their value.

II. To a person considered *by himself,* the value of a pleasure or pain considered *by itself,* will be greater or less, according to the four following circumstances:[5]

1. *Its intensity.*
2. Its *duration.*
3. Its *certainty or uncertainty.*
4. Its *propinquity or remoteness.*

III. These are the circumstances which are to be considered in estimating a pleasure or a pain considered each of them by itself. But when the value of any pleasure or pain is considered for the purpose of estimating the tendency of any *act* by which it is produced, there are two other circumstances to be taken into the account; these are,

5. Its *fecundity,* or the chance it has of being followed by sensations of the *same* kind: that is, pleasures, if it be a pleasure: pains, if it be a pain.
6. Its *purity,* or the chance it has of *not* being followed by sensations of the *opposite* kind: that is, pains, if it be a pleasure: pleasures, if it be a pain.

These two last, however, are in strictness scarcely to be deemed properties of pleasure or the pain itself; they are not, therefore, in strictness to be taken into the account of the value of that pleasure or pain. They are in strictness to be deemed properties only of the act, or other. event, by which such pleasure or pain has been produced; and accordingly are only to be taken into the account of the tendency of such act or such event.

IV. To a *number* of persons, with reference to each of whom the value of a pleasure or a pain is considered, it will be greater or less, according to seven circumstances: to wit, the six preceding ones; *viz.*

1. Its *intensity.*
2. Its *duration.*
3. Its *certainty* or *uncertainty.*
4. Its *propinquity* or *remoteness.*
5. Its *fecundity.*
6. Its *purity.*

---

5   These circumstances have since been denominated *elements* or *dimensions* of *value* in a pleasure or a pain. Not long after the publication of the first edition, the following memoriter verses were framed, in the view of lodging more effectually, in the memory, these points, on which the whole fabric of morals and legislation may be seen to rest.
Intense, long, certain, speedy, fruitful, pure—
Such marks in *pleasure* and in *pains* endure.
Such pleasures seek of *private* be thy end:
If it be *public,* wide let them *extend.*
Such *pains* avoid, whichever be thy view:
If pains *must* come, let them *extend* to few.

And one other; to wit:

7. Its *extent*; that is, the number of persons to whom it *extends*; or (in other words) who are affected by it.

V. To take an exact account then of the general tendency of any act, by which the interests of a community are affected, proceed as follows. Begin with any one person of those whose interests seem most immediately to be affected by it: and take an account,

1. Of the value of each distinguishable *pleasure* which appears to be produced by it in the *first* instance.
2. Of the value of each *pain* which appears to be produced by it in the *first* instance.
3. Of the value of each pleasure which appears to be produced by it *after* the first. This constitutes the *fecundity* of the first *pleasure* and the *impurity* of the first *pain*.
4. Of the value of each *pain* which appears to be produced by it after the first. This constitutes the *fecundity* of the first *pain*, and the *impurity* of the first pleasure.
5. Sum up all the values of all the *pleasures* on the one side, and those of all the pains on the other. The balance, if it be on the side of pleasure, will give the *good* tendency of the act upon the whole, with respect to the interests of that *individual* person; if on the side of pain, the *bad* tendency of it upon the whole.
6. Take an account of the *number* of persons whose interests appear to be concerned; and repeat the above process with respect to each. *Sum up* the numbers expressive of the degrees of *good* tendency, which the act has, with respect to each individual, in regard to whom the tendency of it is *good* upon the whole: do this again with respect to each individual, in regard to whom the tendency of it is *good* upon the whole: do this again

with respect to each individual, in regard to whom the tendency of it is *bad* upon the whole. Take the *balance*; which, if on the side of *pleasure*, will give the general *good tendency* of the act, with respect to the total number or community of individuals concerned; if on the side of pain, the general *evil tendency*, with respect to the same community.

VI. It is not to be expected that this process should be strictly pursued previously to every moral judgment, or to every legislative or judicial operation. It may, however, be always kept in view: and as near as the process actually pursued on these occasions approaches to it, so near will such process approach to the character of an exact one.

VII. The same process is alike applicable to pleasure and pain, in whatever shape they appear: and by whatever denomination they are distinguished: to pleasure, whether it be called *good* (which is properly the cause or instrument of pleasure) or *profit* (which is distant pleasure, or the cause or instrument of distant pleasure,) or *convenience*, or *advantage*, *benefit*, *emolument*, *happiness*, and so forth: to pain, whether it be called *evil*, (which corresponds to *good)* or *mischief*, or *inconvenience*, or *disadvantage*, or *loss*, or *unhappiness*, and so forth.

VIII. Nor is this a novel and unwarranted, any more than it is a useless theory. In all this there is nothing but what the practice of mankind, wheresoever they have a clear view of their own interest, is perfectly conformable to. An article of property, an estate in land, for instance, is valuable. on what account? On account of the pleasures of all kinds which it enables a man to produce, and what comes to the same thing the pains of all kinds which it enables him to avert. But the value of such an article of property is universally understood to rise or fall according to the length or shortness of the time which a man has in it: the certainty or uncertainty of its coming into possession: and the nearness or remoteness of the time at which, if at all, it is to come into possession. As to the *intensity* of the pleasures which a man may derive from it, this is never thought of, because it depends upon the use which each particular person may come to make of it; which cannot be estimated till the particular pleasures he may come to derive from it, or the particular pains he may come to exclude by means of it, are brought to view. For the same reason, neither does he think of the *fecundity* or *purity* of those pleasures.

Thus much for pleasure and pain, happiness and unhappiness, in *general*. We come now to consider the several particular kinds of pain and pleasure.

Chapter VII Of Human Actions in General

I. The business of government is to promote the happiness of the society, by punishing and rewarding. That part of its business which consists in punishing, is more particularly the subject of penal law. In proportion as an act tends to disturb that happiness, in proportion as the tendency of it is pernicious, will be the demand it creates for punishment. What happiness consists of we have already seen: enjoyment of pleasures, security from pains.

II. The general tendency of an act is more or less pernicious. according to the sum total of its consequences: that is, according to the difference between the sum of such as are good, and the sum of such as are evil.

III. It is to be observed, that here, as well as henceforward, wherever consequences are spoken of, such only are meant as are *material*. Of the consequences of any act, the multitude and variety must needs be infinite: but such of them only as are material are worth regarding. Now among the consequences of an act, be they what they may, such only, by one who views them in the capacity of a legislator, can be said to be material,[6] as either consist of pain or pleasure, or have an influence in the production of pain or pleasure.[7]

IV. It is also to be observed, that into the account of the consequences of the act, are to be taken not such only as might have ensued, were intention out of the question, but such also as depend upon the connexion there may be between these first-mentioned consequences and the intention. The connexion there is between the intention and certain consequences is, as we shall see hereafter, a means of producing other consequences. In this lies the difference between rational agency and irrational.

V. Now the intention, with regard to the consequences of an act, will depend upon two things: 1. The state of the will or intention, with respect to the act itself. And, 2. The state of the understanding, or perceptive faculties, with regard to the circumstances which it is, or may appear to be, accompanied with. Now with respect to these circumstances, the perceptive faculty is susceptible of three states: consciousness, unconsciousness, and false consciousness. Consciousness, when the party believes precisely those circumstances, and others, to subsist. which really do subsist: unconsciousness, when he

---

6 Or of *importance*.

7 In certain cases the consequences of an act may be material by serving as evidences indicating the existence of some other material fact, which is even *antecedent* to the act of which they are the consequences: but even here, they are material only because, in virtue such their evidentiary quality, they have an influence, at a subsequent period of time, in the production of pain and pleasure: for example, by serving as grounds for conviction and thence for punishment. See tit. [Simple Falsehoods], *verbo* [material].

fails of perceiving certain circumstances to subsist, which, however, do subsist: false consciousness, when he believes or imagines certain circumstances to subsist, which in truth do not subsist.

VI. In every transaction, therefore, which is examined with a view to punishment, there are four articles to be considered: 1. The *act* itself, which is done. 2. *The circumstances* in which it is done. 3. The *intentionality* that may have accompanied it. 4. The *consciousness*, unconsciousness, or false consciousness, that may have accompanied it.

What regards the act and the circumstances will be the subject of the present chapter: what regards intention and consciousness, that of the two succeeding.

VII. There are also two other articles on which the general tendency of an act depends: and on that, as well as on other accounts, the demand which it creates for punishment. These are, 1. The particular *motive* or motives which gave birth to it. 2. The general *disposition* which it indicates. These articles will be the subject of two other chapters.

VIII. Acts may be distinguished in several ways, for several purposes.

They may be distinguished, in the first place, into *positive and negative*. By positive are meant such as consist in motion or exertion: by negative, such as consist in keeping at rest; that is, in forbearing to move or exert

one's self in such and such circumstances. Thus, to strike is a positive act: not to strike on a certain occasion, a negative one. Positive acts are styled also acts of commission; negative, acts of omission or forbearance.[8]

IX. Such acts, again, as are negative, may either be *absolutely* so, or *relatively*: absolutely, when they import the negation of all positive agency whatsoever; for instance, not to strike at all: relatively, when they import the negation of such or such a particular mode of agency; for instance, not to strike such a person or such a thing, or in such a direction.

X. It is to be observed, that the nature of the act, whether positive or negative, is not to be determined immediately by the form of the discourse made use of to express it. An act which is positive in its nature may be characterized by a negative expression: thus, not to be at rest, is as much as to say to move. So also an act, which is negative in its nature, may be characterized by a positive expression: thus, to forbear or omit to bring food to a person in certain circumstances, is signified by the single and positive term *to starve*.

XI. In the second place, acts may be distinguished into *external and internal*. By external, are meant corporal acts; acts of the body; by internal, mental acts; acts of the mind. Thus, to strike is an external or exterior[9] act: to intend to strike, an internal or interior one.

---

8   The distinction between positive and negative acts runs through the whole system of offences, and sometimes makes a material difference with regard to their consequences. To reconcile us the better to the extensive, and, as it may appear on some occasions, the inconsistent signification here given to the word *act*, it may be considered, 1. That in many cases where no exterior or overt act is exercised, the state which the mind is in at the time when the supposed act is said to happen, is as truly and directly the result of the will, as any exterior act, how plain and conspicuous soever. The not revealing a conspiracy, for instance, may be as perfectly the act of the will, as the joining in it. In the next place, that even though the mind should never have had the incident in question in contemplation (insomuch that the event of its not happening should not have been so much as obliquely intentional) still the state the person's mind was in at the time when, if he *had* so willed, the incident might have happened, is in many cases productive of as material consequences; and not only as likely, but as fit to call for the interposition of other agents, as the opposite one. Thus, when a tax is imposed, your not paying it is an act which at any rate must be punished in a certain manner, whether you happened to think of paying it or not.

9   An exterior act is also called by lawyers *overt*.

What Utilitarianism Is

John Stuart Mill

A passing remark is all that needs be given to the ignorant blunder of supposing that those who stand up for utility as the test of right and wrong use the term in that restricted and merely colloquial sense in which utility is opposed to pleasure. An apology is due to the philosophical opponents of utilitarianism for even the momentary appearance of confounding them with anyone capable of so absurd a misconception; which is the more extraordinary, inasmuch as the contrary accusation, of referring everything to pleasure, and that, too, in its grossest form, is another of the common charges against utilitarianism; and, as has been pointedly remarked by an able writer, the same sort of persons, and often the very same person, denounce the theory "as impracticably dry when the word 'utility' precedes the word 'pleasure,' and as too practically voluptuous when the word 'pleasure' precedes the word 'utility'." Those who know anything about the matter are aware that every writer, from Epicurus to Bentham, who maintained the theory of utility meant by it, not something to be contradistinguished from pleasure, but pleasure itself, together with exemption from pain; and instead of opposing the useful to the agreeable or the ornamental, have always declared that the useful means these, among other things. Yet the common herd, including the herd of writers, not only in newspapers and periodicals, but in books of weight and pretension, are perpetually falling into this shallow mistake. Having caught up the word "utilitarian," while knowing nothing whatever about it but its sound, they habitually express by it the rejection or the neglect of pleasure in some of its forms; of beauty, of ornament, or of amusement. Nor is the term thus ignorantly misapplied solely in disparagement, but occasionally in compliment, as though it implied superiority to frivolity and the mere pleasures of the moment. And this perverted use is the only one in which the word is popularly known, and the one from which the new generation are acquiring their sole notion of its meaning. Those who introduced the word, but who had for many years discontinued it as a distinctive appellation, may well feel themselves called upon to resume it if by doing so they can hope to contribute anything toward rescuing it from this utter degradation.[1]

The creed which accepts as the foundation of morals "utility" or the "greatest Hap-

---

1   The author of this essay has reason for believing himself to be the first person who brought the word "utilitarian" into use. He did not invent it, but adopted it from a passing expression in Mr. Galt's *Annals of the Parish*. [John Galt (1779-1839) was a Scottish novelist.] After using it as a designation for several years, he and others abandoned it from a growing dislike to anything resembling a badge or watchword of sectarian distinction. But as a name for one single opinion, not a set of opinions—to denote the recognition of utility as a standard, not any particular way of applying it—the term supplies a want in the language, and offers, in many cases, a convenient mode of avoiding tiresome circumlocutions.

piness principle" holds that actions are right in proportion as they tend to promote happiness; wrong as they tend to produce the reverse of happiness. By happiness is intended pleasure and the absence of pain; by unhappiness, pain and the privation of pleasure. To give a clear view of the moral standard set up by the theory, much more requires to be said; in particular, what things it includes in the ideas of pain and pleasure, and to what extent this is left an open question. But these supplementary explanations do not affect the theory of life on which this theory of morality is grounded—namely, that pleasure and freedom from pain are the only things desirable as ends; and that all desirable things (which are as numerous in the utilitarian as in any other scheme) are desirable either for pleasure inherent in themselves or as means to the promotion of pleasure and the prevention of pain.

Now such a theory of life excites in many minds, and among them in some of the most estimable in feeling and purpose, inveterate dislike. To suppose that life has (as they express it) no higher end than pleasure—no better and nobler object of desire and pursuit—they designate as utterly mean and groveling, as a doctrine worthy only of swine, to whom the followers of Epicurus were, at a very early period, contemptuously likened; and modern holders of the doctrine are occasionally made the subject of equally polite comparisons by its German, French, and English assailants.

When thus attacked, the Epicureans have always answered that it is not they, but their accusers, who represent human nature in a degrading light, since the accusation supposes human beings to be capable of no pleasures except those of which swine are capable. If this supposition were true, the charge could not be gainsaid, but would then be no longer an imputation; for if the sources of pleasure were precisely the same to hu-

man beings and to swine, the rule of life which is good enough for the one would be good enough for the other. The comparison of the Epicurean life to that of beasts is felt as degrading, precisely because a beast's pleasures do not satisfy a human being's conceptions of happiness. Human beings have faculties more elevated than the animal appetites and, when once made conscious of them, do not regard anything as happiness which does not include their gratification. I do not indeed, consider the Epicureans to have been by any means faultless in drawing out their scheme of consequences from the utilitarian principle. To do this in any sufficient manner, many Stoic, as well as Christian, elements require to be included. But there is no known Epicurean theory of life which does not assign to the pleasures of the intellect, of the feelings and imagination, and of the moral sentiments a much higher value as pleasures than to those of mere sensation. It must be admitted, however, that utilitarian writers in general have placed the superiority of mental over bodily pleasures chiefly in the greater permanency, safety, uncostliness, etc., of the former—that is, in their circumstantial advantages rather than in their intrinsic nature. And on all these points utilitarians have fully proved their case; but they might have taken the other and, as it may be called, higher ground with entire consistency. It is quite compatible with the principle of utility to recognize the fact that some kinds of pleasure are more desirable and more valuable than others. It would be absurd that, while in estimating all other things quality is considered as well as quantity, the estimation of pleasure should be supposed to depend on quantity alone.

If I am asked what I mean by difference of quality in pleasure,, or what makes one pleasure more valuable than another, merely as a pleasure, except its being greater in amount, there is but one possible answer. Of two pleasures, if there be one to which all or almost all who have experience of both give a decided preference, irrespective of any feeling of moral obligation to prefer it, that is the more desirable pleasure. If one of the two is, by those who are competently acquainted with both, placed so far above the other that they prefer it, even though knowing it to be attended with a greater amount of discontent, and would not resign it for any quantity of the other pleasure which their nature is capable of, we are justified in ascribing to the preferred enjoyment a superiority in quality so far outweighing quantity as to render it, in comparison, of small account.

Now it is an unquestionable fact that those who are equally acquainted with and equally capable of appreciating and enjoying both do give a most marked preference to the manner of existence which employs their higher faculties. Few human creatures would consent to be changed into any of the lower animals for a promise of the fullest allowance of a beast's pleasures; no intelligent human being would consent to be a fool, no instructed person would be an ignoramus, no person of feeling and conscious would be selfish and base, even though they should be persuaded that the fool, the dunce, or the rascal is better satisfied with his lot than they are with theirs. They would not resign what they possess more than he for the most complete satisfaction of all the desires which they have in common with him. If they ever fancy they would, it is only in cases of unhappiness so extreme that to escape from it they would exchange their lot for almost any other, however undesirable in their own eyes. A being of higher faculties requires more to make him happy, is capable probably of more acute suffering, and certainly accessible to it at more points, than one of an inferior type; but in spite of these liabilities, he can never really wish to sink into what he feels to be a lower grade of existence. We may give what explanation we please of this unwillingness; we may attribute it to pride, a name which is given indiscriminately to some of the most and to some of the least estimable feelings of which mankind are capable; we may refer it to the love of liberty and personal independence, an appeal to which was with the Stoics one of the most effective means for the inculcation of it; to the love of power or to the love of excitement, both of which do really enter into and contribute to it; but its most appropriate appellation is a sense of dignity, which all human beings possess in one form or other, and in some, though by no means in exact proportion to their higher faculties, and which is so essential a part of the happiness of those in whom it is strong that nothing which conflicts with it could be otherwise than momentarily an object of desire to them. Whoever supposes that this preference takes place at a sacrifice of happiness—that the superior being, in anything like equal circumstances, is not happier than the inferior—confounds the two very different ideas of happiness and content. It is indisputable that the being whose capacities of enjoyment are low has the greatest chance of having them fully satisfied; and a highly endowed being will always feel that any happiness which he can look for, as the world is constituted, is imperfect. But he can learn to bear it imperfections, if they are at all bearable; and they will not make him envy the being who is indeed unconscious of the imperfections, but only because he feels not at all the good which those imperfections qualify. It is better to be a human being dissatisfied than a pig satisfied; better to be Socrates dissatisfied than a fool satisfied. And if the fool, or the pig, are of a different opinion, it is because they only know their own side of the question. The other party to the comparison knows both sides.

It may be objected that many who are capable of the higher pleasures occasionally, under the influence of temptation, postpone them to the lower. But this is quite compatible with a full appreciation of the intrinsic superiority of the higher. Men often, from infirmity of character, make their election for the nearer good, though they know it to be the less valuable; and this no less when the choice is between two bodily pleasures than when it is between bodily and mental. They pursue sensual indulgences to the injury of health, though perfectly aware that health is the greater good. It may be further objected that many who begin with youthful enthusiasm for everything noble, as they advance in years, sink into indolence and selfishness. But I do not believe that those who undergo this very common change voluntarily choose the lower description of pleasures in preference to the higher. I believe that, before they devote themselves exclusively to the one, they have already become incapable of the other. Capacity for the nobler feelings is in most natures a very tender plant, easily killed, not only by hostile influences, but by mere want of sustenance; and in the majority of young persons it speedily dies away if the occupations to which their position in life has devoted them, and the society into which it has thrown them, are not favorable to keeping that higher capacity in exercise. Men lose their high aspirations as they lose their intellectual tastes, because they have not time or opportunity for indulging them; and they addict themselves to inferior pleasures, not because they deliberately prefer them, but because they are either the only ones to which they have access or the only ones which they are any longer capable of enjoying. It may be questioned whether anyone who has remained equally susceptible to both classes of pleas-

ures ever knowingly and calmly preferred the lower, though many, in all ages, have broken down in an ineffectual attempt to combineboth.

From this verdict of the only competent judges, I apprehend there can be not appeal. On a question which is the best worth having of two pleasures, or which of two modes of existence is the most grateful to the feelings, apart from its moral attributes and from its consequences, the judgment of those who are qualified by knowledge of both, or, if they differ, that of the majority among them, must be admitted as final. And there needs be the less hesitation to accept this judgment respecting the quality of pleasure, since there is no other tribunal to be referred to even on the question of quantity. What means are there of determining which is the acutest of two pains, or the intensest of two pleasurable sensations, except the general suffrage of those who are familiar with both? Neither pains nor pleasures are homogeneous, and pain is always heterogeneous with pleasure. What is there to decide whether a particular pleasure is worth purchasing at the cost of a particular pain, except the feelings and judgment of the experienced? When, therefore, those feelings and judgment declare the pleasures derived from the higher faculties to be preferable *in kind*, apart from the question of intensity, to those of which the animal nature, disjoined from the higher faculties, is susceptible, they are entitled on this subject to the same regard.

I have dwelt on this point as being a necessary part of a perfectly just conception of utility or happiness considered as the directive rule of human conduct. But it is by no means an indispensable condition to the acceptance of the utilitarian standard; for that standard is not the agent's own greatest happiness, but the greatest amount of happiness altogether; and if it may possibly be doubted whether a noble character is always the happier for its nobleness, there can be no doubt that it makes other people happier, and that the world in general is immensely a gainer by it. Utilitarianism, therefore, could only attain its end by the general cultivation of nobleness of character, even if each individual were only benefited by the nobleness of others, and his own so far as happiness is concerned, were a sheer deduction from the benefit. But the bare enunciation of such an absurdity as this last renders refutation superfluous.

According to the greatest happiness principle, as above explained, the ultimate end, with reference to and for the sake of which all other things are desirable—whether we are considering our own good or that of other people—is an existence exempt as far as possible from pain, and as rich as possible in enjoyments, both in point of quantity and quality; the test of quality and the rule for measuring it against quantity being the preference felt by those who, in their opportunities of experience, to which must be added their habits of self-consciousness and self-observation, are best furnished with the means of comparison. This, being according to the utilitarian opinion the end of human action, is necessarily also the standard of morality, which may accordingly be defined "the rules and precepts for human conduct," by the observance of which an existence such as had been described might be, to the greatest extent possible, secured to all mankind; and not to them only, but, so far as the nature of things admits, to the whole sentient creation.

Against this doctrine, however, arises another class of objectors who say that happiness, in any form, cannot be the rational purpose of human life and action; because, in the first place, it is unattainable; and they contemptuously ask, What right hast thou to be happy?—a question which Mr. Carlyle [2] clinches by the addition, What right, a short time ago, hadst thou even *to be*? Next they say that men can do *without* happiness; that all noble human beings have felt this, and could not have become noble but by learning the lesson of *Entsagen*, or renunciation; which lessens, thoroughly learned and submitted to, they affirm to be the beginning and necessary condition of all virtue.

The first of these objections would go to the root of the matter were it well founded; for if no happiness is to be had at all by human beings, the attainment of it cannot be the end of morality or of any rational conduct. Though, even in that case, something might still be said for the utilitarian theory, since utility includes not solely the pursuit of happiness, but the prevention or mitigation of unhappiness; and if the former aim be chimerical, there will be all the greater scope and more imperative need for the latter, so long at least as mankind think fit to live and do not take refuge in the simultaneous act of suicide recommended under certain conditions by Novalis. [3] When, however, it is thus positively asserted to be impossible that human life should be happy, the assertion, if not something like a verbal quibble, is at least an exaggeration. If by happiness be meant a continuity of highly pleasurable excitement, it is evident enough that this is impossible. A state of exalted pleasure lasts only moments or in some cases, and with some intermissions, hours or days, and is the occasional brilliant flash of enjoyment, not its permanent and steady flame. Of this the philosophers who have taught that happiness is the end of life were as fully aware as those who taunt them. This happiness which they meant was not a life of rapture, but

---

2 {Thomas Carlyle (1795-1881) was a Scottish author and social critic who wrote a multivolume history of the French Revolution. His theistic view stressed the essential spirituality of the world and its leaders.}

3 {Pseudonym of Friedrich Leopold Freiherr von Hardenberg (1771-1801), a German romantic poet.}

moments of such, in an existence made up of few and transitory pains, many and various pleasures, with a decided predominance of the active over the passive, and having as the foundation of the whole not to expect more from life than it is capable of bestowing. A life thus composed, to those who have been fortunate enough to obtain it, has always appeared worthy of the name of happiness. And such an existence is even now the lot of many during some considerable portion of their lives. The present wretched education and wretched social arrangements are the only real hindrance to its being attainable by almost all.

The objectors perhaps may doubt whether human beings, if taught to consider happiness as the end of life, would be satisfied with such a moderate share of it. But great numbers of mankind have been satisfied with much less. The main constituents of a satisfied life appear to be two, either of which by itself is often found sufficient for the purpose: tranquillity and excitement. With much tranquillity, many find that they can be content with very little pleasure; with much excitement, many can reconcile themselves to a considerable quantity of pain. There is assuredly no inherent impossibility of enabling even the mass of mankind to unite both, since the two are so far from being incompatible that they are in natural alliance, the prolongation of either being a preparation for, and exciting a wish for, the other. It is only those in whom indolence amounts to a vice that do not desire excitement after an interval of respose; it is only those in whom the need of excitement is a disease that feel the tranquillity which follows excitement dull and insipid, instead of pleasurable in direct proportion to the excitement which preceded it. When people who are tolerably fortunate in their outward lot do not find in life sufficient enjoyment to make it valuable to them, the cause generally

is caring for nobody but themselves. To those who have neither public nor private affections, the excitements of life are much curtailed, and in any case dwindle in value as the time approaches when all selfish interests must be terminated by death; while those who leave after them objects of personal affection, and especially those who have also cultivated a fellow-feeling with the collective interests of mankind, retain as lively an interest in life on the eve of death as in the vigor of youth and health. Next to selfishness, the principal cause which makes life unsatisfactory is want of mental cultivation. A cultivated mind—I do not mean that of a philosopher, but any mind to which the fountains of knowledge have been opened, and which has been taught, in any tolerable degree, to exercise its faculties—finds sources of inexhaustible interest in all that surrounds it; in the objects of nature, the achievements of art, the imaginations of poetry, the incidents of history, the ways of mankind, past and present, and their prospects in the future. It is possible, indeed, to become indifferent to all this, and that too without having exhausted a thousandth part of it, but only when one has had from the beginning no moral or human interest in these things and has sought in them only the gratification of curiosity.

Now there is absolutely no reason in the nature of things why an amount of mental culture sufficient to give an intelligent interest in these objects of contemplation should not be the inheritance of everyone born in a civilized country. As little is there an inherent necessity that any human being should be a selfish egotist, devoid of every feeling or care but those which center in his own miserable individuality. Something far superior to this is sufficiently common even now, to give ample earnest of what the human species may be made. Genuine private affections and a sincere interest in the public good are possible, though in unequal degrees, to every rightly brought up human being. In a world in which there is so much to interest, so much to enjoy, and so much also to correct and improve, everyone who has this moderate amount of moral and intellectual requisites is capable of an existence which may be called enviable; and unless such a person, through bad laws or subjection to the will of others, is denied the liberty to use the sources of happiness within his reach, he will not fail to find this enviable existence, if he escapes the positive evils of life, the great sources of physical and mental suffering—such as indigence, disease, and the unkindness, worthlessness, or premature loss of objects of affection. The main stress of the problem lies, therefore, in the contest with these calamities from which it is a rare good fortune entirely to escape; which, as things now are, cannot be obviated, and often cannot be in any material degree mitigated. Yet no one whose opinion deserves a moment's consideration can doubt that most of the great positive evils of the world are in themselves removable, and will, if human affairs continue to improve, be in the end reduced within narrow limits. Poverty, in any sense implying suffering, may be completely extinguished by the wisdom of society combined with the good sense and providence of individuals. Even that most intractable of enemies, dis-

ease, may be indefinitely reduced in dimensions by good physical and moral education and proper control of noxious influences, while the progress of science holds out a promise for the future of still more direct conquests over this detestable foe. And every advance in that direction relieves us from some, not only of the chances which cut short our own lives, but, what concerns us still more, which deprive us of those in whom our happiness is wrapt up. As for vicissitudes of fortune and other disappointments connected with worldly circumstances, these are principally the effect either of gross imprudence, of ill-regulated desires, or of bad or imperfect social institutions. All the grand sources, in short, of human suffering are in a great degree, many of them almost entirely conquerable by human care and effort; and though their removal is grievously slow—though a long succession of generations will perish in the breach before the conquest is completed, and this world becomes all that, if will and knowledge were not wanting, it might easily be made—yet every mind sufficiently intelligent and generous to bear a part, however small and inconspicuous, in the endeavor will draw a noble enjoyment from the contest itself, which he would not for any bribe in the form of selfish indulgence consent to be without.

Justice as Fairness

John Rawls

I

It might seem at first sight that the concepts of justice and fairness are the same, and that there is no reason to distinguish them, or to say that one is more fundamental than the other. I think that this impression is mistaken. In this paper I wish to show that the fundamental idea in the concept of justice is fairness; and I wish to offer an analysis of the concept of justice from this point of view. To bring out the force of this claim, and the analysis based upon it, I shall then argue that it is this aspect of justice for which utilitarianism, in its classical form, is unable to account, but which is expressed, even if misleadingly, by the idea of the social contract.

To start with I shall develop a particular conception of justice by stating and commenting upon two principles which specify it, and by considering the circumstances and conditions under which they may be thought to arise. The principles defining this conception, and the conception itself, are, of course, familiar. It may be possible, however, by using the notion of fairness as a framework, to assemble and to look at them in a new way. Before stating this conception, however, the following preliminary matters should be kept in mind.

Throughout I consider justice only as a virtue of social institutions, or what I shall call practices. The principles of justice are regarded as formulating restrictions as to how practices may define positions and offices, and assign thereto powers and liabilities, rights and duties. Justice as a virtue of particular actions or of persons I do not take up at all. It is important to distinguish these various subjects of justice, since the meaning of the concept varies according to whether it is applied to practices, particular actions, or persons. These meanings are, indeed, connected, but they are not identical. I shall confine my discussion to the sense of justice as applied to practices, since this sense is the basic one. Once it is understood, the other senses should go quite easily.

Justice is to be understood in its customary sense as representing but *one* of the many virtues of social institutions, for these may be antiquated, inefficient, degrading, or any number of other things, without being unjust. Justice is not to be confused with an all-inclusive vision of a good society; it is only one part of any such conception. It is important, for example, to distinguish that sense of equality which is an aspect of the concept of justice from that sense of equality which belongs to a more comprehensive social ideal. There may well be inequalities which one concedes are just, or at least not unjust, but which, nevertheless, one wishes, on other grounds, to do away with. I shall focus attention, then, on the usual sense of justice in which it is essentially the elimination of arbitrary distinctions and the establishment, within the structure of a practice, of a proper balance between competing claims.

Finally, there is no need to consider the principles discussed below as *the* principles of justice. For the moment it is sufficient that they are typical of a family of principles normally associated with the concept of justice. The way in which the principles of this family resemble one another, as shown by the background against which they may be thought to arise, will be made clear by the whole of the subsequent argument.

II

The conception of justice which I want to develop may be stated in the form of two principles as follows: first, each person participating in a practice, or affected by it, has an equal right to the most extensive liberty compatible with a like liberty for all; and second, inequalities are arbitrary unless it is reasonable to expect that they will work out for everyone's advantage, and provided the positions and offices to which they attach, or from which they may be gained, are open to all. These principles express justice as a complex of three ideas: liberty, equality, and reward for services contributing to the common good.

The term "person" is to be construed variously depending on the circumstances. On some occasions it will mean human individuals, but in others it may refer to nations, provinces, business firms, churches, teams, and so on. The principles of justice apply in all these instances, although there is a certain logical priority to the case of human individuals. As I shall use the term "person," it will be ambiguous in the manner indicated.

The first principle holds, of course, only if other things are equal: that is, while there must always be a justification for departing from the initial position of equal liberty (which is defined by the pattern of rights and duties, powers and liabilities, established by a practice), and the burden of proof is placed on him who would depart from it; nevertheless, there can be, and often there is, a justification for doing so. Now, that similar particular cases, as defined by a practice, should be treated similarly as they arise, is part of the very concept of a practice; it is involved in the notion of an activity in accordance with rules. The first principle expresses an analogous conception, but as applied to the structure of practices themselves. It holds, for example, that there is a presumption against the distinctions and classifications made by legal systems and other practices to the extent that they infringe on the original and equal liberty of the persons participating in them. The second principle defines how this presumption may be rebutted.

It might be argued at this point that justice requires only an equal liberty. If, however, a greater liberty were possible for all without loss or conflict, then it would be irrational to settle on a lesser liberty. There is no reason for circumscribing rights unless their exercise would be incompatible, or would render the practice defining them less effective. Therefore no serious distortion of the concept of justice is likely to follow from including within it the concept of the greatest equal liberty.

The second principle defines what sorts of inequalities are permissible; it specifies how the presumption laid down by the first principle may be put aside. Now by inequalities it is best to understand not *any* differences between offices and positions, but differences in the benefits and burdens attached to them either directly or indirectly, such as prestige and wealth, or liability to taxation and compulsory services. Players in a game do not protest against there being different positions, such as batter, pitcher, catcher, and the like, nor to there being various privileges and powers as specified by the rules; nor do the citizens of a country object to there being the different offices of government such as president, senator, governor, judge, and so on, each with their special rights and duties. It is not differences of this kind that are normally thought of as inequalities, but differences in the resulting distribution established by a practice, or made possible by it, of the things men strive to attain or avoid. Thus they may complain about the pattern of honors and rewards set up by a practice (e.g., the privileges and salaries of government officials) or they may object to the distribution of power and wealth which results from the various ways in which men avail themselves of the opportunities allowed by it (e.g., the concentration of wealth which may develop in a free price system allowing large entrepreneurial or speculative gains).

It should be noted that the second principle holds that an inequality is allowed only if there is reason to believe that the practice with the inequality, or resulting in it, will work for the advantage of *every* party engaging in it. Here it is important to stress that *every* party must gain from the inequality. Since the principle applies to practices, it implies that the representative man in every office or position defined by a practice, when he views it as a going concern, must find it reasonable to prefer his conditions and prospects with the inequality to what they would be under the practice without it. The principle excludes, therefore, the justification of inequalities on the grounds that the disadvantages of those in one position are outweighed by the greater advantages of those in another position. This rather simple restriction is the main modification I wish to make in the utilitarian principle as usually understood. When coupled with the notion of a practice, it is a restriction of consequence, and one which some utilitarians, for example, Hume and Mill, have used in their discussions of justice without realizing apparently its significance, or at least without calling attention to it. Why it is a significant modification of principle, changing one's conception of justice entirely, the whole of my argument will show.

Further, it is also necessary that the various offices to which special benefits or burdens attach are open to all. It may be, for example, to the common advantage, as just defined, to attach special benefits to certain offices. Perhaps by doing so the requisite talent can be attracted to them and encouraged to give its best efforts. But any offices having special benefits must be won in a fair competition in which contestants are judged on their merits. If some offices were not open, those excluded would normally be justified in feeling unjustly treated, even if they benefitted from the greater efforts of those who were allowed to compete for them. Now if one can assume that offices are open, it is necessary only to consider the design of practices themselves and how they jointly, as a system, work together. It will be a mistake to focus attention on the varying relative positions of particular persons, who may be known to us by their proper names, and to require that each such change, as a once for all transaction viewed in isolation, must be in itself just. It is the system of practices which is to be judged, and judged from a general point of view: unless one is prepared to criticize it from the standpoint of a representative man holding some particular office, one has no complaint against it.

III

Given these principles, one might try to derive them from *a priori* principles of reason, or claim that they were known by intuition. These are familiar enough steps and, at least in the case of the first principle, might be made with some success. Usually, however, such arguments, made at this point, are unconvincing. They are not likely to lead to an understanding of the basis of the principles of justice, not at least as principles of justice. I wish, therefore, to look at the principles in a different way.

Imagine a society of persons amongst whom a certain system of practices is *already* well established. Now suppose that by and large they are mutually self-interested; their allegiance to their established practices is normally founded on the prospect of self-advantage. One need not assume that, in all senses of the term "person," the persons in this society are mutually self-interested. If the characterization as mutually self-interested applies when the line of division is the family, it may still be true that members of families are bound by ties of sentiment and affection and willingly acknowledge duties in contradiction to self-interest. Mutual self-interestedness in the relations between families, nations, churches, and the like, is commonly associated with intense loyalty and devotion on the part of individual members. Therefore, one can form a more realistic conception of this society if one thinks of it as consisting of mutually self-interested families, or some other association. Further, it is not necessary to suppose that these persons are mutually self-interested under all circumstances, but only in the usual situation in which they participate in their common practices.

Now suppose also that these persons are rational: they know their own interests more or less accurately; they are capable of tracing out the likely consequences of adopting one practice rather than another; they are capable of adhering to a course of action once they have decided upon it; they can resist present temptations and the enticements of immediate gain; and the bare knowledge or perception of the difference between their condition and that of others is not, within

certain limits and in itself, a source of great dissatisfaction. Only the last point adds anything to the usual definition of rationality. This definition should allow, I think, for the idea that a rational man would not be greatly downcast from knowing, or seeing, that others are in a better position than himself, unless he thought their being so was the result of injustice, or the consequence of letting chance work itself out for no useful common purpose, and so on. So if these persons strike us as unpleasantly egoistic, they are at least free in some degree from the fault of envy.

Finally, assume that these persons have roughly similar needs and interests, or needs and interests in various ways complementary, so that fruitful cooperation amongst them is possible; and suppose that they are sufficiently equal in power and ability to guarantee that in normal circumstances none is able to dominate the others. This condition (as well as the others) may seem excessively vague; but in view of the conception of justice to which the argument leads, there seems no reason for making it more exact here.

Since these persons are conceived as engaging in their common practices, which are already established, there is no question of our supposing them to come together to deliberate as to how they will set these practices up for the first time. Yet we can imagine that from time to time they discuss with one another whether any of them has a legitimate complaint against their established institutions. Such discussions are perfectly natural in any normal society. Now suppose that they have settled on doing this in the following way. They first try to arrive at the principles by which complaints, and so practices themselves, are to be judged. Their procedure for this is to let each person propose the principles upon which he wishes his complaints to be tried with the understanding that, if acknowledged, the complaints of others will be similarly tried, and that no complaints will be heard at all until everyone is roughly of one mind as to how complaints are to be judged. They each understand further that the principles proposed and acknowledged on this occasion are binding on future occasions. Thus each will be wary of proposing a principle which would give him a peculiar advantage, in his present circumstances, supposing it to be accepted. Each person knows that he will be bound by it in future circumstances the peculiarities of which cannot be known, and which might well be such that the principle is then to his disadvantage. The idea is that everyone should be required to make *in advance* a firm commitment, which others also may reasonably be expected to make, and that no one be given the opportunity to tailor the canons of a legitimate complaint to fit his own special condition, and then to discard them when they no longer suit his purpose. Hence each person will propose principles of a general kind which will, to a large degree, gain their sense from the various applications to be made of them, the particular circumstances of which being as yet unknown. These principles will express the conditions in accordance with which each is the least unwilling to have his interests limited in the design of practices, given the competing interests of the others, on the supposition that the interests of others will be limited likewise. The restrictions which would so arise might be thought of as those a person would keep in mind if he were designing a practice in which his enemy were to assign him his place.

The two main parts of this conjectural account have a definite significance. The character and respective situations of the parties reflect the typical circumstances in which questions of justice arise. The procedure whereby principles are proposed and acknowledged represents constraints, analo-

gous to those of having a morality, whereby rational and mutually self-interested persons are brought to act reasonably. Thus the first part reflects the fact that questions of justice arise when conflicting claims are made upon the design of a practice and where it is taken for granted that each person will insist, as far as possible, on what he considers his rights. It is typical of cases of justice, to involve persons who are pressing on one another their claims, between which a fair balance or equilibrium must be found. On the other hand, as expressed by the second part, having a morality must at least imply the acknowledgment of principles as impartially applying to one's own conduct as well as to another's, and moreover principles which may constitute a constraint, or limitation, upon the pursuit of one's own interests. There are, of course, other aspects of having a morality: the acknowledgment of moral principles must show itself in accepting a reference to them as reasons for limiting one's claims, in acknowledging the burden of providing a special explanation, or excuse, when one acts contrary to them, or else in showing shame and remorse and a desire to make amends, and so on. It is sufficient to remark here that having a morality is analogous to having made a firm commitment in advance; for one must acknowledge the principles of morality even when to one's disadvantage. A man whose moral judgments always coincided with his interests could be suspected of having no morality at all.

Thus the two parts of the foregoing account are intended to mirror the kinds of circumstances in which questions of justice arise and the constraints which having a morality would impose upon persons so situated. In this way one can see how the acceptance of the principles of justice might come about, for given all these conditions as described, it would be natural if the two principles of justice were to be acknowledged. Since there is no way for anyone to win special advantages for himself, each might consider it reasonable to acknowledge equality as an initial principle. There is, however, no reason why they should regard this position as final; for if there are inequalities which satisfy the second principle, the immediate gain which equality would allow can be considered as intelligently invested in view of its future return. If, as is quite likely, these inequalities work as incentives to draw out better efforts, the members of this society may look upon them as concessions to human nature: they, like us, may think that people ideally should want to serve one another. But as they are mutually self-interested, their acceptance of these inequalities is merely the acceptance of the relations in which they actually stand, and a recognition of the motives which lead them to engage in their common practices. *They* have no title to complain of one another. And so provided that the conditions of the principle are met, there is no reason why they should not allow such inequalities. Indeed, it would be shortsighted of them not to do so, and could result, in most cases, only from their being dejected by the bare knowledge, or perception, that others are better situated. Each person will, however, insist on an advantage to himself, and so on a common advantage, for none is willing to sacrifice anything for the others.

These remarks are not offered as a rigorous proof that persons conceived and situated as the conjectural account supposes, and required to adopt the procedures described, would settle on the two principles of justice. For such a proof a more elaborate and formal argument would have to be given: there remain certain details to be filled in, and various alternatives to be ruled out. The argument should, however, be taken as a proof, or a sketch of a proof; for the proposi-

tion I seek to establish is a necessary one, that is, it is intended as a theorem: namely, that when mutually self-interested and rational persons confront one another in typical circumstances of justice, and when they are required by a procedure expressing the constraints of having a morality to jointly acknowledge principles by which their claims on the design of their common practices are to be judged, they will settle on these two principles as restrictions governing the assignment of rights and duties, and thereby accept them as limiting their rights against one another. It is this theorem which accounts for these principles as principles of justice, and explains how they come to be associated with this moral concept. Moreover, this theorem is analogous to those about human conduct in other branches of social thought. That is, a simplified situation is described in which rational persons pursuing certain ends and related to one another in a definite way, are required to act subject to certain limitations; then, given this situation, it is shown that they will act in a certain manner. Failure so to act would imply that one or more of the assumptions does not obtain. The foregoing account aims to establish, or to sketch, a theorem in this sense; the aim of the argument is to show the basis for saying that the principles of justice may be regarded as those principles which arise when the constraints of having a morality are imposed upon rational persons in typical circumstances of justice.

IV

These ideas are, of course, connected with a familiar way of thinking about justice which goes back at least to the Greek Sophists, and which regards the acceptance of the principles of justice as a compromise between persons of roughly equal power who would enforce their will on each other if they could, but who, in view of the equality of forces amongst them and for the sake of their own peace and security acknowledge certain forms of conduct in so far as prudence seems to require. Justice is thought of as a pact between rational egoists the stability of which is dependent on a balance of power and a similarity of circumstances. While the previous account is connected with this tradition, and with its most recent variant, the theory of games, it differs from it in several important respects which, to forestall misinterpretations, I will set out here.

First, I wish to use the previous conjectural account of the background of justice as a way of analyzing the concept. I do not want, therefore, to be interpreted as assuming a general theory of human motivation: when I suppose that the parties are mutually self-interested, and are not willing to have their (substantial) interests sacrificed to others, I am referring to their conduct and motives as they are taken for granted in cases where questions of justice ordinarily arise. Justice is the virtue of practices where there are assumed to be competing interests and conflicting claims, and where it is supposed that persons will press their rights on each other. That persons are mutually self-interested in certain situations and for certain purposes is what gives rise to the question of justice in practices covering those circumstances. Among an association of saints, if such a community could really exist, the disputes about justice could hardly occur; for they would all work selflessly together for one end, the glory of God as defined by their common religion, and reference to this end would settle every question of right. The justice of practices does not come up until there are several different parties (whether we think of these as individuals, associations, or nations, and so on, is irrelevant) who do press their claims on one another, and who do regard themselves as repre-

sentatives of interests which deserve to be considered. Thus the previous account involves no general theory of human motivation. Its intent is simply to incorporate into the conception of justice the relations of men to one another which set the stage for questions of justice. It makes no difference how wide or general these relations are, as this matter does not bear on the analysis of the concept.

Again, in contrast to the various conceptions of the social contract, the several parties do not establish any particular society or practice; they do not covenant to obey a particular sovereign body or to accept a given constitution. Nor do they, as in the theory of games (in certain respects a marvelously sophisticated development of this tradition), decide on individual strategies adjusted to their respective circumstances in the game. What the parties do is to *jointly* acknowledge certain *principles* of appraisal relating to their common *practices* either as already established or merely proposed. They accede to standards of judgment, not to a given practice; they do not make any specific agreement, or bargain, or adopt a particular strategy. The subject of their acknowledgment is, therefore, very general indeed; it is simply the acknowledgment of certain principles of judgment, fulfilling certain general conditions, to be used in criticizing the arrangement of their common affairs. The relations of mutual self-interest between the parties who are similarly circumstanced mirror the conditions under which questions of justice arise, and the procedure by which the principles of judgment are proposed and acknowledged reflects the constraints of having a morality. Each aspect, then, of the preceding hypothetical account serves the purpose of bringing out a feature of the notion of justice. One could, if one liked, view the principles of justice as the "solution" of this highest order "game" of adopting, subject to the procedure described, principles of argument for all coming particular "games" whose peculiarities one can in no way foresee. But this comparison, while no doubt helpful, must not obscure the fact that this highest order "game" is of a special sort. Its significance is that its various pieces represent aspects of the concept of justice.

Finally, I do not, of course, conceive the several parties as necessarily coming together to establish their common practices for the first time. Some institutions may, indeed, be set up *de novo*; but I have framed the preceding account so that it will apply when the full complement of social institutions already exists and represents the result of a long period of development. Nor is the account in any way fictitious. In any society where people reflect on their institutions they will have an idea of what principles of justice would be acknowledged under the conditions described, and there will be occasions when questions of justice are actually discussed in this way. Therefore if their practices do not accord with these principles, this will affect the quality of their social relations. For in this case there will be some recognized situations wherein the parties are mutually aware that one of them is being forced to accept what the other would concede is unjust. The foregoing analysis may then be thought of as representing the actual quality of relations between persons as defined by practices accepted as just. In such practices the parties will acknowledge the principles on which it is constructed, and the general recognition of this fact shows itself in the absence of resentment and in the sense of being justly treated. Thus one common objection to the theory of the social contract, its apparently historical and fictitious character, is avoided.

V

That the principles of justice may be regarded as arising in the manner described illustrates an important fact about them. Not only does it bring out the idea that justice is a primitive moral notion in that it arises once the concept of morality is imposed on mutually self-interested agents similarly circumstanced, but it emphasizes that, fundamental to justice, is the concept of fairness which relates to right dealing between persons who are cooperating with or competing against one another, as when one speaks of fair games, fair competition, and fair bargains. The question of fairness arises when free persons, who have no authority over one another, are engaging in a joint activity and amongst themselves settling or acknowledging the rules which define it and which determine the respective shares in its benefits and burdens. A practice will strike the parties as fair if none feels that, by participating in it, they or any of the others are taken advantage of, or forced to give in to claims which they do not regard as legitimate. This implies that each has a conception of legitimate claims which he thinks it reasonable for others as well as himself to acknowledge. If one thinks of the principles of justice as arising in the manner described, then they do define this sort of conception. A practice is just or fair, then, when it satisfies the principles which those who participate in it could propose to one another for mutual acceptance under the aforementioned circumstances. Persons engaged in a just, or fair, practice can face one another openly and support their respective positions, should they appear questionable, by reference to principles which it is reasonable to expect each to accept.

It is this notion of the possibility of mutual acknowledgment of principles by free persons who have no authority over one another which makes the concept of fairness fundamental to justice. Only if such acknowledgment is possible can there be true community between persons in their common practices; otherwise their relations will appear to them as founded to some extent on force. If, in ordinary speech, fairness applies more particularly to practices in which there is a choice whether to engage or not (e.g., in games, business competition), and justice to practices in which there is no choice (e.g., in slavery), the element of necessity does not render the conception of mutual acknowledgment inapplicable, although it may make it much more urgent to change unjust than unfair institutions. For one activity in which one can always engage is that of proposing and acknowledging principles to one another supposing each to be similarly circumstanced; and to judge practices by the principles so arrived at is to apply the standard of fairness to them.

Now if the participants in a practice accept its rules as fair, and so have no complaint to lodge against it, there arises a *prima facie* duty (and a corresponding *prima facie* right) of the parties to each other to act in accordance with the practice when it falls upon them to comply. When any number of persons engage in a practice, or conduct a joint undertaking according to rules, and thus restrict their liberty, those who have submitted to these restrictions when required have the right to a similar acquiescence on the part of those who have benefitted by their submission. These conditions will obtain if a practice is correctly acknowledged to be fair, for in this case all who participate in it will benefit from it. The rights and duties so arising are special rights and duties in that they depend on previous actions voluntarily undertaken, in this case on the parties having engaged in a common practice and knowingly accepted its benefits. It is not, however, an obligation which pre-

supposes a deliberate performative act in the sense of a promise, or contract, and the like. An unfortunate mistake of proponents of the idea of the social contract was to suppose that political obligation does require some such act, or at least to use language which suggests it. It is sufficient that one has knowingly participated in and accepted the benefits of a practice acknowledged to be fair. This *prima facie* obligation may, of course, be overridden: it may happen, when it comes one's turn to follow a rule, that other considerations will justify not doing so. But one cannot, in general, be released from this obligation by denying the justice of the practice only when it falls on one to obey. If a person rejects a practice, he should, so far as possible, declare his intention in advance, and avoid participating in it or enjoying its benefits.

This duty I have called that of fair play, but it should be admitted that to refer to it in this way is, perhaps, to extend the ordinary notion of fairness. Usually acting unfairly is not so much the breaking of any particular rule, even if the infraction is difficult to detect (cheating), but taking advantage of loopholes or ambiguities in rules, availing oneself of unexpected or special circumstances which make it impossible to enforce them, insisting that rules be enforced to one's advantage when they should be suspended, and more generally, acting contrary to the intention of a practice. It is for this reason that one speaks of the sense of fair play: acting fairly requires more than simply being able to follow rules; what is fair must often be felt, or perceived, one wants to say. It is not, however, an unnatural extension of the duty of fair play to have it include the obligation which participants who have knowingly accepted the benefits of their common practice owe to each other to act in accordance with it when their performance falls due; for it is usually considered unfair if someone accepts the benefits of a practice but refuses to do his part in maintaining it. Thus one might say of the tax-dodger that he violates the duty of fair play: he accepts the benefits of government but will not do his part in releasing resources to it; and members of labor unions often say that fellow workers who refuse to join are being unfair: they refer to them as "free riders," as persons who enjoy what are the supposed benefits of unionism, higher wages, shorter hours, job security, and the like, but who refuse to share in its burdens in the form of paying dues, and so on.

The duty of fair play stands beside other *prima facie* duties such as fidelity and gratitude as a basic moral notion; yet it is not to be confused with them. These duties are all clearly distinct, as would be obvious from their definitions. As with any moral duty, that of fair play implies a constraint on self-interest in particular cases; on occasion it enjoins conduct which a rational egoist strictly defined would not decide upon. So while justice does not require of anyone that he sacrifice his interests in that *general position* and procedure whereby the principles of justice are proposed and acknowledged, it may happen that in particular situations, arising in the context of engaging in a practice, the duty of fair play will often cross his interests in the sense that he will be required to forego particular advantages which the peculiarities of his circumstances might permit him to take. There is, of course, nothing surprising in this. It is simply the consequence of the firm commitment which the parties may be supposed to have made, or which they would make, in the general position, together with the fact that they have participated in and accepted the benefits of a practice which they regard as fair.

Situations Ethics, The New Morality

Joseph Fletcher

Situationism

A third approach, in between legalism and antinomian unprincipledness, is situation ethics. (To jump from one polarity to the other would be only to go from the frying pan into the fire.) The situationist enters into every decision-making situation fully armed with the ethical maxims of his community and its heritage, and he treats them with respect as illuminators of his problems. Just the same he is prepared in any situation to compromise them or set them aside *in the situation* if love seems better served by doing so.

Situation ethics goes part of the way with natural law, by accepting reason as the instrument of moral judgment, while rejecting the notion that the good is "given" in the nature of things, objectively. It goes part of the way with Scriptural law by accepting revelation as the source of the norm while rejecting all "revealed" norms or laws but the one command—to love God in the neighbor. The situationist follows a moral law or violates it according to love's need. For example, "Almsgiving is a good thing *if . . .*" The situationist never says, "Almsgiving is a good thing. Period!" His decisions are hypothetical, not categorical. Only the commandment to love is categorically good. "Owe no one anything, except to love one another." (Rom. 13:8) If help to an indigent only pau-

perizes and degrades him, the situationist refuses to handout and finds some other way. He makes no law out of Jesus' "Give to every one who begs from you." It is only one step from that kind of Biblicist literalism to the kind that causes women in certain sects to refuse blood transfusions even if death results—even if they are carrying a quickened fetus that will be lost too. The legalist says that even if he tells a man escaped from an asylum where his intended victim is, if he finds and murders him, at least only one sin has been committed (murder), not two (lying as well)!

As Brunner puts it, "The basis of the Divine Command is always the same, but its content varies with varying circumstances." Therefore, the "error of casuistry does not lie in the fact that it indicates the infinite variety of forms which the Command of love may assume; its error consists in deducing particular laws from a universal law . . . as though all could be arranged beforehand. . . . Love, however, is free from all this predefinition."[1] We might say, from the situationist's perspective, that it is possible to derive general "principles" from whatever is the one and only universal law (*agape* for Christians, something else for others), but not laws or rules. We cannot milk universals from a universal!

William Temple put it this way: "Universal obligation attaches not to particular judg-

---

1   *The Divine Imperative*, tr. by Olive Wyon (The Westminster Press, 1947), pp 132 ff.

ments of conscience but to conscientious-ness. What acts are right may depend on circumstances . . . but there is an absolute obligation to will whatever may on each occasion be right."[2] Our obligation is relative *to* the situation, but obligation *in* the situation is absolute. We are only "obliged" to tell the truth, for example, if the situation calls for it; if a murderer asks us his victim's where-abouts, our duty might be to lie. There is in situation ethics an absolute element and an element of calculation, as Alexander Miller once pointed out.[3] But it would be better to say it has an absolute *norm* and a calculating method. There is weight in the old saying that what is needed is "faith, hope, and clarity." We have to find out what is "fitting" to be truly ethical, to use H.R. Niebuhr's word for it in his *The Responsible Self*.[4] Situation ethics aims at a contextual appropriate-ness—not the "good" or the "right" but the *fitting*.

A cartoon in a fundamentalist magazine once showed Moses scowling, holding his stone tablet with its graven laws, all ten, and an eager stonecutter saying to him, "Aaron said perhaps you'd let us reduce them to 'Act responsibly in love.'" This was meant as a dig at the situationists and the new morality, but the legalist humor in it merely states exactly what situation ethics calls for! With Dietrich Bonhoeffer we say, "Principles are only tools in God's hands, soon to be thrown away as unserviceable."[5]

One competent situationist, speaking to students, explained the position this way. Rules are "like 'Punt on fourth down,' or 'Take a pitch when the count is three balls.' These rules are part of the wise player's know-how, and distinguish him from the novice. But they are not unbreakable. The best players are those who know when to ignore them."

2   *Nature, Man and God* (The Macmillan Company, 1934), p. 405.
3   *The Renewal of Man* (Doubleday & Company, Inc., 1955), p. 44.
4   (Harper & Row, Publishers, Inc., 1963), pp. 60–61. Precedents are Samuel Clarke, *Unchangeable Obligations of Natural Religion* (London, 1706), and A.C. Ewing, *The Definition of the Good* (The MacMillan Company, 1947).
5   *Ethics*, tr. by N. H. Smith (The Macmillan Company, 1955), p. 8.

Questions

Section II

1. Did Socrates believe it was better to suffer injustice or to commit suicide?

2. Why did Socrates not allow his followers to break him out of prison?

3. Would this act of civil disobedience have had some justification?

4. For Aristotle, what is the purpose of ethical studies?

5. What might be called the "ingredients" of the "good life"?

6. Define "virtue" and "vice".

7. What is the role of the virtue of prudence in Aristotle's theory?

8. How does his theory of virtue relate to our happiness?

9. What would be one weakness in his theory?

10. What is the Natural Law for Cicero?

11. Compare Aquinas' view of Natural Law with that of Cicero.

12. For St. Thomas, how is the Natural Law promulgated?

13. For St. Thomas, what is the relation of human positive law to the Natural Law?

14. According to Locke, why was the State "created"?

15. In the light of its creation and mandate by the people, how would even massive civil disobedience (revolution) be justified?

16. Show the relationships of the Declaration to the views of Locke and Aquinas.

17. Do you agree with both major imperatives of Kant? Explain your answer.

18. Why could Kant not accept the teachings of Bentham?

19. How did Mill defend Bentham on the ethical criterion of hedonism?

20. Why might it be said that Rawls has rejected the pessimistic attitude toward ethical studies that we see in Ayer?

21. According to Rawls:
    a. In what ways are people equal and unequal?

    b. Besides basic liberties, what would be our rights in the workplace?

    c. As members of a society, what do we owe to each other? Would he be in agreement with Kant? If so, Why?

Section III

When Is Killing Murder?

Introduction

The Old Testament tells us: "Thou shall not commit murder." While this seems to be a rather precise and clear command, the distinction between killing and murder still presents a puzzle to many people. Killing is the destruction of anything living, e.g., a tree, or an ant. All murder is killing, but for an action to be considered murder, at least two conditions must be met: we must have a human being or person, and this person must be "innocent," that is, he/she must have done nothing to place his/her life in jeopardy. His/her killing is therefore unjustifiable, the right to kill is absent. Abortion, for example, is killing; but is it murder? What kind of a being is being killed? That is a metaphysical question, not an ethical one. The readings in this section will focus on various types of killing. The professor can outline the different positions on the controversies, always with an eye toward the distinction mentioned above.

Our writers are Donald Kagan, at the time professor of history and classics at Yale University, with a *New York Times* op. ed. page essay on citizen obligations vis-a-vis the draft. Jesuit Father Norbert Rigali deals with the newly opened debate on the traditional "just war" theory. Burton Leiser of Drake University and Carl Rowan, nationally famous Washington, D.C.-based columnist, take opposite positions on capital punishment. Rowan is an African-American who realizes that race has played a part in capital sentences, a fact that Leiser also mentions in his essay.

I have also included an article on the execution of the first woman in Texas in over a hundred years. It was somewhat controversial because of her gender and her lengthy stay (14 years) on Death Row, during which she claimed to have become a changed person due to her "conversion" to Christianity. Unfortunately, she brutally murdered two people.

On the abortion issue, we have two authors who, while not in favor of abortion on demand, address the problem from interesting viewpoints. Fr. Joseph Donceel, S.J., a long-time professor of philosophy and philosophical psychology at Fordham University, takes up the challenging question of the presence of a "soul" in the early stages of pregnancy. Judith Jarvis Thompson, professor of philosophy at M.I.T., wrote in 1971 on the special situation of rape in a famous and oft-republished article in *Philosophy and Public Affairs*. The subject matter of Fr. Donceel's article is being re-examined by some Catholic theologians and biologists.

The Ru-486 pill presents the possibility of the elimination of abortion clinics, but not of the intentional elimination of a fertilized ovum. This article by Dorothy Wickendem should be related to Fr. Donceel's. The essay by Margaret Carlson of *Time* deals with the question of the parent's right to be informed of a teenager's pregnancy and the rights of rape and incest victims.

Active euthanasia is against the law, but passive euthanasia presents a problem for relatives of the hopelessly ill who must decide to terminate the use of "extraordinary means" to keep the patient alive or to have the "Do not resuscitate" sign posted on a hospital bed. The Euthanasia Society has created the advanced directive or "living will" which is executed while the person is still living and which states the situations in which death would be welcomed. What would be the values and disvalues of these documents?

Just War and Pacifism

Norbert J. Rigali, S. J.

In their pastoral letter on war and peace, the American bishops tried to accept both pacifism as an individual option and a nation's right to defend its interests. The two positions are difficult to reconcile

Less than a decade after Pope Pius XII had expressly rejected conscientious objection to all war as a moral option for Catholics, the Second Vatican Council called upon governments to enact laws to protect the rights of those who for reasons of conscience object to war as such. Only a few years later the Catholic bishops of the United States called for legislative provision to recognize additionally the rights of selective conscientious objectors. Three decades had not yet elapsed since Pius XII's repudiation of conscientious objection, when in their 1983 pastoral letter, "The Challenge of Peace: God's Promise and Our Response," the American bishops went on to present "the pacifist option for individuals" as a second, complementary perspective of the Christian theological tradition, alongside the military option. The two perspectives, just-war theory and nonviolence, the bishops taught, "support and complement one another, each preserving the other from distortion".

If it is true that Christian theological tradition is distorted by the absence of a pacifist perspective, the Christian vision of war and peace had become obscured long before the papacy of Pius XII. His explicit rejection of conscientious objection was readily compatible with the moral theology that had been handed down. In their treatise on war the manuals of moral theology used in seminaries before Vatican II did not even raise the question of conscientious objection to all war. For a manualist it sufficed to conclude from just-war principles that a soldier is not allowed to fight in a war that is clearly unjust but that in cases of doubt about the justice of a war a distinction is to be drawn between subjects ordered to fight and would-be volunteers. Those ordered to fight are obliged to obey, while the volunteers may take up arms only if they become convinced of the justice of the war.

By reintroducing the pacifist option into mainstream Catholic reflections on war and peace, the bishops of the United States have dramatically moved the church—or a significant part of it—and theological tradition in the direction of meeting a need that Vatican II had designated as "a completely fresh reappraisal of war." However, the seed of reevaluation had already been planted by Pius XII himself. By reducing the legitimate

From *America*, March 31, 1984, 233-234. Reprinted with permission of America Press, Inc., 106 West 56th Street, New York, New York, 10019. Copyright 1984 All Rights Reserved.

causes of undertaking war to the single one of defense, he radically transformed just-war theory: The offensive wars sanctioned in the manuals of moral theology were disallowed, and the theory itself was thereby purged of much of the militaristic spirit that frequently enveloped it.

In the process of bringing about a fresh reappraisal of war the bishops of the United States are clearly demonstrating outstanding moral leadership. As seen in their remarkable pastoral letter, the spirit of this leadership is also a spirit of humble service, marked by unwavering awareness that the voice of their letter is not and cannot be the last and definitive word on the subject. Its authors show themselves well aware that, as the pastoral letter carries the Catholic tradition forward, it must also, inevitably, generate from its fresh vantage point new questions and challenges in theology and life, including unpredictable developments. As in Nicodemus's day, still now: The wind blows where it will.

Certainly among the most important theological questions generated by the pastoral letter is one created by the bishops' retrieval of the pacifist option. Theologians may no longer disregard the question: What is the relation of pacifism to just-war theory and of both to the Spirit of Christ in the world?

To this very complex theological question, which has received no definitive answer in 1,600 years, the bishops themselves had to offer some answer, although the fundamental purpose of their pastoral letter lay elsewhere: in applying the just-war perspective to the present situation of the United States. Consequently, their answer to the intricate theological question could be only brief, undeveloped and at best inadequate. It is to their credit that the bishops were willing to pay this price for recovering the pacifist option within mainstream Catholic teach-

ing. In effect, they left to theologians the theological question and restricted themselves essentially to the pastoral role of moral guidance and leadership. The bishops' brief answer creates a problem that demands reflection.

"Does not the pastoral letter . . . really pass over here the question of objective Christian morality?"

On the level of individual choice there exists, the bishops responded, a complementary relation between the military choice and the pacifist response inasmuch as both seek to serve the common good. While they differ with regard to means to be used, both responses maintain that "peace must be pursued and rights defended within moral restraints and in the context of defining other human values". Also with regard to their religious standpoints, the two responses are seen by the bishops as differing. Looking to the Kingdom of God, when peace and justice will be fully realize, the just-war perspective is based on the view that, until history is consummated in the Kingdom: "Efforts to pursue both peace and justice are at times in tension, and the struggle for justice may threaten certain forms of peace". The religious basis for the pacifist response, however, can be either an "understanding of the Gospel and the life and death of Jesus as forbidding all violence" or the desire "to give personal example of Christian forbearance as a positive, constructive approach toward loving reconciliation with enemies".

Despite the complementary relation between the military response and the pacifist option as far as individuals are concerned, a state, said the bishops, has no choice in this matter: "The council and the popes have stated clearly that governments threatened by armed, unjust aggression must defend their people. This includes defense by armed force if necessary as a last resort". A state—even a Christian state, if there is such—may not choose pacifism; it is morally bound to the just-war perspective.

One important question arising from the advanced position taken by the bishops can be formulated: Is the relation between just-war theory and pacifism really, as the bishops say, one of complementary perspectives? To put the question in a different way: If the relation between the two perspectives is truly complementary, why does its complementary character obtain only with regard to individuals and turn into direct opposition and contradiction with regard to society? Why, if it is moral and praiseworthy for an individual Christian to adopt the perspective of pacifism, is it immoral for a society of Christians (or graced non-Christians) to choose it?

Why is it that, if a democratic society chose what for any individual is the good and laudable option of pacifism, there would result an evil, immoral structure of the state, while if everyone chose the other good and laudable option of just-war theory, not only would the state be structured according to the moral law regarding war, but also there would be achieved a universal consensus in accord with Catholic teaching about the state? Why is it, then, that if the pacifist option really complements just-war theory, its acceptance renders impossible a universal acceptance of the Catholic teaching that a nation is morally bound to the just-war theory and may not elect pacifism? It is indeed an odd complementary perspective of Catholic teaching that makes it impossible for a person adopting it to accept the official teaching of the Catholic Church regarding the position that it supposedly complements. How does the pastoral letter avoid seeing this dilemma that derives directly from its own teaching?

The bishops' discussion of the relation between the two perspectives originates from a somewhat individualistic standpoint that reflects their pastoral concern for individuals, but it is inadequate for the theoretical, theological problem that emerges in the course of their pastoral teaching. They introduce discussion of just-war theory and pacifism by speaking not of two competing claims to Christian truth but of "two distinct moral responses" or "moral options" in the face of the Christian's obligation to defend peace: "Those who resist bearing arms and those who bear them" are seen as differing with regard to "the how of defending peace".

What the bishops present here as complementary are, in fact, not the pacifist position and just-war teaching. They are, rather, one individual's choice to bear arms and another's to refuse to bear them, both in the service of peace. An individual's choice not to bear arms is not the pacifist position, just as another individual's opposite choice is not just-war teaching, although the one may result from a person's subscribing to the pacifist position and the other may be rooted in belief in just-war theory. But there are, of course, very many people who uphold one or the other theory but because of health, age, sex or clerical state do not themselves make a personal choice to bear arms or to refuse to do so.

Military Service: A Moral Obligation

Donald Kagan

NEW HAVEN, Conn. The killing of 239 servicemen in Lebanon and the invasion of Grenada have reminded Americans of the military's role in pursuit of the nation's purposes and once again have raised the question of the citizen's obligation to do military service when called upon. This question still is before us because of continuing controversy over a law requiring students seeking Federal aid to register for the draft.

It would seem obvious that in a world of independent and sovereign states that come into conflict and threaten one another's vital interests—sometimes even existence itself—citizens who choose to remain in a particular country are morally obliged to serve in its armed forces when the need arises.

Critics of this view appeal to a higher morality in which an individual may refuse to serve if such service violates his conscience. Some assert the right, even the duty, to refuse service when they do not approve of the national policy that leads to the need for military action, even though they do not oppose serving when they approve the cause. To accept such a claim would be to destroy all governments but especially democracies, which rely on the willingness of their citizens to accept the decisions that duly elected and appointed bodies and officials arrive at, even if they are wrong.

That is not to say that citizens are morally obliged to accept the decision of any

country in which they live, no matter how wicked and despotic—only in legitimate ones. My definition of a legitimate state is one that permits the open advocacy of different opinions, the possibility of changing the laws by peaceful means and, most important, emigration without penalty. A regime that fails to meet these criteria imposes its will by force alone and has no moral claim on the obedience of its subjects.

On the other hand, a nation that meets them has every claim to its citizens' allegiance and especially to the service most vital to its existence. When a citizen has become an adult and has not chosen to leave the country, he tacitly approves of its legitimacy and consents to its laws. He benefits from their protection and has the moral obligation to obey them if he wants to stay. To enjoy the enormous advantages provided by a free society while claiming the right to ignore or disobey the laws selectively, especially those essential to its survival and most demanding of its citizens, is plainly immoral.

Some recusants are pacifists who refuse to fight regardless of the occasion. Their position, though it lacks the absurdity of claiming the right of each citizen to conduct his own foreign policy, is also deficient. Leaving the country would not solve their problem, since wherever they go they will find a state that will be prepared to use force in the national interest when necessary and will ask its citizens to do military service. One solution has been to refuse to serve and accept the legal penalty without complaint. Another has been to accept auxiliary service, such as in the medical corps, which, though dangerous, does not require killing. These responses prove sincerity and courage, but they do not satisfy the moral demands of citizenship. Pacifists in this imperfect world can pursue their beliefs only in free societies and only because their fellow citizens are willing to fight and protect them. There were no protected pacifists in Hitler's Germany and Stalin's Russia; there are none in Yuri V. Andropov's.

Pacifists are not alone in hating the need to kill. Most American soldiers find it impossible to pull the trigger in their first combat experience and find it profoundly painful even later. Yet they do their duty, though there is no way to know if they dislike killing any less than those refusing to fight. A decent, free society is right to allow concern for personal conscience a place in its considerations and to afford special treatment to those who refuse to fight on plausible grounds of conscience. But those who accept such treatment must realize that they are getting a free ride and failing in their moral responsibility as citizens.

For Capital Punishment

Burton M. Leiser

West Des Moines, Iowa—In the face of studies that claim to demonstrate that capital punishment does not deter potential criminals, American public opinion clearly favors a return to the death penalty. Advocates of capital punishment, without knowing precisely why, rightly suspect that the most crucial arguments on the other side are fundamentally unsound and misguided.

For example, studies that claim to have proved the inefficacy of the death penalty as a deterrent to violent crime point out that some states that have retained the death penalty have had higher crime rates than others that have abolished it. Economic, political, social and psychological conditions that affect the crime rate are ignored, as is the fact that harsh penalties are usually removed first from those jurisdictions that have relatively low crime rates.

Contrary to every maxim of scientific inquiry, opponents of the death penalty base their stand upon evidence gathered exclusively from the experiences of murderers, rapists and kidnappers—persons who have obviously not been deterred. A study of those who have not been deterred yields the astounding conclusion that they have not been deterred—an inference any schoolboy could have drawn with no research whatever.

A genuinely scientific study would have to determine how many persons in our society have been deterred from committing certain dangerous crimes by fear of the death penalty. The crucial question is whether law-abiding citizens sometimes refrain from criminal behavior because of fear of penalties they might suffer if caught.

Let everyone ask himself whether he has even been angry enough to kill; if he has, let him ask further whether his fear of the evil that would befall himself and his loved ones if he were caught contributed to his decision not to do so. I would guess that so many of us have been tempted to commit serious crimes and have refrained from doing so because of our fear of the penalties that might follow that we find arguments based upon the contrary assumption completely unconvincing.

Besides, no advocate of the death penalty says that it will deter every potential murderer, only that it will deter some. If some persons are deterred from committing murder because of their fear of execution, then the law will have saved them as well as their potential victims from the consequences of the crimes they may otherwise have committed.

Some arguments are scarcely worthy of serious consideration, but they have influenced courts and legislators. If the law is administered to favor one part of the population over another, the solution is not to do away with the law but to administer it fairly.

The solution for the unconscionably long delay between sentencing and carrying out an execution is not to abolish the penalty but to expedite appeal procedures. We should spend whatever it takes to reduce the period from arrest of a suspect to the final appeal to no more than six months.

Whatever doubts may be entertained about our ability to deter some criminals, it is evident that others can be deterred by nothing short of the threat of death. The threat of a life sentence is no threat at all to a lifer who decides to stab a fellow inmate or a guard. The terrorist who hijacks a plane and threatens the lives of hundreds of passengers is not alarmed if he is caught and sentenced to life in prison, for he expects his comrades to hijack yet another plane and to demand that he be released.

To be sure, some fanatics are so dedicated to their causes that even the threat of death would not stop them. But the hangers-on, the disenchanted, the thrill-seekers, the uncritical fad-followers might think twice before putting their lives on the line.

No incident in recent history demonstrates the deterrent effect of the fear of death more vividly than the tragedy at Kent State University. The shots that rang out across the campus on May 4, 1970, killing four students and wounding nine more, reverberated throughout North America, and tens of thousands of parents called their children, millions of students went into shock, and an era of campus violence came to a sudden and dramatic end. This is not to justify what I believe to have been the lawless behavior of the Ohio National Guard, but it does illustrate the powerful deterrent effect that the threat of death can have upon vast numbers of people.

In a dispute on this issue some 2,000 years ago, a great legal scholar, Rabbi Simeon Ben Gamaliel, argued that the abolition of the death penalty would increase the shedding of innocent blood in the land.

Murderer Who Turned to Christianity

Christopher Burns

PARIS—Her face covered leading newspapers around the world, and breathless foreign journalists reported live from Texas while the minutes ticked down to last night's execution of Karla Faye Tucker.

To much of the world's media, Tucker's case had become a rallying point for opponents of the death penalty, banned years ago in Europe and many other countries.

"We're hoping for a miracle here, if Karla Faye Tucker is to live," said a visibly moved journalist for Fance 2 television as he did a live report in front of the Huntsville, Texas, prison where Tucker died at 7:45 p.m. EST.

Tucker, 38, was the lead story in several French newspapers as well as the nightly news. "This woman will be executed," headlined the front page of the daily *Le Parisien*, with Tucker's face looking toward the sky.

"It has a lot of dramatic elements," said Jean-Luc Allouche, editor in chief of the leftist Paris daily *Liberation*, explaining the world attention. "Even the father of one of the victims opposes her execution.

"And because someone can change between the time of the crime and the execution," he added. "For Karla Faye Tucker, it was 14 years."

Tucker, a former teenage prositute, was sentenced to death for the pickax murder of a man and woman in 1983 when she and a companion were on a three-day drug binge.

She later became a born-again Christian in prison.

This week, Pope John Paul II appealed for mercy for Tucker. But yesterday, Italy's conservative *Corriere della Sera* daily had the headline, "The wall of hate: Tucker must die."

Before Tucker was executed, about 50 protesters stood in the rain in front of the U.S. Embassy in Rome.

"We are hoping until the last moment that the penalty will be suspended," said parliament member Athos De Luca.

But Britain's tabloid *Dalily Mail* said all the fuss over Tucker has been because she is a woman.

"A pardon would be a patronizing act which implies women have an inferior capacity to distinguish between right and wrong, tantamount to insulting women's power of reasoning," *Mail* reporter Nick Hopkins wrote from Huntsville.

"If a woman is responsible enough to vote on the existence of the death penalty, which of course she is, then she is responsible enough to die in the execution chamber," Hopkins wrote.

From New York, Fox News Channel last night aired a series of graphic crime scene photos of Tucker's victims about an hour before she was executed, including one shot showing a pickax plunged in a victim's chest.

Network executives said they aired the photos after extensive debate to show another side to the story about the fight to keep Tucker alive.

"We thought very long and hard about it," said John Moody, Fox News Channel's vice president for news. "The intention is not to disturb people, it is not to cause anybody unease. What we are trying to do is give people full context to the story."

Throwing Away the Key

James Collins

The Supreme Court allows states to keep "sexual predators" locked up beyond their terms in prison

Leroy Hendricks had done his time. In August 1994, after serving 10 years for taking "indecent liberties" with two 13-year-old boys, Hendricks walked out of prison in Hutchinson, Kans.—and was almost immediately transported to the Larned Correctional Mental Health Facility, where he has been locked up ever since. Under a 1994 state law called the Sexually Violent Predator Act, a judge ordered Hendricks confined indefinitely after ruling that his "mental abnormality" made him likely to attack again. Hendricks challenged the constitutionality of that law, but last week, in a 5-to-4 decision, the Supreme Court upheld it.

Hendricks is just the kind of fiend the Kansas legislature had in mind when it passed the Predator Act. His 1984 molestation conviction was his fifth in almost 30 years. The only sure way to make him stop molesting children, he has admitted, would be to kill him. "He's really a poster boy for pedophiles," says Wichita district attorney Nola Foulston. "Sometimes he was a carnival worker. He would ingratiate himself with single mothers by taking their children out for ice cream. The mothers would think, 'What a nice man.'"

The American justice system punishes criminals for what they have done, not for what they might do. Only those deemed dangerous and insane are locked away to protect themselves and society from their potential actions. Hendricks' lawyers argued that the "mental abnormality" clause in the Kansas statute created too low and too vague a standard for committing a person and so was a violation of due process. They also claimed that the law subjected Hendricks to double jeopardy and that it violated the Constitution's ex post facto clause, which forbids the enactment of new laws that extend punishment for past crimes. The court was not convinced. Writing for the majority, Clarence Thomas asserted that the Kansas law's standard for what constitutes a dangerous mental illness was as strict as the standards in many laws the court has long upheld. Thomas further concluded that since the Kansas law was a version of these well-established "civil commitment" statutes, Hendricks' confinement could not be considered "punishment"—because punishment, in constitutional terms, arises from criminal proceedings, not civil ones.

Many legal experts are worried that the decision will allow states to lock up all sorts of people. "Today we're dealing with sexual predators, " says Steven Shapiro, the legal director of the American Civil Liberties Union. "Who is it tomorrow that we're going to label as abnormal and potentially danger-ous?" The dissenting Justices, however, agreed with Thomas that Kansas' criteria for committing someone were valid. Their ob-jection, as expressed by Stephen Breyer in the minority opinion, was that Hendricks has received virtually no treatment even though the law requires it. To Breyer, the state's failure to live up to its promise makes Hendricks' confinement look a lot like pun-ishment.

Six states have sexual-predator laws; similar statutes being considered in at least 30 others are likely to be enacted swiftly. To mark their days to freedom, people like Hen-dricks are going to need new calendars.

Don't Limit Blame for a Soaring Murder Rate

Carl Rowan

The Senate Judiciary Committee has issued a horrifying report that more than 23,700 Americans will be murdered this year—a record—and that an American is twice as likely to be among the victims as was the case 30 years ago.

Sen. Joseph Biden Jr. (D–Del.) says that to find the root causes of our "murder epidemic . . . we need to look no further than three D's"—drugs, deadly weapons and demographics, "fueling a growth in violent teenage gangs."

Those three D's are certainly powerful factors in the record pileup of human carnage, but it would be a mistake to limit the blame to them and thus blind ourselves to a fundamental truth: Ours is a very violent society.

Mothers and fathers are slaying their children. Children are murdering their parents. Husbands are killing wives and vice versa. You can get killed for taking a parking place that someone thinks he is entitled to. Or just shot to death at random while driving down a highway.

The murder statistics don't begin to tell the extent to which violence permeates America.

We see it in the brutal beatings that occur when people of one race "trespass" on the neighborhood of people of another race or ethnic group. We see it in our police departments where cops dare to boast of beating suspects. We see it in the widespread embrace of capital punishment by public officials who delude themselves into believing that state-sanctioned killings will prevent increases in murders, even though the result may be the opposite. We see a spirit of violence in American celebrations of our ability to kill massively in "little wars," never letting our minds form a vision of the faces of the dead women and children.

The leaders of this society foment this spirit of violence, then shriek in outrage against those who murder, crying, "Fry em, fry em!" So they offer us a crime bill that lists several new crimes for which the penalty is to be capital punishment, seeking to deceive us into believing that this will be a barrier against further widespread criminal behavior.

It is easy to deplore, even hate, violent youth gangs. But what do we expect from teenagers who have been victimized in so many ways by social, economic and even physical violence?

We leave a third of America's teenagers bereft of meaningful education—and almost as many jobless—yet we are outraged when they do not uphold "law and order." Youngsters who have no stake in the "order" are not going to show high regard for the law.

The advocates of more executions and more and bigger prisons don't want to face these truths, so they cry "soft on crime" at anyone who dares to talk about the ways in which millions of Americans are alienated.

The spirit of vengeance dominates all our ruling circles, including the U.S. Supreme Court, where the majority says, "Kill em, kill em."

We need some leaders who will give priority to devising programs to ensure all young Americans that they are a respected part of this society and that they have so great a stake in its future that they will both honor and advocate conduct that is in keeping with just rules of law. If we go on responding to alienation with oppression and to every level of personal misconduct with state violence, we shall continue to be cursed by horrible rates of murder and of every other crime of violence.

A Liberal Catholic's View

Joseph F. Donceel, S. J.

I fully agree with the basic Catholic principle that we are never allowed to kill an innocent human being. Therefore, if there is a real human being from the moment of conception, abortion would have to be considered immoral at any stage of pregnancy. The majority Catholic opinion holds nowadays that there is indeed a real human being from the first moment of conception, or, at least, that we cannot be certain that such is not the case. But there is also a minority Catholic opinion, which has good standing in the church, which was the opinion of her greatest theologian, Thomas Aquinas,[1] and which is now slowly regaining favor among Catholic thinkers. This minority opinion holds that there is certainly no human being during the early stages of pregnancy. I would like to show you briefly why Thomas held this position, how it was given up by his successors on account of erroneous scientific theories, and how, even after these theories had been given up, the Catholic church did not return to her traditional view because of a philosophy which was at variance with her official doctrine of the nature of man.

Traditional Catholic philosophy holds that what makes an organism a human being is the spiritual soul and that this soul starts to exist at the moment of its "infusion" into the body. When is the human soul infused into the body? Nowadays the majority of

Catholic thinkers would not hesitate to answer: at the moment of conception. This is known as the *theory of immediate animation*. However, during long centuries Catholic philosophy and theology held that the human soul was infused into the body only when the latter began to show a human shape or outline and possessed the basic human organs. Before this time, the embryo is alive, but in the way in which a plant or an animal is alive. It possesses, as the traditional terminology puts it, a vegetative or an animal soul, not yet a human soul. In more modern terms we might say that it has reached the physiological or the psychological, not yet the spiritual level of existence. It is not yet a human person; it is evolving, within the womb, toward hominization. This is the *theory of mediate or delayed animation*.

Why did Thomas and the great medieval thinkers favor this theory? Because they held the doctrine of hylomorphism, according to which the human soul is the substantial form of man, while the human body is the result of the union of this soul with materiality, with undetermined cosmic stuff, with what was then known as prime matter. Hylomorphism holds that the human soul is to the body somewhat as the shape of a statue is to the actual statue. The shape of a statue cannot exist before the statue exists. It

---

From *Abortion in a Changing World*, Vol. 1, ed. by Robert E. Hall (New York: Columbia University Press, 1970), 39-45.

1   See *Summa contra Gentiles*, II, 88–89; *De Potentia* , Q. 3, Art. 9–12; *Summa Theologica*, I, Q. 118, Art. 1–3.

is not something which the sculptor first makes and subsequently introduces into a block of marble. It can exist only in the completed statue. Hylomorphism holds that, in the same way, the human soul can exist only in a real human body.

Although Thomas knew nothing about chromosomes, genes, DNA, or the code of life, he knew that whatever was growing in the mother's womb was not yet, early in pregnancy, a real human body. Therefore he held that it could not be animated by a human soul, any more than a square block of marble can possess a human shape. The medieval thinkers knew very well that this growing organism would develop into a human body, that virtually, potentially, it was a human body. But they did not admit that an actual human soul could exist in a virtual human body. The Catholic church, which had officially adopted the hylomorphic conception of human nature at the Council of Vienne, in 1312, was so strongly convinced of this position that, for centuries, her law forbade the faithful to baptize any premature birth which did not show at least some human shape or outline.

Under the influence of erroneous scientific reports, however, Catholic thinkers gave up this traditional doctrine. In the early seventeenth century, as a result of a combination of poor microscopes and lively imaginations, some physicians saw in embryos which were only a few days old a tiny human being, a homunculus, with microscopic head, legs, and arms.[2] This view of the fetus implied the *preformation theory*, which held that organic development simply consists of the gradual increase in size of organs and structures which are fully present from the very start. If there really were from the beginning a human body, be it ever so small, there might also from the start exist a human soul. Even a microscopic statue must have a shape. Granted the preformation theory, immediate animation was compatible with the hylomorphic conception of man.

The theory of preformation was eventually replaced by the *theory of epigenesis*, which maintains that the organism, far from being microscopically preformed from the start, develops its organs through a complex process of growth, cleavage, differentiation, and organization.

Why did the Christian thinkers not return to the delayed animation theory, which seems to be demanded by their hylomorphic theory of man? The main reason seems to have been the influence of Cartesian dualism. For Descartes, both man's soul and his body are each a complete substance. The soul is a thinking substance, the body an extended substance. This is no longer hylomorphism. To express it in nontechnical language, this is no longer a "shape in the statue" conception, but rather a "ghost in the machine" conception of the human soul. A full-fledged ghost can manage very well with a microscopic machine. If the soul is no longer the formal cause, the constitutive idea of the body, it might well become its efficient cause, that which produces the ovum's development from the start. Instead of being the idea incarnated in the body, it has turned into the architect and the builder of the body. Just as the architect exists before the first stone of the building is laid, so there can be a real human soul from the first moment of conception, before the emergence of a real human body.[3]

---

2   See H. de Dorlodot, "A Vindication of the Mediate Animation Theory," in E. C. Messenger (ed.), *Theology and Evolution*, pp. 273–83, London, 1949.

3   The anonymous author of an article in Latin, "De Animatione Foetus" (*Nouvelle Revue Théologique*, 11: 163–86, 268–89 [1879]), quotes a certain Michael Alberti Germaniae Medicus, who wrote in 1725 "quod a primis conceptionis initiis anima rationalis in foetu adsit, eo quod sine anima illa conceptio fieri nequeat, quae

This way of explaining embryogeny is not absurd. The Cartesian outlook, although quite unfashionable nowadays, has been held by many great thinkers. This kind of philosophy calls for immediate animation, which is clearly in conflict with the hylomorphic doctrine of man, solemnly endorsed by the Catholic church at the Council of Vienne.

There have been other influences which explain the shift in Catholic opinion. One of them may have been the long-standing opposition of the church to the idea of evolution. Thomas admitted some kind of evolution of the embryo and the fetus in the mother's womb. How could the church admit this evolution in the womb and reject it in the race? Since the Catholic church has finally come around to admitting the evolution of the human body, it might also be willing to return to Thomas's idea of evolution in the womb.[4]

Moreover, once we give up the idea of immediate animation, we can no longer say when the human soul is infused, when the embryo or the fetus becomes a human person. That is why those who want to play it absolutely safe claim that the human soul is present from the moment of conception. They seem to take it for granted that, since we do not know when the human soul is present, we neither can know for sure when it is not yet present. This assumption is false. Let us consider another case, where we do not know when a certain factor is present, while knowing very well when it is not yet present. Nobody can tell with certitude when a child is capable of performing his first free moral choice, but all of us are quite

certain that, during the first months or years of his life, a human baby is not yet a free moral agent. Likewise, I do not know when the human soul is infused, when the embryo becomes human. But I feel certain that there is no human soul, hence no human person, during the first few weeks of pregnancy, as long as the embryo remains in the vegetative stage of its development.

Some people make much of the following objection to my position. They say that from the very first the fertilized ovum possesses forty-six human chromosomes, all the human genes, its code of life—that it is a human embryo. This is undeniable. But it does not make a human person. When a heart is transplanted, it is kept alive, for a short while, outside the donor. It is a living being, a human heart, with the human chromosomes and genes. But it is not a human being; it is not a person.

The objection may be pressed. Not only does the fertilized human ovum possess the human chromosomes; unlike the heart, it will, if circumstances are normal, develop into a human being. It is virtually a human being. I admit this, but it does not affect my position. The fertilized human ovum, the early embryo, is virtually a human body, not actually. Correctly understood, the hylomorphic conception of human nature, the official Catholic doctrine, cannot admit the presence of an actual human soul in a virtual human body. Let me use a comparison again. A deflated rubber ball is virtually round; when inflated, it can assume no other shape than the spherical shape. Yet it does not actually possess any roundness or sphe-

---

tanquam artifex et architecta sui corporis praesto est; a qua deinde actus formationis dependet" (that the rational soul is present in the fetus from the first beginnings of conception, because the conception cannot take place without this soul, which is there *like the maker and the architect of its body;* hence the act of formation depends on it) (my italics). This sounds like pure Cartesianism.

4   "For the evolutionistic way of thinking, it is more probable that hominization occurs not at the moment of conception, but at a later time of embryonic development," writes J. Feiner in the most recent comprehensive treatise of dogmatic theology, *Mysterium Fidei,* edited by J. Feiner and M. Löhrer, vol. II, p. 581, Einsiedeln, 1967.

ricity. In the same way, the early embryo does not actually possess a human soul; it is not a human person.

Experimental embryology tells us that every single cell of the early embryo, of the morula, is virtually a human body. It does not follow that each of these cells possesses a human soul. When embryologists carefully separate the cells of a morula in lower organisms, each one of these cells may develop into a complete organism. Starting with the pioneering attempts of Hans Driesch, such an experiment has been performed on many animal species. We do not see why it might not eventually succeed with the human embryo. As a matter of fact, nature frequently performs it on human ova. Identical twins derive from one ovum fertilized by one spermatozoon. This ovum splits into two at an early stage of pregnancy and gives rise to two human beings. In this case the defenders of immediate animation must admit that one person may be divided into two persons. This is a metaphysical impossibility.

Throughout my exposition I have taken for granted the hylomorphic conception of human nature. This is in line with the purpose of my essay, which is not only to present a liberal Catholic's view of fetal animation, but also to show that this view seems to be the only one which agrees with the official Catholic conception of human nature. In other words, I submit that Catholics should give up the immediate animation theory, because it implies a Cartesian, dualistic conception of man, which conflicts with the doctrine endorsed by the Council of Vienne.

In conclusion I would like to say a few words about the standing of hylomorphism among contemporary philosophers. Very few non-Catholic philosophers hold the doctrine of hylomorphism today. Even among Catholics it has fallen into disrepute, although personally I cannot see how one may avoid dualism without this theory or some theory which resembles it. Hylomorphism is radically opposed to dualism, to the doctrine which considers both the soul and the body as complete substances. Contemporary philosophy, as a rule, is also strongly opposed to this kind of dualism. In this sense, negatively, the doctrine I have defended continues to live; it is stronger than ever, although it may be known by other names.

Both linguistic analysis, the leading philosophy in the English-speaking countries, and existential phenomenology, which tends to dominate the field elsewhere, reject any form of Cartesian dualism.[5] Gilbert Ryle, a leading British analyst, has strongly attacked what he calls "the dogma of the ghost in the machine." And Maurice Merliau-Ponty, possibly France's greatest phenomenologist, defended a doctrine which looks very much like an updated form of hylomorphism. For him there are three kinds of behavior: the syncretic, the amovable, and the symbolic. We might perhaps put it more simply and speak of three levels in man: the level of reflex activity and of instincts, the level of learning, and the level of symbolic thinking. Or again, the physiological, the psychic, and the spiritual level. Each lower level stands to the next higher one in the same relation as data stand to their meaning, as materiality stands to the idea embodied in it. The data are not data if they do not possess some meaning, and there can be no meaning which is not embedded in some data. Each higher level presupposes the lower one; there can be no mind before the organism is ready to carry one and no spirit before the

---

5   Among the few exceptions we must mention J. P. Sartre, whose dualism constitutes one of the weakest and most controversial aspects of his philosophy.

mind is capable of receiving it. I submit that this clearly implies delayed animation.

In my opinion there is a great amount of agreement between the contemporary antidualistic trend of philosophy and the hylomorphic conception of man. It is wise therefore to return to this conception or, at least,to accept the conclusions which follow from it. One of these conclusions is that the embryo is certainly not a human person during the early stages of pregnancy, and that, consequently, it is not immoral to terminate pregnancy during this time, provided there are serious reasons for such an intervention.

Let me insist on this restriction: the opinion which I have defended may lead to abuses, to abortions performed under flimsy pretexts. I would be among the first to deplore and condemn such abuses. Although a prehuman embryo cannot demand from us the absolute respect which we owe to the human person, it deserves a very great consideration, because it is a living being, endowed with a human finality, on its way to hominization. Therefore it seems to me that only very serious reasons should allow us to terminate its existence. Excesses will unavoidably occur, but they should not induce us to overlook the instances where sufficiently serious reasons exist for performing an abortion during the early stages of pregnancy.

A Defense of Abortion

Judith Jarvis Thomson

Most opposition to abortion relies on the premise that the fetus is a human being, a person, from the moment of conception. The premise is argued for, but, as I think, not well. Take, for example, the most common argument. We are asked to notice that the development of a human being from conception through birth into childhood is continuous; then it is said that to draw a line, to choose a point in this development and say "before this point the thing is not a person, after this point it is a person" is to make an arbitrary choice, a choice for which in the nature of things no good reason can be given. It is concluded that the fetus is, or anyway that we had better say it is, a person from the moment of conception. But this conclusion does not follow. Similar things might be said about the development of an acorn into an oak tree, and it does not follow that acorns are oak trees, or that we had better say they are. Arguments of this form are sometimes called "slippery slope arguments"—the phrase is perhaps self-explanatory—and it is dismaying that opponents of abortion rely on them so heavily and uncritically.

I am inclined to agree, however, that the prospects for "drawing a line" in the development of the fetus look dim. I am inclined to think also that we shall probably have to agree that the fetus has already become a human person well before birth. Indeed, it comes as a surprise when one first learns how early in its life it begins to acquire human characteristics. By the tenth week, for example, it already has a face, arms and legs, fingers and toes; it has internal organs, and brain activity is detectable.[1] On the other hand, I think that the premise is false, that the fetus is not a person from the moment of conception. A newly fertilized ovum, a newly implanted clump of cells, is no more a person than an acorn is an oak tree. But I shall not discuss any of this. For it seems to me to be of great interest to ask what happens if, for the sake of argument, we allow the premise. How, precisely, are we supposed to get from there to the conclusion that abortion is morally impermissible? Opponents of abortion commonly spend most of their time establishing that the fetus is a person, and hardly any time explaining the step from there to the impermissibility of abortion. Perhaps they think the step too simple and obvious to require much comment. Or perhaps instead they are simply being economical in argument. Many of those who defend abortion rely on the premise that the

Judith Jarvis Thomson, *Philosophy and Public Affairs*, Vol. 1, No. 1. Copyright 1971 by Princeton University Press. Reprinted by permission of Princeton University Press.

1   Daniel Callahan, *Abortion: Law, Choice and Morality* (New York, 1970), p. 373. This book gives a fascinating survey of the available information on abortion. The Jewish tradition is surveyed in David M. Feldman, *Birth Control in Jewish Law* (New York, 1968), Part 5; the Catholic tradition in John T. Noonan, Jr., "An Almost Absolute Value in History," in *The Morality of Abortion*, ed. John T. Noonan, Jr. (Cambridge, Mass., 1970).

fetus is not a person, but only a bit of tissue that will become a person at birth; and why pay out more arguments than you have to? Whatever the explanation, I suggest that the step they take is neither easy nor obvious, that it calls for closer examination than it is commonly given, and that when we do give it this closer examination we shall feel inclined to reject it.

I propose, then, that we grant that the fetus is a person from the moment of conception. How does the argument go from here? Something like this, I take it. Every person has a right to life. So the fetus has a right to life. No doubt the mother has a right to decide what shall happen in and to her body; everyone would grant that. But surely a person's right to life is stronger and more stringent than the mother's right to decide what happens in and to her body, and so outweighs it. So the fetus may not be killed; an abortion may not be performed.

It sounds plausible. But now let me ask you to imagine this. You wake up in the morning and find yourself back to back in bed with an unconscious violinist. A famous unconscious violinist. He has been found to have a fatal kidney ailment, and the Society of Music Lovers has canvassed all the available medical records and found that you alone have the right blood type to help. They have therefore kidnapped you, and last night the violinist's circulatory system was plugged into yours, so that your kidneys can be used to extract poisons from his blood as well as your own. The director of the hospital now tells you, "Look, we're sorry the Society of Music Lovers did this to you—we would never have permitted it if we had known. But still, they did it, and the violinist now is plugged into you. To unplug you would be to kill him. But never mind, it's only for nine months. By then he will have recovered from his ailment, and can safely be unplugged from you." Is it morally incumbent on you to

accede to this situation? No doubt it would be very nice of you if you did, a great kindness. But do you *have* to accede to it. What if it were not nine months, but nine years? Or longer still? What if the director of the hospital says, "Tough luck, I agree, but you've now got to stay in bed, with the violinist plugged into you, for the rest of your life. Because remember this. All persons have a right to life, and violinists are persons. Granted you have a right to decide what happens in and to your body, but a person's right to life outweighs your right to decide what happens in and to your body. So you cannot ever be unplugged from him." I imagine you would regard this as outrageous, which suggests that something really is wrong with that plausible-sounding argument I mentioned a moment ago.

In this case, of course, you were kidnapped; you didn't volunteer for the operation that plugged the violinist into your kidneys. Can those who oppose abortion on the ground I mentioned make an exception for a pregnancy due to rape? Certainly. They can say that persons have a right to life only if they didn't come into existence because of rape; or they can say that all persons have a right to life, but that some have less of a right to life than others, in particular, that those who came into existence because of rape have less. But these statements have a rather unpleasant sound. Surely the question of whether you have a right to life at all, or how much of it you have, shouldn't turn on the question of whether or not you are the product of a rape. And in fact the people who oppose abortion on the ground I mentioned do not make this distinction, and hence do not make an exception in case of rape.

Nor do they make an exception for a case in which the mother has to spend the nine months of her pregnancy in bed. They would agree that would be a great pity, and hard on the mother; but all the same, all persons have a right to life, the fetus is a person, and so on. I suspect, in fact, that they would not make an exception for a case in which, miraculously enough, the pregnancy went on for nine years, or even the rest of the mother's life.

Some won't even make an exception for a case in which continuation of the pregnancy is likely to shorten the mother's life; they regard abortion as impermissible even to save the mother's life. Such cases are nowadays very rare, and many opponents of abortion do not accept this extreme view. All the same, it is a good place to begin: a number of points of interest come out in respect to it.

1. Let us call the view that abortion is impermissible even to save the mother's life "the extreme view." I want to suggest first that it does not issue from the argument I mentioned earlier without the addition of some fairly powerful premises. Suppose a woman has become pregnant, and now learns that she has a cardiac condition such that she will die if she carries the baby to term. What may be done for her? The fetus, being a person, has a right to life, but as the mother is a person too, so has she a right to life. Presumably they have an equal right to life. How is it supposed to come out that an abortion may not be performed? If mother and child have an equal right to life, shouldn't we perhaps flip a coin? Or should we add to the mother's right to life her right to decide what happens in and to her body, which everybody seems to be ready to grant—the sum of her rights now outweighing the fetus' right to life?

The most familiar argument here is the following. We are told that performing the abortion would be directly killing[2] the child, whereas doing nothing would not be killing the mother, but only letting her die. Moreover, in killing the child, one would be killing an innocent person, for the child has committed no crime, and is not aiming at his mother's death. And then there are a variety of ways in which this might be continued. (1) But as directly killing an innocent person is always and absolutely impermissible, an abortion may not be performed. Or, (2) as directly killing an innocent person is murder, and murder is always and absolutely impermissible, an abortion may not be performed.[3] Or, (3) as one's duty to refrain from directly killing an innocent person is more stringent than one's duty to keep a person from dying, an abortion may not be performed. Or, (4) if one's only options are directly killing an innocent person or letting a person die, one must prefer letting the person die, and thus an abortion may not be performed.[4]

Some people seem to have thought that these are not further premises which must be added if the conclusion is to be reached, but that they follow from the very fact that an

2 The term "direct" in the arguments I refer to is a technical one. Roughly, what is meant by "direct killing" is either killing as an end in itself, or killing as a means of some end, for example, the end of saving someone else's life. See footnote 6 for an example of its use.

3 Cf. *Encyclical Letter of Pope Pius XI on Christian Marriage,* St. Paul Editions (Boston, n.d.), p. 32: "however much we may pity the mother whose health and even life is gravely imperiled in the performance of the duty allotted to her by nature, nevertheless what could ever be a sufficient reason for excusing in any way the direct murder of the innocent? This is precisely what we are dealing with here." Noonan (*The Morality of Abortion,* p. 43) reads this as follows: "What cause can ever avail to excuse in any way the direct killing of the innocent? For it is a question of that."

4 The thesis in (4) is in an interesting way weaker than those in (1), (2), and (3): they rule out abortion even in cases in which both mother *and* child will die if the abortion is not performed. By contrast, one who held the view expressed in (4) could consistently say that one needn't prefer letting two persons die to killing one.

innocent person has a right to life.[5] But this seems to me to be a mistake, and perhaps the simplest way to show this is to bring out that while we must certainly grant that innocent persons have a right to life, the theses in (1) through (4) are all false. Take (2), for example. If directly killing an innocent person is murder, and thus is impermissible, then the mother's directly killing the innocent person inside her is murder, and thus is impermissible. But it cannot seriously be thought to be murder if the mother performs an abortion on herself to save her life. It cannot seriously be said that she *must* refrain, that she *must* sit passively by and wait for her death. Let us look again at the case of you and the violinist. There you are, in bed with the violinist, and the director of the hospital says to you, "It's all most distressing, and I deeply sympathize, but you see this is putting an additional strain on your kidneys, and you'll be dead within the month. But you *have* to stay where you are all the same. Because unplugging you would be directly killing an innocent violinist, and that's murder, and that's impermissible." If anything in the world is true, it is that you do not commit murder, you do not do what is impermissible, if you reach around to your back and unplug yourself from that violinist to save your life.

The main focus of attention in writings on abortion has been on what a third party may or may not do in answer to a request from a woman for an abortion. This is in a way understandable. Things being as they are, there isn't much a woman can safely do to abort herself. So the question asked is what a third party may do, and what the mother may do, if it is mentioned at all, is deduced, almost as an afterthought, from what it is concluded that third parties may do. But it seems to me that to treat the matter in this way is to refuse to grant to the mother that very status of person which is so firmly insisted on for the fetus. For we cannot simply read off what a person may do from what a third party may do. Suppose you find yourself trapped in a tiny house with a growing child. I mean a very tiny house, and a rapidly growing child—you are already up against the wall of the house and in a few minutes you'll be crushed to death. The child on the other hand won't be crushed to death; if nothing is done to stop him from growing he'll be hurt, but in the end he'll simply burst open the house and walk out a free man. Now I could well understand it if a bystander were to say, "There's nothing we can do for you. We cannot choose between your life and his, we cannot be the ones to decide who is to live, we cannot intervene." But it cannot be concluded that you too can do nothing, that you cannot attack it to save your life. However innocent the child may be, you do not have to wait passively while it crushes you to death. Perhaps a pregnant woman is vaguely felt to have the status of house, to which we don't allow the right of self-defense. But if the woman houses the child, it should be remembered that she is a person who houses it.

I should perhaps stop to say explicitly that I am not claiming that people have a right to do anything whatever to save their lives. I think, rather, that there are drastic limits to the right of self-defense. If someone

---

5   Cf. the following passage from Pius XII, *Address to the Italian Catholic Society of Midwives:* "The baby in the maternal breast has the right to life immediately from God.—Hence there is no man, no human authority, no science, no medical, eugenic, social, economic or moral 'indication' which can establish or grant a valid juridical ground for a direct deliberate disposition of an innocent human life, that is a disposition which looks to its destruction either as in end or as a means to another end perhaps in itself not illicit.—The baby, still not born, is a man in the same degree and for the same reason as the mother" (quoted in Noonan, *The Morality of Abortion*, p. 45).

threatens you with death unless you torture someone else to death, I think you have not the right, even to save your life, to do so. But the case under consideration here is very different. In our case there are only two people involved, one whose life is threatened, and one who threatens it. Both are innocent: the one who is threatened is not threatened because of any fault, the one who threatens does not threaten because of any fault. For this reason we may feel that we bystanders cannot intervene. But the person threatened can.

In sum, a woman surely can defend her life against the threat to it posed by the unborn child, even if doing so involves its death. And this shows not merely that the theses in (1) through (4) are false; it shows also that the extreme view of abortion is false, and so we need not canvass any other possible ways of arriving at it from the argument I mentioned at the outset.

2. The extreme view could of course be weakened to say that while abortion is permissible to save the mother's life, it may not be performed by a third party, but only by the mother herself. But this cannot be right either. For what we have to keep in mind is that the mother and the unborn child are not like two tenants in a small house which has, by an unfortunate mistake, been rented to both: the mother *owns* the house. The fact that she does adds to the offensiveness of deducing that the mother can do nothing from the supposition that third parties can do nothing. But it does more than this: it casts a bright light on the supposition that third parties can do nothing. Certainly it lets us see that a third party who says. "I cannot choose between you" is fooling himself if he thinks this is impartiality. If Jones has found and fastened on a certain coat, which he needs to keep him from freezing, but which Smith also needs to keep him from freezing, then it is not impartiality that says "I cannot choose between you" when Smith owns the coat. Women have said again and

again "This body is *my* body!" and they have reason to feel angry, reason to feel that it has been like shouting into the wind. Smith, after all, is hardly likely to bless us if we say to him, "Of course it's your coat, anybody would grant that it is. But no one may choose between you and Jones who is to have it."

We should really ask what it is that says "no one may choose" in the face of the fact that the body that houses the child is the mother's body. It may be simply a failure to appreciate this fact. But it may be something more interesting, namely the sense that one has a right to refuse to lay hands on people, even where it would be just and fair to do so, even where justice seems to require that somebody do so. Thus justice might call for somebody to get Smith's coat back from Jones, and yet you have a right to refuse to be the one to lay hands on Jones, a right to refuse to do physical violence to him. This, I think, must be granted. But then what should be said is not "no one may choose," but only "*I* cannot choose," and indeed not even this, but "I will not *act*," leaving it open that somebody else can or should, and in particular that anyone in a position of authority, with the job of securing people's rights, both can and should. So this is no difficulty. I have not been arguing that any given third party must accede to the mother's request that he perform an abortion to save her life, but only that he may.

I suppose that in some views of human life the mother's body is only on loan to her, the loan not being one which gives her any prior claim to it. One who held this view might well think it impartiality to say "I cannot choose." But I shall simply ignore this possibility. My own view is that if a human being has any just, prior claim to anything at all, he has a just, prior claim to his own body. And perhaps this needn't be argued for here anyway, since, as I mentioned, the arguments against abortion we are looking at do grant that the woman has a right to decide what happens in and to her body.

But although they do grant it, I have tried to show that they do not take seriously what is done in granting it. I suggest the same thing will reappear even more clearly when we turn away from cases in which the mother's life is at stake, and attend, as I propose we now do, to the vastly more common cases in which a woman wants an abortion for some less weighty reason than preserving her own life.

3. Where the mother's life is not at stake, the argument I mentioned at the outset seems to have a much stronger pull. "Everyone has a right to life, so the unborn person has a right to life." And isn't the child's right to life weightier than anything other than the mother's own right to life, which she might put forward as ground for an abortion?

This argument treats the right to life as if it were unproblematic. It is not, and this seems to me to be precisely the source of the mistake.

For we should now, at long last, ask what it comes to, to have a right to life. In some views having a right to life includes having a right to be given at least the bare minimum one needs for continued life. But suppose that what in fact *is* the bare minimum a man needs for continued life is something he has no right at all to be given? If I am sick unto death, and the only thing that will save my life is the touch of Henry Fonda's cool hand on my fevered brow, then all the same, I have no right to be given the touch of Henry Fonda's cool hand on my fevered brow. It would be frightfully nice of him to fly in from the West Coast to provide it. It would be less nice, though no doubt well meant, if my friends flew out to the West Coast and carried Henry Fonda back with them. But I have no right at all against anybody that he should do this for me. Or again, to return to the story I told earlier, the fact

that for continued life that violinist needs the continued use of your kidneys does not establish that he has a right to be given the continued use of your kidneys. He certainly has no right against you that *you* should give him continued use of your kidneys. For nobody has any right to use your kidneys unless you give him such a right; and nobody has the right against you that you shall give him this right—if you do allow him to go on using your kidneys, this is a kindness on your part, and not something he can claim from you as his due. Nor has he any right against anybody else that *they* should give him continued use of your kidneys. Certainly he had no right against the Society of Music Lovers that they should plug him into you in the first place. And if you now start to unplug yourself, having learned that you will otherwise have to spend nine years in bed with him, there is nobody in the world who must try to prevent you, in order to see to it that he is given something he has a right to be given.

Some people are rather stricter about the right to life. In their view, it does not include the right to be given anything, but amounts to, and only to, the right not to be killed by anybody. But here a related difficulty arises. If everybody is to refrain from killing that violinist, then everybody must refrain from doing a great many different sorts of things. Everybody must refrain from slitting his throat, everybody must refrain from shooting him—and everybody must refrain from unplugging you from him. But does he have a right against everybody that they shall refrain from unplugging you from him? To refrain from doing this is to allow him to continue to use your kidneys. It could be argued that he has a right against us that *we* should allow him to continue to use your kidneys. That is, while he had no right against us that we should give him the use of your kidneys, it might be argued that he anyway has a right against us that we shall not now intervene and deprive him of the use of your kidneys. I shall come back to third party interventions later. But certainly the violinist has no right against you that *you* shall allow him to continue to use your kidneys. As I said, if you do allow him to use them, it is a kindness on your part, and not something you owe him.

The difficulty I point to here is not peculiar to the right to life. It reappears in connection with all the other natural rights; and it is something which an adequate account of rights must deal with. For present purposes it is enough just to draw attention to it. But I would stress that I am not arguing that people do not have a right to life—quite to the contrary, it seems to me that the primary control we must place on the acceptability of an account of rights is that it should turn out in that account to be a truth that all persons have a right to life. I am arguing only that having a right to life does not guarantee having either a right to be given the use of or a right to be allowed continued use of another person's body—even if one needs it for life itself. So the right to life will not serve the opponents of abortion in the very simple and clear way in which they seem to have thought it would.

4. There is another way to bring out the difficulty. In the most ordinary sort of case, to deprive someone of what he has a right to is to treat him unjustly. Suppose a boy and his small brother are jointly given a box of chocolates for Christmas. If the older boy takes the box and refuses to give his brother any of the chocolates, he is unjust to him, for the brother has been given a right to half of them. But suppose that, having learned that otherwise it means nine years in bed with that violinist, you unplug yourself from him. You surely are not being unjust to him, for you gave him no right to use your kidneys, and no one else can have given him any such

right. But we have to notice that in unplugging yourself, you are killing him; and violinists, like everybody else, have a right to life, and thus in the view we were considering just now, the right not to be killed. So here you do what he supposedly has a right you shall not do, but you do not act unjustly to him in doing it.

The emendation which may be made at this point is this: the right to life consists not in the right not to be killed, but rather in the right not to be killed unjustly. This runs a risk of circularity, but never mind: it would enable us to square the fact that the violinist has a right to life with the fact that you do not act unjustly toward him in unplugging yourself, thereby killing him. For if you do not kill him unjustly, you do not violate his right to life, and so it is no wonder you do him no injustice.

But if this emendation is accepted, the gap in the argument against abortion stares us plainly in the face: it is by no means enough to show that the fetus is a person, and to remind us that all persons have a right to life—we need to be shown also that killing the fetus violates its right to life, i.e., that abortion is unjust killing. And is it?

I suppose we may take it as a datum that in a case of pregnancy due to rape the mother has not given the unborn person a right to the use of her body for food and shelter. Indeed, in what pregnancy could it be supposed that the mother has given the unborn person such a right? It is not as if there were unborn persons drifting about the world, to whom a woman who wants a child says "I invite you in."

But it might be argued that there are other ways one can have acquired a right to the use of another person's body than by having been invited to use it by that person. Suppose a woman voluntarily indulges in intercourse, knowing of the chance it will issue in pregnancy, and then she does become pregnant; is she not in part responsible for the presence, in fact the very existence, of the unborn person inside her? No doubt she did not invite it in. But doesn't her partial responsibility for its being there itself give it a right to the use of her body?[6] If so, then her aborting it would be more like the boy's taking away the chocolates, and less like your unplugging yourself from the violinist—doing so would be depriving it of what it does have a right to, and thus would be doing it an injustice.

And then, too, it might be asked whether or not she can kill it even to save her own life: If she voluntarily called it into existence, how can she now kill it, even in self-defense?

The first thing to be said about this is that it is something new. Opponents of abortion have been so concerned to make out the independence of the fetus, in order to establish that it has a right to life, just as its mother does, that they have tended to overlook the possible support they might gain from making out that the fetus is *dependent* on the mother, in order to establish that she has a special kind of responsibility for it, a responsibility that gives it rights against her which are not possessed by any independent person—such as an ailing violinist who is a stranger to her.

On the other hand, this argument would give the unborn person a right to its mother's body only if her pregnancy resulted from a voluntary act, undertaken in full knowledge of the chance a pregnancy might result from it. It would leave out entirely the unborn person whose existence is due to rape. Pending the availability of some further argument, then, we would be left with the conclusion that unborn persons whose existence is due to rape have no right to the use of their mothers' bodies, and thus that abort-

ing them is not depriving them of anything they have a right to and hence is not unjust killing.

And we should also notice that it is not at all plain that this argument really does go even as far as it purports to. For there are cases and cases, and the details make a difference. If the room is stuffy, and I therefore open a window to air it, and a burglar climbs in, it would be absurd to say, "Ah, now he can stay, she's given him a right to the use of her house—for she is partially responsible for his presence there, having voluntarily done what enabled him to get in, in full knowledge that there are such things as burglars, and that burglars burgle." It would be still more absurd to say this if I had had bars installed outside my windows, precisely to prevent burglars from getting in, and a burglar got in only because of a defect in the bars. It remains equally absurd if we imagine it is not a burglar who climbs in, but an innocent person who blunders or falls in. Again, suppose it were like this: people-seeds drift about in the air like pollen, and if you open your windows, one may drift in and take root in your carpets or upholstery. You don't want children, so you fix up your windows with fine mesh screens, the very best you can buy. As can happen, however, and on very, very rare occasions does happen, one of the screens is defective; and a seed drifts in and takes root. Does the person-plant who now develops have a right to the use of your house? Surely not—despite the fact that you voluntarily opened your windows, you knowingly kept carpets and upholstered furniture, and you knew that screens were sometimes defective. Someone may argue that you are responsible for its rooting, that it does have a right to your house, because after all you *could* have lived

---

6   The need for a discussion of this argument was brought home to me by members of the Society for Ethical and Legal Philosophy, to whom this paper was originally presented.

out your life with bare floors and furniture, or with sealed windows and doors. But this won't do—for by the same token anyone can avoid a pregnancy due to rape by having a hysterectomy, or anyway by never leaving home without a (reliable!) army.

It seems to me that the argument we are looking at can establish at most that there are *some* cases in which the unborn person has a right to the use of its mother's body, and therefore *some* cases in which abortion is unjust killing. There is room for much discussion and argument as to precisely which, if any. But I think we should sidestep this issue and leave it open, for at any rate the argument certainly does not establish that all abortion is unjust killing.

5. There is room for yet another argument here, however. We surely must all grant that there may be cases in which it would be morally indecent to detach a person from your body at the cost of his life. Suppose you learn that what the violinist needs is not nine years of your life, but only one hour: all you need to do to save his life is to spend one hour in that bed with him. Suppose also that letting him use your kidneys for that one hour would not affect your health in the slightest. Admittedly you were kidnapped. Admittedly you did not give anyone permission to plug him into you. Nevertheless it seems to me plain you *ought* to allow him to use your kidneys for that hour—it would be indecent to refuse.

Again, suppose pregnancy lasted only an hour, and constituted no threat to life or health. And suppose that a woman becomes pregnant as a result of rape. Admittedly she did not voluntarily do anything to bring about the existence of a child. Admittedly she did nothing at all which would give the unborn person a right to the use of her body. All the same it might well be said, as in the newly emended violinist story, that she

ought to allow it to remain for that hour—that it would be indecent in her to refuse.

Now some people are inclined to use the term "right" in such a way that it follows from the fact that you ought to allow a person to use your body for the hour he needs, that he has a right to use your body for the hour he needs, even though he has not been given that right by any person or act. They may say that it follows also that if you refuse, you act unjustly toward him. This use of the term is perhaps so common that it cannot be called wrong; nevertheless it seems to me to be an unfortunate loosening of what we would do better to keep a tight rein on. Suppose that box of chocolates I mentioned earlier had not been given to both boys jointly, but was given only to the older boy. There he sits, stolidly eating his way through the box, his small brother watching enviously. Here we are likely to say "You ought not to be so mean. You ought to give your brother some of those chocolates." My own view is that it just does not follow from the truth of this that the brother has any right to any of the chocolates. If the boy refuses to give his brother any, he is greedy, stingy, callous—but not unjust. I suppose that the people I have in mind will say it does follow that the brother has a right to some of the chocolates, and thus that the boy does act unjustly if he refuses to give his brother any. But the effect of saying this is to obscure what we should keep distinct, namely the difference between the boy's refusal in this case and the boy's refusal in the earlier case, in which the box was given to both boys jointly, and in which the small brother thus had what was from any point of view clear title to half.

A further objection to so using the term "right" that from the fact that A ought to do a thing for B, it follows that B has a right against A that A do it for him, is that it is going to make the question of whether or not a man has a right to a thing turn on how easy it is to provide him with it; and this seems not merely unfortunate, but morally unacceptable. Take the case of Henry Fonda again. I said earlier that I had no right to the touch of his cool hand on my fevered brow, even though I needed it to save my life. I said it would be frightfully nice of him to fly in from the West Coast to provide me with it, but that I had no right against him that he should do so. But suppose he isn't on the West Coast. Suppose he has only to walk across the room, place a hand briefly on my brow—and lo, my life is saved. Then surely he ought to do it, it would be indecent to refuse. Is it to be said "Ah, well, it follows that in this case she has a right to the touch of his hand on her brow, and so it would be an injustice in him to refuse"? So that I have a right to it when it is easy for him to provide it, though no right when it's hard? It's rather a shocking idea that anyone's rights should fade away and disappear as it gets harder and harder to accord them to him.

So my own view is that even though you ought to let the violinist use your kidneys for the one hour he needs, we should not conclude that he has a right to do so—we should say that if you refuse, you are, like the boy who owns all the chocolates and will give none away, self-centered and callous, indecent in fact, but not unjust. And similarly, that even supposing a case in which a woman pregnant due to rape ought to allow the unborn person to use her body for the hour he needs, we should not conclude that he has a right to do so; we should conclude that she is self-centered, callous, indecent, but not unjust, if she refuses. The complaints are no less grave; they are just different. However, there is no need to insist on this point. If anyone does wish to deduce "he has a right" from "you ought," then all the same he must surely grant that there are cases in which it is not morally required of you that you allow that violinist to use your kidneys,

and in which he does not have a right to use them, and in which you do not do him an injustice if you refuse. And so also for mother and unborn child. Except in such cases as the unborn person has a right to demand it—and we were leaving open the possibility that there may be such cases—nobody is morally *required* to make large sacrifices, of health, of all other interests and concerns, of all other duties and commitments, for nine years, or even for nine months, in order to keep another person alive.

6. We have in fact to distinguish between two kinds of Samaritan: the Good Samaritan and what we might call the Minimally Decent Samaritan. The story of the Good Samaritan, you will remember, goes like this:

> A certain man went down from Jerusalem to Jericho, and fell among thieves, which stripped him of his raiment, and wounded him, and departed, leaving him half dead.
> And by chance there came down a certain priest that way; and when he saw him, he passed by on the other side.
> And likewise a Levite, when he was at the place, came and looked on him, and passed by on the other side.
> But a certain Samaritan, as he journeyed, came where he was; and when he saw him he had compassion on him.
> And went to him, and bound up his wounds, pouring in oil and wine, and set him on his own beast, and brought him to an inn, and took care of him.
> And on the morrow, when he departed, he took out two pence, and gave them to the host, and said unto him, "Take care of him; and whatsoever thou spendest more, when I come again, I will repay thee."
>
> (Luke 10:30–35)

The Good Samaritan went out of his way, at some cost to himself, to help one in need of it. We are not told what the options were, that is, whether or not the priest and the Levite could have helped by doing less than the Good Samaritan did, but assuming they could have, then the fact they did nothing at all shows they were not even Minimally Decent Samaritans, not because they were not Samaritans, but because they were not even minimally decent.

These things are a matter of degree, of course, but there is a difference, and it comes out perhaps most clearly in the story of Kitty Genovese, who, as you will remember, was murdered while thirty-eight people watched or listened, and did nothing at all to help her. A Good Samaritan would have rushed out to give direct assistance against the murderer. Or perhaps we had better allow that it would have been a Splendid Samaritan who did this, on the ground that it would have involved a risk of death for himself. But the thirty-eight not only did not do this, they did not even trouble to pick up a phone to call the police. Minimally Decent Samaritanism would call for doing at least that, and their not having done it was monstrous.

After telling the story of the Good Samaritan, Jesus said "Go, and do thou likewise." Perhaps he meant that we are morally required to act as the Good Samaritan did. Perhaps he was urging people to do more than is morally required of them. At all events it seems plain that it was not morally required of any of the thirty-eight that he rush out to give direct assistance at the risk of his own life, and that it is not morally required of anyone that he give long stretches of his life—nine years or nine months—to sustaining the life of a person who has no special right (we were leaving open the possibility of this) to demand it.

Indeed, with one rather striking class of exceptions, no one in any country in the world is *legally* required to do anywhere near as much as this for anyone else. The class of exceptions is obvious. My main concern here is not the state of the law in respect to abortion, but it is worth drawing attention to the fact that in no state in this country is any man compelled by law to be even a Minimally Decent Samaritan to any person; there is no law under which charges could be brought against the thirty-eight who stood by while Kitty Genovese died. By contrast, in most states in this country women are compelled by law to be not merely Minimally Decent Samaritans, but Good Samaritans to unborn persons inside them. This doesn't by itself settle anything one way or the other, because it may well be argued that there should be laws in this country—as there are in many European countries—compelling at least Minimally Decent Samaritanism.[7] But it does show that there is a gross injustice in the existing state of the law. And it shows also that the groups currently working against liberalization of abortion laws, in fact working toward having it declared unconstitutional for a state to permit abortion, had better start working for the adoption of Good Samaritan laws generally, or earn the charge that they are acting in bad faith.

I should think, myself, that Minimally Decent Samaritan laws would be one thing, Good Samaritan laws quite another, and in fact highly improper. But we are not here concerned with the law. What we should ask is not whether anybody should be compelled by law to be a Good Samaritan, but whether we must accede to a situation in which somebody is being compelled—by nature, perhaps—to be a Good Samaritan. We have, in other words, to look now at third-party interventions. I have been arguing that no person is morally required to make large sacrifices to sustain the life of another who has no right to demand them, and this even where the sacrifices do not

---

7   For a discussion of the difficulties involved, and a survey of the European experience with such laws, see *The Good Samaritan and the Law*, ed. James M. Ratcliffe (New York, 1966).

include life itself; we are not morally required to be Good Samaritans or anyway Very Good Samaritans to one another. But what if a man cannot extricate himself from such a situation? What if he appeals to us to extricate him? It seems to me plain that there are cases in which we can, cases in which a Good Samaritan would extricate him. There you are, you were kidnapped, and nine years in bed with that violinist lie ahead of you. You have your own life to lead. You are sorry, but you simply cannot see giving up so much of your life to the sustaining of his. You cannot extricate yourself, and ask us to do so. I should have thought that—in light of his having no right to the use of your body—it was obvious that we do not have to accede to your being forced to give up so much. We can do what you ask. There is no injustice to the violinist in our doing so.

7. Following the lead of the opponents of abortion, I have throughout been speaking of the fetus merely as a person, and what I have been asking is whether or not the argument we began with, which proceeds only from the fetus' being a person, really does establish its conclusion. I have argued that it does not.

But of course there are arguments and arguments, and it may be said that I have simply fastened on the wrong one. It may be said that what is important is not merely the fact that the fetus is a person, but that it is a person for whom the woman has a special kind of responsibility issuing from the fact that she is its mother. And it might be argued that all my analogies are therefore irrelevant—for you do not have that special kind of responsibility for that violinist, Henry Fonda does not have that special kind of responsibility for me. And our attention might be drawn to the fact that men and women both *are* compelled by law to provide support for their children.

I have in effect dealt (briefly) with this argument in section 4 above; but a (still briefer) recapitulation now may be in order. Surely we do not have any such "special responsibility" for a person unless we have assumed it, explicitly or implicitly. If a set of parents do not try to prevent pregnancy, do not obtain an abortion, and then at the time of birth of the child do not put it out for adoption, but rather take it home with them, then they have assumed responsibility for it, they have given it rights, and they cannot *now* withdraw support from it at the cost of its life because they now find it difficult to go on providing for it. But if they have taken all reasonable precautions against having a child, they do not simply by virtue of their biological relationship to the child who comes into existence have a special responsibility for it. They may wish to assume responsibility for it, or they may not wish to. And I am suggesting that if assuming responsibility for it would require large sacrifices, then they may refuse. A Good Samaritan would not refuse—or anyway, a Splendid Samaritan, if the sacrifices that had to be made were enormous. But then so would a Good Samaritan assume responsibility for that violinist; so would Henry Fonda, if he is a Good Samaritan, fly in from the West Coast and assume responsibility for me.

8. My argument will be found unsatisfactory on two counts by many of those who want to regard abortion as morally permissible. First, while I do argue that abortion is not impermissible, I do not argue that it is always permissible. There may well be cases in which carrying the child to term requires only Minimally Decent Samaritanism of the mother, and this is a standard we must not fall below. I am inclined to think it a merit of my account precisely that it does *not* give a general yes or a general no. It allows for and supports our sense that, for example, a sick

and desperately frightened fourteen-year-old schoolgirl, pregnant due to rape, may of *course* choose abortion, and that any law which rules this out is an insane law. And it also allows for and supports our sense that in other cases resort to abortion is even positively indecent. It would be indecent in the woman to request an abortion, and indecent in a doctor to perform it, if she is in her seventh month, and wants the abortion just to avoid the nuisance of postponing a trip abroad. The very fact that the arguments I have been drawing attention to treat all cases of abortion, or even all cases of abortion in which the mother's life is not at stake, as morally on a par ought to have made them suspect at the outset.

Secondly, while I am arguing for the permissibility of abortion in some cases, I am not arguing for the right to secure the death of the unborn child. It is easy to confuse these two things in that up to certain point in the life of the fetus it is not able to survive outside the mother's body; hence removing it from her body guarantees its death. But they are importantly different. I have argued that you are not morally required to spend nine months in bed, sustaining the life of that violinist; but to say this is by no means to say

that if, when you unplug yourself, there is a miracle and he survives, you than have a right to turn round and slit his throat. You may detach yourself even if this costs him his life; you have no right to be guaranteed his death, by some other means, if unplugging yourself does not kill him. There are some people who will feel dissatisfied by this feature of my argument. A woman may be utterly devastated by the thought of a child, a bit of herself, put out for adoption and never seen or heard of again. She may therefore want not merely that the child be detached from her, but more, that it die. Some opponents of abortion are inclined to regard this as beneath contempt—thereby showing insensitivity to what is surely a powerful source of despair. All the same, I agree that the desire for the child's death is not one which anybody may gratify, should it turn out to be possible to detach the child alive.

At this place, however, it should be remembered that we have only been pretending throughout that the fetus is a human being from the moment of conception. A very early abortion is surely not the killing of a person, and so is not dealt with by anything I have said here.

Abortion's Hardest Cases

Margaret Carlson

Afterward, when their daughter was buried and their hearts broken, the Bells could see everything clearly. Until then, they had not thought about their teenager's getting pregnant or what they would do if she did. They did not know that there was any such thing as a parental consent law.

But there is such a law in Indiana, where the Bells live and where their daughter Becky, 17, died after an illegal abortion. In 1984 the state legislature voted to require a minor to get a parent's permission for an abortion or else to convince a judge that she is mature enough to make the decision on her own.

Becky, whose room in Indianapolis is still filled with stuffed animals and riding gear, felt she could do neither. She had gone to Planned Parenthood for a pregnancy test, the Bells learned as they tried to retrace the steps she took during those final days, and there she was told of the Indiana law. No one knows what happened between that moment and her death two months later. When the Bells went through Becky's purse after she died, they found telephone numbers of abortion clinics in Kentucky, which did not require parental consent. "Becky just happened to live in the wrong state," says her father.

Should a teenage girl have the right— and the burden—of deciding about abortion on her own? Isn't abortion at least as serious a medical procedure as a tonsillectomy or a tooth extraction, both of which require parental involvement in most states? Shouldn't the law force a parent and a child to communicate, especially if the child is in trouble?

Last week the Supreme Court faced these tough questions in its first abortion rulings since the landmark *Webster* decision last July. In a 5-to-4 vote, the Justices upheld a Minnesota law requiring unwed teenagers to notify both parents before an abortion if the law allows minors to go to a judge instead. In a 6-to-3 vote, the court upheld Ohio's requirement that a physician notify one parent of a pregnant minor of her intent to have an abortion; it also provided for judicial bypass.

The close votes and the widely divergent opinions reveal a court still divided over abortion and, in these cases, over the state of the family. Justice Anthony Kennedy voted to uphold the Minnesota law, with or without the judicial bypass, reasoning that to keep parents in the dark about a daughter's abortion "is to risk, or perpetuate, estrangement or alienation from the child when she is in the greatest need of parental guidance and support." But even he conceded that at times "notifying one or both parents will not be in the minor's best interest."

Just two days after the court's ruling, pro-life activists were applauding an even more stunning victory: the Louisiana legisla-

---

ture gave final approval to the nation's most restrictive abortion law. The bill would make abortion a punishable criminal act unless the life of the mother was at stake. It allows no exception for victims of rape or incest.

The Louisiana bill and the court's rulings bring to a head the two fierce battles fought this past year: the pro-life movement's push to deny abortion to all pregnant women, even victims of rape and incest; and the pro-choice movement's effort to strike down parental-involvement laws as backdoor ways to restrict abortion that do nothing to improve communication between parent and child.

How to deal with rape and incest and parental involvement are so-called wedge issues, a way for each side in the abortion debate to prove the unreasonableness of the other side. Even those who strongly favor a woman's right to choose find themselves troubled by the notion of a girl's right to choose, so parental consent or notification has been a comparatively easy sell: 33 states have passed such laws. By forcing the pro-choice movement to challenge this trend, the pro-life movement has been able to paint its opponents as anti-family, bent on weakening the bond between the generations, encouraging teenage promiscuity and fostering a libertine attitude toward sex that results in more than 400,000 teenage abortions a year.

If this seems extreme, the same is true—but with the sides reversed—on the equally emotional issue of what to do about a child conceived in the violence of rape or incest. The pro-life movement brooks no exception to the absolute position that all abortions, except those to save the life of the mother, are wrong, even ones intended to terminate the progeny of a rapist. Yet this stance may be their undoing. Louisiana's Governor Buddy Roemer, a self-described "right-to-lifer," has promised to veto the just-passed antiabor-

tion bill because it makes no exceptions for rape and incest.

Sometimes when it is not feasible to make abortions following rape or incest illegal, the movement settles for cutting off Medicaid funds. "Rape and incest are tragedies," says Illinois Congressman Henry Hyde, author of the federal restriction, "but why visit on the second victim, the unborn child that is the product of that criminal act, capital punishment?" Forcing only poor women to have the children of their rapists, says the pro-choice movement, shows how heartless the right-to-life movement is.

Yet this issue, like that of parental involvement, is not so simple. The victim of rape or incest is often herself an innocent child in need of saving. Pamela (a pseudonym) was a seventh-grader in Washington when she was allegedly raped by her stepfather. When her mother discovered she was pregnant, she took her to a Planned Parenthood clinic just ten blocks from the White House to arrange an abortion. "She was pitiful," recalls clinic director Mary Vandenbroucke, who had to break the news that Medicaid would not pay the $400 cost of an abortion, even for a case like Pamela's. Although the mother works two jobs, as a part-time government clerk and a cashier in a fast-food restaurant at night, she takes home just $289 every two weeks. Rather than turn away an indigent victim of incest, Planned Parenthood agreed to perform the procedure for $100.

Because cases like Becky's and Pamela's are so difficult to sort out, they have become this year's combat zone. In the fight to win over the ambivalent majority of Americans, the pro-choice movement is on the wrong side of parental consent: 69% of adult Americans favor laws requiring a teenage girl to get her parents' permission before having an abortion, according to a Time/CNN survey. Similarly, pro-lifers lose support over rape and incest: 84% of those polled believe the Government should pay when a rape victim needs an abortion and cannot afford it, and 77% when incest is involved.

Both sides in the abortion fight could score political points by showing moderation on these issues, and both would remove easy targets for their adversaries. "Parental notification is not a battle pro-choicers should fight in public, although the pro-lifers force them to. It defies the common sense of most people," says William Schneider, resident fellow of the American Enterprise Institute. "The same goes for being against abortion for victims of rape and incest. People think you're from Mars; it offends them." But neither side is backing down. Their reasons show how intractable are abortion's hardest cases.

Parents, Teenage Sex and Abortion

Better than a parent's control over abortion would be a world in which children too young to understand the power of sex did not engage in it, and one in which those unprepared to be pregnant did not become so. Since long before Juliet met Romeo, adults have been trying to convince adolescents barely able to decide what to wear in the morning that they are not mature enough to manage the complicated and overwhelming feelings that come with a sexual relationship. But for just as long, teenagers have been unpersuaded. Surveys show that at least half the young people between the ages of 15 and 19 are sexually active, and 24% of teenage girls will become pregnant by age 18.

Nonetheless, communication about sex between parents and children is stuck in the Dark Ages. Says one Washington psychiatrist: "Parents and children don't want to know about each other as sexual beings. Sex is the point of separation, the country into which a parent does not travel with a child."

That is one reason why school sex-education courses, which put the subject at a clinical remove, have become the norm.

But when sex moves from the private to the open and a teenager is pregnant, children who normally turn to a parent in a time of trouble will usually do so whether or not there is a law requiring it and whether or not they have been talking about sex. In Massachusetts, which requires teens to obtain the permission of both parents or of a judge, about 75% of the girls who have abortions share the decision with their parents. Levels of parental involvement are equally high in neighboring Connecticut and New Hampshire, where such consent is not required. "I see no point whatsoever in the parent-involvement laws," says Jamie Ann Sabino, an attorney who chairs the Lawyer Referral Panel on Judicial Consent for Minors in Massachusetts. "These girls didn't go to their parents because of them."

Teenagers who do not want to talk to their parents often find a way to avoid it: they go before a judge, or they go out of state; they wait until their condition becomes obvious and have a dangerous, second-trimester abortion; or they have a baby by default. Justice Thurgood Marshall described the dilemma in his dissent in the Minnesota case: "This scheme forces a young woman in an already dire situation to choose between two fundamentally unacceptable alternatives: notifying a possibly dictatorial or even abusive parent or justifying her personal decision in an intimidating proceeding to a black-robed stranger."

There is some evidence supporting the contention that parental-involvement laws restrict access to abortions. In a brief, opponents of the Minnesota law, which took effect in 1981, cite a study conducted between 1980 and 1984 indicating that the birthrate for 15-to-17-year-olds in Minneapolis rose 38.4%, while the birthrate for 18-to-19-year-olds, not covered by the law, rose only 0.3%. In the 20 months after Massachusetts put its parental-consent law into effect in 1981, 1 of every 3 teenage abortions was done out of state, while those within the state dropped 43%. Former Superior Court Judge Paul Garrity, who is pro-life by sentiment, feels that the law exists to "harass these kids."

Gaffity, who presided over hundreds of judicial-bypass hearings, also believes that a youngster can be a good judge of whether parents can handle an unwanted pregnancy on top of their own difficulties or even whether the parents want to be involved. Of the teenagers who came before him, Garrity says, "To a person, they were scared to death, but they did know what they wanted." An alcoholic mother, a drug-addicted father, an absent or neglectful parent are some of the reasons teenagers cite for not going home for help. The fact that only half the minors in Minnesota live with both biological parents persuaded Justice Sandra Day O'Connor to agree with the more liberal Justice John Paul Stevens on the need for judicial bypass.

An anomaly in the movement to require a parent's consent to an abortion is that there is no law requiring parental approval of staying pregnant and bearing a child, with its life-changing, lifelong consequences. There are compelling health and safety arguments against pregnancy: teenage girls are 24 times as likely to die of childbirth as of a first-trimester abortion, according to the Alan Guttmacher Institute. While having a child is one part of the full and complex life of a woman, it often turns out to be the defining, and confining, fact of a teenager's existence. Eight out of 10 girls who have babies at 17 or younger drop out of high school. Children born of teenagers are much more likely to grow up in poverty and be undereducated and, poorly housed. Children born of teenage mothers are twice as

likely to die in infancy as are those born of women in their 20s, and they are much more likely to be raised in resentment and rage.

It is unlikely that politicians could write laws to improve communications in unhappy families, or keep teenagers from becoming pregnant, or provide wise and caring parents when they do. Still, making the argument against parental involvement is like arguing for the right to burn the American flag—politically, it is a tough case no matter how right the reasoning. Now that the Supreme Court has put its stamp of approval on some notification laws, the two sides head back to the legislatures. Says Kate Michelman, executive director of the National Abortion Rights Action League (NARAL): "On the heels of this week's court decisions, we again confront the reality that the right to choose literally hangs by a thread in post-*Webster* America."

Rape and Incest

Two wrongs do not make a right, both sides argue. Pro-life advocates say an unborn child, innocent of the actions of the father, should not become a second victim; murder should not follow a rape. The pro-choice side responds that a woman forced to bear a child conceived in rape or incest is violated twice, once by the criminal and then by an uncaring state that forces her to carry and give birth to the incarnation of her assailant.

Until recently, the primary arena for this fight has been Congress, where since 1977 the Hyde Amendment has denied Medicaid funding for abortions unless a woman's life is endangered. A significant triumph for the right-to-life movement in the first years after abortion was legalized, the amendment has become the lightning rod for pro-choice advocates on the Hill. Last year Congresswoman Barbara Boxer introduced a proposal to restore abortion funds for women who are assaulted. "Why should the Government leave their side at such a moment of crisis?" she demanded. Hyde called his opponents "the death squads of the left" and "the pro-killer crowd." California Democratic Congressman George Miller, arguing for the Boxer amendment, implored his colleagues not to turn the "disgusting, violent, solitary act of rape into a gang rape by the Congress of the U.S."

The Boxer amendment passed both houses in October 1989, garnering the votes of otherwise pro-life legislators like South Carolina Republican Congressman Arthur Ravenel Jr. But George Bush vetoed the bill, and the House failed to muster the two-thirds majority required for an override. While Hyde and his supporters contend that abortion is wrong no matter what the circumstances, Bush says abortion should be legal for victims of rape or incest. He just does not want to pay for such abortions, a stance that allowed Boxer to tag him as "a kinder and gentler man [who] executes the cruelest veto on the poorest, most vulnerable victims of society."

Twenty-nine states have legislated the equivalent of the Hyde Amendment and restrict Medicaid funds to women in life-threatening situations. Ten states pay for abortions in which rape and incest are involved; twelve states, including Washington, New York and California, still fund all abortions.

The congressional fight is a holding action until the right-to-life movement can push through a state law that forces the Supreme Court to review *Roe v. Wade.* Louisiana's law might be the one. Right-to-life leaders think they have a chance to override Governor Roemer's threatened veto. But they may lose more conservatives like Garey Forster, a self-described "confused Catholic," who voted against the bill because it was

"too harsh, too final." A doctor can be sentenced to a minimum of one year at hard labor and charged a $10,000 fine; a woman can be punished as an accessory to the crime, just as if she were driving a getaway car.

Short of banning abortion outright, the pro-life movement is lobbying legislatures to impose reporting requirements on victims of rape and incest that would make such abortions nearly impossible to obtain. Says the National Right to Life Committee's spokeswoman, Susan Smith: "We do everything we can to eliminate abortions and to prevent funding for rape and incest, but where it is inevitable we lobby for tight reporting requirements to prevent fraud." The new tactic was explained at the National Right to Life Committee convention in Sacramento last month by Scott Fischbach, the group's field coordinator: Laws that ban some abortions, he said, "can lead up to the point of stopping them all."

Smith and Fischbach scored a temporary victory in Idaho last March with passage of a bill that would have permitted legal abortions only if a woman's life was endangered, if an incest victim was under 18, or if the rape was reported to the police within seven days (when a victim would not yet know whether she was pregnant). Pro-life Governor Cecil Andrus vetoed the bill, calling the seven-day provision punitive and "without compassion." He added, "On the eighth day, [the woman] ceases be the victim and becomes a criminal."

Strict reporting requirements are a vestige of the way the legal system treats rape. It has taken years to reverse the assumption that women fabricate claims of rape and incest or that they somehow bring the crime on themselves. Until recent reforms, a victim's testimony alone was not enough to convict a rapist, although it was enough to convict any other kind of criminal. Even now, a rape victim who goes to court often finds herself on trial as much as her attacker is. As a result, rape is one of the most underreported crimes in America. The Senate Judiciary Committee estimates that a woman is raped every six minutes in the U.S.

The Idaho veto and the pending one in Louisiana have not caused pro-lifers to retreat from their position on rape and incest. National Right to Life Committee spokeswoman Smith cites Pennsylvania's experience to show that women lie about rape. When the state did not require that rape or incest be reported to appropriate authorities, an average of 36 rape-related abortions a month were paid for by the state. When reporting requirements took effect in 1988, that number went down to about three a month.

Relatively few abortions are at stake here—less than 1% of the 1.6 million abortions performed annually result from rape or incest—yet the pro-life movement is determined to fight over each one. The movement insists that its position springs from religious beliefs that allow no compromise. Indeed, the harsh logic of the abortion argument makes the exception for rape and incest vulnerable to a charge of hypocrisy. If all fetal life is sacred, as pro-lifers insist, there should be no distinction between pregnancies that result from consensual sex and those that result from force. Otherwise, bearing a child becomes a woman's punishment for sex.

Whatever the political costs, activists on each side of the abortion debate have vowed to battle it out, somehow assured they can win over the middle. NARAL'S Michelman is determined to convince the public that parental-consent laws are a sham. Pro-life and pro-choice forces in Congress pledge to wage the fight over funds for rape and incest victims again and again, every time Boxer or her allies rider to a bill. "We'll debate this

blue in the face, and there will be blood all over the chamber," says Hyde. And despite the defeat snatched from the jaws of victory in Idaho, and perhaps Louisiana, the pro-life lobby will continue to press for recriminalizing abortion in all the states.

Polls show that most Americans feel ambivalent about abortion and that the two sides in the debate fail to express the moral ambiguity at the heart of the matter. The irreconcilable answers people give to pollsters are, in part, an expression of society's inability to come to grips publicly with so private an issue. In a Los Angeles Times poll last year, 61% of those interviewed said abortion is morally wrong; 57% of them believe it is murder, yet 51 % think it should remain a woman's decision. When rape and incest and parental authority enter into the mix, the numbers become ever more confusing.

What happened last week in Louisiana and the court was as much about the state of the family as it was about abortion. The Louisiana legislation conjures up a world where all children are born into families that will take care of them, whether their conception came about through love or violence. By contrast, the court decisions adressed a world that seems to have spun out of control, where pregnant children have to be forced to talk to their parents. Who would not wish for a Father Knows Best kind of life, where teenagers delayed becoming parents until they were no longer children, where youngsters in trouble could turn to families full of wise advice, where rape and incest were unknown and abortion was an unusual remedy for a rare misfortune? But dealing with the world as it is, the Justices, like most Americans, still find themselves struggling for a messy middle ground.

Drug of Choice
The Side Effects of RU 486

Dorothy Wickenden

In the mid–1980s, as word of the French abortion pill rippled across the world, the new drug was greeted as a thing of awesome powers. Pro-choicers eagerly proclaimed that RU 486 would render both surgical abortion and the anti-abortion movement obsolete. If a woman suspected she was pregnant, she would go to her medicine cabinet and, in peace and privacy, swallow the pill. With this simple act she could banish the emotional, the physical, and even much of the moral trauma accompanying the decision to have an abortion. Described by its inventor, Etienne-Emile Baulieu, as a "contra-gestive" (because it impedes gestation rather than conception), RU 486 would in effect erase the distinction between a contraceptive and an abortifacient. Anti-abortionists, horrified at the euphoria, quickly marshaled their forces against the drug, calling it a "chemical time bomb" and a "death pill."

The pro-choicers have sounded more sober about RU 486 over the past couple of years. Their initial hopes for the drug as "the ultimate act of reproductive privacy" proved to be, as Bill Hamilton of Planned Parenthood puts it, "a myopic dream." The anti-abortionists' continual boycott threats have cowed the patent owner and sole manufacturer, Roussel Uclaf of France, and its parent company, Hoechst AG, a German multinational, into tightly restricting access to the drug. In France, the only country where RU 486 is actually available to women outside of clinical trials, each pill must be registered, and the drug is dispensed only by designated clinics, only after a pregnancy has been confirmed, and only through the seventh week. And though French doctors report impressive success with it as an abortifacient, the procedure turns out to be neither quick nor painless nor totally private. Patients are required to make four visits to a designated clinic, on the second of which they are given synthetic prostaglandin to reduce the risk of hemorrhage and help induce contractions.

But the more recent news doesn't look good for the anti-abortionists. Distribution of RU 486 will start in Great Britain within the next year. Scandinavia and the Netherlands are expected to follow soon, and Sweden has begun testing it as a once-a-month contraceptive. Spain's Ministry of Health has made an official demand for the pill, and Baulieu, who still works for Roussel, says the Soviet Union will likely be next. The World Health Organization continues its own clinical studies on RU 486 in China, India, Hong Kong, and Cuba. Perhaps most alarming of all from the anti-abortionists' point of view,

RU 486 is once again being described as a miracle drug—this time by American doctors who say it may prove just as effective in treating a range of deadly diseases as it is in terminating pregnancy. William Regelson, an oncologist at the Medical College of Virginia, declares, "If RU 486 did not have abortion associated with it, it would be considered a major breakthrough drug."

In the August 22/29 issue of *The Journal of the American Medical Association,* Regelson and two co-authors describe the proven and potential uses for RU 486 in treating some kinds of breast cancer and brain tumors, Cushing's syndrome—a terminal disease characterized by hypertension, osteoporosis, diabetes, and infections—and even AIDS. RU 486 is known as a "hormone antagonist" because it prevents cells from responding to certain hormones as they normally would. It arrests the course of pregnancy by blocking the action of progesterone, without which an embryo cannot survive. Some tumors and cancers thrive on hormones as well, as do all stress-related diseases. Cushing's syndrome, for example, is caused by an excess production of cortisol, which is blocked by RU 486.

A program at the University of Southern California School of Medicine is using RU 486 in a small group of patients with a type of meningioma, or brain cancer, that cannot be cured with surgery. Martin H. Weiss, who heads the study with Stephen Grunberg, says that it is the only medical treatment that has ever been shown to work on these patients; a third of them have been responding to the treatment. George Chrousos, a senior investigator at the National Institutes of Health, who conducted a five-year study of RU 486 on Cushing's syndrome sufferers, describes "miraculous improvement" on eight of the twelve patients in his study within weeks after treatment began. RU 486 may even be helpful to women who *want* to

have a baby. Doctors at the University of California, San Diego, are doing a pilot study of RU 486 as a treatment for endometriosis, a common cause of infertility in women; and many believe that it could be used to induce labor in difficult deliveries, thus reducing the need for Caesarian sections.

All this sounds too good to be true, and some of it may be. The hopes that RU 486 may help AIDS patients, for example, are based on little more than informed speculation, and researchers who had hopes that it might cure glaucoma have been disappointed with the results of their animal studies. Arthur Caplan, director of the Center for Biomedical Ethics at the University of Minnesota, points out that "the rhetoric of the abortion debate has gotten the science inflamed." Doctors, no less than the pro-choice and anti-abortion forces, have their own interests to protect, and it's not surprising that they are among those who tend to make extravagant claims about RU 486.

Anti-abortionists, of course, are quick to downplay its curative potential—well aware that once it is approved in the United States for other uses, doctors could legally prescribe it as an abortifacient as well, as long as abortion itself remains legal. John Willke, president of the National Right to Life Committee, says, "People are using the theoretical possibility of therapeutic use to get the drug into the country on a massive level for lethal use." Yet he insists that his organization objects only to studies on RU 486 as an abortifacient. "We couldn't stop the other research if we wanted to," he declares.

That's true, but they can impede it. Hoechst hastily withdrew the drug in September 1988, only a month after the French government had approved it. A Roussel stockholders' meeting had been the scene of an anti-abortion protest, and the National Right to Life Committee in Washington and Catholic groups in France had issued a boycott threat against Hoechst and Roussel. Extremists proclaimed that I. G. Farben, the ancestor company of Hoechst, manufactured cyanide for Hitler's death camps. Distribution of RU 486 was resumed under orders from the French government, which owns 36 percent of Roussel Uclaf. Undeterred, the anti-abortionists kept up their boycott threats, and in December 1988 Roussel devised a set of criteria that countries have to meet before they can receive the drug: abortion must be legal and accepted by medical, public, and political opinion; prostaglandin must be available; distribution must be strictly controlled; and the patient must be required to sign a consent form declaring that if the treatment fails (as it does in up to 4 percent of women), she will have a surgical abortion. This would eliminate the possibility of babies born with defects—an unlikely prospect, many doctors claim, since RU 486 is taken in a single dose and the drug is metabolized quickly, but one that understandably concerns the manufacturer.

According to Roussel, the United States does not qualify for the drug—even though abortion is legal and supported by a majority of the American public. By "accepted by public opinion," the company clearly means "uncontroversial"—a much tougher standard, which thus far essentially has given a noisy minority veto power over a major medical development. Willke vows that if RU 486 comes to the United States, he'll mount a worldwide boycott of every product made by Roussel and Hoechst, and, he warns, "It'll be a whopper." Hoechst AG owns two New Jersey-based companies: Hoechst-Roussel Pharmaceuticals and Hoechst Celanese Corporation, a chemical company that produces everything from carpet fibers to tire cord. Hoechst Celanese alone has annual revenues in the United States of $6 billion. American pharmaceutical companies, which could push for a li-

cense from Roussel, apparently have no intention of doing so. "Do you have any idea what would happen in the U.S. if the drug were being distributed?" one unnamed senior executive at a drug company told *The Washington Post* when RU 486 was issued in France. "The market is potentially huge and the drug appears worthy. But who needs the headache?"

Some researchers who covet the new wonder drug are exasperated by Roussel's extreme caution about relinquishing it. William Regelson and his coauthors say that the threatened boycott has "largely frozen clinical trials," citing as evidence Roussel's cancellation of a meeting that it was to attend in April 1989 at Memorial Sloan-Kettering in New York to help the National Cancer Institute organize a multicenter study of RU 486 for treating breast cancer. Regelson says he was later told by a Hoechst employee that the company had pulled back because of the hostile political climate. Gary Hodgen, president of the Jones Institute for Reproductive Medicine, who has conducted numerous studies on RU 486 since 1982, says of Roussel and Hoechst, "They have limited access far more strictly than they did in years prior to 1989, no question about that." Baulieu denies these charges. It is high costs and the need for quality control, he insists, that have restricted the number of studies. And apparently not all doctors have had trouble getting the drug. Michael Kettle, who is working on the endometriosis study at San Diego, says that he and his coworkers have received active support from Roussel in their work.

On one point, at least, most people agree: Roussel's tight hold on RU 486 has crimped research in some critical areas. Since the early '80s the National Institutes of Health, which is barred from doing any abortion-related studies, has been conducting clinical trials of RU 486 for its use as a contraceptive and cellular studies on it as a possible future cure for breast cancer. However, one of NIH's most promising studies on RU 486 has come to a halt. Unlike women who use it as an abortifacient, patients with Cushing's syndrome require massive doses on a daily basis for extended periods throughout their lives. Although NIH researchers were excited by the extraordinary progress shown by the patients in the study, for whom no other medical treatment is effective, NIH decided not to continue its study in part because of concerns that it would be unable to obtain the quantities needed to sustain the patients' recovery.

One curious sign of the anti-abortionists' discomfort about RU 486 is their rhetoric. When Willke talks about the drug, he emphasizes the threat that it poses to women's health. He calls it a "chemical Dalkon Shield," "a powerful, poisonous steroid" that "kills unborn babies, will injure and kill women, and will cause an epidemic of fetal deformity." This would seem to be a shrewd tactic. The grisly history of fertility control—DES, Thalidomide, and the early birth control pill, as well as the Dalkon Shield—has made many women dubious about being subjected once again to an experimental drug whose long-term effects are unknown.

But this line of attack has already been shattered by the powerful medical establishment. The American Medical Association and *The New England Journal of Medicine*, among others, have declared that RU 486, when properly administered, is as safe as surgical abortion—one of the most common and least dangerous of all surgical procedures. The AMA has endorsed testing RU 486 here and is supporting efforts to convince Roussel to release it. Moreover, doctors are confident that as research continues, the drug—like the early birth control pill—will either be improved upon or replaced by a more sophisticated successor. NIH researchers hope that within the next several years they will have figured out the appropriate dose of RU 486 to be used as a birth control pill, perhaps taken only once or several times a month, and that it will have fewer side effects than the current pill.

Anti-abortionists should be the first to recognize the power of high-tech medicine to affect the political and ethical climate surrounding abortion. Sonograms have enabled us to peer inside the womb and detect the heartbeats of fetuses as young as six-and-a-half weeks, a development that helped to raise doubts among many whose support for abortion during the early months of pregnancy previously had been unqualified. RU 486 seems to be having precisely the opposite effect—removing some of the moral onus from abortion. Most people—even many in the anti-abortion rank and file—have fewer qualms about the idea of aborting a three-quarter-inch embryo than a fetus at three months, complete with tiny fingers and toes and all of its organs. So a pill that would both enable women to have earlier abortions and result in fewer late ones would doubtless be widely seen here, as it has been in France and other countries, as a welcome medical advance. And once its other potential uses are known, and the clamor for the drug increases, the issue will become even more problematic, not least among those who believe RU 486 should be available to prolong health and save lives but have serious scruples about it as an abortifacient.

On the other hand, Willke's health warnings about RU 486 have doubtless proved effective in raising the specter of lawsuits, which scare drug manufacturers in the United States as much as anti-abortion protesters do. Ever since the Dalkon Shield disaster, pharmaceuticals and insurance companies have retreated almost entirely from the field of birth control. In fact, insurance is no longer available in this country for clinical testing of most contraceptives. And even if a U.S. drug company decided to ignore the threat of political harassment and financial vulnerability, it would first have to wind its way through the byzantine—and politicized—regulatory maze. After getting a license from Roussel, a company would present a protocol to the Food and Drug Administration for its own round of expensive tests on RU 486 and synthetic prostaglandin, and, finally, submit the drug application to the lengthy FDA approval process—an even more complex procedure when two drugs are involved. The FDA, for its part, has already revealed its susceptibility to political pressure: in June 1989, at the urging of Senator Jesse Helms, Representatives Henry Hyde and Robert Dornan, and others, it banned the import of RU 486 into the United States for private use.

Limitations on birth control research, of course, mean fewer and less effective means of family planning for Americans. This only perpetuates the country's staggering rates of teenage pregnancy and abortion, both of which are among the highest in the industrialized world. A report of the National Research Council estimates that between 1.2 million and 3 million unwanted pregnancies occur in the United States each year, and that about half of the 1.5 million abortions each year are due to contraceptive failure.

Steps are being taken, though, to break the impasse. Some members of Congress, galvanized by an administration that, like its predecessor, has been more receptive to the demands of a powerful interest group than to the idea of pressing forward in controversial areas of medical research, have begun to move. In July, at the instigation of Representative Barbara Boxer of California, seventy members signed a letter urging Roussel to make RU 486 available for testing in the United States, in the hope that eventually Roussel will be convinced that the anti-abortionists represent neither the views of estab-

lished medicine nor the will of the public at large. In late October the reauthorization bill for NIH collapsed after conservatives vehemently objected to several abortion-related provisions—among them proposals for new centers to study contraception and infertility, which they claimed might lead to federal funding of research on RU 486. But this month Representative Ron Wyden of Oregon is holding a hearing on RU 486, in an attempt to smoke out the administration's position on the drug, and to raise questions about the extent to which the politics of abortion is impeding research that could save lives.

As for the pharmaceutical companies, eventually they may find the lure of profits more compelling than the fear of boycotts and litigation—especially if RU 486 brings with it some of the health benefits that are predicted. The boycott threat could turn out to be a paper tiger: it will be hard to convince Americans not to buy a laxative made by Hoechst-Roussel Pharmaceuticals because its parent company also owns the company that produces RU 486. And Hoechst-Roussel specializes in prescription drugs rather than over-the-counter products. Even the liability conundrum is not insoluble. Many have proposed devising an insurance scheme for controversial new drugs and devices that would assure companies they would only be liable if culpable error could be proved. An insurance pool would cover unforeseen casualties.

Meanwhile, a group of physicians in San Francisco—unwilling to wait for drug companies and the FDA—has attempted to get the testing started themselves. Theirs would be the first trial in the United States of RU 486 with prostaglandin. (An earlier study, at the University of Southern California, examined the efficacy of the drug alone.) California's attorney general, John Van de Kamp, has proposed that the state invoke a statute that allows California to test, manufacture, and market drugs within its own borders that are not yet approved by the FDA. Three hospitals have agreed to conduct the trials, but the doctors' plan has stalled because Roussel has refused their request for the drug.

However, Baulieu, an irrepressible advocate of his invention, is confident that RU 486 will soon find its way to the United States—and "not through the back door," as the Californians are proposing. "I don't see any reason to have partial distribution," he says. "As in the U.K., the pressure will be so strong that it will go ahead in the USA. Roussel will help when the conditions are better." Baulieu is advocating a joint undertaking that would include Roussel, a nonprofit organization here (most likely Planned Parenthood), and a group of venture capitalists.

The anti-abortionists have raised legitimate questions about how RU 486 might be misused if it becomes a legal commodity here. What happens if a pregnant teenager gets hold of some pills in her second trimester, and thinks they'll solve her problem? Because the U.S. regulatory system is so decentralized, it will be more difficult to maintain the scrupulous controls over distribution that France has imposed. But this country would doubtless require abortion patients to undergo the same series of doctors' visits, to receive the pills and the prostaglandin only at clinics and hospitals, and to sign the same strict consent forms. And the United States isn't exactly slack about drug safety standards. RU 486 could be handled like any prescription drug that poses a threat to the fetus (such as the acne treatment Accutane, with doctors strictly screening patients and the FDA requiring detailed warning inserts along with the prescription). Or, if necessary, it could be deemed a "Class 3" drug, like barbiturates and amphetamines, which doctors cannot prescribe without a special license, and which requires a detailed accounting on the part of physicians and pharmacists to avoid forgeries and other abuses.

There is no denying that RU 486 is an eerie drug. Even the most ardent pro-choice advocates have to ask whether there isn't a critical distinction between a contraceptive and a "contra-gestive. "But RU 486, like abortion itself, isn't going to go away—regardless of the restrictions that are placed on it. As more countries begin using the drug, demand for it here will increase. And if it is not approved and carefully regulated in the United States, a black market will certainly develop, with predictably unpleasant consequences. Thus Willke and his colleagues will have succeeded in creating exactly the circumstance he claims to fear the most: widespread misuse of a potent drug with possibly serious health hazards for women.

Advance Directive
Living Will and Health Care Proxy

Death is a part of life. It is a reality like birth, growth and aging. I am using this advance directive to convey my wishes about medical care to my doctors and other people looking after me at the end of my life. It is called an advance directive because it gives instructions in advance about what I want to happen to me in the future. It expresses my wishes about medical treatment that might keep me alive. I want this to be legally binding.

If I cannot make or communicate decisions about my medical care, those around me should rely on this document for instructions about measures that could keep me alive.

I do not want medical treatment (including feeding and water by tube) that will keep me alive if:

- I am unconscious and there is no reasonable prospect that I will ever be conscious again (even if I am not going to die soon in my medical condition), **or**
- I am near death from an illness or injury with no reasonable prospect of recovery.

I do want medicine and other care to make me more comfortable and to take care of pain and suffering. I want this even if the pain medicine makes me die sooner.

I want to give some extra instructions: [*Here list any special instructions, e.g., some people fear being kept alive after a debilitating stroke. If you have wishes about this, or any other conditions, please write them here.*]

The legal language in the box that follows is a health care proxy. It gives another person the power to make medical decisions for me.

I name_____, who lives at_____
_____, phone number _____,
to make medical decisions for me if I cannot make them myself. This person is called a health care "surrogate," "agent," "proxy," or "attorney in fact." This power of attorney shall become effective when I become incapable of making or communicating decisions about my medical care. This means that this document stays legal when and if I lose the power to speak for myself, for instance, if I am in a coma or have Alzheimer's disease.

My health care proxy has power to tell others what my advance directive means. This person also has power to make decisions for me, based either on what I would have wanted, or, if this is not known, on what he or she thinks is best for me.

If my first choice health care proxy cannot or decides not to act for me, I
name_____, address_____
_____, phone number, _____ as my second choice.

(over, please)

Reprinted by permission of Choice in Dying (formerly Concern for Dying/Society for the Right to Die) 200 Varick Street, New York, New York, 10014, 212-366-5540.

219

I have discussed my wishes with my health care proxy, and with my second choice if I have chosen to appoint a second person. My proxy(ies) has(have) agreed to act for me.

I have thought about this advance directive carefully. I know what it means and want to sign it. I have chosen two witnesses, neither of whom is a member of my family, nor will inherit from me when I die. My witnesses are not the same people as those I named as my health care proxies. I understand that this form should be notarized if I use the box to name (a) health care proxy(ies).

Signature_____

Date_____

Address _____

Witness' signature_____

Witness' printed name_____

Address _____

Witness' signature_____

Witness' printed name_____

Address _____

Notary [to be used if proxy is appointed]_____

Drafted and Distributed by Choice In Dying, Inc.—the National Council for the right to Die. Choice In Dying is a National not-for-profit organization which works for the rights of patients at the end of life. In addition to this generic advance directive, Choice In Dying distributes advance directives that conform to each state's specific legal requirements and maintains a national Living Will Registry for completed documents.

CHOICE IN DYING INC.—
the national council for the right to die
(formerly Concern for Dying/Society for the Right to Die)
200 Varick Street, New York, NY 10014 (212) 366–5540
5/92

Sounding Board: Morals and Moralism in the Debate Over Euthanasia and Assisted Suicide

Christine K. Cassel and Diane E. Meier

The newspaper headlines in early June about Dr. Jack Kevorkian and the "suicide machine" with which Mrs. Janet Adkins took her life captured the attention of the nation and stimulated anew the long-running public debate over assisted suicide and euthanasia. Many aspects of the Kevorkian-Adkins case were extreme, and their disturbing quality evoked some of the medical profession's worst fears about the risks of legalized mercy killings. We believe that the extreme aspects of cases such as this have obscured the central issues. We hope that the observations we make here will help move the debate beyond the polarized pronouncements that followed this assisted suicide to an analysis that recognizes more appropriately the full complexity of the problem.

Mrs. Adkins, the newspapers said, was suffering from the early stages of Alzheimer's dementia, diagnosed after extensive neurologic evaluation. She had sought experimental pharmacologic treatment, which had failed, and had decided that she did not want to live a life of progressive cognitive degeneration. She had heard about Dr. Kevorkian and arranged to fly to Michigan to seek his assistance in committing suicide. Dr. Kevorkian, a pathologist, agreed to help her after a single dinner conversation, and he conducted the procedure in a van in a parking lot because he could not find another place.

When this story hit the press, journalists around the country called on a broad range of people for opinions on the case. In a remarkably consistent series of interviews, physicians, lawyers, and ethicists expressed their abhorrence of Dr. Kevorkian's act and his suicide machine. Indeed, the initial response was so uniform that journalists looking for a debate tried in vain to find a physician who would speak in support of assisted suicide. The comments were familiar ones, asserting that it is never acceptable for a medical professional to take life, regardless of the suffering or circumstances of the patient. The reasons cited for this stance included concern about the erosion of the public's trust in physicians as well as the fear that a loosening of constraints on mercy killing could lead to abuses by unethical or incompetent physicians.

The Kevorkian-Adkins case had many features that gave good cause to fear such abuses, including Kevorkian's unusual ideas and background, the excellent physical health and functional status of Mrs. Adkins and the lack of any procedures to ensure the accuracy of her diagnosis and evaluate her capacity to make this decision. Indeed, because of the lack of careful procedural safe-

From The New England Journal of Medicine, Volume 323: Number 1, September 13, 1990, 750-751. Reprinted by permission of The New England Journal of Medicine.

guards, Dr. Kevorkian's conduct, like that in other unusual cases, such as the one described in "It's Over, Debbie," is clearly unacceptable and was appropriately censured by the medical community.

But the unusual circumstances of these highly publicized cases should not be permitted to obscure the profound and genuine suffering and legitimate wish for release that motivates some patients to consider suicide, as was pointed out by Angell in a *New York Times* essay. Mrs. Adkins faced an inexorable and devastating loss of cognitive ability and independence, characteristics that gave her life its meaning and without which she had no desire to live. Her decision was rational and consistent, according to accounts by her family, and she had long been a member of the Hemlock Society and the Unitarian Universalist Church (organizations that support the right of patients to decide to end their own lives under appropriate circumstances). Her decision does not appear to be unusual, although no data on the number of assisted suicides in the United States are available. The American Hospital Association estimates that many of the 6000 daily deaths in the United States are in some way planned by patients, families, and physicians. A recent *New York Times*-CBS poll found that a remarkable 53 percent of respondents believe that doctors should be allowed to assist a severely ill person in taking his or her own life. An initiative that may go to the legislature in the state of Washington proposes broadening the definition of terminal illness and permitting competent patients aid in dying.

The fear and anxiety that many people feel when contemplating chronic and terminal debilitating illness is rooted, at least in part, in the fear that their suffering will be prolonged by medical technology and that they will have little or no control over its application. In this context, the medical profession's repeated and firm rejection of any participation by physicians in assisted suicide begins to appear self-serving in its emphasis on a professional scrupulosity that seems blind to the expressed needs of the patients.

The public appears to be losing faith in doctors, at least partly because of our paternalistic and sometimes cruel insistence on life at any cost. The very rigidity of this position invites the abuses exemplified by the Kevorkian-Adkins case: when people facing unbearable suffering have no legitimate options, extreme measures result. Opponents of physician-assisted suicide cite the risk of "slippery slope" abuses or mistakes, but a more open process might allow a higher level of public and professional accountability, resulting in the effective limitation of assisted suicide to clearly appropriate cases and enhancing public respect for physicians. In the Netherlands, for example, euthanasia is part of public policy and is circumscribed by explicit guidelines requiring a clear and repeated request from the patient that leaves no uncertainty about the patient's competence and wish to die. These guidelines require that there be severe suffering without the hope of relief; a financially and emotionally uncoerced, informed, and consistent choice by the patient; the absence of other treatment options; and second opinions from other professionals.

The debate over assisted suicide and euthanasia should shift to an examination of the needs and values of patients in a context that recognizes the limits of modern medicine and the inevitability of death. The medical profession in the United States has reflected our society's unwillingness to accept death as part of life and to face it with some humility. Perhaps the public is now ahead of the medical profession in this regard, as patients increasingly seek the assistance of physicians in their time of need, when dying with dignity becomes more important than prolonging life. The rigid view that physicians should never assist in suicide denies the complexity of the personal meanings life can have in favor of a single-minded devotion to its maximal duration. For many people, the transcendent or spiritual meaning of life (and afterlife) creates a context in which death is not the enemy, and is in fact sometimes to be welcomed as an appropriate and timely end, either to a life fully lived or to a life cut short by the ravages of incurable disease. The refusal of physicians to deal with their patients at the level of the personal meaning of life and death is a reflection of how sterile and technological our profession has become.

Finally, in an era in which the discipline of medical ethics has become widely accepted in medical schools and hospitals, we need to teach moral reasoning. A strict proscription against aiding in death may betray a limited conceptual framework that seeks the safety of ironclad rules and principles to protect the physician from the true complexity of individual cases. Patients seeking comfort in their dying should not be held hostage to our inability or unwillingness to be responsible for knowing right from wrong in each specific situation. Physicians should have the intellectual and moral vitality to address ethically complex issues and to con-

front their own feelings about death and the meaning of life. Only then will the profession remain true to its commitment to stand by patients through the whole of life's course, up to and including death.

We do not support an indiscriminate easing of sanctions on physician-assisted suicide. We do support a more careful examination of the issue. Certainly this option should not be seized as an expedient because society chooses not to commit itself to the cost of compassionate and respectful medical care for people with devastating or painful diseases. Certainly those who are most vulnerable need to be protected from neglect or abuse. Human support and comfort, adequate control of pain, and true respect for patients' treatment wishes will go a long way toward reducing the demand for assisted suicide or euthanasia. In circumscribed and carefully defined circumstances, however, it may be right to recognize the inevitability of death in a life of unbearable suffering and to help ease this passage.

The debate surrounding the Kevorkian-Adkins case, along with other important events such as the response to the recent Supreme Court decision about Nancy Cruzan, has uncovered a substantial public desire for more control over the circumstances of death.

Questions

1. Historically, what "ends" justified going to war?

2. What is the newer thinking within Catholic Christianity (and probably much of Protestantism as well)?

3. In what way does Kagan relate civil law (Selective Service Laws) to the Natural Law?

4. Do you think the reasoning in his essay is valid and his conclusions fair to pacificists?

5. Give two reasons why Leiser rejects the contentions of sociological data; namely, that capital punishment is *not* a deterrent to capital crime?

6. Although Leiser doesn't mention execution of the innocent, what *are* the procedures he feels must be rectified in the criminal justice system?

7. In light of all the special circumstances, should Karla Faye Tucker have been executed by the Texas legal system in February of 1998.

8. How do the two conceptions of the human being, hylemorphic and Cartesian, differ?

9. Give two reasons why some Catholics might argue that an abortion, for a good reason, in the first two months of gestation would *not* constitute murder.
    a.

    b.

10. What is the essential feature of the argument that Thompson makes to justify termination of a pregnancy resulting from rape?

11. What is meant by the suggestion that the mother could be a "good Samaritan"?

12. Following through from Thompson's article to Carlson's: Do you think rape or incest victims have a special right to abortion? Explain.

13. Should the possibility of a return to "back alley" abortions convince us to remain with Roe v. Wade? Should girls under 17 be made, by law, to have one parent's permission for an abortion?

14. Should fetal tissue be used to help people with advanced Parkinson's disease?

15. How would you relate the Donceel article to the question of the moral licitness of the use of the Ru-486 pill?

16. Would the Ru-486 pill do away with the need for abortion clinics? Explain.

17. What criteria are ordinarily used and/or suggested for the cessation of positive efforts to keep someone alive?

18. Is death an "evil"? Discuss.

19. Would you think seriously about making out a "living will"? Why or why not?

20. Could active euthanasia ever be justified? Explain.

Section IV

The Use of Sexuality

Introduction

The question of the use and abuse of our sexuality has been an ongoing problem since the beginning of written debate and, perhaps, since the beginning of the race. If there were nothing more to us than the "animal" side of our nature, our sexual life would be simple, although perhaps hectic. However, the presence of the psychological side makes matters much more complicated. Our possession of free will, a rational life and an emotional life constantly interacting, the fact that rearing and nurturing the human young is a long, arduous and serious process are the reasons that "sex" always shows up in any work devoted to ethical studies.

For many ethicians there is only one proper, ethical use of and expression of venereal activity: heterosexual sex between a man and woman who are validly married to each other. This view excludes many other types and/or combinations of sexual expression: auto-eroticism, heterosexual fornication, so-called "unnatural" sex acts, such as sodomy, etc., etc.

Our readings are all from contemporary writers who get right to the point and set the stage for discussion.

In the late 1960s Catholic theologians, working with a commission of clergy and laity, examined the problem of birth control, both the use of man-made products (artificial) to prevent conception and the following of natural periods of fertility and sterility (periodic abstinence or the so-called "rhythm method"). An official, authoritative letter, "Humanae Vitae," which contained some very beautiful reflections on marriage, was issued by Pope Paul VI (1897-1974). However, the section on how to practice "responsible parenthood" caused great consternation and debate both within and without the Roman Catholic Church. Very likely the crucial sentence was: "Each and every marriage act must be open to the transmission of life." In the Catholic Church, this type of letter is termed an "encyclical".

Our next writer, Luther Binkley (Ph.D., Harvard) was a professor of ethics at Franklin and Marshall College in Pennsylvania.

Some believe the publication *Penthouse* has surpassed *Playboy* in its genre of magazine, but the general problem of the male perception of women as presented in *Playboy* remains and has become more serious as abuse of women (sadism) increases.

The remainder of our essays are by contemporary journalists/essayists and deal with procreation techniques and fornication, which of course can cause problems (e.g., abortion, mentioned in the last section).

In this third printing, I have added three articles on the cloning of animals and even

229

humans. It will probably never happen with humans, but it merits discussion, and besides, who knows? Another has been added on the AIDS situation. Finally, the day after the death of the renowned actor Anthony Perkins, many of us were surprised at the news of the cause of his death, which was AIDS-related. His stirring statement forces us to reflect on the somewhat mysterious aspect and the problem of human understanding related to this disease.

Humanae Vitae

Pope Paul VI

Conjugal Love

Conjugal love reveals its true nature and nobility, when it is considered in its supreme origin, God, who is love, "the Father, from whom every family in heaven and on earth is named."

Marriage is not, then, the effect of chance or the product of evolution of unconscious natural forces; it is the wise institution of the Creator to realize in mankind His design of love. By means of the reciprocal personal gift of self, proper and exclusive to them, husband and wife tend towards the communion of their beings in view of mutual personal perfection, to collaborate with God in the generation and education of new lives.

For baptized persons, moreover, marriage invests the dignity of a sacramental sign of grace, inasmuch as it represents the union of Christ and of the Church.

Its Characteristics

Under this light, there clearly appear the characteristic marks and demands of conjugal love, and it is of supreme importance to have an exact idea of these.

This love is first of all fully human, that is to say, of the senses and of the spirit at the same time. It is not, then, a simple transport of instinct and sentiment, but also, and principally, an act of the free will, intended to endure and to grow by means of the joys and sorrows of daily life, in such a way that husband and wife become only one heart and only one soul, and together attain their human perfection.

Then, this love is total, that is to say, it is a very special form of personal friendship, in which husband and wife generously share everything, without undue reservations or selfish calculations. Whoever truly loves his marriage partner loves not only for what he receives, but for the partner's self, rejoicing that he can enrich his partner with the gift of himself.

Again, this love is faithful and exclusive until death. Thus in fact, do bride and groom conceive it to be on the day when they freely and in full awareness assume the duty of the marriage bond. A fidelity, this, which can sometimes be difficult, but is always possible, always noble and meritorious, as no one can deny. The example of so many married persons down through the centuries shows, not only that fidelity is according to the nature of marriage, but also that it is a source of profound and lasting happiness and finally, this love is fecund for it is not exhausted by the communion between husband and wife, but is destined to continue, raising up new lives. "Marriage and conjugal love are by their nature ordained toward the begetting and educating of children. Children are really the supreme gift of

Courtesy of Catholic News Service.

marriage and contribute very substantially to the welfare of their parents."

Responsible Parenthood

Hence conjugal love requires in husband and wife an awareness of their mission of "responsible parenthood," which today is rightly much insisted upon, and which also must be exactly understood. Consequently it is to be considered under different aspects which are legitimate and connected with one another.

In relation to the biological processes, responsible parenthood means the knowledge and respect of their functions; human intellect discovers in the power of giving life biological laws which are part of the human person.

In relation to the tendencies of instinct or passion, responsible parenthood means that necessary dominion which reason and will must exercise over them.

In relation to physical, economic, psychological and social conditions, responsible parenthood is exercised, either by the deliberate and generous decision to raise a large family, or by the decision, made for grave motives and with due respect for the moral law, to avoid for the time being, or even for an indeterminate period, a new birth.

Responsible parenthood also and above all implies a more profound relationship to the objective moral order established by God, of which a right conscience is the faithful interpreter. The responsible exercise of parenthood implies, therefore, that husband and wife recognize fully their own duties towards God, towards themselves, towards the family and towards society, in a correct hierarchy of values.

In the task of transmitting life, therefore, they are not free to proceed completely at will, as if they could determine in a wholly autonomous way the honest path to follow; but they must conform their activity to the creative intention of God, expressed in the very nature of marriage and of its acts, and manifested by the constant teaching of the Church.

Respect for the Nature and Purpose of the Marriage Act

These acts, by which husband and wife are united in chaste intimacy, and by means of which human life is transmitted, are, as the council recalled, "noble and worthy," and they do not cease to be lawful if, for causes independent of the will of husband and wife, they are foreseen to be infecund, since they always remain ordained towards expressing and consolidating their union. In fact, as experience bears witness, not every conjugal act is followed by a new life. God has widely disposed natural laws and rhythms of fecundity which, of themselves, cause a separation in the succession of births. Nonetheless the Church, calling men back to the observance of the norms of the natural law, as interpreted by their constant doctrine, teaches that each and every marriage act (*quilibet matrimonii usus*) must remain open to the transmission of life.

Two Inseparable Aspects: Union and Procreation

That teaching, often set forth by the magisterium, is founded upon the inseparable connection, willed by God and unable to be broken by man on his own initiative, between the two meanings of the conjugal act: the unitive meaning and the procreative meaning. Indeed, by its intimate structure, the conjugal act, while most closely uniting husband and wife, empowers them to generate new lives, according to laws inscribed in the very being of man and of woman. By safeguarding both these essential aspects, unitive and procreative, the conjugal act preserves in its fullness the sense of true mutual love and its ordination towards man's most high calling to parenthood. We believe that the men of our day are particularly capable of seizing the deeply reasonable and human character of this fundamental principle.

Faithfulness to God's Design

It is in fact justly observed that a conjugal act imposed upon one's partner without regard for his or her condition and lawful desires is not a true act of love, and therefore denies an exigency of right moral order in the relationships between husband and wife. Hence, one who reflects well must also recognize that a reciprocal act of love, which jeopardizes the responsibility to transmit life which God the Creator, according to particular laws, inserted therein is in contradiction with the design constitutive of marriage, and with the will of the Author of life. To use this divine gift destroying, even if only partially, its meaning and its purpose is to contradict the nature both of man and of woman and of their most intimate relationship, and therefore, it is to contradict also the plan of God and His will. On the other hand, to make use of the gift of conjugal love while respecting the laws of the generative process means to acknowledge oneself not to be the arbiter of the sources of human life, but rather the minister of the design established by the Creator. In fact, just as man does not have unlimited dominion over his body in general, so also, with particular reason, he has no such dominion over his generative faculties as such, because of their intrinsic ordination towards raising up life, of which God is the principle. "Human life is sacred," Pope John XXIII recalled; "from its very inception it reveals the creating hand of God."

Illicit Ways of Regulating Birth

In conformity with these landmarks in the human and Christian vision of marriage, we must once again declare that the direct interruption of the generative process already begun, and, above all, directly willed and procured abortion, even if for therapeutic reason, are to be absolutely excluded as licit means of regulating birth.

Equally to be excluded, as the teaching authority of the Church has frequently declared, is direct sterilization, whether perpetual or temporary, whether of the man or of the woman. Similarly excluded is every action which, either in anticipation of the conjugal act, or in its accomplishment, or in the development of its natural consequences, proposes, whether as an end or as a means, to render procreation impossible.

To justify conjugal acts made intentionally infecund, one cannot invoke as valid reasons the lesser evil, or the fact that such acts would constitute a whole together with the fecund acts already performed or to follow later, and hence would share in one and the same moral goodness. In truth, if it is sometimes licit to tolerate a lesser evil in order to avoid a greater evil or to promote a greater good it is not licit, even for the gravest reasons, to do evil so that good may follow therefrom, that is, to make into the object of a positive act of the will something which is intrinsically disordered, and hence unworthy of the human person, even when the intention is to safeguard or promote individual, family, or social well-being. Consequently it is an error to think that a conjugal act which is deliberately made infecund and so is intrinsically dishonest could be made honest and right by the ensemble of a fecund conjugal life.

The Church, on the contrary, does not at all consider illicit the use of those therapeutic means truly necessary to cure diseases of the organism, even if an impediment to procreation, which may be foreseen, should result therefrom, provided such impediment is not, for whatever motive, directly willed.

Licitness of Recourse to Infecund Periods

To this teaching of the Church on conjugal morals, the objection is made today, as we observed earlier, that it is the prerogative of the human intellect to dominate the energies offered by irrational nature and to orientate them towards an end conformable to the good of man. Now, some may ask: in the present case, is it not reasonable in many circumstances to have recourse to artificial birth control if, thereby, we secure the harmony and peace of the family, and better conditions for the education of the children already born? To this question it is necessary to reply with clarity: the Church is the first to praise and recommend the intervention of intelligence in a function which so closely associates the rational creature with his Creator; but she affirms that this must be done with respect for the order established by God.

If, then, there are serious motives to space out births, which derive from the physical or psychological condition of husband and wife, or from external conditions, the Church teaches that it is then licit to take into account the natural rhythms immanent in the generative functions, for the use of marriage in the infecund periods only, and in this way to regulate birth without offending the moral principles which have been recalled earlier.

The Church is consistent with herself when she considers recourse to the infecund periods to be licit, while at the same time condemning, as being always illicit, the use of means directly contrary to fecundation, even if such use is inspired by reasons which may appear honest and serious. In reality, there are essential differences between the two cases; in the former, the married couple make legitimate use of a natural disposition; in the latter, they impede the development of natural processes. It is true that, in the one and the other case, the married couple are in agreement in the positive will of avoiding children for plausible reasons, seeking the certainty that offspring will not arrive; but it is also true that only in the former case are they able to renounce the use of marriage in the fecund periods when, for just motives, procreation is not desirable, while making use of it during infecund periods to manifest their affection and to safeguard their mutual fidelity. By so doing, they give proof of a truly and integrally honest love.

Grave Consequences of Methods of Artificial Birth Control

Upright men can even better convince themselves of the solid grounds on which the teaching of the Church in this field is based, if they care to reflect upon the consequences of methods of artificial birth control. Let them consider, first of all, how wide and easy a road would thus be opened up towards conjugal infidelity and the general lowering of morality. Not much experience is needed in order to know human weakness, and to understand that men—especially the young, who are so vulnerable on this point—have need of encouragement to be faithful to the moral law, so that they must not be offered some easy means of eluding its observance. It is also to be feared that the man, growing used to the employment of anticonceptive practices, may finally lose respect for the woman and, no longer caring for her physical and psychological equilibrium, may come to the point of considering her as a mere instrument of selfish enjoyment, and no longer as his respected and beloved companion.

Let it be considered also that a dangerous weapon would thus be placed in the hands of those public authorities who take no heed of moral exigencies. Who could blame a government for applying to the solution of the problems of the community those means acknowledged to be licit for married couples in the solution of a family problem? Who will stop rulers from favoring, from even imposing upon their peoples, if they were to consider it necessary, the method of contraception which they judge to be most efficacious? In such a way men, wishing to avoid individual, family, or social difficulties encountered in the observance of the divine law, would reach the point of placing at the mercy of the intervention of public authorities the most personal and most reserved sector of conjugal intimacy.

Consequently, if the mission of generating life is not to be exposed to the arbitrary will of men, one must necessarily recognize unsurmountable limits to the possibility of man's domination over his own body and its functions; limits which no man, whether a private individual or one invested with authority, may licitly surpass. And such limits cannot be determined otherwise than by the respect due to the integrity of the human organism and its functions, according to the principles recalled earlier, and also according to the correct understanding of the "principle of totality" illustrated by our predecessor Pope Pius XII.

Conflict of Ideals
Changing Values in Western Society

Luther J. Binkley

The stress upon the individual's right to happiness has taken a different turn in the *Playboy Philosophy* of Hugh Hefner. His magazine is best known for its celebration of the freedom that is now coming to the individual as a result of the sexual revolution, but in the articles he has written for the *Playboy Philosophy* the reader can discern many similarities in his over-all position and in Ayn Rand's. His attacks on the average man, on conformity, and on the traditional moral and religious values appear to be much the same as those of Miss Rand, with the exception that his articles are directed to a different audience. Hefner's summary statement of his philosophy sounds almost like the position defended by John Galt, the hero of *Atlas Shrugged*:

> This, then, is the foundation of our philosophy—an emphasis on the importance of the individual and his freedom; the view that man's personal self-interest is natural and good, and that it can be channeled, through reason, to the benefit of the individual and his society; the belief that morality should be based upon reason; the conviction that society should exist as man's servant, not as his master; the idea that the purpose in

man's life should be found in the full living of life itself and the individual pursuit of happiness.[1]

But there are other basic parallels as well. Hefner extolls capitalism and in doing so indicates that like Ayn Rand he believes in selling ideas in the market place:

> To some of us capitalism is almost a dirty word. It shouldn't be. It's time Americans stopped being embarrassed and almost ashamed of their form of government and their economy. It's the best two-horse parlay in the world and perhaps if we were more fully sold on it ourselves, we could do a better job of selling it to other countries.[2]

He also indicates that he fully approves of the American dream of success, as he stresses that *Playboy* presents a total philosophy involving both working hard at a job and expending one's energies in enjoyable use of leisure time:

> Thus *PLAYBOY* exists, in part, as a motivation for men to expend greater effort in their work, develop their capabilities further and climb higher on the ladder of success. This is obviously desirable in

---

1   Hugh M. Hefner, *The Playboy Philosophy: Parts I, II, III,* and *IV* (Chicago: H M H Publishing Co., Inc., 1962–1965), p. 107.
2   *Ibid.*, p. 14.

our competitive, free enterprise system.
. . .[3]

While Ayn Rand stresses the aspect of productive work in an industrial economy, Hefner's *Playboy* is more concerned with the enjoyable use of a man's leisure. Miss Rand is primarily concerned with the decline of the individual in a collectivized society, while Hefner is more concerned with freeing man from the traditional moral and religious convictions which have hampered him in the free and enjoyable expression of his sexuality. Yet, amazingly enough, their philosophies agree in stressing the primacy of the individual's right to happiness, the supremacy of capitalism to other economic systems, the belief that government should not interfere with the free circulation of any ideas, and the importance of each man developing his own rational code of values.

But there are important differences to be found between the positions of Ayn Rand and Hugh Hefner, especially concerning the nature and degree of self-interest which each justifies. Ayn Rand, the reader will recall, maintains that the individual ought not to be concerned with others unless the others are of use to the individual; and even then, she holds that it is immoral to sacrifice oneself for others. Hefner, on the other hand, defends what he calls "enlightened self-interest" which "includes a concern for others. The individual should be willing to assist those less fortunate, for a society—and each individual in it—benefits from a concern for the welfare of all."[4] While many people have interpreted *Playboy* as sanctioning any form of sexual behavior from which an individual would get pleasure, Hefner himself maintains that even in sexual relationships he does not sanction selfishness:

> We are opposed to wholly selfish sex, but we are opposed to any human relationship that is entirely self-oriented— that takes all and gives nothing in return. We also believe that any such totally self-serving association is self-destructive.[5]

While it is true that Hefner recognizes that sex and love are not the same thing, and that each can exist without the other, yet he maintains that "the best sex, the most meaningful sex, is that which expresses the strong emotional feeling we call love."[6]

Nevertheless, many of the features of *Playboy* seem to extoll sex as a commodity to be enjoyed as other commodities in our affluent society. For many people who do not read Hefner's *Playboy Philosophy*, but glance at the playmates of the month and read the cartoons, John Crane's analysis sums up the image of the ideal man conveyed:

> It is a universe for rather elegant and refined consumers, and girls are the grandest of all consumer goods. A girl is something, like a sports car or a bottle of Scotch or an Ivy League suit, that is meant to be used and enjoyed by men. But always with flair, with polish. There needs to be no entangling, no stifling alliances or obligations. Girls are playthings, and once enjoyed will have to be set aside and replaced with others new and fresh![7]

Hugh Hefner in the first issue of *Playboy* sought to describe "What is a Playboy?" in the sense in which he uses the term:

---

3   *Ibid.*, p. 13
4   *Ibid.*, p. 100
5   *Ibid.*, p. 51.
6   *Ibid.*, p. 179.
7   John Crane, "Philosophy and Phantasy in Playboy Magazine and What This Suggests About Us," quoted in *ibid.*, p. 7.

He can be many things, providing he possesses a certain *point of view*. He must see life not as a vale of tears, but as a happy time; he must take joy in his work, without regarding it as the end and all of living; he must be an alert man, an aware man, a man of taste, a man sensitive to pleasure, a man who—without acquiring the stigma of the voluptuary or dilettante—can live life to the hilt. This is the sort of man we mean when we use the word *playboy*.[8]

Playboy magazine has played a significant role in popularizing a new attitude toward sex. We shall examine Freud's views in a later chapter, for it was really Freud who brought a new approach to our understanding of sex and its relationship to the rest of our lives. In addition to popularizing Freud, *Playboy* also refers approvingly to the Kinsey Reports on male and female sexual behavior as helping to remove American sexual hypocrisy. Largely because of the wide diversity of sexual practices which Kinsey and his staff found in their study, *Playboy* has campaigned for the repeal of the outmoded laws regulating sexual behavior between consenting adults. Just as Ayn Rand objects to the interference of the state with the business of a corporation, so Hefner and his staff oppose society's attempts to force all individuals to conform to one sexual norm. Hefner maintains that "a man's morality, like his religion, is a personal affair best left to his own conscience."[9] In its attacks on our traditional puritanical laws and attitudes concerning sexual behavior *Playboy* has even won the support of many clergymen. Harvey Cox, an American theologian, who is very critical of *Playboy* in most respects, maintains that: "Moralistic criticisms of *Playboy* fail because its antimoralism is one of the

few places in which *Playboy* is right."[10] We shall see, in a later chapter, that many Christian moralists agree with Hefner concerning the necessity for a more enlightened attitude toward sexual behavior, although they do not subscribe to the hedonistic way of life recommended by *Playboy*.

Hefner's philosophy and his magazine offer an individual pleasure and joy as a way of life; only one must be reasonably young, attractive and wealthy to enjoy it fully. His appeal to formulate a new morality "based upon honesty, understanding and reason rather than hypocrisy, superstition and ignorance"[11] is one that many people in our age would fully endorse. What many of these people would not be able to accept is the extolling of the individual's pleasure as the proper way of life in a world in which there are still persons who lack the basic necessities for life itself. To some of these individuals, no way of life is acceptable which does not place its primary concern upon helping others to achieve a decent standard of living. The *Playboy Philosophy* offers instead a modern version of hedonism, a justification for pursuing pleasure as the main goal of one's life. In a rather rhetorical passage Hefner justifies this way of life as fully consistent with the American dream:

> No conflict exists between the pleasure a modern American finds in material things and his struggle to discover a new scientific truth, or evolve a new philosophy, or create a work of art. The good life, the full life, encompasses all of these—and all of them satisfy and spur a man on to do more, see more, know more, experience more, accomplish more. This is the real meaning, the purpose, the point of life itself: the continu-

---

8   Hefner, *Playboy Philosophy*, p. 3.
9   *Ibid.*, p. 19.
10   Cox, *The Secular City*, p. 178.
11   Hefner, *Playboy Philosophy*, p. 162.

ing, upward striving and searching for the ultimate truth and beauty.[12]

Hefner's *Playboy Philosophy* offers little of help to those concerned with eliminating racial injustice, poverty, and the lack of equal opportunity for all people in education, housing, and jobs. In fact, Hefner's defense of his philosophy as "an upward striving and searching for the ultimate truth and beauty" has a hollow ring. One would expect that a writer dedicated to showing that morality is relative to the individual, would also maintain that truth and beauty are in the same camp.

In the search for a satisfactory way of life many youth have been so disillusioned by the hypocrisy of our society that they have joined the ranks of what Kenneth Keniston calls "the uncommitted." These are the individuals who feel that they can not accept the cult of the organization man, of the rugged individualist, or of the pleasure-centered Playboy. But they are also unable to conform to the traditional Western value systems which are reinforced by organized religion. Some of these join the ranks of the alienated, and in a sense drop out of any sincere search for a way of life which they could accept. They become detached observers and while they are given to over-examining their own lives, they become more or less dedicated to the proposition that one ought not to commit himself to any values, movements or persons. Dr. Keniston finds that in our day it is not unusual to discover individuals choosing alienation as their way of life. Characteristically this kind of self-chosen alienation "takes the new form of rebellion without a cause, of rejection without a program, of refusal of what is without a vision of what should be."[13] One of the alienated students studied by Dr. Keniston summarized his reaction to "the American way of life" as follows: "I have no feeling of relationship to an over-all American society defined in terms of success and security. These are not ideals that give me any pleasure."[14]

---

12   *Ibid.*, p. 17.
13   Kenneth Keniston, *The Uncommitted: Alienated Youth in American Society* (New York: Dell Publishing Co., Inc., 1967), p. 6.
14   *Ibid.*, p. 59.

Prof Weighs Ethics of Surrogate Motherhood for Pay, Calls it "Degrading"

Robert Schwaneberg

Just as this society does not permit the sale of votes, judicial decisions or sexual favors, so it should not allow the sale of pregnancy and delivery through surrogate motherhood, according to Professor Michael Walzer of the Institute for Advanced Study at Princeton.

Walzer was invited to speak last week to the state bioethics commission's Task Force on New Reproductive Practices, which is developing a recommendation to the Legislature on whether surrogate motherhood should be allowed.

The debate over surrogate motherhood, Walzer said, is "in part an argument about where we should draw the limits of the market."

Those limits, he said, are constantly being disputed, as seen in the current legislative battle over whether New Jersey should continue to allow sale of handguns to private citizens.

They also vary from society to society, he noted. Britain bans the sale of blood, which is allowed in the United States.

What is undeniable, Walzer said, is that there are certain things that may not be exchanged for money. In contemporary American society, he said, votes, athletic victories, visas, untested medicines, cars without seat belts and flammable pajamas are but a few examples of things that may not be bought.

The existence of such "blocked exchanges," Walzer said, "suggests a free market, even in a capitalist society, isn't really free." In fact, in Walzer's theory of "distributive justice," such limits on the marketplace are essential to a just society.

"We can only understand how justice works in a particular society when we understand what the social goods in that society mean to the people in that society," Walzer explained.

"It is unjust when goods are distributed for the wrong reasons," he continued. "When wealth buys college admissions or judicial decisions, that's an example of injustice.

"We limit what can be exchanged for what. And the most important limits are on what money can buy."

Walzer, through his philosophical analysis, arrived at precisely the same point as state Supreme Court Chief Justice Robert Wilentz, who said in striking down a surrogate motherhood contract in the celebrated Baby M case: "There are, in a civilized society, some things that money cannot buy."

Anne Reichman, a bioethics commission staffer, noted that Walzer and Wilentz are both supported by a developing line of legal

From *The Newark Star-Ledger*, Sunday, October 9, 1988, 48. Reprinted by permission of *The Newark Star Ledger*.

scholarship that seeks to distinguish among things that may be sold, such as inventions, those that may be freely given but may not be sold, such as body organs, and those that may neither be given nor sold—inalienable rights such as religious freedom.

On the other hand, Reichman said, some jurists contend that allowing the free market to operate more freely could cure some social ills, such as the black market in babies. She noted that Judge Richard Posner of the U.S. Court of Appeals for the 7th Circuit in Chicago contends that overly restrictive adoption regulations have resulted in a shortage of babies available for adoption, while there is a corresponding oversupply of children placed in foster care. Both problems, in Posner's analysis, could be cured by allowing payments to parents of children in foster care as incentives to relinquish the children for adoption.

Reichman noted that the state Supreme Court viewed the payment of money to a surrogate mother "as a major evil," but left open the possibility of surrogacy on a voluntary basis.

Similarly, Walzer said his analysis would allow surrogate motherhood "as an act of friendship or love," just as the citizens of Great Britain may donate, but may not sell, their blood.

"Surrogacy falls well outside the world of market relations," Walzer continued. In our culture, he explained, to carry and bear a child is "an emotionally charged experience," and a surrogate mother may be unable to predict or control the attachment she will feel toward the child she bears.

Yet the typical surrogate motherhood contract gives "no weight" to those feelings, he continued. He said it would be undesirable to see "a growing number of women who are emotionless about childbirth."

"It would be especially unjust, in a democratic society, if these individuals are marked by class," Walzer continued. "I think we have to expect that surrogate mothers, like wet nurses not too long ago, will come from the ranks of the poor. Few women are likely to rent out their bodies who don't need the money."

Reichman, however, noted that while those women who have acted as surrogate mothers may not be wealthy, they are "actually quite far from the poverty line."

Alan Weisbard, the bioethics commission's executive director, added that while most surrogate mothers were pleased to be paid, many said it was not the central reason they agreed to act as surrogates.

Walzer replied that if surrogacy for pay is allowed, the rapid commercialization of the process, aided by advances in medical technology, would rapidly lead to exploitation—and degradation—of women who act as surrogates.

To Fool (or Not) with Mother Nature

"The issue is how far we play God, how far we are going to treat mankind as we would animal husbandry." So says Leo Abse, a British M.P. who has long felt that policymakers have not dealt seriously enough with the issues raised by developments like the test-tube baby, and plans to lead a parliamentary debate on the matter this week. But for philosophers and theologians, as well as scientists, the Oldham experiment sharpens some long-standing moral and religious questions. Is in-vitro fertilization to be applauded as a humanizing technique, allowing some infertile couples the joy of procreation? Or is it dehumanizing, a step that is to be condemned because it puts the moment of creation outside the body into a mechanical environment.

To some thinkers, the Oldham experiment poses no problems. Says Rabbi Seymour Siegel, professor of ethics at Manhattan's Jewish Theological Seminary: "The Browns were trying to obey the commandment to have children. When nature does not permit conception, it is desirable to try to outwit nature. The Talmud teaches that God desires man's cooperation."

For many others, in-vitro fertilization is fraught with moral dangers. British Geneticist Robert J. Berry, a consultant to a board set up by the Church of England to consider issues like the ones raised by the Brown baby, accepts the procedure for couples who want a child, but he is still troubled. "We're on a slippery slope," he warns. "Western society is built around the family; once you divorce sex from procreation, what happens to the family?"

For the Roman Catholic Church, which first came out against in-vitro fertilization in the 1950's, the Oldham experiment promised yet another round in Rome's long fight against advances in procreation and birth control. Although the Vatican has yet to take official notice of the test-tube pregnancy, a top official quickly reiterated the church's position that "interference with nature is not acceptable" in any form. For that reason the Papacy has condemned artificial insemination, even with the husband as donor. The church is also opposed to the use of contraceptive devices for the same reason; the Browns' motive is the opposite—to have a child. But that may not matter. Says the Rev. William B. Smith, a spokesman for the Archdiocese of New York: "It's the contraception argument backward. Pius XII talked about not wanting to change the home into a laboratory. I call it switching the marital bed into a chemistry set." Catholics and other Christians who believe that life begins at conception are also troubled by the fact that in test-tube fertilization, many fertilized eggs die.

Some skeptics doubt that enough embryo transplants have been done on primates and other mammals to justify trials on man and also wonder if the patients know enough about the risks to give "informed consent." Protestant Theologian Paul Ramsey insists that the rights of the child-to-be should be considered. He argues that test-tube procreation is "immoral" because of the uncertainties involved: the parents' right to have children is never so absolute as to justify such "induced risk" to the child. Ramsey sees a further risk in Britain's birth watch: possible stigma or damage to the Brown child's self-image because of all the notoriety.

The ethical questions raised by scientific advances in procreation can only become more urgent as new techniques are explored and developed. Robert Edwards, Steptoe's partner in the Oldham experiment, has advocated test-tube selection of the offspring's sex, though only to reduce such sex-linked diseases as hemophilia. Politician Abse fears that "we are moving to a time when an embryo purchaser could select in advance the color of the baby's eyes and its probable IQ."

As for Lesley Brown, she has less difficulty reconciling herself to such anxieties. "I realize that this is a scientific miracle," she told the *Daily Mail*. "But in a way, science has made us turn to God. We are not religious people. But when we discovered that all was working well and I was pregnant, we just had to pray to God to give our thanks. It seemed right and natural."

The Ultimate Cloning Horror

Charles Krauthammer

Last year Dolly the cloned sheep was received with wonder, titters and some vague apprehension. Last week the announcement by a Chicago physicist that he is assembling a team to produce the first human clone occasioned yet another wave of Brave New World anxiety. But the scariest news of all—and largely overlooked—comes from two obscure labs, at the University of Texas and at the University of Bath. During the past four years, one group created headless mice; the other, headless tadpoles.

For sheer Frankenstein wattage, the purposeful creation of these animal monsters has no equal. Take the mice. Researchers found the gene that tells the embryo to produce the head. They deleted it. They did this in a thousand mice embryos, four of which were born. I use the term loosely. Having no way to breathe, the mice died instantly.

Why then create them? The Texas researchers want to learn how genes determine embryo development. But you don't have to be a genius to see the true utility of manufacturing headless creatures: for their organs— fully formed, perfectly useful, ripe for plundering.

Why should you be panicked? Because humans are next. "It would almost certainly be possible to produce human bodies without a forebrain," Princeton biologist Lee Silver told the London Sunday Times. "These human bodies without any semblance of consciousness would not be considered persons, and thus it would be perfectly legal to keep them 'alive' as a future source of organs."

"Alive." Never have a pair of quotation marks loomed so ominously. Take the mouse-frog technology, apply it to humans, combine it with cloning, and you are become a god: with a single cell taken from, say, your finger, you produce a headless replica of yourself, a mutant twin, arguably lifeless, that becomes your own personal, precisely tissue- matched organ farm.

There are, of course, technical hurdles along the way. Suppressing the equivalent "head" gene in man. Incubating tiny infant organs to grow into larger ones that adults could use. And creating artificial wombs (as per Aldous Huxley), given that it might be difficult to recruit sane women to carry headless fetuses to their birth/death.

It won't be long, however, before these technical barriers are breached. The ethical barriers are already cracking. Lewis Wolpert, professor of biology at University College, London, finds producing headless humans "personally distasteful" but, given the shortage of organs, does not think distaste is sufficient reason not to go ahead with something that would save lives. And Professor Silver not only sees "nothing wrong, philosophically or rationally," with producing headless humans for organ harvesting;

he wants to convince a skeptical public that it is perfectly O.K.

When prominent scientists are prepared to acquiesce in—or indeed encourage—the deliberate creation of deformed and dying quasi-human life, you know we are facing a bioethical abyss. Human beings are ends, not means. There is no grosser corruption of biotechnology than creating a human mutant and disemboweling it at our pleasure for spare parts.

The prospect of headless human clones should put the whole debate about "normal" cloning in a new light. Normal cloning is less a treatment for infertility than a treatment for vanity. It is a way to produce an exact genetic replica of yourself that will walk the earth years after you're gone.

But there is a problem with a clone. It is not really you. It is but a twin, a perfect John Doe Jr., but still a junior. With its own independent consciousness, it is, alas, just a facsimile of you.

The headless clone solves the facsimile problem. It is a gateway to the ultimate vanity: immortality. If you create a real clone, you cannot transfer your consciousness into it to truly live on. But if you create a headless clone of just your body, you have created a ready source of replacement parts to keep you—your consciousness—going indefinitely.

Which is why one form of cloning will inevitably lead to the other. Cloning is the technology of narcissism, and nothing satisfies narcissism like immortality. Headlessness will be cloning's crowning achievement.

The time to put a stop to this is now. Dolly moved President Clinton to create a commission that recommended a temporary ban on human cloning. But with physicist Richard Seed threatening to clone humans, and with headless animals already here, we are past the time for toothless commissions and meaningless bans.

Clinton banned federal funding of human-cloning research, of which there is none anyway. He then proposed a five-year ban on cloning. This is not enough. Congress should ban human cloning now. Totally. And regarding one particular form, it should be draconian: the deliberate creation of headless humans must be made a crime, indeed a capital crime. If we flinch in the face of this high-tech barbarity, we'll deserve to live in the hell it heralds.

Neti and Ditto

Christine Gorman

Two Cute New Clones Are Too Close for Comfort

It was bad enough when Scottish researchers cloned a sheep named Dolly and commentators started writing about virgin births and Frankenstein. But then one week later, researchers at the Oregon Regional Primate Research Center let it be known that they had cloned a pair of rhesus monkeys, named Neti (for nuclear embryo transfer infant) and Ditto, that squinted in the glare of the TV lights and clung to each other for dear life.

It was two clones too many—or, more to the point, clones too close to human for comfort. Politicians—with one eye on re-election and another on the polls (a TIME/CNN survey reported that 3 out of 4 Americans believe such research is "against the will of God")—wasted no time. The President, proclaiming that "each human life is unique, born of a miracle that reaches beyond laboratory science," banned the use of federal funds for human cloning, while Republican Representative Vernon Ehlers of Michigan introduced not one but two anticloning measures.

Lost in the rush of legislative activity was the fact that Neti and Ditto were not so much a step toward a brave new world as a diversion. They were produced from embryos, which makes them clones only in the way that identical twins or triplets are clones. The same technique has already been used with sheep, cattle, rabbits, pigs and even humans— although in the last case the embryonic clones were destroyed. What makes Dolly special is that she was cloned from an adult sheep, not from an embryo. She is the only mammal ever born that is identical to her biological mother.

She may not be the last, however. As NIH director Dr. Harold Varmus told a congressional subcommittee last week, it could take just one infertile couple, arguing that cloning provides their only chance to bear a child, to turn public opinion around.

Cloning Ban Fails in Senate

Helen Dewar and Rick Weiss

WASHINGTON—Senate Republican leaders' plans for swift enactment of a ban on human cloning collapsed yesterday amid complaints that the proposed legislation went too far and threatened to impede promising biomedical research.

Both sides in the argument over how far to go in curtailing experimentation with cloned human embryos vowed to press ahead with efforts to come up with an anti-cloning bill that can be enacted by Congress this year.

In the interim, the Food and Drug Administration has said it has the authority to block anyone who attempted to apply to humans the technology that allowed Scottish scientists to clone Dolly the sheep, the flrst mammal cloned from an adult cell.

Yesterday's initial showdown demonstrated how hard it might be to pass a law governing human cloning, with both sides claiming the high moral ground and raising many of the same ethical and religious issues that have stoked political fires over abortion.

The dispute was further complicated by senators' own deeply personal concerns.

Somberly telling his colleagues that he lost his father, mother and a brother to cancer and that he, his wife and daughter have also had the disease, Sen. Connie Mack (R-Fla.) warned against hasty action that might retard research on cancer and other diseases.

Listen, he said, to the scientific community and to patient groups "who represent people like myself."

The Republican-sponsored bill was stalled when its supporters, including Majority Leader Trent Lott (R-Miss.) could muster only 42 votes—18 short of the required 60—for a procedural motion to bring the measure to the floor for debate and votes.

Twelve Republicans, including conservatives such as Mack and Sen. Strom Thurmond (R-S.C.) as well as most party moderates, joined all Democrats in voting to block the bill.

The bill, sponsored by Sens. Christopher S. Bond (R-Mo.) and Bill Frist (R-Tenn.) would permanently ban a procedure known as "human somatic cell nuclear transfer," in which a nucleus from a person's cell would be introduced into a human egg to create a human embryo. Scientists in Scotland used a similar procedure to clone Dolly last year. Violators would be subject to prisom terms of up to 10 years.

Many foes of the bill supported an alternative offered by Sens. Dianne Feinstein (D-Calif.) and Edward M. Kennedy (D-Mass.) that would permit the cloning of human embryos for research purposes but would impose a 10-year moratorium on the implantation of cloned embryos in a woman's uterus to develop.

Bill Would Ban Female Mutilation

Associated Press

ALBANY, N.Y.—The state Legislature has sent Gov. George Pataki a bill that would make it a crime to mutilate the genitals of any female under the age of 18, even with a parent's consent.

New York would become one of only a handful of states to ban the procedure, if the measure is signed into law by Pataki.

"This barbaric procedure has absolutely no medicinal benefits and deserves to be made illegal in New York state," said state Sen. Dale Volker, a sponsor of the bill.

Female circumcision is a practice in which a woman's genitals are partially or totally removed. It is a cultural ritual that is performed in parts of Africa, the Middle East and Southeast Asia, usually on pre-pubescent girls.

Some immigrants to the United States have continued the practice. According to the Centers for Disease Control, an estimated 27,000 females in New York have had or will undergo the procedure.

"We don't know whether it has been widely practiced here or not, but we know the largest population who use this practice are in the states of New York or California,"

Assemblywoman Barbara Clark, who sponsored the bill in her chamber, said Saturday.

"Our prenatal clinics have reported seeing incidents of women who have had this procedure done. They just can't be sure when and where it was done," she said. "But we do know it has happened to women in New York state."

The practice has led to trauma, infections, internal injuries, infertility, childbirth complications and even death. Critics of female circumcision say it is performed as a means of curbing a woman's sexual pleasure and to guard her chastity.

It already has been banned by the federal government and by a few states, including California. It also has been made illegal in many European and African counties.

Under the New York legislation, anyone who mutilates a female's genitals could be convicted of a felony and sentenced to a maximum of four years in prison. In addition, any parent or guardian who allows such a procedure to be performed on his or her child could face the same penalty.

The bill would allow female circumcision to be performed by a doctor if it is deemed medically necessary.

Research on Anti-H.I.V. Drugs

Lawrence K. Altman

CHICAGO, Feb. 5—Efforts to make it easier to take combinations of drugs to combat the AIDS virus have met with mixed results, scientists said here today.

Because those combination therapies can require taking more than a dozen pills several times a day and rigidly adhering to time schedules revolving around meals and sleep, scientists are trying several approaches to ease the burden.

One is to reduce the daily number of drugs taken after several months. Another is to reduce the number of times that some of the pills are taken each day in therapies that most experts believe patients will need to continue for their lifetimes.

A crucial problem in combination therapy is that H.I.V., the AIDS virus, often becomes resistant to one or more of the drugs. Often it is because the person cannot tolerate the drug regimen. But the reasons are not always clear in other cases.

To try to reduce the incidence of resistance, scientists have developed laboratory tests to guide the initial choice of drugs and then to monitor the combination. Progress has been made. But such tests are not ready for everyday use largely because not enough time has passed to correlate their use with outcomes from treatment, scientists said at the Fifth Conference on Retrovirus and Opportunistic Infections.

Scientists have also concocted new combinations of the 11 licensed anti-H.I.V. drugs. A hope is that they will be more powerful, have fewer unwanted effects and save many of those who failed on the combinations that came into widespread use about two years ago.

At the same time, leaders spoke of the development of promising new varieties of existing classes of anti-H.I.V. drugs as well as new classes of anti-H.I.V. drugs. The hope is that doctors will have greater flexibility in treating individuals with a resistant virus by juggling the new drugs coming along with existing ones.

But even now there is no clear consensus about which drug to give first. And the growing number of choices is "leaving clinicians in a quandary about what is best to start with," said Dr. Scott Hammer, an AIDS expert at the Beth Israel Deaconess Medical Center in Boston.

The meeting ended on a discouraging note. The last two talks came from French and American researchers who reported failure in two trials that reduced triple drug regimens to two or just one drug.

In the French study, participants took triple drug therapy (AZT, 3TC and indinavir) for three months. Then one-third of the group stayed on triple therapy. Each of the remaining thirds took different combinations of two of the three drugs (one AZT and

---

3TC; the other AZT and indinavir). The study stopped ahead of schedule when it became clear that two drugs were less effective in suppressing H.I.V.

The American study was conducted by the Federal AIDS Clinical Trial Group. Participants took the same triple drug therapy as in the French study, but for twice as long, 24 weeks. Then they were divided into three groups. One group continued on the triple therapy. A second group took AZT and 3TC and a third took indinavir alone. Again, triple therapy proved superior in the study in keeping H.I.V. suppressed.

Actor Anthony Perkins Dead

LOS ANGELES (AP)—Anthony Perkins, who played the murderous motel keeper Norman Bates in Alfred Hitchcock's "Psycho" and multiple sequels of the movie, died yesterday. He was 60.

Perkins died in his Hollywood home from complications of the AIDS virus, his publicist, Leslee Dart, said. He died peacefully in his bedroom with his wife and sons at his side.

Earlier this week, Perkins put together a statement about his condition, Dart said.

"I chose not to go public about this because to misquote 'Casablanca,' I'm not much at being noble but it doesn't take much to see that the problems of one old actor don't amount to a hill of beans in this crazy world,' " he said.

"There are many who believe that this disease is God's vengeance, but I believe it was sent to teach people how to love and understand and have compassion for each other. I have learned more about love, selflessness and human understanding from the people I have met in this great adventure in the world of AIDS than I ever did in the cutthroat, competitive world in which I spent my life."

From *Newark Star-Ledger*, September 13, 1992.

Questions

Section IV

1. What is an "Encyclical?" How may its contents be viewed by non-Catholics?

2. How was "Humanae Vitae" received by Roman Catholics?

3. How is Natural Law thought used in the Encyclical?

4. How and why was the phrase "open to the transmission of life" criticized by some?

5. What is the message that Binkley and Crane are trying to convey to women concerning the use of sex?

6. Do you think the content of the reading is fair to men?

7. Conceding the positive aspects of extra-marital heterosexual intercourse what would be some of the negatives for both sexes?

8. Should surrogate motherhood be termed "unnatural?"

9. What are the various types of surrogate motherhood? What are the potentially bad consequences of their use as Walzer sees them?

10. Granted that there is a natural process of procreation why do some ethicists believe there is nothing unethical in the "in vitro fertilization" procedure?

11. What are some of the ethical problems and/or consequent dangers that some ethicists see and fear with regard to "in vitro fertilization?"

12. Why do some ethicists object to the use of any man-made (artificial) contra-conceptive device?

13. What is the effectiveness rate of condoms regarding prevention of AIDS and pregnancy?

14. Should condoms be distributed free of charge in high schools?

15. Using the reading of Sections I and II: Why do many moral philosophers and theologians consider sodomitic intercourse to be immoral?

16. What is the difference between a homosexual orientation and homosexual venereal activity?

17. Using various theories of Ethics— what should be our attitude toward people who have contracted the AIDS virus?

18. Could the cloning of animals be justified on a utilitarian basis?

19. What are the dangers involved in the cloning of humans?

Section V

Business Ethics

Introduction

In 1966 Fr. Thomas Garrett, S. J., of the University of Scranton, authored a textbook entitled *Business Ethics*. This work represented one of the first efforts by a philosopher (one who had also studied economics) to address this topic in a general manner. Richard DeGeorge, in 1982, wrote another fine textbook, and this opened a floodgate of writings on the subject.

For whatever economic reasons, industrialists had historically closed plants or abandoned areas in which they had operated for decades, leaving thousands out of work; people wondered whether there was any truth at all in what they saw, heard or read in the various media. Many companies developed Codes of Ethics, as did whole professions, along with political structures such as counties, townships, etc. Civil rights laws and affirmative action legislation in the 1960s triggered heated controversy.

Our writers have addressed these issues going back over 20 years. Most recently, Dr. Gerald Williams has published *Ethics in Modern Management* (1992). Dr. Williams was a manager for AT&T and Bellcore for many years, completing his Ph.D. at N.Y.U. before retiring. He now conducts business and management seminars throughout the country and is an adjunct professor of ethics at Seton Hall University.

The Coopers and Lybrand accounting firm brought together examples culled from Codes of Ethics of various companies. Students have brought the Codes from their own companies, which include banks, and these echo the ones in the Newsletter. Discussion might well ensue as to whether there is an invasion of any civil rights, e.g., privacy, in these Codes. The questions at the end of the Section will raise this issue.

I leave it to the individual teacher to add to, delete, discuss and analyze the readings in this book. I think you will find many of them quite different from those found in the usual anthologies in this field.

In this third printing I have added several articles dealing with sexual harassment, abuse of the Internet, health benefits of retirees, the Tobacco Industry, and the environment.

Employment and Wages

Gerald J. Williams

Good Management or Good Morals?

Good managers, as elementary textbooks in business administration readily point out, will attract capable people into the business, keep their turnover low, secure their loyalty to the company and its objectives, and maintain and increase their productivity wherever possible. A business that wants to keep good employees will have to offer competitive salaries along with some kind of health insurance coverage and savings and pension plans as part of its basic wage package—to the extent that its size and financial resources let it. To motivate and satisfy employees, managers also need to provide them with on and off-the-job training; give them effective job-performance feedback; allow them to participate in decisions affecting the structure and objectives of their jobs and how their performance on those jobs will be measured; provide opportunities for them to move to higher-paying positions with more responsibility; tell them whether or not they are promotable; see to it that they have formal and informal avenues of appeal to higher supervision without fear of retaliation from their immediate bosses; and provide them with safe working conditions.

While all of these practices constitute "good management," they have a moral dimension as well. A company's managers may ignore or abuse them ostensibly in the interest of the company's bottom line, but such actions are morally wrong whenever they involve some form of injury or injustice to an individual or a failure to render the respect due someone as a person.

What moral claims, rights, do employees have against their employers as far as employment and wages are concerned?

Let's start, in this chapter, with rights to employment and just wages.

Is There a Moral Right to Employment?

In the last 10 years or so, many American plants and industries elected to shut down or relocate their operations or downsize their work forces, putting many thousands of people out of work. According to one estimate, "These and similar cutbacks will bring the number of American professional and managerial positions eliminated since 1979 to over 1.5 million."

Some downsizing of American corporations was probably accomplished by ordinary attrition and retirements, but many of the employees affected by these changes had to start over with new employers, perhaps in totally different careers, and some of them likely suffered economic loss along with a severe psychological blow to their self-esteem.

From *Ethics in Modern Management* by Gerald J. Williams, 41-52 and 125-136. Copyright 1992 by Gerald J. Williams. Quorum Books an imprint of Greenwood Publishing Group, Inc., Westport, CT. Reprinted with permission.

Someone might argue that the people involved in these shutdowns, relocations, and force reductions also suffered a violation of their right to employment, but the argument so stated begs the question of whether such a moral right can be shown to exist and exactly against whom it may be asserted. Let's explore one possible answer to that question.

All of us are all born into some kind of economic system which may range from the relatively simple practices of primitive tribes to the complex transactions we find in highly industrialized, technology—oriented societies. While many of us could, if we had to, scratch out a living by farming, or hunting, or gathering, most of us in the highly industrialized countries, at least, get our access to material resources by way of a "job" (using the term in its widest sense to include all occupations and professions), by "work." There are, of course, people who don't need a job because they depend on the work of others, they live on their investments or have inherited wealth, or they are physically or psychologically unable to work.

I argued earlier that every human being has a moral right to acquire and use some share of material resources to insure living at a decent level of physical and psychological well-being, and it seems to follow that if most people are subject to an economic system in which a job is the means by which they obtain resources, then they have a moral right to a job; the economic system owes them employment. One weakness of this argument as stated is that a society can, through its economic system, insure that everyone enjoys some minimal level of material prosperity without providing everyone with a job, through various forms of welfare programs. But the argument is strengthened if its premises include the proposition that our sense of worth as human beings depends on our making a contri-

bution to our own and our family's and society's well-being, which depends, in turn, on our doing it through a job. In the abstract, then, it sounds like a case can be made for a moral right to employment, but we need to expose what that means in concrete terms, in the actual circumstances and conditions of a particular economic system. The "system," after all, is just a handy collective term of reference to the myriad individual economic transactions going on every day among the members of a particular society.

In a capitalistic economic system like our own in the United States, the private sector of the economy provides most job opportunities, so the thrust of the argument for a moral right to employment appears to fall on private employers. In effect, are all industries and businesses morally obligated to employ some minimum number of people to achieve a satisfactory level of employment in the society in which they operate?

The answer seems to be "no," if that society has adopted as its preferred economic system one whose very nature requires extensive freedom for its commercial enterprises in order to generate a maximum level of material prosperity for its members. In the capitalistic system, this freedom includes the right to hire and keep on the payroll only those employees needed to meet the demands for a particular business's products and to operate efficiently at a satisfactory level of profit. It also seems to include taking on only those people whose education, skills, and personality traits are judged best suited to the operations the business engages in.

One very large assumption being made here is that the option to live under the capitalistic system can be shown to be freely chosen by the members of a society either through some direct democratic process or by the notion of an implicit social contract among them. In other words, by continuing to live under the system without political protest, they indirectly indicate their preference for it. Given this assumption, the freedom of employers to hire and retain employees as they see fit entails that no member of the society in which they operate has a moral claim on any specific job offered in the private sector.

Because the capitalistic economic system responds as it does to market forces affecting levels of employment, it cannot guarantee a job to everyone who wants one, at least not on any long-term, continuous basis. There will likely always be those people whose particular skills, for whatever reason, simply are not needed by any business enterprise. Based on the arguments offered here, it may be true that they have no moral right to any specific job in any business, but they still have a right to work. Their society, then, which has decided on a capitalistic economic system has an obligation to provide them with work through its political structure. Welfare programs by themselves are not enough. This means that the government may need to provide training in advanced skills for those who lose their jobs because they cannot cope with the sophisticated technology required in today's employment market. Government may even have to offer jobs as the "employer of last resort." These jobs have to be more than just "make-work"; they should be directed at meaningful kinds of public service not easily provided by the private sector like rebuilding and constructing transportation facilities; building parks, campgrounds and public monuments; or working in libraries and health-care institutions.

The funds for all these functions have to come from some form of tax on those who own, work for, and are retired from viable economic enterprises. These people have a right to use natural resources for their own benefit, but their right to the yield of these resources is not exclusive because, in light of the earlier arguments I offered for entitlement to natural resources, some of the productive potential of those same resources belongs to the people who are unemployed though no fault of their own.

Fair Hiring Practices

Take a hypothetical case where one or the other of an employment agency's client companies ask the agency not to send minority candidates to them for job interviews because they prefer to hire people who fit a certain profile, white, blond, blue-eyed, and good looking, who fit the corporate "front-office image." May these companies argue that since no individual person has any moral claim on the jobs they are offering, they have a right to employ whomever they wish—even if that means establishing discriminatory criteria that are not job-related?

The natural-law moralist (or anyone committed to a rights-based moral theory) would point out that while there is no positive duty to hire a particular individual for a specific job, screening practices based on race, gender, age, or religious preference violate the right of everyone to be treated with the dignity due a human person and are immoral. Consequently, employers have a negative duty not to discriminate on characteristics that have nothing to do with performing the job. Utilitarians, I think, would come to the same conclusion, although their judgment would, of course, depend on weighing the consequences these practices would produce on the whole. Cultural relativists would decide that if there were no laws against discrimination, hiring and promotion policies would follow whatever customs were acceptable in society. Many employers, for example, probably appealed to "community standards" to justify not hiring or promoting black people prior to the 1960s civil rights legislation.

Are the employment agencies morally wrong if they comply with discriminatory practices and refuse to send minority or other applicants on interviews for positions they are qualified to fill? Is an agency's cooperation formal or material in this instance? I believe that the natural law moralist would consider it formal since the agencies have agreed to become an extension of a client's employment office and are performing a direct act of discrimination that is morally wrong in itself. The utilitarian, on the other hand, would likely want to weigh the consequences for the agency if it should lose clients by a refusal to cooperate in discriminatory practices and try to determine whether or not a better state of affairs would result overall from complying with them. The cultural relativist would approve compliance with an employer's wishes if discrimination were an accepted social practice and not against the law.

Affirmative Action and Preferential Treatment

There are many interpretations of just what "affirmative action" means. The approach to this effort may range all the way from setting specific numbers of minorities to be moved into positions over a given time period so that the proportion of the positions they hold begins to approach their numerical distribution in the general population, to establishing the overall principle that employment and promotion opportunities are open to all, regardless of gender, race, religion, age, or disabled status.

It's very likely that both natural-law and utilitarian moralists would agree that everyone should have an equal opportunity to compete for any job he or she is qualified to do and would endorse this sense of affirm-

ative action. Cultural relativists, again, would fall back on society's customary practices and wouldn't agree to the idea of equal opportunity just on its face. But what about preferential treatment (popularly referred to as "setting quotas"), the practice of hiring or promoting members of minority groups in preference to those from nonminority groups?

One rationale for this practice is to redress past injustices committed by American industry and government agencies in their hiring and promotion practices against blacks, women, hispanics, American Indians and any other minority groups. It is designed to insure that members of minority groups are represented in the offices and opportunities a society has to offer in proportion to their numbers in society.

But while the fact of past discrimination is not disputed, this particular remedy for it often is. The key rebuttal against preferential treatment centers on the contention that the person who receives it is not, in most cases, at least, the person who suffered the injustice, and the person (usually a white male) who is being passed over for a position or office because of the preferential treatment being given to a member of a minority group is not the one who committed the injustice in the first place. Therefore, the argument goes, preferential hiring and promotion commit the very offense they are supposed to remedy, namely, selection of a person purely on the basis of some characteristic which has nothing to do with performing a function or job. Setting specific numerical quotas for minorities is, on this view, just plain immoral. What needs to be implemented is a going-forward policy of equal opportunity, selecting people just on their qualifications for a position.

One reply to this argument, offered by Daniel Maguire, claims that its premise exonerating white males is false. While a particular white male may not have directly discriminated against a minority person, he shares in a kind of collective guilt on the part of his society that has failed to care enough or do enough to stop past discrimination. Further, some of these acts of discrimination have quite likely benefitted him personally. On Maguire's view, we must render to others what they deserve in legal justice, the debt we owe to the common good by virtue of our social personhood. He thinks that invidious American individualism has blinded us to this social obligation; we confuse justice with equality when we should be concerned with justice as fairness. We focus incorrectly on the kind of justice that governs interpersonal transactions among equals instead of on distributive and legal justice that govern interrelationships among members of a community. Therefore, while affirmative action quotas as a remedy for legal and distributive injustice may be unequal, they are not unfair.

I suspect that many Americans would not accept Maguire's argument, especially if they have tried to influence legislators to outlaw discriminatory practices in the marketplace, or have worked diligently within the limits of their own authority in the business world to hire and promote people from minority groups. They would likely resist the idea that they shared in a collective guilt for discrimination and, if passed over for a particular position just because they were white males, would deeply resent the explanation that they were simply paying the price for their past sins.

Maguire refers to St. Thomas Aquinas' contention that the community, not just the ruler, is where distributive justice resides, is its subject, and that the members of the community are "pleased and satisfied with a just distribution"). Aquinas suggests that a particular member of the community may have an obligation to be sure that another individual or family is receiving a just share of the community's goods. This means, if I understand him correctly, that even as individuals we are responsible for seeing the common good realized in our fellow community members' situations, and we may even have to give up something we have to insure that happens.

I would like to pick up on Aquinas' idea that the members of a community are pleased with a just distribution and give it my own extended interpretation as a possible rationale for preferential treatment in hiring and promotion.

Concretely, this abstract idea might mean that the people in a society, in "seeing" that members of its subgroups are proportionately represented in all its offices and positions, in the government, in business and industry, in the arts, in academia, and in sports see an affirmation of the value of human personhood that underlies all accidental differences in people. That affirmation should be regarded as a desirable social goal benefitting every individual member of society, and promoting that goal by means that rely on what are ordinarily irrelevant factors in the selection of individuals for offices and positions is not unjust because those factors are now relevant from the standpoint of effecting distributive justice. In the business world, for example, members of minority groups who come in contact with the people in higher levels of management derive a sense of contentment and affirmation of their own personhood when they see that they are "represented" in reasonable proportion in those levels—even if they acknowledge that they personally may not have the talent required to reach them. On this line of argument, then, preferential treatment may be the only way to establish the balance that should exist in these structures in a society, and are not unjust—any more, for example, than drafting a subgroup of young males to fight a society's wars is considered unjust discrimination.

Natural-law moralists might arrive at different conclusions on preferential hiring and promotion depending on how they see justice at work in the practice. The idea of social rather than commutative justice might persuade some of them that this practice is morally justified. Others might see it as reverse discrimination, a violation of the rights of individuals who were not responsible for past social injustice. Or they might argue that it is simply a case of selection of people for a position on irrelevant grounds, an act of disrespect for the people who were passed over in the process and morally wrong in itself.

The utilitarian moralist's approach to preferential treatment would, of course, be to predict the overall good and bad consequences that would result from the practice. If it appeared that it would generate more good than bad consequences on the whole, then it would be morally required—even if the individual white males would have to be passed over for positions they were clearly qualified for. These white males would not be claiming that they had been treated unfairly.

The cultural relativist would try to determine whether society approved or disapproved of preferential treatment, either by law or custom, and act, accordingly.

The basic principle governing hiring and promotion for both natural-law and utilitarian moralists is, I believe, that in the overall interest of society's well-being, managers are obliged to stick to qualifications alone in their selections for jobs and promotions unless a persuasive case has been made for instituting and following preferential treatment for some determinate period of time. (Cultural relativists will fall back on society's practices in this matter.) Does that mean managers must flip a coin, so to speak, when several equally-qualified candidates—e.g.,

black, hispanic, female, white male—present themselves for a position? In an extreme situation, that might be a reasonable thing to do, but choices in these cases are ordinarily justified in some minimal way, such as by deciding that one applicant is better than the others because he or she has better communication skills or would be easier to work with and, consequently, would be more likely to contribute to the smooth operation of the enterprise. It would probably even be morally acceptable to hire or promote a fully-qualified relative or friend, since no one individual applicant has any prima facie title to the position under consideration.

Wages

Employees' wages are generally determined by the market: whatever it takes to attract and keep productive people. In larger industries, it is commonly assumed that competitive salaries include basic wages and bonuses plus assorted benefits like paid holidays, vacations, sick days, medical and dental insurance, and savings and pension plans. In smaller businesses, wages are very often simply a function or what an enterprise can afford; benefits may or may not be a part of the package.

What wages are employees morally entitled to? Are they entitled to a certain level of benefits in addition to a basic wage? Their employment, as was argued earlier, is their access to their fair share of material resources, so at a minimum it seems that their jobs must provide them with wages and benefits at a level that will assure their living in some minimal but decent set of conditions. That appears to be the rationale, for example, behind the federal minimum hourly wage in certain job categories. What is clear, I think, is that shareholders and company officers have no right to a disproportionate share of a company's revenues if that forces employees and their families to accept levels of wages and benefits that won't suffice to support them at a decent human level of existence.

Not every business may be able to afford this ideal. Does this mean that those that can't because they simply aren't big enough should be required to go out of business on moral grounds, grounds of justice? At least two practical reasons, I think, argue against it. First, small enterprises provide a living for their owners, at least (think of "mom and pop" kinds of establishments). Second, they likely employ many people who lack the education and skills needed to work in larger and more sophisticated industries. Low-paying jobs may well be the financial stop-gap these workers need until they can acquire the skills that will get them into better-paying jobs. Or it may be the case that they are the second wage earner in a family and want this income just to supplement the family's minimal living requirements until the principal wage earner has a job that takes care of them. In any case, since it isn't possible to require a particular business to pay wages larger than it can legitimately afford, what these people can't earn toward their minimally decent standard of living needs to come from the government as a matter of distributive justice. That amount will be based on appropriate economic statistics, such as "what it takes to sustain a family of four."

Some More Thoughts About Wages

Equal Pay for Equal Work

The principle "equal pay for equal work" is currently established as part of U.S. labor law. People performing the same kind of work must be paid the same salaries unless the fact that some of them can do the work faster or more efficiently because they have been at it longer than other, newer, employees justifies paying them more. Race, gender, age, and handicaps have no bearing on pay treatment where equal work is concerned.

Does social justice require that employees with dependents, families to support, for example, should be paid more than people with no dependents but who are doing the exact same work? It seems like a case could made for that requirement if a person's dependents gain their rightful access to resources solely through his or her work efforts. It is unlikely, however, that such disparate treatment would ever be accepted in the United States. Single people would surely argue that an employer only has to pay the market wage for a particular job and is not in the business of caring for social justice. They might argue further that the person with dependents probably freely chose to found a family and spend his or her income that way instead of on sports cars, expensive vacations, or high living in general. He or she does not have a right to a subsidy for that life-style choice, a subsidy derived from paying lower salaries to co-workers without such obligations. If distributive justice is at issue, they might argue, it constitutes an obligation falling on society in general; special welfare or family-subsidy programs may well be called for but they should be a responsibility shared by everyone in the community on some equitable basis.

In the United States, at least for many years, this issue did not arise because the productivity and general financial success of large enterprises allowed them to pay the same level of wages and benefits to all employees doing the same kind of work and those with dependents earned enough to care for them decently. The size and profit levels of smaller businesses probably would never be enough to try to pay their employees with dependents anything other than the going market rates, so government would have to provide those people with some sort of family subsidy.

Equal Pay for Comparable Work

In recent years the notion of "equal pay for comparable worth" or work has influenced some states in the United States to require paying people in government jobs having widely different content (tree trimmers and typists, perhaps) the same salaries if it can be demonstrated that these jobs require the same relative levels of education, skill, knowledge, and experience. The spur for this approach to establishing salaries was the incontrovertible fact that for years women were paid lower wages for many kinds of work that required the same skills and knowledge demanded in jobs held by men who were paid higher wages for doing them.

Is equal pay for comparable work a requirement of justice? One business ethicist, Richard DeGeorge, argues that it is not. He thinks that the market is still the most efficient allocator of jobs because even though skill and knowledge requirements may look the same for many jobs, other factors (probably like long hours, risk or physical environment) have to be considered. What is morally required is that no class of people may be excluded from obtaining these higher-paying jobs on irrelevant grounds. If females have been traditionally excluded from them just because they were female, that discriminatory practice has to be discontinued.

I think DeGeorge makes a good case.

Who Gets What Share of the Return on Resources?

There is probably some relationship between the amount of material resources a company uses and its obligation to distribute the return realized from those resources to society's members. What that return is, of course, doesn't depend solely on the amount of resources used, but also on how well a company manages them and how productive its workers are. Managers and workers, then, have a right to a fair share of the return in proportion to their contribution to the enterprise's success, with emphasis on the word "fair." Top managers usually think that they make the biggest contribution and as a result expect the biggest relative share of the wages and bonuses paid by the enterprise. In some cases, however, their salaries and perks often appear to be, to the social justice sceptic at least, a disproportionate share of a company's total compensation package.

Shareholders, of course, have a right to a fair share of their companies' return. Some people might argue that as the owners of the business, they have first claim on the return and the right to the largest relative share. The shareholders, however, through their investment in companies, are simply accessing resources and are entitled, like everybody else, to a fair share of the return on those resources. "Fair" in this case certainly includes compensation for the risk taken in making those investments, but it does not include compensation that might depend on paying substandard wages or benefits to employees.

Closing Down an Operation

Gerald J. Williams

A Plant Closes

A few years ago, the Chrysler Corporation decided to close down one of its plants that had been operating in a community for over 30 years. Although the plant ranked well in productivity compared with the company's other plants, the reason management gave for closing it was overcapacity; the demand for the particular models produced there was down.

As might be expected, the news of the closing was a shock to the community because of its devastating economic impact. Over 4,000 jobs would be lost. A large number of the employees being terminated had put in over 20 years of service, and their chances to earn better pensions based on longer service were obviously jeopardized. The community's tax base would be eroded; property values would drop; supporting businesses, industries, and religious and cultural institutions from food stores to parochial schools would be severely affected.

Critics of the closing claimed that the company was acting unjustly toward the community because it had violated a contract made 31 years ago when it began operations there. Roads and schools were built and police and fire services probably expanded with tax money; churches undertook building programs; small businesses and industries were established in support of the company and its workers. Workers signed on with the company and bought houses and began to raise families. All of this activity was probably undertaken with the expectation and understanding that the plant would be there indefinitely, and that the community could count on its long-term commitment.

Critics also doubted that the company's basic rationale for the closing, overcapacity, was legitimate in view of the fact that it had opened new plants in foreign countries. They suspected that some of the vehicles produced there would find their way back into the United States.

Finally, critics pointed out that the workers had no say in the decision to close the plant (Windsor, 1990).

Are the arguments offered by the critics sound? Let's establish a hypothetical third-person dialogue between plant officials and the community and examine these arguments critically.

We'll begin with the idea of a "contract" the community might claim was made with it when the plant opened. Unless there was some sort of formal written agreement entered into with city officials, it was at best implicit. But what could such a contract guarantee? Did the fact that the plant was built in that particular community automat-

From *Ethics in Modern Management* by Gerald J. Williams, 41-52 and 125-136. Copyright 1992 by Gerald J. Williams. Quorum Books an imprint of Greenwood Publishing Group, Inc., Westport, CT. Reprinted with permission.

ically constitute a promise that the company would never leave? Did the employees who signed up to work at the plant automatically establish a claim to long-term employment, wages, and benefits?

The company, it may be presumed, would argue in rebuttal that it never offered guarantees of that kind. It probably located where it did for many reasons: the community might have offered a good source of dependable workers and easy access to the transportation facilities needed to bring in raw materials and deliver finished products; it may have been attractive to managers who would have to transfer and make their homes there because it had good schools, shopping, and recreational facilities; its political climate may have been favorable to business. But, at best, the company could only guarantee that it would remain in the community as long as its operation there was profitable. Surely the community's political, social, religious, and cultural leaders and the owners of supporting businesses and industries had to understand that. After all, in a free-market economic system, buyers and sellers are free to enter and leave the market as they see fit. At the time of locating the plant, all predictions may have indicated the likelihood that it would operate for a long time, but that could never have been assured independently of economic conditions that could change drastically. No company can afford to operate a plant indefinitely at a loss; eventually, unprofitable operations have to be shut down. So the company surely would reject the idea that it had entered into any kind of contract with the community. Besides, the company had stayed in the community for 30 years—certainly not a fly-by-night commitment by any means.

Finally, the company might have suggested that the political and social organizations in the community owed it a great deal. The income available to the community's

members to care for health needs, educate their children, support their religious programs, and enjoy recreational and cultural activities was largely generated, directly or indirectly, by the plant. It was likely that the company had donated generously to cultural and social organizations over the years. Its managers and employees may have assumed leadership roles in numerous civic enterprises like United Way campaigns, youth organizations, church communities and local government bodies.

The community's leaders would probably respond to this rebuttal by stressing several points. First, when a company starts up an operation in a community, it is well aware that political and social entities will incur costs to support it. Tax rebates may have been offered to attract the company to the community. Roads, sewage systems, schools, libraries, service, and protective services will likely be expanded, and these costs may be laid directly at the doorstep of the company. Unless the company were to pay outright for all of them, members of the community pay some share of these costs. That all these amenities are in place serves the company's interests if only in terms of insuring its ability to attract and retain managers and employees. That's one reason the company "owes" the community. Nor will all taxes assessed on the company pay just for the expense incurred on its behalf because as a member of the community, the company is also a citizen and is obliged to pay a share of the ongoing costs needed to insure that the community will provide an environment that will contribute to its members' welfare.

Second, the company knows full well that employees who build homes and establish families near the place they work are assuming some sort of long-term financial stability from their employer in terms of wages and benefits. Why else would they incur protracted financial obligations?

Third, the businesses established to serve the new market provided by the company and its employees are under no obligation to invest in the community; but many of these businesses do serve the plant's operation directly, and indirectly, of course, by the services they offer its employees. It seems like the company owes them something, too.

Finally, while the community's members obviously benefit from the company's payroll, as devoted and hard-working employees they contribute directly to the company's success. What they receive in wages, they earn. And while the company's managers and employees may contribute much time and effort to leadership roles in the community's organizations, they and their families also benefit from the services offered by those same organizations.

In view of its awareness of all kinds of expectations on the part of employees and of the relationships established with political, social, and business entities, a company surely knows that its commitment to an operation in a community must be long-term.

In the specific case we are considering, the second challenge to the company's decision to close the plant was that it had opened new plants in foreign countries; therefore, the claim of overcapacity was spurious. Further, it could be argued, if the vehicles produced in the foreign plants did show up in the U.S. market, jobs belonging to American workers had in effect been exported to foreigners willing to work for lower wages and benefits.

The company might have responded to this point by pointing out that it has a primary fiduciary responsibility to earn a profit for its shareholders. This U.S. plant was no longer profitable because demand for the models made there was down, but they could be made, perhaps, at a profit overseas.

Further, people in those countries also have a right to access resources on behalf of themselves and their families, and the company was really killing two birds with one stone: generating profits for shareholders and providing jobs for people in underdeveloped countries. Finally, it was probably unlikely that vehicles produced in the foreign countries would replace those produced in the closing plant on a one-to-one basis; so American jobs weren't really being replaced. (And, even if the company had no intention of importing any of the vehicles produced in those plants to the United States, there still might be a lesson here for U.S. workers: if they and the companies they work for plan to remain competitive, especially in the international market, salaries and benefits may need to be reduced to compete with what foreign workers receive.)

The third criticism of the company's decision was that the employees had no voice in it. A totalitarian-like action was taken that would have serious economic and psychological effects on human beings; it's no small matter, after all, to take away a person's livelihood, jeopardize his or her life plans for self and family, and contribute to the possible destruction of his or her religious and civic organizations without any consultation with the person beforehand. Such an action is an extreme violation of human dignity.

The company's rejoinder would likely have been to point out that these employees had no right of ownership in the company and, consequently, no say in decisions that affect its organizational structure and fundamental mode of operation. Decisions at that level belong to the owners of the company, its shareholders, and are entrusted by them to the managers they have appointed to run it. The employees' say in the operation of the company is limited to those policies, procedures, wages, and benefit decisions that management agrees are open to discussion with them, either by management directive or by contract with the union.

Let's see whether we can derive some practical principles from the valid points made in these hypothetical arguments and counter-arguments and try to further derive some conclusions about the moral limits on closing down a company's operations in a community.

Given a political system which endorses a competitive, free-market economic system, where profit is the *sine qua non* of any ongoing private economic enterprise, no business can commit itself unreservedly to an indefinite operation in any given community. It is always vulnerable to conditions beyond its control. Consider just a few simple examples:

- The natural resources on which its operation depends like coal, gas, or oil, for instance, may simply be depleted.
- The market for its product may disappear. Nobody, for instance, is interested in buying asbestos insulation anymore.
- Even though the company's managers might agree that the employees deserve their wage and benefit bill, the company's revenues and level of efficiency may not be sufficient to meet it and still turn an acceptable profit.
- State or local taxes may be so high that the company cannot pay them and also earn a reasonable profit. This could well be true in the case of small, marginal operations.
- Government regulations like environmental protection restrictions may make it impossible to deliver a product at a price consumers are willing to pay. Large manufacturers may be able to survive, but smaller ones might have to close down.

The employees of a particular business and the members of the community where it is located must be aware of and understand these limitations, especially if they themselves are committed to a free-market, competitive economic system. (If they're not, they need to establish a political system that won't allow it.) They must be aware that they are taking some risk when going to work for a particular company or offering that company tax or wage incentives to locate in their community. It's also likely true that the smaller the company or the more restricted or specialized its product, the greater that risk may be. Employees also need to recognize that the company's shareholders are exercising their moral right to access material resources through their ownership of their company's assets and are entitled to a reasonable return on their investment.

A company that establishes an operation in a community, especially if it does so as a result of political or labor-related incentives that may have been offered to it, surely understands that its employees and the members of the community have some legitimate long-term economic expectations about it. They expect to exercise their moral right to access material resources through their employment in the company. The company cannot exist purely to generate profits for its owners; in the wider social context it is a mechanism for people other than the owners to meet their economic needs. A company also knows full well that the community will incur long-term costs in terms of roads, schools, sewage treatment systems, and other supporting services and institutions that will serve the company's operation. Both the company and the community will benefit from these expenditures, and each has to pay its fair share. So, while a company may not make a formal, iron-clad contract that it will remain in a location for a long period of time, it makes an indirect commitment to stay there as long as it is profitable. That condition is an important qualifier, of course, because no one is held to the impossible. An operation that can't make a profit cannot stay in existence indefinitely.

A company, by virtue of settling in a community, becomes a member of it. That means that its owners and managers have an obligation to support the structures needed by the community to promote the welfare of its members. The company is obliged to pay its fair share of taxes and should be willing to support, as a matter of philanthropy, educational and cultural programs not furnished out of the public treasury. (Corporate executives commonly describe their companies as "good corporate citizens," so this is usually not seen as an unreasonable burden, at least by large companies.)

Moral Limits on Closing Down a Company's Operations

What might we conclude now about the moral limits on closing down a company's operations in a community?

No company is obliged to remain in a community when the company clearly can no longer sustain a profitable operation there. However, if the profit turndown is short-term and the company has profitable operations elsewhere, they should carry the loser until its own profitability is restored— assuming that to be a likely expectation.

Unless it has explicitly let it be known from the beginning that its operation will last for a limited time in a location, a company does have some long-term commitment to its employees and the community in which it operates, as long as it can sustain a reasonable level of profitability there. It would be morally questionable, therefore, for a company to shut down an operation just because the company could pay lower wages and benefits in some other location

and could pay higher dividends to its shareholders as a result. While shareholders do have a right to access material resources for their needs through their ownership of businesses, that right is limited by the rights of others to that same access. It is true that a company exists to produce profits for its owners, but, in the larger context of social and distributive justice in a free-market economic system, it exists to provide for other people working in and living under that system as well.

For these reasons, it would be unjust for a company to move an operation to a foreign country and substitute foreign workers for its domestic workers just to maximize its stockholders' earnings. There is nothing wrong with investing in a foreign country and operating there at lower wage and benefit costs and earning dividends for shareholders; people in other countries have a right to use resources in their own and their families' interests. But they should not obtain their jobs by directly replacing workers in another country. It would also be morally questionable, I think, for a company to replace, on a one-to-one basis, its products made in a domestic operation with the same products made in a foreign country, if doing that would result in a loss of domestic jobs.

While it is true that employees do not (unless they are shareholders) own the companies they work for and cannot have the definitive say in whether an operation should shut down or not, respect for their dignity as persons demands that they be heard from on a decision that will profoundly affect their lives. They certainly need some advance notice so that they can begin to plan for what has to be a traumatic experience.

At the very least, the company has to listen to its employees' objections, consider their economic needs, and hear out any possible alternatives they may have to offer to the closing. The employees might be willing to adjust their wages and benefits, agree to increase productivity levels, or even offer to buy the operation as a way of saving their jobs.

The company is obviously obliged to honor all commitments to employees in the event that closing down is its only option. Wages, benefits, and pensions due have to be paid. But the company could also offer to relocate employees who are willing to move to its operations in other locations at its expense. These employees might also need help with losses due to a devalued real estate market. An employment service could be made available to help employees who can't move to positions in other company locations, and training programs could be set up to help equip them with any skills new jobs might require.

To what degree is this assistance a matter of justice or just a nice gesture? I think it depends on how the implicit long-term contract is interpreted. If employees came on board with the company knowing that it might not be staying around long, it seems clear that they would not have a claim to assistance of this kind in strict justice. But if they were hired and told about all the long-term benefits the company had to offer, encouraged, perhaps, to make a long-term commitment to it, the claim in justice would be stronger. It seems to be a growing practice today, however, for companies to state formally that all benefit packages (except those mandated by law, like vested pensions) may be discontinued at any time. In that case, it would be hard to argue that justice demands special treatment over and above commitments owed to employees strictly for work done or as termination benefits negotiated in a union contract.

In virtue, again, of an implicit long-term contract to the community, the company may have some obligations toward that community before it can pick up stakes and move on:

- It is morally questionable whether a company could move just to avoid paying higher taxes, unless they clearly are the cause of the company's inability to make a reasonable profit. Shareholders are obliged to absorb their fair share of the legitimate costs of sustaining the communities their companies operate in.

- Even if a company were justified in moving out, any tax concessions originally offered to attract it to the community and accepted by the company and, to the extent they can be identified, costs of civic improvements supported by taxes and incurred directly to support the company should be calculated. A reasonable estimate should be made of any shortfalls not covered by the ordinary taxes that were levied on the company over the years and those shortfalls made up.

- Private civic institutions that spent money on improvements indirectly benefiting the company might be entitled to donations in some proportionate amount.

- Independent businesses established to supply a company's operation probably have little or no claim in justice on the company when it shuts down. Their owners had to realize that there was some risk in staking their success on just one or a few large industries. The company might, however, help them out, at least for a short time, by ordering supplies or services from them for its other operations, if it has any.

Again, any moral obligations a company has because it decides to shut down are qualified by its ability to meet them. No one is held to do the impossible.

It's clear that the conclusions I have proposed are based on what the notions of right and justice require relative to closing down a plant. The utilitarian moralist, of course, would have to weigh all the consequences for the company's shareholders, managers, employees, and the community and decide, in each situation, whether the good would outweigh the bad. The cultural relativist would have to rely on the local, state, or federal laws that might govern plant closings, or, in the absence of such laws, find out what society's customs or mores would tolerate.

Summary

We examined, as an example of what a company might owe a community, a case where an automobile manufacturer decided to close down a 30-year operation in a community because, it claimed, the demand for its model built there was down, and the plant was over capacity.

The economic effects on the community threatened to be devastating. Further, critics of the closing saw it as a breach of contract with the community because of all the services the community had provided the company over the years, and because the company, implicitly, at least, had made a long-term commitment to remain in the community.

Another criticism of the closing stressed the fact that the employees had no say in a decision that profoundly affected their lives.

The critics were particularly harsh because they suspected that the company really intended to replace the automobile built in this plant with models made in newly-opened plants in foreign countries.

When a plant closes, all of a company's wage, benefit, and pension commitments to employees must be met. Depending on what kinds of long-term promises for continued employment, raises, and pensions were held out by the company, there may be some obligation in justice to relocate employees willing to move to other company operations at company expense, assist these employees with losses caused by a depressed real estate market, and offer retraining and reemployment services for those employees who can't move.

It would be morally questionable for a company to move just to avoid paying higher taxes, unless those taxes made it impossible for the company to earn a decent profit. Shareholders have to do their fair share of sustaining the communities their companies operate in.

Any shortfalls in tax concessions or ordinary taxes levied on the community for civic improvements made in the company's interests should be calculated, if possible, and made up.

Independent businesses established to supply a company's operations probably have no claims against it in justice, although the company might help them out by directing to them business from another one of its operations for a period of time.

The moral conclusions just derived depended on notions of rights and justice, for the most part. The utilitarian moralist would approach this issue by weighing and comparing all the good and bad consequences affecting companies and communities when deciding the morality of closing down a plant. The cultural relativist would be guided by relevant laws, and if there weren't any, by his or her understanding of what society's customs or mores required in this matter.

Report Hails Affirmative Action as Key to Minority Progress

Jodi Enda

WASHINGTON—Defying a tidal wave of movements aimed at ending racial preferences, the Clinton administration has concluded affirmative action has successfully put more minorities into the nation's most prestigious universities and on the road to high-paying jobs.

Black and Latino students are more likely to be admitted to elite institutions than white or Asian students with similar grade-point averages and test scores, according to the President's Economic Report, due out today. A copy of the report's chapter on race was obtained by KRT News Service yesterday.

The report argues using ethnicity as one factor in college admissions is a way to open the doors of economic opportunity and, eventually, pare the income gap between whites and minorities And it asserts few white students are harmed.

"Over the last number of decades there has been very substantial progress in narrowing income differences, but the progress has been uneven," said Janet Yellen, chair of the President's Council of Economic Advisers, which wrote the report. While the current economic boom has brought "signs of improvments," she said in an interview, "substantial differences persist."

Although African-Americans in particular have benefited from the healthy economy, with large drops in unemployment and poverty rates, they still earn far less than whites, the report says.

In 1996, Asian familes had the highest median income, with $49,100, followed closely by white families, at $47,100, according to the report. African-American and Latino families earned far less, $26,500 and $26,100, respectively, the report says.

But it isn't income alone that makes it harder for blacks and Latinos to keep up with whites. Whites have accrued 10 times more wealth—savings and assets, such as homes—than blacks and Latinos, the report states.

"Much of the minority middle-class is only two paychecks away from poverty because they don't have the wealth to fall back on," said Christopher Edley, a Harvard law professor and adviser to President Clinton's initiative to reduce racial tension and promote equality.

The Council of Economic Advisers, which issues a report annually, included a chapter on racial inequality for the first time this year to coincide with the race initiative. The report found Latinos have lost more ground than African-Americans the past quarter-century. But it attributes much of

279

that to a large influx of immigrants, who they expect eventually will assimilate and earn higher wages.

"Hispanics who have been here longer improve their situation really quite rapidly," Yellen said.

For African-Americans, the outlook is not as rosy, according to White House officials.

"The strong evidence of continuing disparities show both that history still poisons the present and that we have current problems that require renewed public and private attention," Edley said.

Despite recent gains, black men still earn a median of 74 cents for every dollar earned by white men; black women earn 83 cents for every dollar earned by white women. Latinos, whose ranks have doubled since 1980, earn less: 63 cents for men and 71 cents for women, compared to their white counterparts.

The civil rights movement of the 1960s vastly improved the incomes of African-Americans by opening whole new job markets, particularly in manufacturing. But wages stagnated, starting in the mid-1970s, and have only recently begun to climb again relative to whites, Yellen said.

Black women, who nearly achieved parity with white women in the 1970s, lost significant ground as their white counterparts leapfrogged into better paying professions, explained Cecilia Conrad of the Joint Center for Political and Economic Studies, an independent public policy research organization.

"We have to appreciate that the glass has been filling, but we also need to focus on what remains to be done, whether that's a politically appealing story or not," Edley said.

Perhaps the most sensitive political issue this year is affirmative action, which has absorbed recent blows at the ballot box and in the courts. Clinton has defended it, while aknowledging the government might need to find new ways to accomplish its goals of diversity in the face of the current backlash.

The economic report takes the argument one step further, contending black and Hispanic students admitted based, in part, on their ethnicity, ultimately succeed in the nation's most elite universities. Affirmative action hasn't made notable strides in the 80 percent of colleges and universities that most students attend, partially because many of them admit most applicants, officials said.

"There seems to be very little merit to the counterargument that putting people with less preparation into college harms them, Yellen said. "Everybody who goes to an elite institution tends to do better."

Stephan Thernstrom, who along with his wife, Abigail, wrote "America in Black and White: One Nation Indivisible," argues minorities who go to college ill-prepared "feel inferior."

Thernstrom, a leader in the movement to end what he calls racial preferences, said yesterday he is "suspicious" of the administration's findings and disagrees with its conclusions. He noted initiatives are brewing in 17 states to do away with affirmative action in state universities, government employment and public contracting.

A similar measure adopted by California voters in 1996 brought a dramatic drop in minorities who applied and were admitted to state-run graduate schools.

Truth in the Marketplace: Advertisers, Salesmen, and Swindlers

Burton M. Leiser

The advertising industry and those that are allied with it, including general merchandising and salesmanship, have been subjected to severe criticism in recent decades because of widespread and flagrant abuses, most of them having to do with fraud and deception. So much advertising is offensive and obtrusive, so much of it is in poor taste, and so much publicity has been given to the "hidden persuaders,' the "motivational researchers,' and the Madison Avenue "men in the grey flannel suits" that it is easy to lose perspective and assume that the advertiser is a callous huckster concerned only with selling his product and earning his commissions, and not at all bothered with ordinary standards of taste, decency, or morality. Yet there can be no doubt that the advertiser sometimes performs a valuable service, not only for those who employ him, but for the general public as well.

Case 11. An Adman's Confession

One day when I was young in advertising I slipped a piece of paper into my typewriter and wrote an advertisement for a life insurance company. It was addressed to young husbands and fathers. One of the coupons received in reply came from a traveler in Rio de Janeiro, whose home was in New Jersey. He was thirty-eight years old, married, and the father of three children. He wanted information on a policy that, in case of his death, would guarantee his family an income of $3,000 a year.

On the man's return to New Jersey, the policy was written and the first payment made. A few days later he went to his dentist to have a wisdom tooth extracted. Somehow the cavity became infected, the infection spread and he died.

That incident made a deep impression on me. Many times in the intervening years I have been reminded that somewhere in New Jersey there are a mother and three children, now grown up, who, without the slightest suspicion of my existence, have had their whole lives changed by the fact that one day I put together some words that were printed in a magazine, and read in a faraway country by their husband and father, who was influenced to do what I suggested.[1]

Advertisements perform a vital function in almost any society, for they help to bring buyers and sellers together. Even Plato, idealist and anti-materialist that he was, ac-

---

Reprinted with permission of Macmillan Publishing Company from *Liberty Justice and Morals*, Second Edition by Burton M. Leiser. Copyright 1973 by Burton M. Leiser.

1. Bruce Barton (a founder of Batten, Barton, Durstine and Osborne advertising agency), "Advertising: Its Contribution to the American Way of Life," *Reader's Digest*, **66**:103ff. (April, 1955).

corded the merchant a place in his ideal state, for it was obvious that under the most primitive, Spartan conditions, division of labor was still essential. If everyone was to do his own job well, people had to be relieved of the irksome tasks of producing everything for themselves and of grubbing aimlessly for the necessities of life. The merchants who brought their wares to early marketplaces relieved people of the need to wander about finding each of the many items they needed. The invention of a central location for shopping was probably as important to the growth of civilization as was the invention of the wheel, though it seems to have been overlooked by historians. The success of a market or of a merchant must have depended from earliest times on some form of advertisement—that is, of some means of attracting shoppers to the merchant's place of business, of "turning him toward" the merchant, as the Latin origin of the word indicates. Peddlers who hawked their wares through ancient streets were croaking out ads of a kind, and those who invented tunes or chanted "Cockles and mussels, alive alive-o" were performing the first singing commercials.

More important, perhaps, is the fact that certain goods and services cannot be made available at all without appropriate advertising. If it is morally right for women, under some circumstances, to seek abortions, then it is also morally right to inform them of the availability of safe abortions. If the decimation of fur-bearing animals is wrong, then it is right for the public to be informed of the availability of artificial furs. The advertisement by a domestic manufacturer of products whose purchase can contribute to a drop in unemployment and a rise in the standard of living is at least offering potential buyers information without which they would not be able to make informed, independent moral decisions as to purchases they are thinking of making.[2] When there is no advertising, people may be unaware of the availability of services that may decisively enhance the quality of their lives. Many poor persons, for example, would be far better off if they could be professionally advised of their legal rights as tenants, consumers, and employees and assisted in writing contracts, wills, and other documents. Legal advertisements could help make them aware of the availability of such advice.[3]

Some professional organizations have banned all forms of advertising, presumably because the practice is "unbecoming" to professional persons, but more realistically because it is likely to lead to price competition. The American Bar Association (ABA) has argued that competitive advertising would "encourage extravagant, artful, self-laudatory brashness in seeking business and thus could mislead the layman. . . . It would inevitably produce unrealistic expectations. . . . and bring about distrust of the law and lawyers."[4] Pharmacists contend that advertising would force them to cut down on professional services and would reduce their image to that of mere retailers.[5] Physicians insist that ads by members of their profession would be confusing, however truthful they might be, because patients are incapable of understanding fee information; such ads should be banned, they say, because people would select doctors on the basis of cost

2   This does not address the question of the desirability of preferential purchases of domestic over foreign goods. It only points out that important moral questions are involved and that ads can help the consumer make more informed decisions.

3   *Consumers Union of United States, Inc.* v. *American Bar Association*, 427 F Supp. 506 (E.D. Va., 1976).

4   Ibid.

5   *Virginia State Board of Pharmacy* v. *Virginia Citizens Consumer Council, Inc.*, 96 S.Ct. 1817 (1976).

rather than quality of professional care.[6] The courts have held that these contentions are based upon the assumption that people are ignorant, that they must be protected from exploitation by knowledgeable professionals, and that the professionals are not to be trusted. As the court in the ABA case put it, the ABA is assuming that "the public will not be able to accurately evaluate its [the advertising's] content, for either they are intellectually incapable of understanding the complexities of legal services or they will fall prey to every huckster with a promise, law license, and a law book." If the public is so likely to fall prey to hucksters, the court said, that is all the more reason for giving it more rather than less information. In the pharmacy case, the court concluded that an alternative to the "highly paternalistic approach" of the professionals was "to assume that this information is not in itself harmful, that people will perceive their own best interests if only they are well enough informed, and that the best means to that end is to open the channels of communication rather than to close them."

In short, the utility of advertisements rests upon the fact that potentially valuable information is passed from one person to another. The right of the advertiser to hawk his wares is parallel to the consumer's right to hear the advertiser's message. Although such communication may not be deserving of the broad protection that John Stuart Mill and the authors of the United States Constitution have conferred upon other forms of speech and artistic presentations, similar considerations justify granting advertisers

relatively broad rights—rights which have recently gained some degree of recognition in American courts.[7]

On the other hand, some kinds of advertisements are immoral on their face, for they promote personally or socially harmful products or services. From the point of view of an antiabortionist, an advertisement informing pregnant women of the availability of abortions is immoral. The advertisement of cock fights, dog fights, or other cruel exhibitions, or of slave auctions (when slavery was legal), insofar as they encourage, aid, and abet wrongful behavior, are wrong. If racism and sexism are immoral, then help wanted ads that specify racial, religious, or sexual preferences or exclusions are immoral.[8]

The Sophists and Modern Advertising

The business of advertising is persuasion. Most advertisements are placed in the interests of commerce, their business being to persuade potential customers to buy some product or service. But some advertising is used for other than commercial purposes: to gain votes for a political candidate, for example, or for a bond issue, or for some other political proposition. Some are directed toward persuading people to change their personal habits, not to engage in certain practices, or to lend their support to some charitable cause. Examples would be advertising campaigns conducted by associations dedicated to discouraging smoking or drug abuse, and fund-raising campaigns of the Red Feather or United Fund agencies.

---

6   *Health Systems Agency of Northern Virginia* v. *Virginia State Board of Medicine,* 424 F. Supp. 267 (E.D. Va., 1976).

7   Cf. the cases cited in notes 2–4.

8   Some periodicals continue to carry help-wanted advertising that is discriminatory, despite the fact that it is contrary to American public policy. The *Chronicle of Higher Education,* for example, publishes notices of academic vacancies in certain Arab universities that obviously indicate Jewish applicants will not be accepted. The managing editor of the *Chronicle* has explained that because such discrimination is not contrary to the law of the states that place the ads, the ads do not violate any American law, and will therefore continue.

Because the fundamental aim of advertising is persuasion, it is natural that all the devices and techniques of persuasion should be employed by advertisers to achieve their aim. Because of the tremendous financial stake that business has in advertising, it is not surprising that great efforts have gone into perfecting the art, to developing new techniques, and to finding out just what factors motivate people to do one thing or another, so that advertisers may exploit that knowledge in order to motivate persons to do what they want them to do. This has given rise to the charge that advertisers "manipulate" the public, that they wield an unconscionable amount of power over the general populace, and that they are capable of molding people to their will. Phrased in this way, these charges are grossly exaggerated. But advertisers admit, and even boast, that they are able to create desires in people for products and services that they had never wanted before and that they can motivate them to change their life-styles, to some extent at least, to conform with the desires of their clients. One may argue that this may be very good and that from the skills of the advertising profession much of America's prosperity has been derived. If people had not been motivated to purchase automobiles and vacuum cleaners, great industries would never have been born, and millions of people would not be employed as they are today. In the case of the automobile, to the extent that advertising has contributed to the growth of the industry, it has helped to make America and the rest of the world what they are today and has done its part to change a whole way of life. Whether this is good or evil is not altogether clear, but its existence is indisputable. To the extent that advertisers have persuaded people to buy soap, it may be argued, they have contributed to the cleanliness of the American people and therefore to their high standards of hygiene

and health. Anyone who has visited the Middle East, where vast numbers of people have never been reached by the salesmen of Proctor and Gamble and Lever Brothers, and where governments are spending vast sums of money to introduce habits of personal hygiene to the populace, can appreciate the positive achievements of both the advertising and the soap and detergent industries.

But one may argue, too, that these "benefits" are mitigated by serious disadvantages, and in spite of the good that has derived from advertising, the evil that has resulted from it may be enough to cause grave reservations about the practitioners of the art. Because of false, deceptive, and misleading advertising, millions of people have been bilked out of vast sums of money. They have been inveigled into enrolling in "plans" and "schools" that promised to give them great benefits, when in fact the "Plans" were ineffective, the "schools" did not employ teachers, and the benefits were totally illusory. They have been persuaded, by false promises of swift cures for the illnesses and ailments that afflicted them, to buy nostrums and remedies that were ineffective and on occasion damaging or even deadly. They have been bilked into purchasing merchandise, or land, or burial plots, or services that were either worthless or nonexistent. They have been conned into paying outrageously inflated prices for products that provided no benefit to anyone but their makers.

The art of persuasion was highly developed in ancient Greece by a group of men who came to be known as Sophists. The Sophists' greatest critic was Plato, who devoted many of his dialogues to excoriating them for their verbal trickery and for their unscientific attitudes. The Sophists claimed to be teachers, and some of them were in fact paid large sums of money by wealthy Greeks who hired them to teach their sons the art of persuasion, which they called rhetoric, on the theory that it was the key to a successful career. The Sophists claimed—correctly, no doubt—that their art gave men power over others that they could not readily achieve in any other way. In one of Plato's dialogues, a supporter of sophism argues that if he were pitted against a physician in a contest over a public health measure that came before the senate, he would be able to persuade the senators to vote in accordance with his views, whereas the physician would be helpless.

Plato, in inquiring into the nature of this art of persuasion, has Gorgias, a Sophist, explain to Socrates that rhetoric is the art of persuasion that is used in law courts and at public gatherings, and deals with justice and injustice. This is not very far from the claim that might be made by a modern public relations firm that attempts to influence legislation on behalf of a major industry. Socrates points out that there is a difference between belief and knowledge; for there can be no false knowledge, whereas people can have false beliefs as well as true beliefs. With this distinction in mind, he suggests that there must be two kinds of persuasion—one that produces belief (whether true or not) and the other that produces knowledge. And Gorgias, the Sophist, concedes that rhetoric is concerned only with producing beliefs in its subjects and is not concerned to give them scientific certainty or even reasoned arguments for such beliefs as they may have. He concedes also that the rhetorician (or—in modern terms—the advertising man or the public relations expert) is interested only in producing the desired belief, but does not particularly care whether the beliefs he propagates are true or false. To Socrates this is tantamount to an admission that rhetoricians are not *teachers* or *instructors* of men in any true sense. Instead they are merely manipulators of men. Though they may deal with law courts and assemblies over matters in which right and wrong, justice and injustice are at stake, they are not teachers of what is right and what is wrong, or of what is just and what is unjust. They may attempt to influence men on questions of public policy having to do with medicine, architecture, commerce, and engineering, but their efforts—though they may be more persuasive, in one sense, because of their knowledge of the techniques of persuasion—cannot be compared to those of experts in those fields, who may be less accomplished as public speakers and who may not be familiar with the gimmicks of the public relations man but who are able to bring their expert knowledge on the *subject* to bear in the discussion. When the Sophist is more persuasive than the doctor in a question where public health is at stake, it is a case of the ignorant being more persuasive with the ignorant public than the expert is able to be. The Sophist does not have to know the facts that are relevant to the issue, for he has devices that enable him to convince the public (that is, those who do not have knowledge about the subject themselves) that he knows more about the subject than those who really do know the facts. He merely *seems* to know, even when he knows nothing.

Socrates presented an intriguing analysis that is worth pondering. He distinguished between genuine arts and fraudulent ones.[9] A genuine art is a tech-

---

9   These are not the exact terms used in his dialogues, but they give a more accurate picture of Plato's meaning, in modern terms, than the translations that I have seen thus far. For example, W. C. Helmbold calls gymnastics and medicine *arts*, whereas makeup and cookery are called *knacks*. *Knack*, in modern English, is very far, in my opinion, from what Plato had in mind. See Helmbold's translation of Plato's *Gorgias* (Indianapolis: Bobbs-Merrill, 1952), pp. 23 ff. Compare other translations of the same passages for similarly inept renderings.

nique for achieving some genuine benefit to humanity, whereas a fraudulent art (which ought not, properly speaking, to be called an art at all) is a technique that masquerades in the form of an art, that makes a pretext of conferring a benefit upon those who apply to its practitioners, but that actually does them no good at all and may even cause considerable damage to them.

As examples of genuine arts, Socrates offers gymnastics and medicine, both of which are concerned with the health of the body. The gymnastics teacher prescribes a regimen of exercise, diet, work, and rest that is designed to preserve the body's health, and the medical doctor prescribes a similar regimen, in addition to such drugs and other treatments as he may deem necessary, to restore health to a person who has lost it. Both of these people are genuinely concerned for the health of the persons who consult them, and both of them base their prescriptions upon scientific knowledge that they have gained about the body and about what is necessary for good health.

As opposed to the gymnastic teacher and the medical doctor, there are the makeup artists and the confectioners. (In modern terms, the former would be called beauticians, cosmetic salesmen and manufacturers, girdle and brassiere manufacturers, and fashion designers, and the latter would be called gourmet chefs, convenience-food packers, bakers, candy makers, and so on.) These people are not interested in the true well-being of those who consult them or purchase their products. Their principal concern is that their customers should derive *pleasure* from their services and products, regardless of whether it is to their real benefit or not. The use of these means, Socrates says, is deceitful, for to the extent that they succeed, they merely cover up the truth and offer a false sense of security and well-being.

The Sophists of those days, like some of the image makers of today, imagined that they wielded much power, for, as they put it, they were able to cause men to be put to death, to be sent off into exile, and to lose their fortunes. They did these things without regard to the rightness or the justice of their actions.

Socrates asked whether it was worse to do injustice or to be the victim of injustice, and concluded, for his own part, that it was bad to be the victim of injustice, but that it was far worse to be the perpetrator of injustice. For in his view the unjust man was doomed to be wretched and unhappy. Injustice, as he saw it, was a psychological disease, a disorder of the mind that consisted of the individual's inability to control his emotions and desires. A rational person whose personality was not afflicted with the disease of injustice would know that the pleasures of the moment are detrimental to himself in the long run, and, though he might be sorely tempted to give in to his desires for them, he would control his impulses in order to maintain both his physical and his psychological health. Similarly, greed, avarice, and anger can lead a man to perform acts that will harm others; but from Socrates' point of view, the harm that the tyrant does to himself is far greater than any hurt that he can inflict upon his victims. For every time that he gives in to an impulse to hurt another man, he gives rein to an irrational part of his personality, he permits it to overcome his own instincts for self-preservation (like the man who becomes addicted to tobacco when he knows how damaging smoking may be to his health in the long run), and he brings himself ever closer to the time when those baser instincts will take complete control of him. When that time comes, Socrates said, they will destroy him as a human being as surely as anarchy and revolution will destroy a state. Real power, then, is not the power that one wields over other men—the power to expropriate their money, to send them off into exile, or to put them to death—but power over one's own desires, impulses, and emotions. Self-control is the sign of a well-ordered personality, of a healthy and sound man; and the self-controlled man does what is fitting and right to other men, and behaves toward them in accordance with the principles of justice. Such a person, Socrates maintained, is happy, whereas the person who lacks self-control and lets his irrational impulses rule his behavior toward others, prompting him to behave unjustly, is unhappy and wretched, however much outward appearances may deceive us into thinking otherwise. And the truly just man, he concluded, is not interested in persuading his fellow citizens to enjoy themselves at the expense of their physical or their psychological well-being. He tries, as far as possible, to fulfill the principal task of a citizen: to bend all his efforts toward persuading his fellow citizens to improve themselves, to become the masters of themselves, to behave rationally rather than impulsively, and to behave justly toward one another.[10]

The Sophist, then, and (one may suppose) his modern counterpart, the stereotype of the advertising man, may be characterized as one who attempts to wield power over other men for selfish ends; who devotes himself to the pseudoart, or the fraudulent art, of rhetoric, whereby he attempts to inculcate beliefs in other men without regard to the truth of those beliefs, and who furthers the ends of such other fraudulent arts as makeup and confectionary, playing upon the desires of other men rather than trying to improve them. To the extent that this characterization is true, it would follow, in Plato's scheme, that these men are unjust and that they are therefore not acting in their own best interests, though they may imagine that the financial profits that they earn are indicative of the extent to which they are acting in their own best interests.

In spite of the strong arguments that Plato offers in support of his point of view, it cannot be accepted uncritically. Certain assumptions that Plato makes run counter to common sense and have not been satisfactorily established by other means.

His attempt to prove that the unjust man is worse off than the just man seems more a wish that one would like to see fulfilled than a true picture of reality. Too often one sees those who have lived by nefarious practices waxing rich, respected in their communities, and—to all appearances, at least—smug and happy with themselves and their families while honest and conscientious men and women groan under their burdens and live with a broken spirit and even with broken health. That the perpetrator of injustice *should* be more wretched than his victim is devoutly to be desired, perhaps, but it is not a fact of life.

Plato's "fraudulent arts" may not be the unmitigated evils that he paints them as being. There may be some virtue in pleasure seeking, in enjoying the pleasure of the moment and not thinking always of the long-range consequences of every action. The skills of the confectioner do give much pleasure to people, and the skills of the beautician, the corset maker, and the cosmetic manufacturers may be valuable *precisely because* they make the unshapely shapely, the unseemly seemly, and the ugly beautiful, if only for a

10   These doctrines can be studied best in Plato's dialogue, *The Gorgias*, though they are discussed in many other dialogues in the Platonic corpus. I would recommend particularly *The Republic, The Symposium*, and *The Protagoras*, in that order. Plato's assaults on the Sophists are scattered throughout his writings. His theory of justice received many different expressions, from the early Socratic dialogues (e.g., *The Apology, The Crito*, and *The Euthyphro*) through the lengthy *Republic* to the late dialogues *The Statesman* and *The Laws*.

time. Can it be said unequivocally that man ought never improve upon nature, especially when nature has not been overly generous? A woman who has lost her hair because of a childhood illness can hardly be blamed for wearing a wig, and the suggestion that the wigmaker is guilty of helping her to perpetrate a fraud is extraordinarily narrow and shortsighted. Perhaps changes in style and fashion are a conceit artificially nurtured by Sophists and their followers, but they do give a great deal of pleasure to many people, including not only the vain people who change with every breeze of fashion, but those who enjoy looking at them as well.

Finally, it is not always possible to explain all the reasons for every move to each individual who ought to make it. Time does not always permit all the facts and the reasons to be presented and digested, and not everyone is prepared to grapple with all of the arguments that might be presented on every side of every issue. There are excellent reasons for the use of soap, and some that may not be so excellent. There may also be good reasons for not using soap. Many arguments might be marshalled in favor of the use of one brand of soap as against the use of some other. But it scarcely seems worth anyone's while to get all of those facts and arguments together and to weigh them in order to make a reasoned judgment on the matter. It is not so momentous as to justify much expenditure of time or energy, unless one happens to live in a place where large numbers of people are endangered because of lack of proper hygienic practices. On the other hand, if one has to decide whether to submit to an electroshock treatment, or whether a certain dam should be constructed, it might be worthwhile to get as much information as possible on the matter before doing so, in order to be sure that a proper judgment is being made.

The Sophist and his modern counterpart, the advertising man, may have their place, then. The art of persuasion, as opposed to the art of teaching, is not evil in itself. Only the perverse uses of that art are evil, those practices that make use of lies and deceptions in order to persuade people to do what the advertisers or their clients know they ought not to do. This is the aspect of advertising to which we now turn.

Caveat Emptor

The ancient maxim *Caveat emptor* ("Let the buyer beware") was coined, no doubt, because merchants in those days were known for their sharp practices. The meaning of the maxim might have been, "Buyer, be careful, for those from whom you make your purchases are not always truthful. They do not always represent their products as honestly as they might. They have a reputation for charging more than a product is worth. They sometimes sell you one thing and then, in the dark recesses of their stalls, wrap another for delivery to you. Be careful, then, lest you be cheated." This *might* have been the meaning of the maxim at one time. Later, though, it is evident that it acquired a wholly new meaning. It was raised from the status of a *warning* based on general knowledge of certain unsavory practices engaged in by some merchants to that of a *principle*: "In any commercial transaction, if there is a dispute between buyer and seller, the burden of proof shall be upon the buyer. If he has any complaints or reservations about his purchase, let him make them before he signs the sales agreement or takes delivery of the merchandise, for once the sale is consummated, the purchase is completed, and the officials of the state are obliged to enforce its provisions, whether the customer is satisfied or not."

In all the centuries that men have been selling things to one another, many devices have been perfected for making things appear to be what they are not, and for wording sales pitches and sales contracts so that they seem to say what they do not say—always to the advantage of the seller, for he is the one who writes the agreement or buys pads of printed forms that have been written by his attorneys to afford him the greatest possible protection against any action that might be brought against him by a disgruntled customer. The customer is presented a printed form and is asked to sign it. He seldom reads it, and if he does read it he does not understand all of its implications, and he hardly ever takes it to his own attorney for advice. If he does and his attorney advises him not to sign it because of possible trouble later on, he is confronted with the choice of complying with the dealer's terms or not having the product that he wants to buy. In almost all cases, then, customers make their purchases on the *seller's* terms, and not on those that would be in their own best interests. In addition, the law has been heavily weighted in the seller's favor, for until quite recently, the consumer had no advocate to argue for him before the legislatures, there was no organized consumer lobby, and very little publicity was given to any but the most flagrant abuses. Manufacturers and retail associations, on the other hand, sent well-paid lobbyists to work on their behalf at the legislative level, and assured themselves of legislative courtesies by contributing heavily to the election campaigns of those who were sympathetic to their goals.

Case 12. The Television Set

Mrs. Amanda Jones was a poor black woman who lived with her three children in a small rented house in a Midwestern town. She worked as a sorter in a cannery, standing on her feet for eight hours every day. For years she saved a portion of every week's earnings so that her boys could go to college some day.

One day, attracted by an ad in a local newspaper, she went to a discount store to purchase a color television set on very easy terms—$20 down and $20 per month. A few days later the set was delivered, and she and her children sat down to enjoy their new possession. Three weeks later, the set caught fire because of an overheated transformer. When Mrs. Jones called the store the following morning, she was given a long runaround. At last, the manager explained that the store was not responsible for any defect in the merchandise. It was covered by a warranty, he explained, and would be repaired by the manufacturer. The nearest authorized repair station was 300 miles away. Mrs. Jones paid a mover to pack her set and deliver it to the service outlet, and then to return it to her. The service outlet, after examining the set, concluded that it was not authorized to replace the set, but made the necessary repairs. It returned the set to Mrs. Jones at her expense, and enclosed a bill for $125 for the labor, because under the warranty, which Mrs. Jones had not read carefully, only defective parts were covered. By this time, Mrs. Jones had paid nearly $600 for her television set, though she had used it for less than three weeks.

When it was reinstalled, she noticed that human figures had a sickly green cast to them. No amount of dial-twisting and adjusting helped. The set was hopelessly out of adjustment. In anger and frustration, she complained again to the manager of the store from which she had purchased the set and threatened to make no further installment payments unless he repaired the set. (The interest on these installment payments, incidentally, added another $90 to the cost of her set, a fact that she did not fully appreciate because she had never sat down to figure it out.) The manager assured her that he had no responsibility for her problems, that that was for her and the manufacturer to work out, and that she was fully responsible for continued payment of her debt to his firm.

When Mrs. Jones tried her set once more, the green picture faded and the sound went out. She wrote an angry letter to the store and to the manufacturer, and tore up the next bill that came to remind her of the monthly installment that was due. After several reminders from the store, she received a letter from the attorney of a collection agency, informing her that her account had been turned over to him and that if she did not pay the full amount due, she would have to go to court.

Mrs. Jones was only too happy to learn that she would go to court for she felt that at last justice might be done. But to her sorrow, she found that the judge would not listen to her complaints about the set; the only question before him was whether she had failed to make payments in accordance with her contract. Because she admitted that she had failed to make the necessary payments, she was required, under terms of the contract, to make full payment of the entire amount due, plus a 10% "service charge," plus court costs and the fees of the finance company's attorneys, as well as her own attorney's fee. Because she could not possibly pay this amount in one lump sum, the judge imposed a garnishment on her wages. Her employer, assuming she must be a "deadbeat," informed her that she was no longer needed. As a result of her continuing inability to pay the judgment, the court ordered the sheriff to seize everything she had that was of any value, except those items that she needed to exist, and to sell them at public auction. At last, the savings account in which she had deposited her sons' future tuition was attached, more than $1,000 was withdrawn from it to pay all the expenses she had incurred, and Mrs. Jones and her children were left with nothing.

Case 12 actually happened and illustrates only a few of the practices engaged in by businesses when the merchandise they sell is defective. Efforts to correct these abuses are often countered by new methods that effectively leave the consumer in the same vulnerable position he had been in prior to the enactment of the legal remedy.

An example of this is the "specious cash sale," a gimmick that was developed by New York merchandisers when the state legislature passed laws designed to protect people like Mrs. Jones from some of the abuses just described.

In the state of New York legislation was passed a few years ago placing some of the responsibility for defective merchandise on the retailer who sold it. In some cases the customer who purchased the item on the installment plan would be permitted to withhold payment until he was given satisfaction for any claims he may have had about defects in the merchandise he had purchased. In order to get around this, merchants assigned the debts to finance companies and banks, who would then collect, regardless of any claims that might be made against the original seller. In 1970 a new law gave the consumer the right to file claims against the bank or finance company in an installment transaction when the dealer failed to make good on any legitimate complaints that the purchaser might have. As a result, these financial institutions refused to deal with retailers who acquired a reputation for being unscrupulous.

The boycotted dealers had to find a way to continue their practices so that they could stay in business and at the same time protect themselves and the finance companies against their customers' complaints. The solution consisted of the "specious cash sale." The retailer, after making the sale, sent his customer to a finance company that lent him the money for the sale. The customer then returned to the merchant and made a "cash" purchase.

Now if the merchant cheated his customer, overcharged him, or refused to replace defective merchandise, the customer was without recourse. He had already paid the merchant for the merchandise and the finance company had lent him the money in a separate transaction. Both the dealer and the finance company were thus in the clear.

In 1971, because of pressure from a million-member consumer lobby and labor unions, the state legislature closed the loophole for some purchases, but not for all. Under the new legislation, when the finance-company personnel are related to the dealer, when the dealer and the finance company are under common control, or when the dealer prepares the forms for paying the loan, the buyer will have the right to redress against the finance company as well as against the dealer.

Four out of five states still adhere to the old doctrine, which gives the finance company or bank that buys an installment contract from a dealer complete immunity against any complaint that the purchaser may have against the dealer. In opposing proposed rulings by the Federal Trade Commission that would do away with these practices, the American Industrial Bankers Association asserted that their practices were "time honored and recognized" and "practiced in the marketplace for many, many years." Consumer groups, on the other hand, have alleged that many cases of consumer fraud would have been impossible were it not for the doctrine that permits such transfers of indebtedness to take place without a corresponding assumption of responsibility for the original sale.[11]

Because there are so many kinds of fraud and deception in business practices, it is impossible to discuss them all here. A few of the more common types, however, will serve to indicate how varied these practices are and how difficult the moral and legal issues involved may be.

It should be noted that not all practices fall under the category of truth telling. In some of the instances to be discussed, it may be argued that no falsehood has been uttered and that the moral issue of truth telling does not arise. If the moral issue of truth telling must be confined within the rigid limits set by the distinction between "stating what is true" and "stating what is false," the discussion that follows clearly goes beyond those limits. But the moral issues surrounding truth telling are actually more subtle than that distinction allows, for the two alternatives set forth—stating what is true and stating what is false—are not exhaustive. In real human discourse there are other possibilities, including telling the truth in a misleading way; not saying anything that is false, but not providing all the information that is needed to make an informed decision; and using various devices to make things seem to be what they are not, without saying anything in words at all. In short, "stating what is true" and "stating what is false" are contraries. "Telling the truth" and "not telling the truth" are contradictories, whose meaning is not exhausted by the contraries just mentioned. Part of the complexity of the problem is bound up with the extremely complicated meanings of these phrases.

The Confusion of Needs and Desires

At a recent conference on business ethics, the founder and president of a high-technology, multinational corporation explained that a corporation is "a group of persons whose purpose is to provide goods and services to those who need them." This is surely a most commendable goal toward which to bend one's efforts. He then went on to ex-

---

11   See Robert J. Cole, "New Law Bars Unscrupulous Ruse to Deprive a Debtor of Legal Rights," *New York Times*, August 19, 1971, p. 51.

plain that *needs* are whatever the public will buy in the marketplace. Now if people need whatever they buy, then a corporation is merely fulfilling its purpose if it sells those goods and services to them. And any corporation that helps a person acquire what he or she needs would be doing what anyone ought morally to do, for it is *prima facie* right for one person to strive to meet the needs of another whenever he can reasonably do so. But people don't always need what they buy. From the fact that a person buys a given item, it does not necessarily follow that he *needs* that item, though it is reasonable to conclude that he wants or *desires* it. Men walking down Broadway may be seduced into purchasing the services of a prostitute or a supply of heroin or cocaine. Although they *desire* those goods or services when they pay for them, they can be said to need them only in the most extended sense of that word. In that same extended sense, purchasers of slaves in the eighteenth century needed the slaves they purchased. Few people today would argue that the slave traders performed a valuable or morally commendable service. There also are corporations that fail to meet the most elementary standards of morality, though they cater to their customers' desires (or create those desires) and sell them products and services.

People need far more than such elementary necessities of life as food, drink, clothing, and shelter. An inventor developed a plastic tube that can be implanted in the leg of a person whose circulation has been obstructed to serve as an artificial blood vessel, thus saving the leg from being amputated. Persons afflicted by grave circulatory disorders *need* that product, and the inventor performed a valuable service by making it available to them. Like the insurance ad that induced a young man to purchase a policy just a few days before his untimely death, thus assuring his widow and small children

of a modest income, an advertisement about such a product would help to reduce the amount of suffering in the world and add to the sum of human happiness. By any utilitarian standard, it would be moral.

Suppose, however (contrary to the facts), that the manufacturer of the artificial blood vessel decided to increase his profits by selling his product to people who did not need it. An appropriate strategy might be to direct a well-organized advertising campaign to the medical profession to persuade physicians that circulatory bypasses ought to be employed in many conditions that are presently treated by chemical means. By offering large research grants to university professors interested in pursuing projects related to circulatory disorders, the manufacturer might succeed in commissioning a number of studies that could be cited in ads in support of his product. By offering entering medical students new instruments with his company's logo, and by sending them small gifts throughout their careers, he would attempt to build loyalty to his firm among those most likely to use or prescribe his products. Finally, if salesmen drop subtle hints about the financial advantages the physician would enjoy if he were to perform circulatory bypass surgery more often, an unscrupulous manufacturer might attempt to sell his product at the expense of persons who don't need it and would be subjected to unnecessary surgery.

Such an advertising campaign and sales tactics would be immoral, for they would contribute to the corruption of scientific researchers and the medical profession and contribute to public cynicism about the reliability of science and medicine and the trustworthiness of the academic community. If successful, such tactics would subject numerous patients to needless and potentially dangerous surgery with the expense, suffering, and possible loss of life that that entails.

In earlier times, when people had a simpler way of judging one another's motivations, those responsible would have been called *greedy.*

Testimony at hearings before a United States Senate subcommittee revealed that such unscrupulous practices are not uncommon among pharmaceutical firms.[12] The case described illustrates the contrast between advertising that fulfills the conditions of morality (that it be truthful and honest, and that it contribute to human happiness and diminish human suffering) and that which does not (for it is untruthful, deceitful, corrupting, and damaging to innocent persons). However, the advertiser's motives are not especially important, for in general, motives have little, if anything, to do with the moral quality of acts. The term *greed*, for example, is not especially helpful, for it contains a moral condemnation. Only *after* a moral judgment has been rendered would one be able to determine whether he was greedy. The inventor of the artificial blood vessel readily conceded that he was motivated by a desire to make a profit. The profit motive does not render the invention and the marketing of such a life-saving device immoral or amoral. One's motive is not a sufficient determinant of the moral quality of one's act. One must be judged on the act and not on psychological attitudes. Because products cannot perform their intended function without being marketed and advertised, there can be no doubt of the moral desirability of advertising them, however much the manufacturer may be motivated by the desire for profit. After all, that desire is not evil in itself. Greed is an unrestrained desire for money, regardless of the harm its acquisition may do to others, and is con-demned for that reason. It should not be confused with the desire for profit.

False Claims of Need

Part of the American scheme of things seems to be the creation of needs, the introduction of a conviction into the minds of people that they ought to have something that they had never needed before, often because it had never existed before. Not only Americans, but people the world over today feel that certain items that would have been regarded as luxuries by their grandparents—or even by themselves a few years ago—are necessities today. Yesterday's luxury has become today's necessity. Electric refrigerators, hair driers, canned foods, soup mixes, and instant potatoes are considered by many to be necessities, though the "need" for some of them has been created. The automobile is probably the most outstanding example of a product whose increasing use has in fact created a genuine need for itself by driving all the competition—not only the horse, but passenger railroads and commuter bus services—out of business. Cosmetics of all kinds are generally regarded by American women as being quite necessary, though women in other countries, including some very advanced nations, feel no particular compulsion about using them, and some American women are now beginning to question the necessity of using them as well. The need for razor blades was created some years ago by clever advertising by the Gillette Company, which convinced men that they were "cleaner" and more attractive if they were "clean-shaven" than if they wore beards or long sideburns. Many members of the new generation have not only called these premises into question, but have acted

---

12   Cf. the Hearings on Effect of Promotion of Advertising Over-the-Counter Drugs before the Subcommittee on Monopoly of the Select Committee on Small Business of the U.S. Senate (92nd Congress) beginning in 1971.

upon the assumption that it is not necessary to shave in order to be attractive.

Vaginal deodorants are another example of a created need. Full-page advertisements in women's magazines and on television are designed to convince women of the need for these deodorants and of the effectiveness of particular brands.

The executive vice president of the American Advertising Federation, Jonah Gitlitz, objected to legislation that would require warning signs on poisonous products on the ground that such warnings are "opposed to the whole concept of advertising." "We are opposed to the whole concept of warnings in advertising," he said, "because our primary purpose is to sell. If we do inform, it is only in order to sell."[13]

The principle that the merchant should inform his customer only when it will help him to sell his product, and its corollary—that the customer should not be informed of anything that might deter him from making a purchase, even when such information may be vitally important to him—are just a step from the swindler's principle—that the customer may be told anything, whether it is true or false, so long as he is persuaded to buy.

The swindler's principle operates in much the same way as that of the respectable advertising man. He too is interested in persuading his customer that the latter has a need for a product or service that the swindler is prepared to sell him, even though he knows that the customer does *not* need it, even when he knows the customer's well-being may be seriously compromised by his purchase. But the principle that the sale must be made, whatever moral principles must be bent, prevails. A few examples may be instructive.

In the 1930s complaints began to pour in to Better Business Bureaus and the Federal Trade Commission (FTC) about the Holland Furnace Company, a firm that had some 500 offices throughout United States and employed more than 5,000 persons. Salesmen, misrepresenting themselves as "furnace engineers" and "safety inspectors," gained entry to their victims' homes, dismantled their furnaces, and condemned them as hazardous. They then refused to reassemble them, on the ground that they did not want to be "accessories to murder." Using scare tactics, claiming that the furnaces they "inspected" were emitting carbon monoxide and other dangerous gases, they created, in the homeowners' minds, a need for a new furnace—and proceeded to sell their own product at a handsome profit. They sold one elderly woman nine new furnaces in six years for a total of $18,000. The FTC finally forced the company to close in 1965, but in the meantime, it had done some $30 million worth of business per year for many years.

Similar frauds have been perpetrated by home repair men who climb onto the roof, knock some bricks from the chimney, and persuade the homeowner that he must replace his chimney—at highly inflated prices—or suffer serious consequences. And some automobile repair shops and transmission dealers have been accused in a number of states of declaring that perfectly good transmissions were "burned up" or "shot" and needed replacement or rebuilding at enormous cost.[14] Again, the gimmick is to create a "need" for something when in fact there is no need at all. That is, to persuade the consumer that he ought to buy something that he really ought *not* to buy; to persuade him that it is in his best interests to pay a large sum of money for a given product or

---

13   *Consumer Reports*, Vol. 36 (September 1971), p. 526.
14   Warren G. Magnuson and Jean Carper, *The Dark Side of the Marketplace* (Englewood Cliffs, N.J.: Prentice-Hall, 1968), Chapters 1 and 2 *et passim*.

service when in fact it is highly detrimental for him to do so, and he gains no benefit whatever from his purchase.

False Claims of Effectiveness

An ad in a magazine directed at the teen-age market carries a picture of a young girl whose tears are streaming down her cheeks. "Cry Baby!" the ad proclaims.

> That's right, cry if you like. Or giggle. You can even pout. Some things you can do just because you're a woman. And, also because you're a woman, you lose iron every month. The question is, are you putting that iron back? You may be among the 2 out of 3 American women who don't get enough iron from the food they eat to meet their recommended iron intake. . . . But One-A-Day Brand Multiple Vitamins Plus Iron does. . . . One-A-Day Plus Iron. One of the things you should know about, because you're a woman.

Two claims, at least, are made or implied by this advertisement. The first is that most American women do not get enough iron in their diets to make up for the "deficiency" that results from menstruation. The second is that One-A-Day tablets will fill the gap. As for the first claim, the American Medical Association pointed out long ago that "the average diet of Americans is rich in iron." This statement was made during the AMA's campaign against Ironized Yeast, which also claimed to offer beneficial results from the Vitamin B that was included in its compound. The AMA showed that Vitamin B was found in sufficient quantities in the average American diet to require no special supplement.[15] Now, if there is no significant lack of iron in the average person's diet (and

this includes the average woman), there is no deficiency for One-A-Day tablets to fill. To be sure, some Americans do suffer from a lack of certain vitamins and minerals because they do not have an adequate diet. But the answer to this is not for them to take One-A-Day pills, but to eat more nutritious food.

Prior to 1922, Listerine had been advertised as "the best antiseptic for both internal and external use." It was recommended for treating gonorrhea and for "filling the cavity, during ovariotomy." During the years that followed, it was also touted as a safe antiseptic that would ward off cold germs and sore throat, and guard its users against pneumonia. Mothers were urged to rinse their hands in Listerine before touching their babies, and, after prayers, to "send those youngsters of yours into the bathroom for a good-night gargle with Listerine." During the Depression the promoters of Listerine warned those who had jobs to hold on to them. To do that it was necessary to "fight colds as never before. Use Listerine."[16] Gerald B. Lambert, a member of the family that manufactured the product, told how Listerine came to be advertised as a mouthwash. He was deeply in debt, and, needing some cash to bail himself out, he decided to move into the family business. In discussing the advertising of the mixture, his brother asked whether it might be good for bad breath. Lambert was shocked at the suggestion that "bad breath" be used in advertising a respectable product. In the discussion that followed, the word *halitosis*, which had been found in a clipping from the British medical journal *Lancet*, was used. The word was unfamiliar to everyone at the meeting, but immediately struck Lambert as a suitable term to use in a new adver-

---

15   See James G. Burrow, *AMA: Voice of American Medicine* (Baltimore: Johns Hopkins Press, 1963), p. 268, and Arthur J. Cramp, *Nostrums and Quackery and Pseudo-medicine* (Chicago: University of Chicago Press, 1936), Vol. III, pp. 29–31.
16   James H. Young, *The Medical Messiahs* (Princeton, N.J.: Princeton University Press, 1967), pp. 147 f.

tising campaign. The campaign caught on, Lambert paid off his debt, and in eight years made $25 million for his company.[17]

Now, how effective is Listerine for the ailments it claimed to cure? The AMA pointed out that the manufacturers of these antiseptics exaggerated the germ-killing powers of their products, that they did not tell of the hazardous germs that were not affected by Listerine, and that they failed to mention that the ability of a compound to kill germs in a test tube or on a glass plate in the laboratory is no indication of its capability of killing them in the mouth, the teeth, the gums, or the throat, let alone in other parts of the body.[18]

A recent case that is merely an echo of similar cases that go back many years is that in which the Federal Trade Commission ordered the ITT Continental Baking Company to stop promoting Profile bread as being less fattening than ordinary bread because it had fewer calories per slice. The advertisers neglected to mention that Profile bread had fewer calories per slice because it was sliced thinner, and that the difference between Profile and other bread slices was 58 as opposed to 63 calories, a rather insignificant amount.

In addition, it had been claimed that people could lose weight by eating two slices of Profile before every meal. This was so, the FTC held, only if the consumer ate a lighter meal; and Profile bread had no special virtue, in this respect, over any other brand of bread.[19]

A similar misrepresentation was discovered in ads sponsored by the General Foods Corporation, claiming that two Toast 'ems Pop-Ups contained at least as many nutrients as a breakfast of two eggs, two slices of bacon, and two slices of toast. In a commercial showing a child mulling over such a breakfast, a voice told parents whose children were unhappy at breakfast that "two hot Toast 'ems provide 100 per cent of the minimum daily requirements of vitamins and iron. . . . As long as you know that—let them think it's just a big cookie." General Foods signed a consent order prohibiting it from making false nutritional claims for Toast 'ems or any other consumer food product.[20]

These are only a few of the better-known nationally advertised products that do not do what they claim to do.

---

17   See David Ogilvy, *Confessions of an Advertising Man* (New York: Atheneum, 1963), p. 86. Also Gerald B. Lambert, "How I Sold Listerine," in *The Amazing Advertising Business,* ed. by the Editors of *Fortune* (New York: Simon & Schuster, 1957), Chapter 5.
18   Young, op. cit., p. 155.
19   *Consumer Reports,* Vol. 36 (September 1971), pp. 525 f.
20   Ibid., p. 561.

Unshackling Net Speech

John F. Dickerson

In Its First Foray into Cyberspace, the Supreme Court Says the First Amendment Applies There Too

One of the key ideas behind the Internet was to build a computer network that could withstand a nuclear holocaust. Last week the Net proved its resilience in the face of another sort of attack. The Communications Decency Act, signed into law by President Clinton last year, was designed to protect children by prohibiting "indecent" speech or images from being sent through cyberspace. But even before Congress passed the legislation, free-speech advocates were blasting it as an unacceptable infringement on the First Amendment.

Now the Supreme Court has agreed that the CDA is precisely that. The court, while disagreeing about some issues in the case, unanimously concluded that reducing online communication to a safe-for-kids standard is unconstitutional. "The interest in encouraging freedom of expression in a democratic society," wrote Justice John Paul Stevens, "outweighs any theoretical but unproven benefit of censorship."

It was a decisive—though not unexpected—victory for civil libertarians. Opponents of the CDA, led by the American Civil Liberties Union and the American Library Association as well as dozens of other plaintiffs, including Planned Parenthood and Hu-

man Rights Watch, had argued that the statute was so vaguely worded and ill defined that discussions in online chat rooms about abortion or contraception could have attracted the vice squad. Says Ira Glasser, executive director of the A.C.L.U.: "It would have criminalized all sorts of speech that would never have been criminalized before."

And that, said the court, could have crippled the Internet, which now has some 50 million users. Indeed, wrote Stevens in his 15-page opinion, the CDA threatened "to torch a large segment of the Internet community." Clearly the Justices, like many newbies before them, were swept up in the global reach and boundless potential of the medium. "Any person with a phone line can become a town crier with a voice that resonates farther than it could from any soapbox," Stevens observed.

Minutes after the ruling was handed down, the court could have seen that phenomenon in action. At the click of a mouse, the text of the opinion was piped across the Net and plastered on computer sites from New York City to Australia. A laptop computer in New York was used to "Netcast" the audio portion of an A.C.L.U. press conference to all corners of the earth. Chat rooms and message boards were choked with Net folk weighing in about what it all meant. Computer jocks even ventured forth into the

From *Time* July 7, 1997. © 1997 Time Inc. Reprinted by permission.

sunlight for real-time, nonvirtual victory parties. "Let today be the first day of a new American Revolution—a Digital American Revolution!" said Mike Godwin, attorney for the Electronic Frontier Foundation, addressing a crowd of revelers in San Francisco.

CDA proponents were every bit as vociferous in defeat as their counterparts were in victory. Members of the anti-porn group Enough Is Enough, led by former Gary Hart co-scandalist Donna Rice Hughes, demonstrated outside the Supreme Court with signs that read HONK IF YOU HATE PORN and CHILD MOLESTERS ARE LOOKING FOR VICTIMS ON THE INTERNET.

Legislators seized the moment as well. "Parents are going to have to realize that a computer without any restrictions to children is just as dangerous to their minds and development as a triple-X store," said retiring Indiana Senator Dan Coats, co-author of the CDA. "The court has ignored the clear will of the Executive Branch and the Congress and the clear will of the American people."

In fact, though, the court did not rule that government cannot regulate the Internet. Nor did it alter the long-standing legal prohibition against obscenity, which remains unprotected speech, both on and off the Net. It simply said that the CDA as written was fatally flawed because in trying to protect children it would also keep adults from getting material they have a legal right to see. That gives CDA forces hope that they'll be able to revisit the issue. "The opinion gives us a good road map to what the courts will allow," says Bob Flores, senior counsel of the National Law Center for Children and Families. Vows Don Hodel, the recently installed president of the Christian Coalition: "We won't accept this as the last word."

Nor, evidently, will the President. The White House began backing away from its support of the clearly doomed CDA months ago. But Administration officials have recently come at the problem from a new angle. They propose to fight technology with technology. This week President Clinton will convene a meeting of Internet providers, family groups and others during which he'll propose to protect kids from indecency with a software fix.

While the details have yet to be worked out, White House staff members hope to talk Website operators into a kind of universal rating system. Combining it with software browsers used to access much of the Net, parents could in theory set their own comfort level and filter out the naughty bits. "If we are to make the Internet a powerful resource for learning, we must give parents and teachers the tools they need to make the Internet safe for children," Clinton said last week. "With the right technology and rating systems, we can help ensure that our children don't end up in the red-light districts of cyberspace."

Good luck. Software filters and online ratings systems have been around since before the CDA was born, and they've always been beset with problems. Recently, for instance, when Microsoft began backing a ratings standard known as RSACI and started including the filter as part of its browser, Internet Explorer, the company quickly found that the "solution" could keep large numbers of viewers away from its news site, MSNBC. Microsoft quietly removed the rating. The problem should have been foreseen. News, after all, frequently covers violent, adult-oriented subjects, which puts many news stories into the same verboten range as porn. While RSACI officials have proposed offering a news exemption, it's hard to see how that could work. Readers of the sex-oriented newspaper Screw, for instance, might well consider it just as newsworthy as the New York *Times.*

Still, the First Amendment notwithstanding, many Americans feel that parents have a legitimate right to protect their kids from inappropriate material. "You can't connect every high school in America to the Net unless there's some way to ensure that kids won't see what they're not supposed to," says Lawrence Lessig, a Harvard Law School professor and author of an essay, "Reading the Constitution in Cyberspace," that was cited repeatedly by Justice O'Connor in a minority opinion. "It can't be the case that Congress has no power to regulate here."

It can be the case, however, that Congress's power is largely symbolic. Even if the government figures out a constitutional way to impose limited censorship online, these rules can apply only within the U.S.— and the Internet is international. If parents want to control what their children see, they'll probably have to resort to an old-fashioned, low- tech solution: they'll have to supervise their kids' time online.

Invasion of Privacy

Joshua Quittner

For the longest time, I couldn't get worked up about privacy: my right to it; how it's dying; how we're headed for an even more wired, underregulated, overintrusive, privacy-deprived planet.

I mean, I probably have more reason to think about this stuff than the average John Q. All Too Public. A few years ago, for instance, after I applied for a credit card at a consumer-electronics store, somebody got hold of my name and vital numbers and used them to get a duplicate card. That somebody ran up a $3,000 bill, but the nice lady from the fraud division of the credit-card company took care of it with steely digital dispatch. (I filed a short report over the phone. I never lost a cent. The end.)

I also hang out online a lot, and now and then on the Net someone will impersonate me, spoofing my E-mail address or posting stupid stuff to bulletin boards or behaving in a frightfully un-Quittner-like manner in chat parlors from here to Bianca's Smut Shack. It's annoying, I suppose. But in the end, the faux Quittners get bored and disappear. My reputation, such as it is, survives.

I should also point out that as news director for Pathfinder, Time Inc.'s mega info mall, and a guy who makes his living on the Web, I know better than most people that we're hurtling toward an even more intrusive world. We're all being watched by computers whenever we visit Websites; by the mere act of "browsing" (it sounds so passive!) we're going public in a way that was unimaginable a decade ago. I know this because I'm a watcher too. When people come to my Website, without ever knowing their names, I can peer over their shoulders, recording what they look at, timing how long they stay on a particular page, following them around Pathfinder's sprawling offerings.

None of this would bother me in the least, I suspect, if a few years ago, my phone, like Marley's ghost, hadn't given me a glimpse of the nightmares to come. On Thanksgiving weekend in 1995, someone (presumably a critic of a book my wife and I had just written about computer hackers) forwarded my home telephone number to an out-of-state answering machine, where unsuspecting callers trying to reach me heard a male voice identify himself as me and say some extremely rude things. Then, with typical hacker aplomb, the prankster asked people to leave their messages (which to my surprise many callers, including my mother, did). This went on for several days until my wife and I figured out that something was wrong ("Hey...why hasn't the phone rung since Wednesday?") and got our phone service restored.

It seemed funny at first, and it gave us a swell story to tell on our book tour. But the interloper who seized our telephone line continued to hit us even after the tour ended. And hit us again and again for the next six months. The phone company seemed powerless. Its security folks moved us to one unlisted number after another, half a dozen times. They put special pin codes in place. They put traces on the line. But the troublemaker kept breaking through.

If our hacker had been truly evil and omnipotent as only fictional movie hackers are, there would probably have been even worse ways he could have threatened my privacy. He could have sabotaged my credit rating. He could have eavesdropped on my telephone conversations or siphoned off my E-mail. He could have called in my mortgage, discontinued my health insurance or obliterated my Social Security number. Like Sandra Bullock in The Net, I could have been a digital untouchable, wandering the planet without a connection to the rest of humanity. (Although if I didn't have to pay back school loans, it might be worth it. Just a thought.)

Still, I remember feeling violated at the time and as powerless as a minnow in a flash flood. Someone was invading my private space—my family's private space—and there was nothing I or the authorities could do. It was as close to a technological epiphany as I have ever been. And as I watched my personal digital hell unfold, it struck me that our privacy—mine and yours—has already disappeared, not in one Big Brotherly blitzkrieg but in Little Brotherly moments, bit by bit.

Losing control of your telephone, of course, is the least of it. After all, most of us voluntarily give out our phone number and address when we allow ourselves to be listed in the White Pages. Most of us go a lot further than that. We register our whereabouts whenever we put a bank card in an ATM machine or drive through an E-Z Pass lane on the highway. We submit to being photographed every day—20 times a day on average if you live or work in New York City—by surveillance cameras. We make public our interests and our purchasing habits every time we shop by mail order or visit a commercial Website.

I don't know about you, but I do all this willingly because I appreciate what I get in return: the security of a safe parking lot, the convenience of cash when I need it, the improved service of mail-order houses that know me well enough to send me catalogs of stuff that interests me. And while I know we're supposed to feel just awful about giving up our vaunted privacy, I suspect (based on what the pollsters say) that you're as ambivalent about it as I am.

Popular culture shines its klieg lights on the most intimate corners of our lives, and most of us play right along. If all we really wanted was to be left alone, explain the lasting popularity of Oprah and Sally and Ricki tell-all TV. Memoirs top the best-seller lists, with books about incest and insanity and illness leading the way. Perfect strangers at cocktail parties tell me the most disturbing details of their abusive upbringings. Why?

"It's a very schizophrenic time," says Sherry Turkle, professor of sociology at the Massachusetts Institute of Technology, who writes books about how computers and online communication are transforming society. She believes our culture is undergoing a kind of mass identity crisis, trying to hang on to a sense of privacy and intimacy in a global village of tens of millions. "We have very unstable notions about the boundaries of the individual," she says.

If things seem crazy now, think how much crazier they will be when everybody is as wired as I am. We're in the midst of a global interconnection that is happening much faster than electrification did a century ago and is expected to have consequences at least as profound. What would happen if all the information stored on the world's computers were accessible via the Internet to anyone? Who would own it? Who would control it? Who would protect it from abuse?

Small-scale privacy atrocities take place every day. Ask Dr. Denise Nagel, executive director of the National Coalition for Patient Rights, about medical privacy, for example, and she rattles off a list of abuses that would make Big Brother blush. She talks about how two years ago, a convicted child rapist working as a technician in a Boston hospital riffled through 1,000 computerized records looking for potential victims (and was caught when the father of a nine-year-old girl used caller ID to trace the call back to the hospital). How a banker on Maryland's state health commission pulled up a list of cancer patients, cross-checked it against the names of his bank's customers and revoked the loans of the matches. How Sara Lee bakeries planned to collaborate with Lovelace Health Systems, a subsidiary of Cigna, to match employee health records with work-performance reports to find workers who might benefit from antidepressants.

Not to pick on Sara Lee. At least a third of all FORTUNE 500 companies regularly review health information before making hiring decisions. And that's nothing compared with what awaits us when employers and insurance companies start testing our DNA for possible imperfections. Farfetched? More than 200 subjects in a case study published last January in the journal Science and Engineering Ethics reported that they had been discriminated against as a result of genetic testing. None of them were actually sick, but DNA analysis suggested that they might become sick someday. "The technology is getting ahead of our ethics," says Nagel, and the Clinton Administration clearly agrees. It is about to propose a federal law that would protect medical and health-insurance records from such abuses.

But how did we arrive at this point, where so much about what we do and own and think is an open book?

It all started in the 1950s, when, in order to administer Social Security funds, the U.S. government began entering records on big mainframe computers, using nine-digit identification numbers as data points. Then, even more than today, the citizenry instinctively loathed the computer and its injunctions against folding, spindling and mutilating. We were not numbers! We were human beings! These fears came to a head in the late 1960s, recalls Alan Westin, a retired Columbia University professor who publishes a quarterly report Privacy and American Business. "The techniques of intrusion and data surveillance had overcome the weak law and social mores that we had built up in the pre-World War II era," says Westin.

The public rebelled, and Congress took up the question of how much the government and private companies should be permitted to know about us. A privacy bill of rights was drafted. "What we did," says Westin, "was to basically redefine what we meant by 'reasonable expectations of privacy'"—a guarantee, by the way, that comes from the Supreme Court and not from any constitutional "right to privacy."

The result was a flurry of new legislation that clarified and defined consumer and citizen rights. The first Fair Credit Reporting Act, passed in 1970, overhauled what had once been a secret, unregulated industry with no provisions for due process. The new law gave consumers the right to know what was in their credit files and to demand corrections. Other financial and health privacy acts followed, although to this day no federal law protects the confidentiality of medical records.

As Westin sees it, the public and private sectors took two very different approaches. Congress passed legislation requiring that the government tell citizens what records it keeps on them while insisting that the information itself not be released unless required by law. The private sector responded by letting each industry—credit-card companies, banking, insurance, marketing, advertising—create its own guidelines.

That approach worked—to a point. And that point came when mainframes started giving way to desktop computers. In the old days, information stored in government databases was relatively inaccessible. Now, however, with PCs on every desktop linked to office networks and then to the Internet, data that were once carefully hidden may be only a few keystrokes away.

Suddenly someone could run motor-vehicle-registration records against voting registrations to find 6-ft.-tall Republicans who were arrested during the past year for drunk driving—and who own a gun. The genie was not only out of the bottle, he was also peering into everyone's bedroom window. (Except the windows of the very rich, who can afford to screen themselves.)

"Most people would be astounded to know what's out there," says Carole Lane, author of Naked in Cyberspace: How to Find Personal Information Online. "In a few hours, sitting at my computer, beginning with no more than your name and address, I can find out what you do for a living, the names and ages of your spouse and children, what kind of car you drive, the value of your house and how much taxes you pay on it."

Lane is a member of a new trade: paid Internet searcher, which already has its own professional group, the Association of Independent Information Professionals. Her career has given her a fresh appreciation for what's going on. "Real privacy as we've known it," she says, "is fleeting."

Now, there are plenty of things you could do to protect yourself. You could get an unlisted telephone number, as I was forced to do. You could cut up your credit card and pay cash for everything. You could rip your E-Z Pass off the windshield and use quarters at tolls. You could refuse to divulge your Social Security number except for Social Security purposes, which is all that the law requires. You'd be surprised how often you're asked to provide it by people who have no right to see it.

That might make your life a bit less comfortable, of course. As in the case of Bob Bruen, who went into a barbershop in Watertown, Mass., recently. "When I was asked for my phone number, I refused to give them the last four digits," Bruen says. "I was also asked for my name, and I also refused. The girl at the counter called her supervisor, who told me I could not get a haircut in their shop." Why? The barbershop uses a computer to record all transactions. Bruen went elsewhere to get his locks shorn.

But can we do that all the time? Only the Unabomber would seriously suggest that we cut all ties to the wired world. The computer and its spreading networks convey status and bring opportunity. They empower us. They allow an information economy to thrive and grow. They make life easier. Hence the dilemma.

The real problem, says Kevin Kelly, executive editor of Wired magazine, is that although we say we value our privacy, what we really want is something very different: "We think that privacy is about information, but it's not—it's about relationships." The way Kelly sees it, there was no privacy in the traditional village or small town; everyone knew everyone else's secrets. And that was comfortable. I knew about you, and you knew about me. "There was a symmetry to the knowledge," he says. "What's gone out of whack is we don't know who knows about us anymore. Privacy has become asymmetrical."

The trick, says Kelly, is to restore that balance. And not surprisingly, he and others point out that what technology has taken, technology can restore. Take the problem of "magic cookies"—those little bits of code most Websites use to track visitors. We set up a system at Pathfinder in which, when you visit our site, we drop a cookie into the basket of your browser that tags you like a rare bird. We use that cookie in place of your name, which, needless to say, we never know. If you look up a weather report by keying in a zip code, we note that (it tells us where you live or maybe where you wish you lived). We'll mark down whether you look up stock quotes (though we draw the line at capturing the symbols of the specific stocks you follow). If you come to the Netly News, we'll record your interest in technology. Then, the next time you visit, we might serve up an ad for a modem or an online brokerage firm or a restaurant in Akron, Ohio, depending on what we've managed to glean about you.

Some people find the whole process offensive. "Cookies represent a way of watching consumers without their consent, and that is a fairly frightening phenomenon," says Nick Grouf, CEO of Firefly, a Boston company that makes software offering an alternative approach to profiling, known as "intelligent agents." Privacy advocates like Grouf—as well as the two companies that control the online browser market, Microsoft and Netscape—say the answer to the cookie monster is something they call the Open Profiling Standard. The idea is to allow the computer user to create an electronic "passport" that identifies him to online marketers without revealing his name. The user tailors the passport to his own interests, so if he is passionate about fly-fishing and is cruising through L.L. Bean's Website, the passport will steer the electronic-catalog copy toward fishing gear instead of, say, Rollerblades.

The advantage to computer users is that they can decide how much information they want to reveal while limiting their exposure to intrusive marketing techniques. The advantage to Website entrepreneurs is that they learn about their customers' tastes without intruding on their privacy.

Many online consumers, however, are skittish about leaving any footprints in cyberspace. Susan Scott, executive director of TRUSTe, a firm based in Palo Alto, Calif., that rates Websites according to the level of privacy they afford, says a survey her company sponsored found that 41% of respondents would quit a Web page rather than reveal any personal information about themselves. About 25% said when they do volunteer information, they lie. "The users want access, but they don't want to get correspondence back," she says.

But worse things may already be happening to their E-mail. Many office electronic-mail systems warn users that the employer reserves the right to monitor their E-mail. In October software will be available to Wall Street firms that can automatically monitor correspondence between brokers and clients through an artificial-intelligence program that scans for evidence of securities violations.

"Technology has outpaced law," says Marc Rotenberg, director of the Washington-based Electronic Privacy Information Center. Rotenberg advocates protecting the privacy of E-mail by encrypting it with secret codes so powerful that even the National Security Agency's supercomputers would have a hard time cracking it. Such codes are legal within the U.S. but cannot be used abroad—where terrorists might use them to protect their secrets—without violating U.S. export laws. The battle between the Clinton Administration and the computer industry over encryption export policy has been raging for six years without resolution, a situation that is making it hard to do business on the Net and is clearly starting to fray some nerves. "The future is in electronic commerce," says Ira Magaziner, Clinton's point man on Net issues. All that's holding it up is "this privacy thing."

Rotenberg thinks we need a new government agency—a privacy agency—to sort out the issues. "We need new legal protections," he says, "to enforce the privacy act, to keep federal agencies in line, to act as a spokesperson for the Federal Government and to act on behalf of privacy interests."

Wired's Kelly disagrees. "A federal privacy agency would be disastrous! The answer to the whole privacy question is more knowledge," he says. "More knowledge about who's watching you. More knowledge about the information that flows between us—particularly the meta information about who knows what and where it's going."

I'm with Kelly. The only guys who insist on perfect privacy are hermits like the Unabomber. I don't want to be cut off from the world. I have nothing to hide. I just want some measure of control over what people know about me. I want to have my magic cookie and eat it too.

How You're Spied On

Everyday events that can make your life a little less private

Bank Machines
Every time you use an automated teller, the bank records the time, date and location of your transaction.

Prescription Drugs
If you use your company health insurance to purchase drugs, your employer may have access to the details.

Employee ID Scanners
If you rely on a magnetic-stripe pass to enter the office, your whereabouts are automatically recorded.

Browsing on the Web
Many sites tag visitors with "magic cookies" that record what you're looking at and when you have been surfing.

Cellular Telephone
Your calls can be intercepted and your access numbers cribbed by eavesdroppers with police scanners.

Credit Cards
Everything you charge is in a database that police, among others, could look at.

Registering to Vote
In most states, voter-registration records are public and online. They typically list your address and birth date.

Making a Phone Call
The phone company doesn't need a court order to note the number you're calling—or who's calling you.

Supermarket Scanners
Many grocery stores let you register for discount coupons that are used to track what you purchase.

Sweepstakes
These are bonanzas for marketers. Every time you enter one, you add an electronic brushstroke to your digital portrait.

Satellites
Commercial satellites are coming online that are eagle-eyed enough to spot you—and maybe a companion—in a hot tub.

Electronic Tolls
In many places, drivers can pay tolls electronically with passes that tip off your whereabouts.

Surveillance Cameras

They're in banks, federal office buildings, 7-Elevens, even houses of worship; New Yorkers are on camera up to 20 times a day.

Mail-Order Transactions

Many companies, including mail-order houses and publishers, sell lists of their customers. Why do you think you're getting that Victoria's Secret catalog?

Sending E-Mail

In offices, E-mail is considered part of your work. Your employer is allowed to read it—and many bosses do.

Online Browser Tricks

Find Your Cookie

Your cookie is the string of text that identifies you to cookie-catching Websites. Use your computer's Find command to get any file with the word cookie in its name. You should be able to figure out by its title which one is your "magic cookie." Look at it using a word- processing program to find out who is stashing cookies in your browser.

Rig Your Cookie

Both Netscape's and Microsoft's browsers give you the option of being warned whenever a Website asks for your cookie. That way, you can refuse to proceed if you don't want to reveal anything about yourself.

Disable Your Cookie

Go to www.luckman.com and get a free "anonymous cookie," a program that disables cookies, among other things.

Know What Your Boss Knows

On Netscape's browser, in the Location field, type about:global. This shows everyplace you've visited, in some cases going back months. In Microsoft's Internet Explorer, you can list every site you've visited for the past 20 days by opening the Go menu and choosing the Open History item. You can erase this stuff by selecting the Clean Cache option on either browser.

Surf the Web Anonymously

You can browse the Web from behind a privacy curtain by first connecting to www.anonymizer.com. The free account imposes a 60-second delay on all browsing; a pay option lifts that annoying restriction.

Protect Yourself

Just say no to telemarketers If you don't want to get an unlisted telephone number (cost: $1.50 a month), practice the mantra "I don't take phone solicitations." Once you buy, you're put on a chump list that's sold to other marketers.

Consider removing your name from many direct-mail and telemarketing lists

Write to:

Direct Marketing Association
Mail/Telephone Preference Service
P.O. Box 9008 (mail)
or P.O. Box 9014 (phone)
Farmingdale, NY 11735

Pay cash whenever possible The less you put on your credit cards, the fewer details anyone has about your buying habits.

Be wary about buying mail order Many mail-order companies sell their customer lists. So call the company to check its procedures (unless you like catalogs).

Give your Social Security number only when required by law Many organizations, from school to work, use it as your ID number. Resist them. (Experts say it often helps if you can tell someone in authority about your concerns.)

Think twice before filling out warranty cards or entering sweepstakes. These are data mines for marketers. Besides, most products are guaranteed by your sales receipt. And have you ever won anything in a sweepstakes?

Be careful when using "free blood-pressure clinics" Typically, your data will be used by marketers and pharmaceutical companies.

Avoid leaving footprints on the Net You're being watched even as you browse. And search engines index your postings to public forums such as Usenet by your name.

Tobacco Fighters Find Another Smoking Gun

Marianne Lavelle

The universe of people who still believed tobacco companies' claims that they did not market cigarettes to minors was small to begin with. But that universe compressed still further with last week's revelation of R. J. Reynolds Tobacco's past effor ts to target customers as young as 14. On Thursday, Rep. Henry Waxman, a leading tobacco opponent, released 81 internal RJR documents produced between 1973 and 1990 describing the company's efforts to attract new young smokers to RJR brands such as Camel . The documents, many marked "secret" or "confidential," make such recommendations as "If our company is to survive and prosper, over the long term we must get our share of the youth market," and "The brand must increase its share penetration among the 14-to-24 age group." RJR claims that the memos are taken out of context and that some mentions of underage smokers are the result of typographical errors.

The documents come as another blow to the industry's hope for a sweeping settlement of state lawsuits seeking to recoup health care costs. Under the proposed deal, the industry would pay hundreds of billions and agree to curbs on marketing in return for protection from future lawsuits. But Senate Majority Leader Trent Lott recently expressed doubts that the package would pass Congress. And though the industry put out one brush fire last week by settling a lawsuit by the state of Texas for $15 billion, a Minnesota lawsuit set to begin this week promises to make public even more damaging industry documents.

A new plan. Following the latest document disclosure, Sen. John McCain raised the possibility of scaled-down tobacco legislation that would let the courts and the states deal with the pending lawsuits and would focus solely on limiting youths' access to cigarettes, curbing advertising to the young, and establishing penalties if youths' tobacco use fails to drop by set targets.

But industry analysts such as David Adelman of Morgan Stanley Dean Witter point out that Congress would face major legal obstacles in attempting a youth-only bill. Supreme Court rulings suggest that proposed congressional restrictions on tobacco advertising would violate the First Amendment. Such a bill might also run afoul of the Constitution's due process and private property requirements by forcing the industry to pay fines if youth smoking rates don't drop. The comprehensive settlement deal would do these things legally because the cigarette industry would voluntarily exchange those rights for protection from lawsuits.

Adelman still believes Congress will pass the overarching settlement, arguing that the new documents are "on people's minds today but won't be a month from now." John Coale, a private lawyer who helped broker the deal, agrees, noting that President Clinton, in his 1998 budget proposal, is already assuming an additional $10 billion in revenue from the tobacco-settlement money. "The best sign I see is that everyone's spending the money," Coale says. "When that starts happening, it's not easy to give up."

Firm to Pay $10 Million in Settlement of Sex Case

Kenneth N. Gilpin

In an agreement that dwarfs any previous award in a sexual harassment suit, the American subsidiary of a big Swedish drug maker said yesterday that it would pay nearly $10 million to settle accusations by the Equal Employment Opportunity Commission on behalf of former employees of the subsidiary.

In addition to the monetary payment, the subsidiary, Astra U.S.A., of Westborough, Mass., acknowledged that it allowed a hostile working environment for female employees and apologized.

"Astra is sorry for the instances of sexual harassment that took place under previous management," Ivan R. Rowley, president and chief executive of Astra U.S.A., said in a statement. "As a company we are ashamed of the unacceptable behavior that took place. To each person who suffered, I offer our apologies."

The award, which amounts to $9.85 million plus interest, eclipses in size the previous record in a sex harassment case, a $1.3 million settlement agreed to by Management Recruiters International in a suit that was resolved last year.

Jim Lee, regional counsel for the commission, said yesterday that of the 120 former female employees of Astra who had been interviewed in the inquiry, about 80 had been identified as able to file claims. But others may not have yet come forward.

The commission began its investigation in May 1996, shortly after Business Week magazine reported accusations of sexual harassment had been made at the company, a subsidiary of Astra A.B.

Lars Bildman, who was Astra U.S.A.'s president and chief executive for 15 years before being dismissed in June 1996, was accused of replacing mothers and older female employees with beautiful young single women who were pressured into having sex with company executives. Former Astra employees said Mr. Bildman demanded that a full work day be followed by evenings of drinking and parties.

Paul Igasaki, chairman of the E.E.O.C., said that the commission had found that Mr. Bildman and other Astra executives "engaged in a pattern and practice of sexually harassing female sales representatives, including incidents of quid pro quo sexual harassment and creating a hostile work environment." The agency said that "sexual harassment was part of the 'Astra Way,' "

In a Federal lawsuit filed in 1996, six former Astra employees contended that executives created "an organized pattern of sexual harassment" to "satisfy their personal desires."

The pattern started early.

"At initial training classes female employees were told that their performance evaluation depended upon their social skills and their socialization with senior management officials," the commission said. "The investigation showed that because senior management officials engaged in this behavior, lower management officials, employees, agents and customers followed suit."

Although it has settled with the commission, there are still two outstanding sexual harassment lawsuits pending against Astra U.S.A.

Robert Sanders, director of the E.E.O.C. office in Boston, said that the women who filed those suits must choose between becoming a party to the settlement or pursuing their claims independently.

Under the terms of the settlement, Astra, which has instituted training to deter sexual harassment and replaced its entire senior management since the accusations were originally filed, will have its policies monitored for the next two years by an individual who is not an employee.

In June 1996, Astra U.S.A. dismissed Mr. Bildman and George Rodman, vice president for marketing and sales, after its own investigation of the accusations. A third executive, Edward Aarons, director of institutional business, resigned. Two district sales managers, William Reed and Robert Packin, also resigned.

Mr. Bildman last week pleaded guilty to filing false Federal tax returns in an agreement that will send him to prison for 21 months and pay the Government more than $300,000 in back taxes and interest. He still faces considerable legal hurdles.

On Wednesday, Astra filed a $15 million lawsuit against Mr. Bildman, accusing him of spending more than $2.2 million in company money to renovate three of his homes. Part of the money it is seeking in its suit is to recover costs related to the E.E.O.C. investigation, Astra said.

Rain Forest Losses Increase in Brazil

Stan Lehman

SAN JOSE DOS CAMPOS, Brazil—Breaking years of silence, Brazil's government conceded yesterday that destruction of the Amazon rain forest reached record levels in 1995 before finally leveling off in the last two years.

The findings reinforced environmentalists' fears that the pace of destruction of the vital region continues to accelerate.

Until yesterday, the destruction remained shrouded in mystery: Satellite photos showing the devastation remained rolled up, gathering dust, while the government insisted it didn't have the money to analyze them. The most recent figures were from 1994.

Silence suited the government, which maintained it could not say whether destruction was up or not until the official numbers were in.

The latest figures show deforestation nearly doubled from 5,958 square miles in 1994 to 11,621 square miles in 1995—a 95 percent increase.

And, although the rate dropped in 1996 to 7,200 square miles, it was still 21 percent higher than 1994. In 1997—with the numbers only 80 percent complete—the Amazon lost 5,200 square miles of forest.

Perhaps most alarmingly, the slowdown was largely due to abnormally heavy rainfall in the region rather than govenment policy.

"These numbers are no reason to celebrate," Brazil's Environment Minister Gustavo Krause said at the presentation of the study based on satellite images of the forest.

But he also credited enforcement of forest protection laws for some of the improvement, including a moratorium on new concessions for logging mahogany and virola wood enacted in 1996.

Between 1978 and 1996, more than 200,000 square miles—or 12.5 percent—of the Amazon's rain forest were destroyed.

Eduardo Martins, president of Brazil's Environmental Protection Agency, said the main cause of the destruction was the burning and logging of huge tracts of land to create grazing pastures for livestock.

In 1995 and 1996, deforestation of small plots measuring 37- to 124-acres accounted for about a quarter of the destruction, he said.

"The government will spare no efforts to strengthen its commitment to reduce the deforestation," said Martins. "It will intensify its monitoring, control and inspection of the region."

But at the same time, he said, the government could not turn a blind eye to the need to develop the 2 million-square-mile region and improve the quality of life for its 20 million people.

He said the government would increase aid to small farmers to diminish their dependency on slash-and-burn techniques and will no longer grant land ownership titles in areas that have been deforested without authorization.

The government also will guarantee that no deforestation takes place in the 10 percent of the Amazon designated as nature reserves, he said.

Krause said the government was implementing 10 measures to protect the rain forest and promote its sustainable development, including offering credits to farmers who plant crops suited to its ecosystem and restricting farm credit in areas covered with virgin forest.

But Joao Paulo Capobianco of the Social-Environmental Institute, a nongovernmental organization, said the worst offenders were no longer small farmers but the logging industry.

Krause admitted that foreign loggers, mostly from Asia, had invested $100 million in the region in 1997 alone. He had no figures on how much of the deforestation they were responsible for, but said the companies had been fined about $1 million for illegal logging last year.

Corporate Ethics
Recent Developments in Legislation and Regulation Compel Re-Examination and Monitoring of Ethics Codes

Because of the broad interest in the subject of corporate ethical conduct, Coopers & Lybrand recently undertook a study of the ethics codes of 21 major corporations in a variety of industries. The study indicates that many of these companies—and it can be assumed others as well—are broadening and updating their codes to include a wider range of issues.

This C&L *Comment* discusses the types of issues most often stressed in today's ethics codes, means of implementing them, and auditing techniques useful in monitoring compliance. It is hoped that the discussion, together with the current compliance background (see Exhibit 1), will be useful in developing formal ethics policy statements or updating existing ones.

Findings of the Study

The companies in our study have generally tailored their ethics codes to suit the particular environments in which they operate and to meet their specific needs. But there are some common themes running through the codes. In past years, we found that ethics

policies primarily covered dealings with suppliers, conflicts of interest, treatment of confidential information, and antitrust matters. Afterwards, references to political contributions and questionable payments were added. More recently, several companies have included in their ethics codes policies on hiring of minorities and environmental protection.

The results of our most recent study of ethics statements showed that the topics most frequently addressed were:

☐ Basic guidelines (including legal compliance).

☐ Conflicts of interest.

☐ Proprietary information.

☐ Political contributions and activities.

☐ Outside activities.

☐ Off-book transactions.

☐ Improper transactions and payments.

Presented here, under each of these headings, are capsule summaries representing the thrust of the policies.

Basic guidelines. A general statement of ethical standards often serves as the intro-

From Coopers & Lybrand Newsletter (New York, NY), June 1978, Vol. 20, No. 6. Reprinted by permission.

duction to an ethics code. Besides an admonition to observe laws in both letter and spirit, the introduction frequently contains statements along these lines:

☐ Adherence to the highest standards of ethical conduct is expected of all employees.

☐ No code of conduct can specify the appropriate moral conduct and ethical behavior for every situation; employees should exercise good judgment.

☐ The policy will be subject to continuous refinement and updating since ethical behavior is dynamic; that is, sensitive to changes in values and customs that are certain to take place over time.

The latter point is highly significant in that the effectiveness of any ethics policy is undoubtedly based in part on its applicability to the current business, economic, and social environment.

Conflicts of interest. Conflicts of interest in codes of ethics generally refer to any circumstance that could cast doubt—or, in some cases, even the appearance of doubt—on an employee's ability to act with total objectivity with regard to the company's interests. Activities held to represent unacceptable conflicts of interest include:

☐ Engaging in financial, business, or other relationships with outside suppliers, customers, contractors, or competitors that might impair the independence of an employee or not be in the best interest of the company.

☐ Accepting gifts, bonuses, or hospitality (except of nominal value) from a supplier, customer, etc.

☐ Rendering services to any person, firm, or organization for compensation without prior approval.

Proprietary information. Codes that include mention of proprietary information usually cover:

☐ Disclosure of trade secrets; confidential information of a technical, financial, or business nature; or other "insider information."

☐ Use of such information for personal benefit, including buying or selling of securities of an entity or property in which the company has indicated a prospective interest.

☐ Use of insider information in connection with trading in company securities.

Consideration might be given to extending coverage to include confidential treatment of proprietary information of customers and other outsiders, where applicable.

Political contributions and activities. Prohibited areas with respect to political contributions and activities focus on:

☐ Use of company funds for supporting any U.S. political parties or candidates.

☐ Making foreign political payments, even when permitted by law, or a statement that political contributions made in foreign countries may be made in accordance with local law but must have company authorization.[1]

☐ Indirect contributions for political purposes made through consultants, suppliers, customers, other third parties or by reimbursement to employees for personal contributions or payments.

---

1   The Foreign Corrupt Practices Act generally makes illegal foreign political payments by SEC-registered companies and any other "domestic concern" (including individuals) when intended to influence an official's actions to gain or retain business.

☐ Applying pressure that infringes upon the right of an employee to decide whether, to whom, and in what amount a personal political contribution will be made.

☐ Payments to public officials to obtain business or preferential treatment for the company.

☐ Acceptance of public office or active participation in politics by an employee who holds himself out as a representative of the company rather than an individual citizen.

Most companies are probably aware of what activities are allowed with respect to domestic politics. Companies should also consider the content of their ethics codes relating to foreign political payments and other prohibited activities in light of the Foreign Corrupt Practices Act.

Outside activities. This topic was found to encompass the following guidelines:

☐ Permission must be obtained to hold outside directorships.

☐ Employees are expected to devote their full time to the company's interests during regular hours of employment.

☐ Employment and business commitments outside of regular hours of employment are prohibited if they tend to impair an employee's ability to meet job responsibilities.

☐ Permission is needed to serve as an officer, employee, or consultant of another organization.

Off-book transactions. Because of the often direct relationship between illegal or otherwise improper payments and inaccurate books and records, the subject of off-book transactions has received increasing attention in ethics statements. Typical provisions in the policies studied include the following:

☐ A payment is prohibited if no record of its disbursement is entered into the company's accounting records.

☐ All transactions in the conduct of company business must be properly reflected in the books and records.

☐ No secret or unrecorded fund of corporate monies or other assets shall be established or maintained.

☐ Making false or fictitious entries in the books and records of the company or its subsidiaries, and issuing false or misleading documents (e.g., invoices) or reports is prohibited.

☐ No off-book funds or transactions are allowed.

Although the maintenance of accurate books and records by SEC registrants is now mandated by law under the Foreign Corrupt Practices Act, comprehensive ethics policies should still cover this topic, as it is of key importance.

Improper transactions and payments. Other transactions related to improper and/or illegal payments that are prohibited by ethics policy statements include:

☐ Issuing or authorizing any official company document that is false or misleading.

☐ Knowingly accepting and treating as accurate a false or misleading document prepared by a person outside the company.

☐ Offering bribes, kickbacks, or other illegal payments on behalf of the company, directly or indirectly.

☐ Giving unusual gifts and entertainment to a supplier, customer, etc.

Other categories of ethics guidelines. In addition to the above-mentioned topics, which were covered most frequently in the policy statements studied, other categories of guidelines were provided in some instances. Those additional topics are listed in Exhibit 2. Many of the policy statements provided administrative guidance, as discussed later.

Additional topics for consideration. Although generally not covered in the ethics codes included in the study, there are several topics that, because of significant current interest, should be considered in developing or updating policies.

Executive perquisites. The SEC's interest in perquisites or "perks" is an outgrowth of its investigations of illegal or unauthorized payments. In the course of these investigations, cases surfaced in which corporate funds were used at least in part for executives' personal benefit without proper disclosure. The Commission issued an interpretative release in 1977 emphasizing its view that existing provisions of the securities acts require registrants to disclose in registration statements, reports, proxy, and information statements *all* forms of remuneration received by officers and directors. In addition, the IRS has recently indicated it is concerned as to whether perks have been treated properly as to income taxes.

GM Retirees Vow to Keep Fighting

Robert Lewis

The U.S. Supreme Court may get the last word in a 10-year fight by retirees of General Motors Corp. to secure the lifetime health-care benefits they say GM promised them in the 1970s and early 1980s.

Attorney Raymond Fay, lead counsel for 84,000 nonunion retirees who first sued GM in 1989, says he will ask the Supreme Court to overturn last month's federal appeals court decision upholding the company's right to cut benefits.

"This decision jeopardizes the position of retirees everywhere," Fay says, "because [if it stands] retirees can no longer count on the word of their employer to guarantee them benefits for life."

In an 8 to 5 split, judges on the 6th Circuit Court of Appeals in Cincinnati held that despite verbal and written assurances of free, lifetime retiree health benefits, GM was within its rights to later begin charging annual deductibles and copayments, as well as to cancel vision and hearing-aid coverage.

Their reasoning: Other provisions in company documents "unambiguously reserved GM's right to amend or terminate" benefits.

"We see no ambiguity," the majority opinion held, "in a summary plan description that tells participants both that the terms of the current plan entitle them to health insurance at no cost throughout retirement and that the terms of the current plan are subject to change."

Legal experts say if the ruling stands it could open the floodgates to broadscale corporate cutbacks in retiree health benefits.

"Our fear is that employers will read this case and revisit the question of whether or not they can cut their retiree benefits," Mark Machiz, associate solicitor of the Department of Labor's Pension and Welfare Benefits Administration, told reporters.

"Giving employers a free hand to break their promises of health benefits to retirees assures that no retiree will ever be certain of his or her health benefits," says AARP Executive Director Horace B. Deets.

AARP, which had supported the retirees' suit, will continue to back their effort in the Supreme Court, he adds.

In a scathing dissent, Boyce F. Martin Jr., the court's chief judge, said GM was caught in a classic case of corporate shortsightedness.

"When General Motors was flush with cash and health-care costs were low," he wrote, "it was easy to promise employees and retirees lifetime health care. Rather than pay off those perhaps ill-considered promises, it is [now] easier for the current regime to say those promises were never made."

The majority decision, he said, gives GM "the freedom to eliminate healthcare coverage completely."

GM declined to comment on the decision. But in a statement the company noted that it had not eliminated retiree health coverage and that its benefits were competitive with other large corporations.

And GM insisted in court arguments that it had reserved the right to change or eliminate retiree health benefits, even while telling employees they could count on free lifetime coverage.

The plaintiffs are salaried employees or the dependents of salaried employees who retired between 1974 and 1988. After 1988 GM began reserving the right to cut benefits in ways that were consistent with federal law, attorneys for the retirees say.

GM also promised free, lifetime healthcare benefits to blue-collar employees in contracts with the United Auto Workers Union. Those agreements remain in effect and have not been modified.

Fay estimates that more than one-fifth of the 84,000 plaintiffs are surviving spouses of GM retirees. Many plaintiffs, he adds, are in advanced age and have serious health problems.

The average age of retirees who had taken early retirement is now 73, he says. Many plaintiffs are in their 80s.

QUESTIONS

Section V

1. Give 3 ethical rules which should be followed from top management down to middle-management.

2. What is the "reason for being" of business corporations?

3. To whom do they owe their primary loyalty: employees, stockholders, the public or their "host" city?

4. How would utilitarians look at a company's obligations?

5. Are a just wage and a "living" wage the same?

6. How should a "just wage" be determined?

7. When companies cannot pay a just wage should the government (under distributive justice) help out?

8. Do employees have any right to demand a profit-sharing plan?

9. How would you define "discrimination?"

10. In what ways has there been discrimination in the American workplace" since the civil war?

11. What is the meaning of "Affirmative Action?"

12. If we grant past discriminatory practices have occurred, who should make restitution?

13. Can there be such a phenomenon as racial guilt?

14. In a succinct manner state Dr. Williams' view on the Affirmative Action issue.

15. Why do many American companies re-locate either to different states on even foreign foreign countries?

16. Even if we grant a right of re-location in some instances (justice) what conditions might the principle of "love of neighbor" demand?

17. What is the value to both employer and employees of a company having a "Code of Ethics?"

18. Why might "moonlighting" and "kickbacks" be detrimental to a business firm?

19. What is the difference between false advertising and misleading advertising?

20. What ethical principles should be applicable to the advertising industry?

21. Why must "off-book transactions" be considered unethical and illegal?

22. Why is "Business Ethics" not a contradiction in terms or in reality?

23. Concerning use of the "Internet," is there any way to have a security system which will protect our privacy—financial, personal, and sexual?

24. How can sovereign nations be prevented from damaging the environment on a global level? Why must the "Rain Forests" be saved?

25. Besides the cigarette, what are the new discoveries with regard to cigars and chewing tobacco?

26. Under what circumstances (if any) might companies have the right to renege on Retirment Agreements?